Writing

SUCCESSFUL GRANT PROPOSALS

from the
TOP DOWN
and
BOTTOM UP

Editorial Board

Writing
SUCCESSFUL
GRANT
PROPOSALS

from the
TOP DOWN
and
BOTTOM UP

ROBERT J. STERNBERG
Oklahoma State University

Los Angeles | London | New Delhi
Singapore | Washington DC

Los Angeles | London | New Delhi
Singapore | Washington DC

FOR INFORMATION:

SAGE Publications, Inc.
2455 Teller Road
Thousand Oaks, California 91320
E-mail: order@sagepub.com

SAGE Publications Ltd.
1 Oliver's Yard
55 City Road
London EC1Y 1SP
United Kingdom

SAGE Publications India Pvt. Ltd.
B 1/I 1 Mohan Cooperative Industrial Area
Mathura Road, New Delhi 110 044
India

SAGE Publications Asia-Pacific Pte. Ltd.
3 Church Street
#10-04 Samsung Hub
Singapore 049483

Printed in the United States of America

A catalog record of this book is available from the Library Congress.

978-1-4129-9928-1

This book is printed on acid-free paper.

Acquisitions Editor: Reid Hester
Assistant Editor: Eve Oettinger
Editorial Assistant: Sarita Sarak
Production Editor: Libby Larson
Copy Editor: Amy Rosenstein
Typesetter: C&M Digitals (P) Ltd.
Proofreader: Bonnie Moore
Indexer: Sylvia Coates
Cover Designer: Michael Dubowe
Permissions Editor: Karen Ehrmann
Marketing Manager: Lisa Sheldon Brown

Certified Chain of Custody
SUSTAINABLE Promoting Sustainable Forestry
FORESTRY www.sfiprogram.org
INITIATIVE SFI-01268
SFI label applies to text stock

12 13 14 15 16 10 9 8 7 6 5 4 3 2 1

Contents

Foreword

In various roles, I have seen the development of science policy: as a psychological scientist at Stanford; as a federal science administrator leading the National Science Foundation; and as a higher education administrator overseeing the University of California, San Diego, and later the University of California system.

Through these lenses, I have witnessed the ups and downs of science funding. I have participated in battles between Congress and the administration over what is good science, defending specific research projects that were criticized as wasteful and later found to be of tremendous value to the nation. I have fought for quality science education to train the next generation of scientists. And, I have encountered the varying levels of appreciation for different fields of science.

Broad science policy sets the stage for the progress of science. But, at the heart of it all is you, the researcher, and your research idea. You do the painstaking work of taking a novel idea, embedding it in the larger body of scientific work, translating the idea to a research plan, and making the case to independent scientific panels and federal agencies that this idea should be funded.

The process, as a whole, allows the best ideas to rise to the top and produces knowledge that leads to innovation, improves health, undergirds national security, and enhances learning to produce a literate population. Research is critical to the nation's economic growth and helps to address complex societal issues. The nation needs this knowledge base and owes its gratitude to scientists like you who continue the search for discovery.

This book attempts to glean the insights and strategies of both insiders and outsiders, that is, those who can look back on years of overseeing the grant process at funding agencies and share how the process has changed and what appeals to the agency and review panels, as well as scientists who have been successful in getting grant money, even handling inconsistent streams of funding over time.

The authors combine a dose of common sense and creative ideas to produce helpful recommendations for grant seekers. New investigators will benefit especially from the book, although there are nuggets of advice to motivate even experienced scientists.

The book pulls together in one place recommendations for seeking grants from a number of funders supporting basic, applied, and translational research—each with its own processes and culture—and includes the National Institutes of Health, National Science Foundation, U.S. Department of Defense agencies, Institute of Education Sciences, and even private foundations.

Regardless of the funder, the best ideas still must be communicated, must be tailored for the particular organization, and must stand apart from other great ideas. The reader will see that the sciences of mind, brain, and behavior are of interest to federal and private funders precisely because a solid understanding of what these sciences contribute is needed to advance their missions.

Reports released by the National Science Board indicate that international competition in science is increasing, while federal and state funding for research in the United States continues to decrease, especially when considering inflation-adjusted dollars. To be sure, agency leaders are trying to determine how to stretch their limited budgets to cover as many awards as possible and to make sure that newer investigators stay the course.

Finding motivation to compete for limited dollars can be challenging. There are no magic formulas, but as you will read here, successful grant getters find inspiration in many places!

Federal policy surrounding science may change with new administrations and new members of Congress. What will not change is the need for inquiry and discovery.

I hope the insights shared on the following pages will give you the boost needed to "keep at it." I am confident that we will see brighter opportunities in the future for funding science. The return on the investment is just too great.

Richard C. Atkinson

Preface

Writing a successful grant proposal is like constructing a building. It needs to be built from the bottom up, starting with a strong foundation and then relying on successive "floors" that rest perfectly atop it. Like a building, it also needs to be built at a conceptual level from the top down: A vision is needed and then a plan that ensures that the structure is sound and consistent with that vision. In editing this volume, my colleagues and I aimed to create a book that would help grant writers achieve the goal of constructing successful proposals.

This book is sponsored by the Federation of Associations in Behavioral and Brain Sciences (FABBS). As stated on its website, "FABBS is a coalition of scientific societies that share an interest in advancing the sciences of mind, brain, and behavior. Understanding the human element of many of society's challenges in healthcare, education, conservation behavior, human conflicts, economic decision making and more is a key component to improving the welfare of individuals and our society."

The goal of the proposed book is to provide comprehensive advice on how to build a successful grant proposal, from the top down and from the bottom up. The book provides advice on planning, executing, submitting, and revising grant proposals to maximize their chances of success.

Our motivation in editing the book was to provide a service to all investigators in the behavioral and brain sciences seeking to improve their grant writing. The audience for the book is thus behavioral, cognitive, and social scientists, as well as researchers from aligned fields (e.g., neuroeconomics), the large majority of whom are writing grants and are becoming increasingly frustrated chasing after elusive grant dollars. The book should be relevant to senior as well as junior investigators, because over the course of people's careers, the grant-getting game changes. The book also should appeal to graduate and postdoctoral students who are preparing to write grants.

The book has several special features that we hope will enhance its value to readers.

- *Editorial board.* The editorial board, drawn from the FABBS and FABBS Foundation Boards, includes some of the most successful grant getters in the field of brain and behavioral sciences.
- *Selection of chapter authors.* Part II contains chapters by experts who either have given or have received grants describing how to write effective proposals for various granting agencies. Thus, the chapter authors are seasoned professionals in our field who have experience working with the agencies that are targets of grant proposals.
- *Integrative summary.* Part III culls from the book what is common to the different funding agencies so that grant proposers can learn general as well as specific strategies.
- *Dual strategies.* The book discusses both agency-specific and agency-general strategies. Chapters have been written by people who have given grants as well as people who have applied for them.

Robert J. Sternberg

About the Contributors

Terrance L. Albrecht, Ph.D., is Associate Center Director for Population Sciences and Leader of the Population Studies and Disparities Research Program at the Karmanos Cancer Institute and Professor and Division Director in the Department of Oncology at WSU School of Medicine, where she directs transdisciplinary cancer research in clinical communication, health behavior, and epidemiology. Her cancer research focuses on health disparities affecting underserved adult and pediatric populations in southeast Michigan and has been continuously funded for many years by the National Institutes of Health and other federal agencies. She has served as a permanent and ad hoc member of numerous federal grant review panels, including a previous appointment as Chair of the Community Influences on Health Behavior Study Section.

Jon Atherton is Director of Strategy and Sustainability at the Community Alliance for Research & Engagement within the Yale School of Public Health. Before immigrating to the United States, he was an advisor on urban renewal policy at the Office of the Deputy Prime Minister in London. He has developed numerous National Institutes of Health–funded research collaborations at Yale and has written two successful training fellowships with colleagues at the Center for Interdisciplinary Research on AIDS.

Richard C. Atkinson is president emeritus of the University of California and professor emeritus of cognitive science and psychology at the University of California, San Diego. He is a former director of the National Science Foundation and was a long-term member of the faculty at Stanford University. His research has been concerned with problems of memory and cognition.

Eva L. Baker is Distinguished Professor in the Graduate School of Education & Information Studies at the University of California, Los Angeles (UCLA), and Director of the National Center for Research on Evaluation, Standards, and Student Testing (CRESST). She conducts research in learning, assessment, and technology. At UCLA, she has been responsible for obtaining more than $124 million in grant funding.

Robin A. Barr is Director of the Division of Extramural Activities at the National Institute on Aging (NIA), National Institutes of Health (NIH). With 25 years and counting of experience at NIH, he has served as a program administrator, training officer, and now has responsibility for supervising review, and grants management as well as coordinating the different program areas. He has attended countless review meetings, advised hundreds, if not thousands, of applicants and speaks regularly on how to obtain funding to diverse communities. Once upon a time, he even obtained funding from NIA himself.

Bettina L. Beard is a senior research psychologist and human factors engineer at the National Aviation and Space Administration Ames Research Center. She has initiated, sponsored, and served as Contracting Officer's Technical Representative for numerous contracts and grants at the National Aeronautic and Space Administration (NASA). Dr. Beard is currently working in the air-traffic control domain with funding from both NASA and the Federal Aviation Administration.

Susan E. F. Chipman managed the Cognitive Science program at the U.S. Office of Naval Research (ONR), as well as more applied programs in advanced training technology for 22 years until retiring in August 2006. Previously, she was Assistant Director of the National Institute of Education, where she was responsible for managing research programs in mathematics education, cognitive development, computers and education, and social influences on learning and development. In these positions, she reviewed and made funding decisions on hundreds of proposals and conducted a number of very large grant competitions. During a brief period as a visiting assistant professor at the University of Michigan, she wrote successful proposals for both a **National Institute of Mental Health** (NIMH) Small Grant and an NIMH postdoctoral fellowship. Her job responsibilities at ONR included the development of competing mega-proposals to obtain funds that were then used to fund external research grants. She earned an A.B. in mathematics, an M.B.A., and an A.M. and a Ph.D. in experimental psychology from Harvard University and is a Fellow of both the American Psychological Association and the Association for Psychological Science. She was named an honorary lifetime member of the Cognitive Science Society in recognition of her contributions to the field and also received the American Psychological Association's award for federal research managers. She is currently engaged in independent scholarly activities.

M. Brent Dolezalek is Senior Program Associate at the James S. McDonnell Foundation (JSMF), a private foundation in St. Louis, Missouri. He received his B.A. in psychology from Washington University in St. Louis and M.S. in industrial/organizational psychology from San Francisco State University. His background in psychology, expertise in technology, and decade of experience with JSMF has put him on the frontlines of grant making.

John F. Dovidio is Professor of Psychology at Yale University. He has served as Editor of the *Journal of Personality and Social Psychology–Interpersonal Relations and Group Processes, Personality and Social Psychology Bulletin,* and *Social Issues and Policy Review.* He has received the Kurt Lewin Award and the Donald Campbell Award for his scholarly accomplishments in social psychology.

Howard Eichenbaum is Professor of Psychology and Director of the Center for Memory and Brain at Boston University. In his academic appointments at Wellesley College, the University of North Carolina, the State University of New York at Stony Brook, and Boston University, he has been continuously funded by grants from the National Institutes of Health, the National Institute on Aging, the National Science Foundation, and the U.S. Office of Naval Research for more than 20 years and is currently principal investigator on a **National Institute of Mental Health** Silvo O. Conte Center for Neuroscience Research.

Susan T. Fiske is Eugene Higgins Professor of Psychology and Professor of Psychology and Public Affairs, Princeton University. She has been funded by the National Science Foundation, the National Institutes of Health, and private foundations, but lately she has found the grant-getting process more frustrating. Author of research in social cognition and social neuroscience, she is President-Elect of the Federation of Associations in Behavioral and Brain Sciences.

Susan M. Fitzpatrick is Vice President of the James S. McDonnell Foundation (JSMF) and Adjunct Associate Professor in the Department of Anatomy and Neurobiology and the School of Occupational Therapy at Washington University. Her experience as an academic scientist and a not-for-profit executive provide Susan with experience in both grant seeking and grant making. During her two decades with JSMF, Susan has been directly involved with grant programs awarding more than $300 million in support of research. Susan is currently serving as President, Association for Women in Science.

Nathan A. Fox is Distinguished University Professor at the University of Maryland, College Park. His research on individual differences in infant temperament has been funded continuously by the National Institutes of Health for the past 20 years, and he is a recipient of a MERIT award from the National Institute of Child Health and Human Development. He has also received funding from the National Science Foundation and a Distinguished Investigator Award from the Brain and Behavior Research Foundation. He is a Fellow of the American Association for the Advancement of Science and the American Psychological Society.

Morton Ann Gernsbacher is a Vilas Research Professor and the Sir Frederic Bartlett Professor at the University of Wisconsin-Madison. She's held grants from the National Institutes of Health (NIH), the National Science Foundation (NSF), the Air Force Office of Scientific Research, the Army Research Institute, the Centers for Disease Control and Prevention, and several large and small private foundations. She has served two terms as a member of a NIH standing study section, has chaired multiple grant review panels for the Department of Defense, and is currently serving her second term as a member of an NSF Advisory Committee. She has also worked directly with small private foundations to shape their grant-making priorities and craft their grant-application procedures. She is the immediate past president of the Federation of Associations in Behavioral & Brain Sciences Foundation.

Nathan Hansen is an Associate Professor in the Department of Psychiatry at the Yale University School of Medicine. He serves as the Director, Global Mental Health and HIV Prevention Research in the Division of Prevention and Community Research within the Department of Psychiatry. He also serves as Director, Development Core, Deputy Director, Office of International Training, and Associate Director of Training in the Center for Interdisciplinary Research on AIDS at Yale University. Dr. Hansen oversees training activities across six National Institutes of Health–funded training programs, including two T32 programs in substance use and HIV prevention, an R25 training program for diverse scholars, and three D43 international training programs.

Jeannette R. Ickovics is Professor of Epidemiology and Public Health and of Psychology at Yale University. She is the Founding Director of the Social and Behavioral Sciences Program at the School of Public Health. As Principal Investigator of a National Institutes of Health (NIH) training grant since 1999, she has trained more than 50 pre- and postdoctoral fellows—a next generation of prevention scientists. Dr. Ickovics' research lies at the intersection between public health and psychology. She investigates the interplay of the psychological, medical, and social factors that influence the health of the person and of the community. She uses this lens to examine the challenges faced by those marginalized by the health care system and by society. Her community-based research—more than $20 million funded by NIH, the Centers for Disease Control and Prevention, and private foundations—is characterized by methodological rigor and cultural sensitivity.

Robert W. Levenson received his Ph.D. from Vanderbilt University in clinical psychology. He is currently a Professor in the Department of Psychology at the University of California–Berkeley where he is a member of the behavioral neuroscience, clinical science, developmental, and social/personality programs. He currently serves as Director of the Institute for Personality and Social Research, Director of the Clinical Science Program, and is the former Director of the Predoctoral Training Consortium in Affective Science (a National Institute of Mental Health [NIMH]–funded multidisciplinary training program). His research program is in the area of human emotion, studying the organization of physiological, behavioral, and subjective systems; the ways that these systems are impacted by neuropathology, normal aging, and culture; and the role that emotions play in the maintenance and disruption of committed relationships. Dr. Levenson's research is supported by NIMH and the National Institute on Aging (including a MERIT award). He is past President of the Society for Psychophysiological Research and past President of the Association for Psychological Science.

Cynthia H. Null is a Technical Fellow at the National Aeronautics and Space Administration (NASA). She received a B.A. in mathematics from Albion College, and an M.A. and Ph.D. in quantitative psychology from Michigan State University. Her career began with an academic appointment at the College of William and Mary, where she was on the faculty for 18 years before joining NASA. She has been the managing editor of the journal *Psychometrika* since 1984.

Lynn Okagaki is Dean of the University of Delaware's College of Education and Human Development. Prior to this appointment, Dr. Okagaki served in the Institute of Education Sciences (IES). From 2002 through 2005, she was the Institute of Education Sciences Deputy Director for Science. In that role, she established the IES scientific peer review system. She then served as Commissioner for Education Research and Acting Commissioner for Special Education Research. She designed the IES research goal structure, which creates a stream of research from applied exploratory research through intervention development to efficacy and effectiveness evaluations.

Lisa S. Onken is Chief of the Science of Behavioral and Integrative Treatment Branch and the Associate Director for Treatment in the Division of Clinical Neuroscience and Behavioral Research at the National Institute on Drug

Abuse (NIDA). At NIDA, she created and oversees the behavioral and integrative treatment development program, a program of research designed to facilitate the development of treatment interventions from basic science to implementable interventions. Prior to joining the National Institutes of Health, she worked as both a researcher and a clinician in a variety of settings.

Denise C. Park is the codirector of the Center for Vital Longevity at the University of Texas at Dallas and Distinguished University Chair of Behavioral and Brain Sciences. She has been continuously funded by the National Institute of Aging for more than 30 years and presently holds a National Institutes of Health MERIT award.

Louis A. Penner is a Professor of Oncology in the School of Medicine at Wayne State University and a member of the Population Studies and Health Disparities Program at Karmanos Cancer Institute, Detroit Michigan, as well as an Associate Faculty Member in the Research Center for Group Dynamics at the Institute for Social Research at the University of Michigan. In the last nine years, he has been the principal investigator or a coinvestigator on grants totaling more than $12 million, which have come from the National Institutes of Health and various private foundations. He currently is a member of the Social Psychology, Personality, and Interpersonal Processes Study Section for the National Institutes of Health.

William (Bill) T. Riley is Chief of the Science of Research and Technology Branch, Behavioral Research Program, Division of Cancer Control and Population Sciences at the National Cancer Institute (NCI). He previously served as a Program Director at the National Institute of Mental Health and at the National Heart, Lung, and Blood Institute. This chapter was written while at the National Heart, Lung, and Blood Institute. Prior to joining the National Institutes of Health (NIH), he was an extramural researcher in academic and private sectors, and was the principal investigator of approximately 30 NIH grants and contracts.

Emilie F. Rissman is a professor in the Department of Biochemistry and Molecular Genetics at the University of Virginia School of Medicine. Her entire faculty career has been at Virginia and over those 26 years, she has trained 11 Ph.D. students and 13 doctoral fellows. She has been well funded with grants from the National Institute of Mental Health, the National Institute of Child Health and Human Development, the National Institute of Neurological Disorders and Stroke, the National Science Foundation, NARSAD, and Autism Speaks. She is a past President of the Society for Behavioral Neuroendocrinology, an Editor for *Endocrinology*, and is on the editorial board for several other journals.

Eduardo Salas is Trustee Chair and Pegasus Professor of Psychology at the University of Central Florida (UCF). He also holds an appointment at the Institute for Simulation and Training. He previously was Branch Head and Senior Research Psychologist at the Naval Air Warfare Center in Orlando, where he directed and funded multimillion-dollar research programs. At UCF, he has generated over $45 million in contracts and grants from agencies like the National Science Foundation, the U.S. Office of Naval Research, the Army Research Institute, the U.S. Army Research Laboratory, and several other foundations and organizations.

Marissa L. Shuffler, M.A., is a graduate research associate at the Institute for Simulation and Training, University of Central Florida. Ms. Shuffler has worked in applied research in the behavioral sciences for more than seven years and has successfully led or supported numerous grant and contract efforts for various military agencies, including serving as a lead writer on two winning indefinite delivery, indefinite quantity proposals valued at more than $20 million each. She is currently completing her doctorate in Industrial/Organizational (I/O) Psychology at the University of Central Florida, and holds a master's degree in I/O Psychology from George Mason University.

Robert J. Sternberg is Provost, Senior Vice President, Kaiser Family Foundation Chair in Leadership Ethics, and Regents Professor of Psychology and Education at Oklahoma State University. During his years as a professor at Yale, he held roughly 50 grants and contracts totaling $20 million from various granting agencies, such as the National Science Foundation, the U.S. Office of Naval Research, the Army Research Institute, the Institute of Education Sciences, and the Spencer Foundation. He is currently president of the Federation of Associations in Behavioral and Brain Sciences.

Tracy L. Waldeck, Ph.D., is Branch Chief for Extramural Policy within the Division of Extramural Activities. During her 10 years with the National Institutes of Health (NIH), National Institute of Mental Health (NIMH), Dr. Waldeck has been actively involved in developing extramural policy at the NIH and was an active participant with the NIH Enhancing Peer Review Initiative. In her current role as Branch Chief with NIMH, she interacts with applicants and grantees in all aspects of the grant application, review, and award process.

Joseph L. Young is retired from government service after more than 30 years as a program officer, first at the U.S. Office of Naval Research and then at the National Science Foundation, responsible for review, funding, and monitoring of research grants in cognitive and perceptual psychology.

Dr. Young is a Fellow of the American Psychological Association (APA), the Association for Psychological Science, the American Association for the Advancement of Science, and the American Educational Research Association and a recipient of the APA Meritorious Research Service Citation. Since his retirement, Dr. Young has remained active as a consultant and as a Scientific Review Officer at SRA International, responsible for organizing peer review for a number of government agencies, primarily the Congressionally Directed Medical Research Programs of the Department of Defense.

PART I

General Information About Obtaining Grants

1

Securing a Research Grant

Robert J. Sternberg

When I started as an assistant professor in 1975, I was offered $5,000 in seed money from my university to start up my research. I had no extramural (outside) funding. A quarter century later, I had more than $6 million in extramural funding. But, there were some years that I seemed to have the golden touch in getting grants and other years in which everything I touched seem to turn to lead. Oddly, I never could predict which grant proposals would get funded, even after years of experience writing proposals.

That is the first lesson you need to learn about securing research grants. The grant-getting process is uncertain: One never knows which grant proposals will be funded, nor even how long one's funding will last. It is not uncommon for budgets to be cut in midstream, leaving the principal investigator with expenses and commitments that were made in good faith but that no longer can be met. Worse, those multiyear projects can disappear with the drop of a hat if Congress decides, for one reason or another, not to budget certain funds or if a foundation decides that its interests have changed and your work is no longer of interest to them.

Note: This chapter draws in parts upon Sternberg, R. J. (2003). Obtaining a research grant: The view from the applicant. In J. M. Darley, M. P. Zanna, & H. L. Roediger (Eds.), *The complete academic: A career guide* (2nd ed., pp. 169–184). Mahwah, NJ: Erlbaum.

Although the funding landscape is fraught with booby traps, there are steps you can take to maximize your chances of avoiding those traps—of securing and maintaining your funding, at least to the extent possible. This chapter discusses some of those steps.

Before making suggestions, I should add that my comments are based on experiences (a) of my own in trying to get funded, (b) that my colleagues have had in seeking funding, (c) that I've had reviewing grants, and (d) of serving on a panel that funded research (sponsored by the Air Force Office of Scientific Research [AFOSR]). I hope my experiences are helpful. But, do not limit yourself to learning from my experience! Talk to others in your department or unit who are experienced in getting grants, and ask them for tips. You might even ask to see their old grant proposals, just to get a concrete sense of what successful proposals look like. Most important, read as much of this book as possible to learn from the diverse experiences of the chapter authors.

In the granting enterprise, to some extent, you "make your own luck." First, let's consider why you should apply for a grant. Next, let's discuss the kinds of organizations that fund research. Then, let's talk about the actual process of getting funded. Then, let's consider techniques to maximize the chances of your getting funded. Finally, let's consider how proposals are evaluated.

There are many different kinds of grants. Some grants fund research, but others instead fund travel, teaching, or development of particular commercial products. This chapter focuses on research grants. Other chapters in this volume focus on other aspects of grants.

Why Apply for a Research Grant?

Why should you apply for a research grant? There are several reasons.

First, it will provide you with funds to do your research. Even relatively inexpensive research costs *something* and having a research grant helps ensure that you can accomplish the research you would like to do. Even if you do relatively inexpensive research, having a grant means you will no longer have to rely on departmental funds or perhaps your own.

Second, research grants help support students. Many graduate students and postdoctoral fellows are supported partly or exclusively by research grants, and without such grants, some members of the next generation of researchers might never have the opportunity to be trained. Moreover, you are helping your department by investing your grant funds in students so that the department (or university) can invest in other things.

Third, a research grant can free you from responsibilities you may wish to delegate to others. For example, you may use the research grant to pay someone other than yourself to test participants or to prepare stimulus materials under your direction. Although there are fun parts of research, copying documents, coding data, and preparing each piece of research material are probably not among those fun activities but rather are ones you would rather delegate to others paid off grants.

Fourth, research grants can provide you with summer salary if your institution pays you for less than 12 months. Many universities do, in fact, pay salaries for less than 12 months. A research grant can provide one, two, or sometimes even three months of summer support, thus supplementing the researcher's income. Of course, when you take summer salary, you are expected to work on the research during the time you are drawing the salary. Many investigators find that, as a result of teaching obligations, it is hard to devote the time they would wish to research during the nine or so months in which they are teaching. So having summer support can greatly accelerate one's research enterprise while providing needed funds for living expenses.

Finally, obtaining a research grant marks you as a serious (and fundable!) scholar and can help you when it comes time for promotion and tenure decisions. At a major research institution, getting a grant may be a *sine qua non* for promotion or tenure. Even at an institution that emphasizes teaching, having a research grant can set you apart from your colleagues.

Thus, it makes sense to apply for a research grant as soon as one possibly can once one begins one's career. Some scholars even apply during their postdoctoral years to get a head start on their research.

Who Funds Research and How Do They Fund It?

There are many different kinds of funding organizations. Some of these organizations are very specific in the kinds of research they fund, whereas others are more general. The main types of organizations that fund university research are universities, governmental organizations, nongovernmental organizations, foundations, and corporations. Much more detail is contained in subsequent chapters of this book.

Intramural (Internal) Grants

Universities often have limited funds to support the research of their own students and faculty members. These funds may be available to anyone who applies or may only be available to certain individuals, such as new faculty members, junior faculty members, or faculty members who have not succeeded in gaining external support. The funds are typically awarded on a competitive basis. Universities are often willing and eager to provide first small seed grants to new faculty, so be sure to check on the availability of funding from your own institution.

In my experience, universities are more likely to provide funds to early-career researchers than to later-career researchers, on the view that those in early career need some initial funding to kick-start their careers. However, there are various kinds of exceptions. For example, at my previous university, Tufts, my colleagues and I in the Office of the Dean of Arts and Sciences initiated a program to help senior faculty who had gotten off track in their research to get back on track again. At my current university, Oklahoma State, my colleagues and I in the Office of the Provost have initiated a program of funding for planning grants to support creative interdisciplinary research that helps to support the land-grant mission of the university. In sum, it always pays to check whether there are special intramural programs in your institution that will fund your research, no matter where you are in your career.

Extramural (External) Grants

Governmental Organizations

Governmental funding organizations are sponsored by national, state, and local governments. Examples of governmental organizations in the United States are the National Science Foundation (NSF), the National Institutes of Health (NIH), the United States Military (e.g., Army Research Institute, Office of Naval Research, and Air Force Office of Scientific Research), and the U.S. Department of Education (e.g., the Institute of Education Sciences [IES]). National organizations such as these have regular grant competitions and you can find out about these competitions either through your grants and contracts office or through the agencies' websites. State and local governmental organizations may have research funds but may not have regular competitions for them.

Government grants are typically for 3 years, although they may be for less time (such as a year) or for more time (typically up to 5 years). It is important to realize that a commitment by the government to fund your research for a specified period of years does not guarantee you will actually get the funding you were promised. Many variables can intervene. The agency's budget may be cut by the government, resulting in your budget's being reduced or sometimes even eliminated. The agency may be dissatisfied with your progress and terminate your funding (which is relatively rare but does happen). Or, the agency may change its priorities and decide your project no longer fits its goals. You should thus be optimistic that commitments to you will be met, but you should by no means feel certain of it.

Most grants require progress reports at least once a year, and it behooves you to do such reports with the utmost of care and to put your research in the most positive light possible. Some agencies also conduct site visits: Members of a team come to the site of the research to evaluate the quality of the work. These visits also should be taken very seriously.

As you will learn in later chapters, governmental organizations have diverse programs. Some fund only research of a particular kind or in a particular area. Others are more wide ranging. Grants.gov is a source of information about a wide variety of governmental grants. Typically, there are many steps in submitting grant proposals to government agencies, so it behooves you to start the process of preparing the proposal early. The best way to start is to look on the appropriate website to see what is available and to determine what might be a good match to your own research. It is also an excellent idea to talk to a relevant program officer before you start writing to ascertain his or her views on the appropriateness of your ideas for the particular program he or she heads.

My best experience with a governmental grant was my first: I was funded by NSF my first year as an assistant professor, despite the fact that the grant proposal I wrote was anything but exemplary. I learned then that granting agencies often go out of their way to fund new investigators if they possibly can. My worst experience was with the U.S. Department of Education: We got all "excellent" ratings from outside reviewers, something that had never happened to me before. But, the program director turned down the grant because she thought it too similar to another proposal we had submitted that they had funded. We pointed out that the other grant proposal had not, in fact, been funded. After further investigation, she conceded this fact, but unwilling to admit she had made a mistake—an event not uncommon in life—she refused to reconsider.

Nongovernmental Organizations

Nongovernmental organizations are entities that are not tied to any one government or that are tied to multiple governments but that are run somewhat independently of these governments. Examples of nongovernmental organizations are the World Bank, North Atlantic Treaty Alliance, and World Health Organization. These organizations are less likely to have regular funding competitions, and you need to consult their websites or, if you have contacts, individuals within the organizations to find out about funding opportunities.

My best experience with a nongovernmental organization was funding that created a program for enhancing the intelligence of Venezuelan college students. The proposal was a real shot in the dark, and this grant gave me an opportunity to visit Venezuela several times in the early 1980s, to learn Spanish, and to write a book that I otherwise never would have written. My worst experience was with the same organization. When the political party in power was thrown out, I learned that the nongovernmental organization was not as nongovernmental as I had thought. The new president had campaigned on the silliness of programs to increase intelligence and indicated he would not support them if elected. When he was elected, the "nongovernmental" organization proved to be more "governmental" than we had thought and that was the end of the funding.

Foundations

Foundations are privately owned and operated, and typically are more targeted and mission-oriented than government in the particular kinds of research they will fund. Examples of foundations are the Spencer Foundation, the W. T. Grant Foundation, the John Templeton Foundation, the James McDonnell Foundation, and the MacArthur Foundation. There are hundreds of foundations that fund research, but the chances are that only a small number, if any, will fund the particular kind of research you want to do.

Foundations generally run with small staffs. This means that you need to rely heavily on website and other documents because their staff members often are already hard-pressed to meet all the demands on their time. Nevertheless, there are occasionally foundation officers who will be willing to talk to you about your grant proposal. The foundation website will probably indicate the level of assistance that is available.

My best experience with foundation funding was with a grant from the James S. McDonnell Foundation we had through the Partnership for Child Development, then at Oxford University. It enabled us to collaborate with other psychologists as well as epidemiologists, parasitologists, anthropologists, and economists on a project investigating the effects of parasitic illnesses on children's cognitive abilities. The project enabled us to do research in parts of the world in which we never had imagined we would work—Jamaica, Kenya, Tanzania, Zambia, and other locations, collaborating with individuals who taught us lessons we never would have learned from our typical research. My worst experience with foundation funding was submitting a proposal and hearing—nothing. I just never got a response, despite my having cleared the proposal through the foundation office.

Corporations

Corporations generally are private entities. They may be for-profit or nonprofit. Corporations tend to be the most selective in the kinds of research they fund. Typically, they are interested in research that will improve sales of their products or services. You need to be especially careful in selecting corporations to which to apply for funding.

Sometimes corporations have rules regarding publication of data that render problematical the receipt of funding from them. For example, they may insist on reviewing potential publications before they are submitted, or they may have a nondisclosure policy that forbids publication at all. If the research does not go the way they hoped, they may lose interest in continuing funding of the research and may even hamper the research enterprise. It is therefore important to carefully check the terms to which you agree to make sure that the terms suit you as well as the corporation. Universities sometimes will not approve corporate-funded research if the corporation places too many constraints on publication of the data—for example, requiring approval of the corporation before any documents based on the research are published.

My best experience with corporate funding was when a large testing organization agreed to fund what was, to that time, what I considered to be the most important research project I had ever done—one that showed that tests of creative and practical thinking could double prediction of college freshman grade-point average over standardized test scores taken the senior year of high school. That experience became my worst, however, when the corporation cut off our funding immediately upon learning that supplementing its test with our test resulted in much better prediction (and also reduction in ethnic-group differences) relative to the use of its test alone.

When we apply for research funding, we often investigate funding organizations that we think other researchers are *less* likely to apply to. Organizations like NSF and NIH receive huge numbers of proposals, because their funding priorities meet the needs of so many researchers and because these organizations are so visible. Ask yourself whether there might be organizations interested in your research that are not as widely sought after.

The Need for Entrepreneurial Spirit

In the past, researchers could apply to the major funding organizations such as NSF and NIH and expect that if they had a reasonably good proposal, they would be funded. This was the case when I started my career. Moreover, my advisor, Gordon Bower, told me that when he started his career, anything that was even reasonably good had substantial probability of being funded. But, with the increase in the number of researchers in the field and the decreases in research budgets, many good or even excellent proposals fail to get funded. It therefore behooves you to think about places where your colleagues are less likely to apply and hence where you may have a better chance of funding.

Another issue you may have to face is that the areas of heaviest funding may not correspond to what you most want to investigate. I have faced this issue many times in my own career. You therefore may find yourself facing a choice of writing a proposal that is your dream research project, but without much hope of funding, or writing one for research that is not quite as high on your priority list but that is higher on the list of priorities for agencies that are providing funding.

Also, find out whether an organization requires a *preproposal*. A preproposal is a brief document, often as little as three to five pages, that describes the concept of the proposed research, how the research would be executed, and the rough budget for the research. Preproposals are commonly required by foundations and corporations, and by some governmental organizations as well (such as the military ones). Preproposals require a little extra work initially but often can end up saving you a lot of time later on. If the organization does not accept your preproposal, at least you have saved yourself the bother of having to write a full proposal, a process that typically is quite time-consuming.

Even if an organization does not request a preproposal, often, a program officer will be willing to chat with you or communicate by snail mail or e-mail regarding ideas you have. The program officer often can give you an idea of whether your idea sounds appropriate for the program he or she administers. Thus, it often makes sense to talk to the program officer, to make sure you are targeting your proposal to the right agency or group within that agency.

Grants Versus Contracts

Most funding takes the form of either a grant or a contract, although there are hybrids as well. A grant is a sum of money that you are given with minimal restrictions to accomplish the research you have proposed. Although major changes in what you plan to do may require approval, generally, granting agencies are somewhat flexible, realizing that plans change as time goes on. Contracts are agreements for prespecified and generally fixed deliverables—in other words, products that you agreed in advance to provide. You are expected to do pretty much what you said you would do and then turn over the products to the contracting agency. There is typically somewhat less flexibility in contracts than in grants. Nevertheless, there often can be some flexibility if you negotiate with whoever awarded the contract. Should you wish to change the terms of the contract, however, it is important that you get permission rather than doing so unilaterally without such permission from the funder.

In much earlier times, when I started my career in the mid-1970s, granting agencies did not closely monitor whether funds from a grant were being spent on the activities specific to that grant. For example, my graduate advisor generously and selflessly supported some of my research on human intelligence, and without that support, I doubt my career ever would have jump-started. Today, however, granting agencies monitor such expenses extremely carefully. You must make sure that expenses from a grant are for research under that grant only. Transferring money between grants or across programs of research without permission can land one in serious trouble.

The Process of Getting Funded in Brief

1. *Think up an idea.* The first step to getting funded is having an idea. The idea does not have to be the greatest one since sliced bread, and as I will say later, it's often better if it isn't the "greatest" idea. You just need a good idea, or, at least, one you can sell to a granting agency. People come up with ideas in different ways. Some do it based on reading articles and deciding what needs to be done next; others do it by observing problems in the world around them; still others combine these and perhaps other techniques. Everyone has to find his or her own preferred ways of generating ideas.

It usually helps you to get funded if the idea is theory-based—that is, it derives from some kind of existing theory or theory you are newly proposing. Innovative methodologies can also be of interest to many funding agencies.

In thinking about what to propose, keep in mind that many grant proposals represent collaborations. You might want to collaborate either with people in your own institution or in other institutions. Within your institution, you may choose to work with people in your own department or in another. Some of the best proposals are collaborative. And, some programs even *require* that proposals be collaborative.

2. *Operationalize the idea.* Next, you need to put the idea into terms that represent a program of research and/or development. In other words, you need to do something with the idea.

3. *Find out who might be interested in your idea.* There are thousands of sources of funding, although most psychologists stick to a much smaller number of sources. Find out what funding organizations might be interested in what you have to offer. You can get tips from colleagues, your department chair, the grants and contracts office of your college or university, or from books and the Internet. Electronic bulletin boards also can be helpful. You can list relevant keywords, and then when calls for proposals come out that use the keywords you provided, you will be notified of the funding opportunities. These days, Internet search is usually a great source of ideas for finding funding agencies, but there is no substitute for knowledgeable individuals who have worked before with the agencies in which you are potentially interested.

4. *Write your proposal.* Next, you write the proposal that presents your idea. Different organizations have different specific requirements as to the format and content of a proposal. But, typically you will need to state (a) what your "big" idea is, (b) why the idea is important, (c) what the theory is behind the idea, (d) what research previously has been done on the idea, (e) what research you propose to do, (f) how you plan to analyze the data from the research, (g) how you plan to manage and share the data with others, (h) how much money you will need to do the research and how you will allocate the funds, (i) how you will handle human-subjects issues (such as informed consent and debriefing), (j) why you are the person (or team) to do the research (i.e., your qualifications), and (k) what resources are available that will enable you to get the research done (such as space, available equipment, the time you have available to do the research, and so on).

When I talk to junior investigators about writing proposals, I emphasize to them the importance of having a story to tell. What is the story behind the research project you propose? What is lacking in the story is the ending: If you were to do the research, how would it all end? You want the readers of your proposal to be interested enough to find out.

A good story always has a setting or context, but it also has a novel twist to keep it interesting. What is the novel twist of your story? What makes your story different from that of others? You need a twist to generate interest both in your proposed research and in the proposal describing it.

Most agencies have rather strict guidelines regarding length. You therefore may not get to tell your story at the length you would have wished to tell it. Thus, as when you tell any story, you must stick to the main ideas and the most important points. What details do readers need and what details, although interesting to you, may not be so interesting to them? What details are crucial to how the research will be done and which ones are secondary? Your judgment as to what is critical will be important, given the length constraints imposed by most funding agencies.

Most importantly, do not assume that readers will be interested in your story because you are. It is your job to interest them. All story authors know they have to catch a reader quickly or lose that reader. You need to do the same. If you can't motivate a reader quickly, the reader may read the proposal, but his or her excitement may be lost quickly, as well as his or her desire to see the proposal funded.

5. *Be sure to proofread and check over your proposal.* Reviewers typically donate their time to evaluating proposals. They do not want to see and may have little patience with typographical or word-processing errors in what they read.

When you proofread, be sure to proofread with the agency guidelines in mind. I once submitted a proposal for which the margins were not according to the prescribed guidelines. The proposal was immediately declined because of the margins! I lost that funding cycle because of bad margins. This is not a mistake I ever made again. You can do better: Don't make it the first time. Make sure margins, fonts, and all aspects of the proposal meet the guidelines.

6. *Solicit feedback on your proposal.* You may find, as I often have, that others readily can see flaws in your proposal that just are invisible to you. Therefore, ask colleagues for feedback before you finalize your proposal. Also, read over your proposal from the standpoint of a reviewer. After I write a proposal, I always read it over as though I were a reviewer, and I try to ask myself the questions I would ask were I reading the proposal for the purpose of reviewing it. Reading over your proposal with a critical eye can often resolve problems in advance so that reviewers do not have to bring them up.

I once wrote, with colleagues, a proposal for the military that I thought was compelling. We even went to great lengths to line up military subjects at several bases. I solicited feedback from the program officer and found out, to my horror, that for the basic research program to which I was applying (called "6–1" in military parlance), military subjects were neither required nor even wanted. Had I submitted the proposal without getting that feedback, it would have been rejected summarily.

7. *Get the proposal approved by your institution.* Almost all institutions have a formal approval process that a grant proposal needs to go through before the proposal can be submitted. This is so because the grant actually goes to the institution rather than to you. You may be the principal investigator or a coinvestigator, but the actual allocation of funds goes to the institution, not to you.

Part of the approval process may be human-subjects approval, if, in fact, you are using human participants. Such approval can take time and so you should be sure to submit your human-subjects forms to your institutional review committee well in advance. Monitoring of rights of human participants has been tightening up over the years, and you may find that getting approval is nontrivial, even if the research seems to be benign. NIH has started requiring potential principal investigators to get training in human-subjects protection, and at the time this chapter is being written, other governmental organizations are expected to follow suit.

During the last few years, I have gone into academic administration, first as a dean and now as a provost. One of the most annoying experiences I have—it just happened the week before I wrote this chapter—is when investigators submit proposals to the university for approval the day the proposal is due or without sufficient lead time for an administration to process the proposal. In the case of the proposal that was submitted to me last week, the budget had a problem and I could not sign it. Do NOT wait until the last minute to submit the proposal to your university.

8. *Send out the proposal on time.* Most funding agencies have deadlines. You therefore need to pay attention to the time frame in which you are allowed to send out your proposal. Deadlines tend to be strict. If you miss a deadline, you probably will have to wait until the next round of funding takes place.

There is one thing you cannot do. You cannot send out minor variants of the same proposal to different agencies and, if more than one version is funded, accept funding for all of them. To meet the ethical requirements for submitting proposals, you must ensure that the research you propose to the different agencies is substantively and substantially different.

9. *Revise the proposal, if necessary; otherwise, abandon it for now.* Relatively few proposals are funded the first time around. Typically, they need to be revised. Therefore, expect to have to do a revision if your proposal is turned down. If you receive really awful reviews or simply can't see how to revise the proposal into an acceptable form, stuff the proposal into a file drawer and wait. You may never see how to revise the proposal, but more likely, incubation will enable you to see things in a more positive light after some time has passed.

Agencies have different policies on revisions. At NIH, you now are allowed only one revision. At NSF, you can do multiple revisions. But, whatever you do, make sure each revision counts. You cannot afford to do a sloppy revision because, at worst, you lose the ability to submit a third time, and at best, you lose another funding cycle and lead reviewers to believe that you are not serious about revising the proposal.

Sometimes, you really are best off abandoning the proposal for the time being. For example, at NIH, if you are not judged to be in the top half of submitters, you will not get a priority score. Such proposals may be funded on the second round but typically aren't. So ask yourself whether you truly are ready to do a fundable revision, and if not, consider filing the proposal away for a while until you either have other proposal ideas or can review your proposal and see what you need to do to make it fundable.

If you wait, don't wait too long because ideas have a limited shelf life. I once did a proposal on concept naturalness and received back reviews suggesting that the concept of concept naturalness was itself unnatural. The reviewers just weren't interested. I shelved the proposal, only to find a few years later the topic had become hot and it seemed like everyone was studying concept naturalness! Indeed, the topic had peaked by the time I became interested in it again. I was too early the first time around and then I waited too long and was too late for a second try.

10. *Resubmit and explain what you have changed.* If you do resubmit, you typically will be expected to indicate how you have responded to the earlier reviews. You should follow all or most of the suggestions of the reviewers. If you have chosen not to follow a suggestion of a reviewer or a panel of reviewers, explain why you have decided not to.

You can afford to pass on a few suggestions and explain why but if you find yourself passing on more than a few reviewer suggestions, then you probably are not ready to do a resubmission. Wait a while until you get over the feeling that the reviewers have dissed you unforgivably!

11. *Get funded, or if not, start over.* You may get funded, in which case, congratulations. Enjoy your funding. But, whether or not you get funded, you soon will be back to writing proposals. For most of us, writing proposals is not a one-time thing. It is a regular part of a research career. Sometimes you will succeed, other times not. But, whatever happens, soon you will be back to proposal writing again.

These items are the bare bones of the proposal-writing process. But, of course, some proposals get funded and others do not. What can you do to maximize the chances of your proposal's getting funded? One thing is to have the right frame of mind.

Your Frame of Mind

1. *Believe in yourself.* Proposal writing is a time-consuming process. At times, you may draw a blank. Or, you may become dissatisfied or even disgusted with what you have written. Moreover, when you get reviews back, you may feel even worse about yourself. It is easy to give up. If you still believe in your idea, don't give up! Believe in your ability to get funded. Reverses are the rule, not the exception. The people who succeed in getting funded and staying funded are those who believe in themselves. They do not believe that every idea they ever have is a good idea. No one has only good ideas. Rather, they believe that, over the course of time, they will be able to produce research ideas that are worthy of funding, and that, ultimately, will get funded.

That said, sometimes we start writing and find that an idea that we thought we had worked out is not in fact ready for prime time. The details we thought we had straight in our mind now elude us. If you feel the proposal getting away from you, there is nothing wrong with shelving it for a few weeks or even a funding cycle and trying again when you feel your head is clearer.

2. *Go for it.* For several years, I thought that it was not worth applying for a grant to pursue my interests in the psychology of wisdom because granting agencies would find the topic just too flaky. In fact, our first proposal was rejected. We then wrote a different proposal, sent it to three foundations, and one foundation funded it for three years. I was shocked! Shocked! But, the lesson is one I should have learned earlier. If you tell yourself you can't get funded, you won't get funded, because you will never try. You have to *go for it.* You may or may not succeed, but the only way to know is to try.

3. *Don't worry about having the greatest idea.* What is the correlation between the quality of ideas in a proposal and its getting funded? If I had to venture a guess for my own career, it's probably about zero. Really bad ideas generally don't get funded. But, sometimes, really good ideas don't get funded either. There are a number of reasons for this. Sometimes, really creative ideas do not fit into existing *zeitgeists,* and reviewers may not understand them, know what to make of them, or see the value of them (Sternberg, Kaufman, & Pretz, 2002). Other times, really creative ideas threaten those who read about them. Reviewers may have a vested interest in another point of view and may not be thrilled to read that what they have been thinking all along has been wrong. Still other times, really creative ideas just seem crazy. So if you have an idea that you think is good but not world-shattering,

don't worry about it. And, if you think you have an idea that is world-shattering, be sure to express it in a way that makes as much contact as possible with the frames of mind of the reviewers. I have sometimes soft-pedaled ideas that I thought might antagonize reviewers in the hope that they then would react more positively. I do not "sell out" on the ideas, but I do soften the way I present them. Often, this technique has worked.

Sometimes ideas can be "ahead" of their time, as with the concept naturalness idea about which I wrote a proposal too early. Many of us have had the experience of applying for a grant, being turned down because the reviewers do not see the relevance of the problem or the research on the problem, and then reading some years later about funded research that does essentially what we proposed. If your ideas are particularly novel, then you have to go to even greater efforts to convince potential reviewers of the importance of the work.

4. *Persist!* During the 30 years I was at Yale, my group was fairly successful in obtaining grant funding. Some colleagues assumed we must have had a wonderful track record in getting grants. False! We probably had more grant proposals turned down than any other individual or group of which I knew at the time. We just wrote more grant proposals. I found that the rate at which my proposals got funded held more or less steady during my career before I entered administration, with minor fluctuations from time to time. The principal key to getting funded, therefore, is to write a lot of proposals.

Many people give up after being turned down once or twice. They conclude that their research—or they—are just never going to be funded. They are right. Their lack of persistence has guaranteed that they will not get funded because they have stopped writing proposals. When we get turned down, a frequent event, we just keep trying, and eventually something works out.

5. *Thicken your skin.* One reason many grant writers do not persist is that they are dismayed by the negativity and often even what seem like the personal insults contained in reviews. No one enjoys being flayed alive—metaphorically speaking—so it is easy to give up. A key lesson is never to take reviews personally and to ignore the tone if it is sarcastic or insulting. Simply concentrate on what is constructive in the reviews, and if you think you can respond to the reviews, do so without responding to their tone. Just take the substance of what is said and respond to that.

I went through a period of my career in which I thought several agencies just "had it in" for me. But, then I realized that these agencies were funding only about 10 percent of the proposals that were submitted, so that even good to excellent proposals were being rejected. I realized I was making a mistake in taking the rejections personally. And, I persisted, despite the large number of proposals being turned down. When I was a dean at Tufts, our faculty member in Arts and Sciences with the greatest success in getting funded—in the biology department—told me that only roughly 1 in 10 of his proposals was being funded. He just kept sending out proposals!

6. *Focus—don't be distracted.* There are almost always many things you would rather do than write a grant proposal. Few people delight in writing proposals; most proposal writers would rather be doing something else. Moreover, there are always many other things to do. Your course preparations need to get done. You may have scholarly articles begging you to write them up. Your committee work may be falling behind. Personal commitments may be on hold and need to be given more attention. Truly, anyone can find excuses not to write a proposal. But, if you wish to do research, chances are good you will need at least some funding. So, you need to focus on proposal writing and find a way to make sure that your proposals get done, regardless of all the other things that genuinely need attention as well. You have to *make the time.*

Many institutions give most credit—for tenure and promotion—for your getting funded. But, many will look at whether you have at least tried. They are more likely to look favorably on someone who has tried and not yet succeeded than on someone who never even gave it a shot.

7. *Find your right audience.* You can end up wasting a lot of time by submitting a proposal to a funding organization that simply does not fund the kind of work you are proposing. Before you write your proposal, make sure that the agency or agencies to which you are applying actually fund the kind of work you are proposing. Some funding agencies release the names of the individuals who serve on and head various grant panels, so that you can know in advance who is likely to evaluate your proposal. Even if you obtain such a list, though, you still will not know to what external referees the proposal will be sent for outside evaluation.

Now that you have gotten started, here are some things to attend to in writing the proposal itself.

Your Proposal

1. *Tell your story.* You may think science is somehow the opposite of story telling, but this is not the case. As noted earlier, good science tells a story. The story begins with a problem. It typically continues with people who, in the past, have tried to solve the problem (or who may not have correctly identified just what the problem is). And, it continues with how you

plan to solve the problem or at least contribute to its solution. So, a good grant proposal has a narrative quality to it that holds the whole thing together. It has a big idea, like the plot of a story, and it develops the idea in a way that gives the whole proposal coherence, just like a story. If you cannot figure out the story behind your grant proposal, do not expect your reviewers to do so.

2. *Justify the scientific importance and interest of the research.* Because you have probably thought a lot about the research you are proposing, it may be obvious to you why the research is important. But, do not expect it to be obvious to the reviewers of your proposal. You have to justify to them the importance of the research. Do not assume that others will see this importance without your stating it. If you really do not know why the research is important, do not expect the reviewers to.

An ineffective argument for the importance of research is to point out that X, Y, and Z have been done, but A, B, and C have not yet been done, and your goal is to do A, B, and C. The fact that something has not been done does not, in itself, make that thing important. There are an infinite number of studies that could be done that have not been done and never will be done because no one will care about the results. You need to show why your particular set of studies is worth doing.

3. *Be clear, and then try to be clearer.* If you are writing a proposal about a specific area, chances are you have at least some expertise in that area. You therefore may assume that reviewers have the same kind and level of background you have. They may not. You must therefore be extremely clear in your presentation of ideas. Moreover, because you have thought about your ideas many times, it is easy, in writing, to leave gaps. After all, it should be obvious what you meant. But, it rarely is obvious to anyone but yourself. Be as clear as you possibly can be, and after you have done that, try to be clearer yet. When you write, write for someone who is generally knowledgeable in your broad area of research (such as cognitive psychology, social psychology, developmental psychology, or whatever), but who is not necessarily specialized in the particular problem within the area or areas you are studying. (For tips on how to write clearly, you may wish to consult Sternberg and Sternberg [2010].)

4. *Organize the hell out of your proposal.* Actually, I think this is a statement made to me years ago by my graduate advisor, Gordon Bower. Proposals tend to be technical. They also tend to be complex. It is easy for a reviewer to get lost in the thicket. You therefore want to make sure your writing is as organized as possible.

Organize your proposal in a hierarchical way. Make sure the major points stand out and that the minor points are properly subordinated. No reviewer possibly can remember everything you have written. By writing hierarchically, you ensure that the reviewer will remember the most important things—the things you really want him or her to remember.

5. *Sell your ideas.* After you have paid attention to how you present your ideas, you need to think about how you are going to sell your ideas. Good ideas typically do not sell themselves (Sternberg & Lubart, 1995). You have to sell them. No matter how good you may think your ideas are, do not expect it to be obvious to reviewers why your ideas are so great. You have to convince them. It therefore is important to write the proposal in a way that is not only descriptive but persuasive as well. You are not just saying what you want to do. You are telling the reader why anyone in his or her right mind will want to fund you to do it.

6. *Be comprehensive but selective in your literature review.* Usually, you are writing under the constraint of only being allowed a certain number of pages in your proposal. Thus, although it might be possible to devote the whole proposal to literature review, you need to be selective. Cite as much as possible of the research that is *directly* relevant to your proposal, but skip the stuff that, while peripherally relevant, does not bear directly on what you propose.

When people in my group at Yale wrote proposals, we tried to keep in mind likely reviewers of these proposals. Most reviewers consider their work in the area to be important. After all, they may feel that they would not have been asked to review the proposal if their work were not important. So, they will not be thrilled to see their classic book or article roundly ignored. The lesson is to try to cite likely reviewers, whenever possible.

Although you cannot be certain of who will review your proposal, you can make reasonable guesses. People who are central to the field, people who have reviewed your articles (should you know who any of them are), people you run into at professional meetings and symposia on topics of interest to you—these are among the likely reviewers. Write with them in mind, as you would wish they would do for you. Have you ever gotten an article or proposal to review and turned first to the references to see if you were cited? Others may well do the same!

7. *Be respectful in your literature review.* Sometimes, the research one proposes is designed to set the record straight—perhaps to correct the errors the researcher sees in past work. But, even if you believe past work has led to wrong conclusions, which you are going to correct, it is important to be

respectful of this work. First, disagree though you may with those who came before you, these very scientists are the ones who created the methods or results that are serving as the basis for your work. Hence, you owe them a debt, because you are building or rebuilding on their work. Second, it is unprofessional and, arguably, immature, to be disrespectful. Third, and pragmatically, the people who did this past work are those most likely to review your proposal, and if you are disrespectful toward them, you endanger the viability of your own proposal.

8. *Have a strong theoretical basis for your proposal.* One of the main reasons I have seen for rejections of proposals is that there is no theory, or the theory is only sketchily portrayed, or the theory is only marginally relevant to the research that is proposed. It is therefore important for you to pay close attention to the theory section of your proposal. Explain the theory clearly, and also the hypotheses that derive from it that are relevant to your research. Be sure you show how the hypotheses derive from the theory. Don't expect reviewers to see the derivation of the hypotheses on their own. Then, when you are describing the research, make sure it is clear how the research tests the hypotheses that you generated from the underlying theory.

9. *Follow directions.* Funding agencies, especially governmental ones, have many rules to follow in the preparation of a proposal. Just following all these rules and doing all of the required paperwork can become enormously time-consuming and, at times, can be frustrating. Yet it is imperative that you follow all of these nitty-gritty rules lest your proposal be returned or even rejected because you disobeyed the rules. I once had a proposal sent back and then had to wait for the next granting deadline because I had inadvertently not answered a few questions on a form.

Today, college and university grant and contract offices generally check for these mechanical kinds of errors, but ultimately, it is your responsibility, not theirs, to follow the guidelines. You do not want your proposal to be rejected because it did not follow the guidelines. If it must be rejected, it should be because of the science. Therefore, do not make yourself vulnerable by ignoring or flouting the rules. Be creative in your science, not in the mechanics of writing the proposal.

10. *Make sure your budget is reasonable and matches the proposed research.* Reviewers of grants are typically experienced and can recognize rather quickly when a project is underbudgeted or overbudgeted. If you underbudget, you are showing that you do not understand the full cost of the research, and your underbudgeting calls into question whether you really understand the resources your research requires. If you overbudget, you may

give the impression of being more concerned about the money than about the research or even of being greedy. It therefore is important that your budget be reasonable. Some organizations state the evaluation of budgets is separate from evaluation of the merits of the work. My own experience, though, is that unrealistic budgeting can sour the way reviewers perceive the work you propose. You typically will be asked to provide a justification for your budget, and this justification should make explicit why you are requesting the level of funding and allocation of funds you have requested. Unfortunately, budgets are often cut before funding is awarded.

In budgeting, keep in mind that most institutions charge "overhead." Overhead is a portion of the grant or contract that the university takes out for its own use. In theory, overhead pays for things such as space, library usage, heating, electricity, costs to the university of administering the grant, and so forth. Rates of overhead vary widely among universities, and can reach 65 percent or more. The overhead may be computed on the whole grant or only on salaries and wages. For example, if the overhead rate is 50 percent, then the university will take 50 cents out of your grant for every dollar you spend. Rates of overhead are negotiated between the university and the funding organization.

Universities differ in their flexibility regarding overhead. Generally, though, they are willing to do some negotiation. For example, my own institution typically charges a fairly high rate of overhead but is willing to pay less if the funding institution writes a letter saying it is their policy to pay less. You thus may have some leverage in negotiating rates, although probably not much.

Universities also may charge benefits on salaries and wages. This is money taken out of the grant to pay for employee benefits such as health care, retirement plans, life insurance, disability insurance, and so forth. Benefit rates vary widely across universities. From the researcher's standpoint, the important thing to realize is that you do not get to spend the entire amount of money that a funding agency allocates to you.

It is important also to realize that universities have policies regarding grant spending, and it is wise to check these policies. For example, when a grant is used to pay for a professional trip, the university may have a maximum daily amount that it will reimburse lodging or food expenses.

Foundations often are unwilling to pay overhead, or they may agree to pay only a small percentage (such as 10 percent). Sometimes, the overhead is called by another name, such as "administrative costs." If you are thinking of applying to an agency that does not pay overhead or that pays only a minimal amount, make sure your university will support the proposal. Hard to believe though it may be, universities often lose money even on grants that pay full overhead. So, they may be reluctant to accept grants with little or no overhead, especially if you have not also been funded with grants that pay overhead at the full rate.

Evaluation of Proposals

Each funding organization has its own criteria for evaluating proposals and its own timeline for doing evaluations. Evaluations may take just a few weeks, but typically require four to six months or even more.

Evaluations may be internal, external, or both. Internal evaluation means that employees of the funding organization evaluate the proposal. Such evaluations are common with foundations and corporations. External evaluation means that reviewers outside the funding organization—often people like you—evaluate the proposal and provide their evaluations to the funding organization. In writing your proposal, you need to keep in mind the reviewers who are likely to evaluate your proposal, and write with these potential evaluators in mind.

When proposals are sent out for review, they are sent out with the explicit understanding that the proposal is a privileged document. This means that a reviewer is not permitted to show or even discuss the proposal with others and certainly is not permitted to use any of the ideas in the proposal for his or her own research. Usually, reviewers are asked to destroy the proposals after they are done reviewing them. In my experience, reviewers are honest in adhering to these guidelines. After all, they do not want people stealing their ideas! Of course, there can be a bad apple in any basket and there is no guarantee that things will go as they should. But in my experience, reviewers generally take their ethical responsibilities seriously.

Different organizations use different criteria in evaluating proposals, but certain criteria tend to be common across many different funding organizations. A first criterion most organizations use for evaluating proposal is that of whether the proposal even fits the kinds of research the organization sees itself as funding. A second criterion is likely to be the scientific (or educational or commercial) value of the research. Organizations typically look for some degree of originality in a proposal, as well as quality of the way in which the research is designed and is to be executed. A third criterion is whether the data analysis is appropriate for the research that has been proposed. A fourth criterion often is the appropriateness of the budget. And, a fifth criterion is the level of qualifications of the proposer and the facilities available to the proposer. This last criterion is important because it helps ensure that the research will get done, and get done well.

Now you are almost ready to write your grant proposal. All you need are some ideas and to set aside the time to put these ideas into the form of a proposal. Perhaps you would rather watch a football game, go for a picnic, or check out a new movie. But, when these things are over, they are over. When you do a piece of research, it can have a lifelong impact on your career, and if it is really important, it can impact the field forever.

Final Thoughts

Would you like to get a grant? Chances are, you can and even will. Of course, you need an idea, but chances are, you have that idea, or even more than one. So, the main thing you need to do is organize yourself and your time to write a grant. You want to give it your best shot, but don't wait until you get every thought and every sentence perfect. Wait too long, and the time for doing the research may well be past! Find out the organizations that fund the kind of research you would like to do, and go for it. Most of all, remember the importance of persistence. Some lucky people are funded the first time around. Probably, many more are not. You may have to revise the proposal once or even twice. Or, you may have to submit the proposal elsewhere. Or, you may have to write a new proposal. But, if there is one key to getting funded, it is persistence. Keep trying, and sooner or later, you will be funded. That's what we do. We know that not every grant we write will be funded. But we don't give up, and eventually, one proposal or another, some time or another, gets funded. Then, we're off and running.

References

Sternberg, R. J., Kaufman, J. C., & Pretz, J. E. (2002). *The creativity conundrum: A propulsion model of kinds of creative contributions.* New York: Psychology Press.

Sternberg, R. J., & Lubart, T. I. (1995). *Defying the crowd: Cultivating creativity in a culture of conformity.* New York: Free Press.

Sternberg, R. J., & Sternberg, K. (2010). *The psychologist's companion* (5th ed.). New York: Cambridge University Press.

2

Guide to Professional Begging

Emilie F. Rissman

My husband and I are both scientists. We are Ph.D.s working in a medical school. The university covers some of our salary, paying us to perform tasks such as teaching graduate courses, the occasional lecture to medical students, and serving on various committees. However, our major role is to conduct research, and to perform this function, which is of course the reason we selected this career many years ago, we must write grants, many many grants. When our kids were little, we tried to be writing for different deadlines, so that there was always one functional adult in the house. The kids figured out this pattern of behavior pretty quickly; in fact, our neighborhood is full of other academics, and the girls could pretty much tell when a neighbor was writing a grant based on the condition of their yard.

Professional begging requires a skill set that is continually changing and needs to be honed and refined on a routine basis. In these particularly difficult economic times, it is easy to become discouraged. Continual rejection is never fun, and writing and rewriting grants takes a lot of time away from

Note: The author thanks Drs. Diane Witt (National Science Foundation [NSF]), Jim Deschler (NSF), James Gnadt (National Institute of Neurological Disorders and Stroke), Lisa Freud (National Institute of Child Health and Human Development), Janine Simmons (National Institute of Mental Health [NIMH]), and Nancy Desmond (NIMH) for years of good counsel and advice. The author is also grateful to the National Institutes of Health (NIH) and NSF for past, current, and hopefully future research funding.

the actual doing of science, the most rewarding part of the job. One essential skill is to have fun in the process. I know this sounds ridiculous; the phrase "I am writing a grant" is usually uttered in a morose manner more typically used to pronounce the death of a relative or friend. However, most of us selected academics because we enjoy learning new things, and grant writing is the perfect excuse to read and think about the literature in your own field and to expand your knowledge base to other areas. The push for "translational" research also necessitates that many of us have to stretch our interests and move from discovery for its own sake to discovery for its potential application to a real-world health issue.

In this short chapter, I intend to cover the process of grant writing from the hunt for appropriate funding vehicles to the challenges of revising an application that has not been funded. If my tone sounds a bit whimsical, this is because I am hoping to help you to take the "heaviness" out of the process and enjoy yourself. In my household these days, we spend about 50 percent of our time writing grants; if this was an onerous task, we would be miserable and likely divorced but we are still happy and happily married. Of course, our yard is a disaster area.

Finding the Right Funding Vehicle

NIH is the largest funding agency in the country, probably in the world, but don't quote me. NIH is always the first place to go for funds for your research program. Look for these three little words, "Requests for Applications," more affectionately known as the RFA. The RFA is a call for proposals on a selected topic that at least one of the institutes is interested in funding. The money for the RFA is a set-aside. This is a special pot of gold just for this topic, and it must be spent. This is the best-bet mechanism and whenever you find an RFA that relates to your work, you MUST submit an application. That said, it is certainly the case that you will have lots of competition; in fact, the RFAs are often the result of conferences or symposium called by NIH. Invited extramural scientists in attendance assist the program staff to identify important gaps in our knowledge, in an area that they are familiar with; thus, the scientists essentially help to draft what will become the RFA. These folks likely have the upper hand in terms of getting their applications funded when the RFA is released. However, regardless of this, you MUST apply. You will not get 100 percent of the grants you do not apply for.

Typically, there is not an RFA, so the regular R01 mechanism is your best shot. I always suggest going to NIH first because their grant budgets are larger than those at the other big funder in town, NSF. This is because NIH adds the indirect costs on top of your budget whereas NSF takes it out of the budget you submit. However, if your work is not costly, and/or is so basic that there is little possibility that it will ever be translational, NSF is a fine option. Moreover, if you are a new investigator without a track record of NIH or NSF funding (National Research Service Award [NRSA] fellowships do not count), you can and should dual submit the same proposal to both agencies. Both NIH and NSF have changed their submission rules recently, and these changes make it even more essential that you get the grant right the first time. The major change instituted a few years ago at NIH is that you can only revise and resubmit once (they used to allow two resubmissions). NSF is now calling for preproposals, which will be reviewed. Approximately one third of the preproposals will receive the green light, at which point the principal investigator (PI) can write and submit a full proposal. Full proposals will be reviewed only once a year. This means you have to send in proposals at least a year before you need the money. That takes a lot of skill and likely the development of at least two different research projects.

Both NIH and NSF have a variety of grant mechanisms other than the standard R01-type grant. For more high-risk exploratory work, NIH has an R21. According to the guidelines, pilot data are not required for the R21, but given the tight budgets, it is a good idea to have some proof of principle. The R21 grants are typically for only two years and the budget is half of what an R01 will fund. Many other specialized programs exist. For example, if you are reentering science after an absence of no more than eight years, NIH has a special grant; if you work at a small college, both agencies have grant mechanisms; if you are an underrepresented minority, there are several additional options at both NSF and NIH; or if you are an established scientist who wants to learn a new technique, there are programs for you to do so. Once you find a program that appears to suit your needs, contact the responsible program officers to get the full lowdown. I will elaborate on this in the next section.

Finally, there are private foundations that fund basic research. Typically, these are disease-oriented. If you do an Internet search for a disease that is related to your research and "research funding," you can find the appropriate groups. Most foundation grants are small, with a few exceptions. But, the good news is that the applications are typically short. I have received foundation grants for my work and I will continue to write for these funds. Without sounding preachy, I would advise you to apply only if you truly in your heart of hearts believe your work is going to help diagnose, understand, and/or treat the disease in question. Private foundations represent patients and their families; they are looking for cures, and if you can help that is terrific; if you cannot, I'd skip it.

Program Staffers Are Your Friends

Now that you have identified an agency or group to apply to for funds, it is time to plan and to talk. If you are going to NIH for the first time, read the mission statements for the institutes (mental health, child health and human development, etc.) where you feel your work might be most relevant. For an RFA, the program staffers at NIH who are organizing the call for proposals are listed at the end of the announcement. If you are sending in a regular grant, and you have no history with any staffers at the appropriate institute, do a search on the program staff members to get a feeling for the types of projects they have in their portfolio. There are other types of program announcements that staffers send out and that reflect their area of interest. Once you have figured out whom to talk to, send an e-mail, introduce yourself, and ask for a phone date to discuss your science and ideas for an application. If you have not contacted the correct program officer, they will suggest someone else. Before the call, write out your aims, and some alternatives. If you are submitting a grant to NSF, you need to find the correct program director to talk with. Now that the timing for applications has changed, it is even more important to make contact with a staffer at NSF before you submit an application.

Program staffers at NIH and at NSF are an amazing group of people. Nearly all are former bench scientists who left the lab for a variety of reasons. In fact, at NSF they have one-year to two-year appointed program staffers called "rotators" who are lab scientists at colleges and universities. These people come on a temporary basis to NSF to learn about grants administration and to keep the agency's knowledge of current science up to date. The program staffers are scientists; they want to talk about your science, and they are there to help you—let them. They are just as unhappy as you are about the funding climate; they sincerely want to help you get a grant and once that happens, they can guide you through the rest of the red tape. Another way to find and stay connected with the appropriate NIH and NSF program people is to visit their "booths" at large meetings. Private foundations also have program development staffers, and I have found them to be exceptionally nice and helpful. Sometimes they have a science background, sometimes not, but they are committed to turning good research ideas into funded projects.

In addition to helping you hone your research ideas, NIH program staff members can suggest the appropriate study sections, they can give you a heads up on RFAs that might be coming out, and especially if they attend the study section meeting when your grant is being reviewed, they can help guide you through the critiques. At NSF, program directors are extremely powerful.

At NSF, program and review are combined. The program directors run the study sections. They also decide which external reviewers are asked to review your proposal. NSF runs panels in-house and in addition, all grants go out for external reviews, much like journal articles. Moreover, the panels and external reviews are only *advisory;* the final decision on funding is made by the program director. In contrast, at NIH, the decisions are made by the numbers, although program officers can occasionally fund proposals "out of order" if they feel the grant is going to make an exceptionally important contribution. Program staffers are ready, willing, and able to work with you to find alternative funding mechanisms if you have an idea that is not an exact fit for an R01-type grant. For example, NIH has fellowship grants for investigators at all levels. So, if you want to learn a new technique and the best way to do that is to spend three months at a colleague's lab (sort of a mini-sabbatical), NIH has a program for just that type of thing. NSF has all kinds of mechanisms—conference grants, center grants, training grants, network grants, postdoctoral fellowships, and so on. One particularly interesting vehicle is the EAGER, or Early-concepts Grants for Exploratory Research. This grant is for timely, novel, potentially risky, but high payoff projects over a one-year or two-year period. Decisions on these grants are made *internally;* they are not evaluated by a panel. Both agencies try out new mechanisms and the program staffers know about all of them before the public does.

Planning the Application

Pilot Data

Once you know what type of application you are writing, you need to begin to make a plan. I always start with the aims and then write the experiments. This way, I can figure out beforehand if and what types of pilot data are needed. Pilot data are essential, even for proposals that claim this is not a requirement. Depending on the type of studies you conduct, you may or may not be able to generate data quickly. One rule that should be understood is that if your pilot data are weak, do not include them in the grant. Your job is to convince the reviewers that you have a solid basis for the hypotheses you present. If you include weak data, even if the numbers per group are low, and you can think of lots of ways to optimize the experiment, you are undermining your application.

One special type of pilot data is production of engineered mice, knockouts, transgenics, and so on. Fifteen years ago, you could write a grant that included an aim in which you would collaborate with a company, or another laboratory and produce a mouse to test your hypothesis. Or, if the appropriate knockout mouse was already made, you could include a letter from the lab head stating that he would send the mice to you, as part of a collaborative arrangement. Now this does not fly. You have to have the mouse in your laboratory, or it must be available for purchase. Having the animals in hand speaks to the feasibility of the project. Given the funding pressures, it is easy to reduce the priority of a proposal that does not have all the needed resources lined up and "shovel ready."

Collaborators

Another important aspect of the application that needs lead time is identifying collaborators and/or consultants to join you on the application. The scientific effort used to be single-lab based. That is less and less the case. Team-based science is practical if you have a good team and it can be more efficient than individual R01s. I would make a distinction here between "big" science—program project grants and the like—and an R01-type grant in which different types of expertise are required. In my work, I am interested in gene discovery. Gene discovery requires biostatistical expertise that I do not possess. For that reason, I must collaborate with bioinformaticians. If you are proposing a new method or technique that your laboratory is not doing on a routine basis, such as analysis of gene expression or sequencing data, you need a collaborator. The best situation is if someone in your department, or at least on your campus, can collaborate with you. Ideally, this would be someone that you have a track record with and with whom you have at least one coauthored publication. If you have this ideal collaborator, all you will need is his or her biosketch and a letter that states what his or her role will be on the project. It is best for you to draft the letter for your consultant since you probably have the best vision for what his contribution will be to the grant.

If there is no one on your campus that is expert in the technique you have proposed, and/or the method is only done in a few places, it is clear that you will need to strike up an arrangement with an expert. If you have a distant colleague that you know, that is great; if the right person is someone you do not already know, my suggestion is to buy a plane ticket and work out the collaboration in person. If you have enough lead time in these cases, it is well worth the effort to conduct a pilot study with the long-distance collaborator to demonstrate that this is a viable relationship and that together you will be able to do great things.

In the past, NIH did not allow co-PIs, but that has changed and now grants can have co-PIs, coinvestigators, and/or consultants. My definitions of these partners are as follows. A consultant will give you advice, on statistics or a lab method. But, the work will be done in your laboratory. A coinvestigator is someone that is doing part of the work, say one or two studies in an aim, in their laboratory. In my case, my bioinformatics collaborator is a coinvestigator on my grant. This typically comes with some percentage effort. So, the coinvestigator may be recovering part of his or her salary from your grant. The amount of effort the coinvestigator is spending should be less than your own effort. Finally, the co-PIs should be contributing equally in terms of expertise, effort, and the execution of the work in the application. If your application has co-PIs, you need to include a leadership plan.

Other Eyes

An additional advantage to collaborators is having more people to read drafts of the grant. Ask people in advance if they are able to read your application; tell them when you can give them the draft and when the grant is due. This is important, not only for their insights but also because this forces you to finish the document ahead of time. For really comprehensive instructions on the actual writing of the proposal, I am a big fan of *The NIH and NSF Grant Application Writer's Workbook* by Russell and Morrison (© 2010 Grant Writers' Seminars & Workshops LLC). This team has put a lot of thought into the essence of each section of the proposal. They have tips on how to organize and structure each section. The book is available online for $75 and is money well spent. If you have never written a grant application, I suggest you buy the book now and read it carefully and far ahead of time.

Which Study Section?

My best advice on how to understand study sections is to serve on one. If you have received funding from NSF or NIH, in my opinion, you owe them. Plus, if you have written a grant that was strong enough to get funded, you are qualified to review other grants. If you are a junior person, I would not suggest that you join a panel until you have your own grant funded (it simply takes too much time). But, you can offer to serve as an ad hoc reviewer, which is an excellent way to learn the ropes.

For some scientific disciplines, there may be only one study section that is appropriate for your application. If that is the case, look over the roster online. Note the permanent members and determine if any of them has a conflict of interest with your program. A conflict can be defined as a previous coauthorship, a close competitor or rival, or even a dear friend. In addition to the permanent members, every panel meeting will have ad-hoc reviewers. Often these people are called on for a grant that employs methods that the permanent members are not knowledgeable in, or when the member that is knowledgeable has a conflict of interest in evaluating the proposal. If you look back over the rosters, you can see whom the panel uses for ad hocs. The ad hocs are often not present at the panel meeting, and instead join the meeting on the phone just for the proposals they reviewed. This, obviously, puts them at a disadvantage. If they have an opinion that is different from the panel reviewers, their view is typically the minority.

If your application potentially could be reviewed by more than one panel, you need to think long and hard about which group you should suggest in the cover letter. Your program officer can help you with this decision. My suggestion is to go with the panel that has members whose work you know. Even if you have never met them, if you have read their papers it is likely they have read yours (or your advisor's, if you are junior). If your work is similar to theirs, they can understand your motivation and methods. If you don't know many of the panel members, look them up on PubMed.

If you are lucky enough to apply through an RFA, typically new panels are brought together to review these grants. This is an additional reason to discuss your proposal with the program officer in charge of the RFA. She or he will want to bring in panel members with expertise in the science the panel will receive. This is also the primary reason for "letters of intent." So be sure to submit the letter to get the appropriate people on the panel.

A final thought on study-section etiquette. Never ask anyone on a panel about how the grant review went down. Also never assume that you know who reviewed your grant; you are probably wrong and it really doesn't matter.

The Look of the Grant

Although I defer to Russell and Morrison for most of the writing, I do have a few suggestions on the appearance of the document. The most important of these is to use graphics. In addition to graphics for pilot data, I think cartoons that illustrate your hypotheses and aims are extremely useful. Just drawing a cartoon of an aim is a great exercise, which lets you streamline the study. Cartoons do take up space, which is at a premium, so the idea here is to use the cartoon in place of some of the written text. Another nice approach is that if your aims build on a model (which they should), you can literally show that in the cartoons by using the same basic figure and adding pieces as you go through the proposal. In your cartoons, use color judiciously. Think of the grant like you would a poster; use bright colors to catch the reviewer's attention and to stress important points, but don't go wild. Another issue is the size of the pictures; make them large, and do not skimp. Write the embedded figure legends in large fonts so after you import them into the document, the reviewers can read them.

The other more obvious feature about the appearance of the grant is that you should use wide margins and large fonts. For the same reason that cartoons and pictures are a good idea, reviewers get tired of looking at packed applications. Less is always better. Less verbiage, more diagrams, indents, and spaces—try to make the document attractive and fun to read. I know this is easier said than done, but it is something to strive for.

The Cover Letter

The cover letter used to be optional, but smart grant writers always wrote one. This letter helps route your application to the correct institute at NIH. You should have identified the correct institute at the front end of the application so this is straightforward. You also indicate in the cover letter which study section you believe has the expertise to review your application. In addition, if you have any conflicts with permanent members of the panel, this is the place to declare them.

How to Do It All Again and Again

The Score and the Summary Sheet

In the old days, months after the study section meeting you would get a summary sheet in the U.S. mail. Now within a few days after the meeting, the scores are on the Commons. Chances are high (around 90 percent) that seeing the score will not be a pleasant experience. In fact, the bottom half of the applications will not receive a score, and instead that fateful "ND" for not discussed will be on your screen. Knowing this, I like to wait until the end of the day on the Friday after the panel meeting to check for the score. That way, if it is bad, you have the weekend to get over it and if it is good you can celebrate. Unless you are in the upper 10 percent, and even then there are no certainties, you will need to resubmit the application. If the proposal received an ND, you may consider not resubmitting and instead shift focus a bit and fashion a new proposal. But, those decisions depend on the summary sheet.

The summary sheet takes six to eight weeks to appear on Commons. When you get it, read it carefully, get angry, run around the block, and then read it again. If the application received an ND, you will get the reviewers' comments and their scores, but you will not get a summary of the discussion. The NIH has five categories (Significance, Investigator, Innovation, Approach, Environment) that are individually scored and an overall score. The overall score is not just an average; it is a metric that takes the individual scores into account; thus, you can intuit how the individual scores were weighted. In my experience, two of the categories—Significance and Approach—are the most important. After you have digested the summary sheet, send an e-mail to your program officer and make a phone date to discuss the comments and to solicit his or her advice on the next step.

If you decide to revise and resubmit, generally you have to wait out one cycle at the NIH since typically by the time you get the summary sheets, the next deadline is either just past or a few weeks away. If you can make the deadline, and the panel is not asking for more pilot data, or you have data that can address the issues, go for it. This will save you four months. In addition, the closer you resubmit relative to the initial review, the more likely it is that the panel members will remember the original application and perhaps you will be lucky enough to have one or more of the original reviewers assigned to the revision. The panel is a bit of a moving target. You can never be sure that any of the members that reviewed your application the first time will be there when your revision is reviewed. Even if they are at the meeting, they may not be assigned to review your revision. This of course makes it more difficult for you. However, the new reviewers will definitely read your one-page introduction and the summary sheet from the first review.

Addressing the Reviewers' Concerns

The introduction is extremely important. You only have one page to convince the reviewers that either you have made the required changes and/or the critiques from the first review were off base. You can organize this a number of ways. One is by category. If all the weaknesses were in a few categories, this makes sense. Just list the categories with weaknesses. If more than one reviewer had the same issue, you only have to address it one time. Alternatively, if one reviewer had most of the concerns, I would organize the introduction around that one review. My advice on this section is to make sure the writing is clear and that you completely understand and address the comments. If feasibility is an issue, new data are always a plus. If the problem is experimental design, it is possible that the reviewer has a good point. Alternatively, your write-up of the methods may be lacking. Be sure to give yourself plenty of time to write the introduction. It is the most important part of the revised grant.

One common concern I have already mentioned is feasibility. The funding levels are so low now that the reviewers can write off a proposal if they do not think all the expertise, methods, or tools are in place. In some cases, pilot data are needed, but in others a new collaboration may make all the difference. Alternatively, there may be another approach that is less novel but gets the job done. For example, you may have proposed a high-tech method that is state of the art, but, in fact, the method you have used in the past is nearly as effective. Don't be too wedded to the original proposal; changes show that you have taken the panel's analysis to heart.

Recycling

In general, if the proposal had a decent initial score, it is worth the effort to revise. There is one category that can be deadly, however. This is Significance. It is difficult to argue this one without major revisions to the basic idea of the grant. The other deathblow is ND. When grants had two chances for re-review, it was occasionally the case that a grant with an ND on the first review could ultimately make the pay line. Now, I think that is virtually impossible. However, it might be possible to use a different mechanism for proposal with an ND score. For example, if you submit an R01 and the panel thinks you need more preliminary data, you might be able to revise the application and resubmit it as an R21. You will need the advice of your program officer for this sort of situation.

Another obvious route is to revise the ND application and send it to a different funding agency. One big distinction between NIH and NSF these days is that NSF is still actively interested in funding basic science. If, for example, your failed NIH grant was considered weak because it had little implication for human health, revise it and send it to NSF. If you really want to do the project and you think it is important, maybe you can get some private funds to collect more data and try again.

Perseverance

One of my mentors once told me that persistence is the most important feature of a successful scientist. I actually do not agree, but I do think that perseverance is key for getting or staying funded. You have to get a thick skin and be adaptable. Think about doing something new if that is what it takes to stay funded. Move into an area that is more applicable to human health if you want an NIH grant. Work with other people to push your project in a translational direction. Most of all, try to have some fun in the process. Learning about a different field or a new method can be stimulating. Don't shy away from reinventing yourself.

3

Mistakes That Grant Proposers Make

Robert W. Levenson

*T**he moment has arrived. Your grant proposal is up for discussion. The buzzing in the room lessens and the committee becomes silent as the reviewers begin to speak. Each is clearly awestruck by your brilliance. There really is no score high enough to reflect the quality of the research you have proposed. Funding is not in question, only whether the review committee is free to recommend more than you actually requested . . .*

The alarm clock rings harshly and you wake up to face the realities of another day of working on your grant proposal.

Writing grant proposals has become a ubiquitous part of academic life. Beginning prior to graduate school with fellowship applications, continuing during the predoctoral and postdoctoral years, and reaching a crescendo as you move up the career ladder, the drumbeat of drumming up funding to support yourself, your research team, and your work becomes increasingly incessant. In this chapter, I will offer a number of suggestions aimed at helping you avoid common mistakes and thus write better, more effective, and hopefully more fundable grants. All of the suggestions in this chapter come from personal experience, with many grants written (some successful, some not); many colleagues' and students' grants commented on; and many, many grants reviewed (again, some successful and some not). The structure and content of grant applications can differ greatly across funding agencies and grant types (e.g., federal agencies versus private foundations, research versus training grants). For these reasons, it is impossible to write a one-size-fits-all tome on grant structure or content. Instead, this chapter focuses on the more common elements, suggesting generalized solutions based on the habits and practices of successful grant writers, topped off with a big dollop of common sense.

To help organize this chapter, I have created a "to-do" list of suggestions for dealing with a number of potential pitfalls and opportunities that every grant writer encounters. There are many other items that could be included, but these are some of the most basic.

Follow Instructions; Avoid Destruction

For about a decade, the Association for Psychological Science sponsored a session on grant writing at its annual convention called "Show Me the Money." Jane Steinberg of the National Institutes of Mental Health was the originator, and I had the privilege of serving as coleader and as one of the regular speakers. Over the years, the representatives from the federal agencies and foundations changed but, regardless of the individual speaker, there was one message that always seemed to emerge (most often as the first item on each speaker's list): "Follow the instructions."

You would think that this item would be so obvious that it would not need to be mentioned. After all, how can you write an application without knowing what the funders want to read? But, the consistency of this message, stated by so many different speakers representing so many different funding organizations, clearly suggests that there are many applicants who choose to commence writing without thoroughly and carefully reading the instructions. Nobody wants to be the voice of conformity, but in this case, that voice clearly needs to be heard. Improvisation may be a wonderful quality for jazz musicians, but grant applicants are better served by following the notes on the page. Page limits, section headings, required tables, minimum fonts, maximum margins, styles for references, and all of their brethren are best followed to the letter. Fortunately, for those who bristle at all of this conformity or who are severely instruction-resistant, the newer electronic formats for grant submission enforce some degree of compliance in many subtle and not so subtle ways. However, rest assured that even the most restrictive text field designed by the greatest geniuses at Adobe cannot foil the resolute efforts of the exceedingly "I-do-it-my-own-way" grant writer. So, before you start to put pen to paper, go to the relevant website, download the instructions for the grant you are applying for, read them over carefully (maybe even twice), and then COMPLY!

But, why is this so important? Why should you allow some silly instructions to silence your unique voice and cramp your unique grant-writing style? First, some violations of instructions are deemed sufficient by some funders to turn your application away without further review. This kind of outcome can be extremely costly to you in terms of time lost. Moreover, it can deny you the benefit of receiving reviewers' comments, which are the mother's milk when it comes to revising and improving your application. Second, even if your grant makes it to review, you run the risk that your tinier-than-tiny fonts, wider-than-wide margins, missing section on "innovation," or extra half-page of text "hidden" in a footnote in the appendix (thus cleverly circumventing the maximum length requirement) will be encountered by a reviewer who has entered the absolutely grumpiest phase of her or his fatigue cycle and who will soon cast an unwanted cloud of doom over your noncompliant but otherwise brilliant prose.

There's yet another reason for reading the instructions. They often parallel the guidelines given to reviewers to help them evaluate the extent to which applications realize the funders' mission and goals. So, if the instructions say to include a section on how your research reflects issues of diversity, or how it is innovative, or how it reflects the foundation's founder's vision of promoting world peace, you can be pretty sure that reviewers will be asked to score the proposal in terms of these very same things.

Try to Cull Mr./Ms. Excitement

You spend weeks on "flaw patrol," searching your application for anything that could serve as a launching pad for a negative review. Some minor bugs were found, but you have carefully exterminated each and every one. Surely, a flawless proposal like yours will turn out to be a true gem. You say to yourself: "What's not to like about a proposal with no fatal flaws?" You send out your unblemished masterpiece and wait to hear back. Finally, the reviews arrive and, true to your ministrations, no fatal flaws have been found. You scan ahead to the bottom line and, much to your surprise, your immaculate creation has not done well enough to be funded.

What is the point here? First, there is absolutely no doubt that grants that are fatally flawed are fated to fail. However, a lack of flaws is not always synonymous with success. For the latter to be the outcome, there needs to be something beyond flawlessness, something that elevates the proposal from the middle of the pack to nearer the top. If someone prepared verbatim transcripts of grant-review sessions, performed the requisite text analysis, and then correlated categorical word counts with outcomes, I'd wager an indirect cost percentage or two that the category that would emerge as most predictive of ultimate success would be "excitement." Although truly egregious (a.k.a. "bonehead") mistakes are sometimes encountered in grant applications, most proposals manage to pass the fatally flawed test. However, proposals that generate true excitement among the reviewers are much less common.

One way to approach this "excitement thing" is to think about your grant application in a manner similar to how a writer might think about a novel. From the outset, the writer wants the reader to start caring about the characters and situations, and tries to hook them in so that they will eagerly work their way through the twists of the plot, reading page after page to find out how it all turns out. Similarly, with a grant application, you want the reader to be interested in and to care about your research questions early on and to be eager to know what the answers will be. So how do you make this happen?

Like Snoopy starting his novel with "It was a dark and stormy night," it's likely that every successful grant writer has her or his own tricks (and just as reading successful novels is a great way to become a better novelist, the same is true about reading successful grants). One thing that might be helpful is to think about your audience—the people who will be reading and evaluating your applications. Who are the typical grant reviewers? Well, you can be sure that they are going to be successful grant getters and good scientists. Granting agencies like to recruit reviewers who have strong grant-getting records and recognized expertise in the domains under review. Good scientists tend to be curiosity junkies. For them the drugs of choice are often unexplained anomalies, unexpected connections or disjunctions, interesting observations, and abiding mysteries. Viewed from this perspective, the first step in getting good scientists excited about your proposal is to get them thinking about your underlying questions.

A few simple observations are worth considering when selecting research questions and framing them in an application. First, fairly or not, research that aims to tweak paradigms, tidy up loose ends, or provide the one missing modification after hundreds of prior paradigmatic variations does not tend to generate a great deal of reviewer excitement. Of course, it may generate admiration and gratitude accompanied by statements along the lines of "someone should do this." But, these kinds of sentiments tend not to carry grants over the funding threshold. Second, and from the other extreme, research that is more grandiose than grand is similarly doomed. Science is ultimately incremental; thus, overpromising or overreaching can seem naïve at best and unseemly and arrogant at worse. Third, the fuse for igniting reviewers' interest is short; thus, you are best served by "getting to the good part" quickly. Although there are many positive correlates of being able to delay one's own gratification, delaying reviewer gratification is not a very good grant strategy. So, if you start your proposal by excavating all of the areas that surround the issue but are not the real issue; if you endlessly dance around the point and never get to it; and if you obscure your research question in a fog of tangents and asides, you may find that you have missed the time-limited window for launching the reviewer on the royal road to excitement.

Aim High, Aim Often, Aim at Others

As far back as I can remember, NIH grants have always started out with a one-page specific aims section. Of course, there is always an abstract, and now there might be a mini-section with a few sentences on relevance, but the grant show doesn't really start until the specific-aims section appears. The specific-aims section is arguably the most important part of the grant for both you and for the reviewers. It provides a précis of the proposed work in one convenient place. I suggest that you be ambitious and work toward comprehensiveness, striving for a specific-aims section that states the underlying problem, explains its importance, sketches the methods that will be used, lists the hypotheses to be tested, and touches on the significance of the expected findings. Further, I suggest that you be extremely strict about limiting all of this to one page and not consider yourself done until all of those extra sentences that you plan to trim later are duly lopped off.

Why so much emphasis on making this section all-inclusive and combining this with a draconian enforcement of the length limit? Doing so provides a critical test bed for perfecting the underlying logic of your research proposal. It forces you to distill all aspects down to their essences and to find a way of piecing things together that is economical, coherent, logical, and compelling. A one-page, comprehensive specific aims section is totally unforgiving, revealing problems in the clarity of your thinking and presentation, weaknesses in the logic of your research, vagueness in your methods, and failures in the all important "so what" realm. If the rationale for the research is weak, its logic unclear, its hypotheses murky, and its grand purpose not so grand, all of this will be exposed. Given the luxury of length, additional verbiage has a way of camouflaging weaknesses (at least from the writer, but not so often from the reviewer). The brevity of the specific aims section works to reveal these weaknesses. But, when this section reaches the point of being clear, complete, cogent, and compelling, it provides a strong backbone and invaluable outline for writing the rest of the proposal.

In addition to helping you develop and refine your research logic, the specific-aims section also plays a critical role in the communal aspects of grant writing. Although it may not always take a village, many grant applications will be helped by input from at least some of the neighbors. Getting feedback on your grant applications from colleagues (especially those who have been successful grant getters) can be incredibly useful in helping improve your grant-writing skills and in increasing the likelihood that a particular proposal will reach that exalted and highly desired state of being fundable. Unfortunately, the lives of successful scientists and grant getters are extremely busy, and, thus, it can be quite difficult for them to find the time necessary to read your full proposal and give you extensive feedback. But, relief is on the way. Because the specific-aims section provides a taste of your entire grant in a single bite-sized piece, it is perfect for sharing. In my experience, most colleagues will be willing to read and give you feedback on a single page. And, some may even be willing to read several iterations of that page. Thus, it is a good idea to work on your specific-aims section first, to refine it to the point where it is ready to show to others, and then to ask key colleagues to read it. For those eager for immediate feedback, the one-page specific-aims section is an ideal length for real-time reading and feedback over a cup of coffee, but even sans beverage, it should be pretty easy to get feedback quickly.

Any specific-aims section worth its caffeine is worth rewriting numerous times, and you should plan to go through multiple cycles of feedback (from your own reading and that of others) and revision before you move on. It is worth remembering that, in addition to serving as a vehicle for getting feedback from colleagues, the specific-aims section is going to live many lives. It will provide a framework to help you craft the rest of your proposal. It will be used by reviewers when they need to quickly refresh their memories about your grant (e.g., often the last thing read before your grant is discussed and scored). It will be used by program staff when they have to explain the research and make the case for its being worth funding. And, hopefully it will be used by you many, many times as you share your successful grant application with admiring students, staff, and colleagues.

Be Ready for a Twosome

Rejection and failure are never welcome visitors when they arrive at our professional doorsteps. Although some develop thick skins and habituate to their sting, most of us never get to that point. Why, you may ask, am I starting off this section with such a gloomy, depressing thought? The reality is that, unless you are one of those mythic creatures who encounter only success in their professional life, rejection and failure are inevitable parts of the grant-getting enterprise. Given typical percentile cutoffs for funding (in recent years sometimes falling below the 10th percentile at some NIH institutes), it is a simple, unarguable fact that most applications will fail. Moreover, among those grant applications that are ultimately funded, many (perhaps most) will not be funded on the first round, but will need to be revised and submitted again (and perhaps again and again). This is all pretty sobering when you consider that the group of scientists who are submitting these applications is already highly selected, a very impressive lot by any standards.

Okay, by now I hope you have read the preceding paragraph and wept. Before sitting down to write your grant application, before putting in the hundreds of person hours it takes to produce an application regardless of its ultimate fate, it is critical that you get to the point where you are ready for a twosome. Your proposal may well not be funded the first time around. However, this first-round failure will most likely be accompanied by two extremely useful consolation prizes: Reviews and resubmission! If your funding agency provides an opportunity to revise your grant application and resubmit, reviews are your lifeline. Reviews can provide valuable insights as to what went right and what went wrong, and even more importantly, illuminate a path that could lead toward greater success the next time around. Until recently, NIH grants could be revised and resubmitted three times. Although that third round meant more interim rejections with all of their attendant pain and misery, it also meant more reviewer feedback and additional opportunities to address the concerns that were raised in the reviews. Reading reviews, going to school on their contents, and revising your application accordingly has always been the royal road to grant-getting success. And, you can be assured that even the most highly successful grant getters have been down this multiple-submission road before and will continue to go down it in the future.

Having provided all of this background, there are two extremely unfortunate responses to initial failure that you clearly want to avoid. The first is *paralysis*, when the venomous sting of rejection causes you to give up and never try again. Like graduate students who never publish their dissertations, academia is rife with those who try grant writing once, fail, and never try again. This is a terrible shame. The effort to produce the first application is significant and it is likely that much of that effort will be very useful when preparing the revision or next application. In an ideal world, all unsuccessful grant writers would allow themselves a respectable period of mourning, dust off their slightly battered egos, and be ready to try again.

Another unfortunate and all-too-common unproductive response is to engage in "solipsistic review myopia" (to invent a term). Here, you read the reviews and then expend an incredible amount of time and energy convincing yourself that (a) the reviewers were ill informed and/or biased; (b) the grant-review process was unfair and/or corrupt; (c) you are so much smarter than the reviewers that they might never be able to understand or appreciate your brilliance; or (d) you are going to hatch an elaborate plot to seek revenge against all who stood in your way. There is probably a time and place for a quick dip into the shallow end of the miserable pool of failure and for railing against the unfairness of it all. But, however cathartic a place this is to visit, it's definitely not a productive place for a long stay.

One thing that can be immensely helpful is to show your reviews to a colleague who is experienced in the world of grants. Such a person can often read between the lines to help you see which issues are real and which are imagined, to help you determine if the surgery that is needed is minor or major (e.g., do you need to start over?), and to help you pick up any lifelines that are being thrown your way by helpful reviewers. One thing that savvy grant writers learn is how to gauge the excitement the reviewers had for the basic idea (flaws and issues notwithstanding). Reviews that signal excitement and an interest in seeing a revision are harbingers of likely success. Reviews that signal the opposite (boredom and disinterest) suggest a trip back to the proverbial drawing board. Over time, we all get better at reading our own reviews objectively. However, human nature being what it is, it's probably always worth getting a second opinion about your reviews from a dispassionate and savvy other.

Remember: People, People Who Need People Are the Luckiest People in the World

Someday, grants may be reviewed by machines, using advanced text analysis and artificial intelligence to provide completely objective and valid reviews. But, until that day (which is to say, probably never), it is worth remembering that grants are reviewed by people. Because of this, it is important that we not leave our knowledge of human nature at the door when entering the world of grant writing. To this end, I offer a few specific kernels of advice:

> *Progress in the field of emotion research has been greatly hampered by the theories of Kutcher and Ashton, which, in their murkiness, have impeded a generation of investigators.*

Don't bite the hand that feeds you. Academia is an incredibly small, inbred world. When you find yourself singling out particular researchers for your most caustic critiques and your most barbaric barbs, please realize that it is almost certain that at least one of your reviewers will either be, have collaborated with, have studied under, or have great admiration for one of those researchers. In service to your own well-being and likely success in grant writing, when it comes to anything remotely ad hominem, assume zero degrees of separation and temper your criticisms accordingly.

> *The proposed research is unique in being the first to examine bottom-up attentional control as a possible explanation for the social deficits found in autism and other related developmental disorders.*

There's nothing new under the sun. Stating boldly that nobody before you has done, said, thought, imagined, intuited, or studied something is the equivalent of throwing bloody chum into a tank of sharks. There's nothing quite as likely to wake up a drowsy reviewer (or room full of reviewers) as an assertion of primacy. Because of this, it will only take seconds before someone comes up with a purported prior instance. And, others are likely to chime in quickly with additional examples that counter your claims. Remember—regardless of whether these examples are ultimately on or off point, relevant or irrelevant, or real or imagined, you won't be there to argue the point. Most important, once these counterexamples are raised, extremely deadly aspersions of "sloppy scholarship" cannot be far behind. There is no winning strategy here, and no way to redeem yourself. Thus, a word to the wise: It's a good idea to make clear how your work differs from that which has come before but to avoid claims of absolute primacy.

> *The notion that adolescence is a time of accelerated neural development was refuted by Willis' empirical studies and the highly influential Magno-Contextual theory.*

We all live in silos. In some areas of science, large groups of researchers work on a single problem and everyone knows everyone else and their work. In social science, it is quite a different scenario. In many areas, small groups of scientists stake out separate territories and conduct their work blithely unaware of the work of those in other areas. Viewed from inside our own silos, the players, ideas, discoveries, and failures are all so well known that they assume mythic stature. Thus, it is impossible to think that others might not share our insider's knowledge. But, they don't. For this reason, when writing grants it is important to include all of the critical details about studies, theories, controversies, people, and findings. In the previous example, more information is needed about those legendary studies (what was done and what was found), that renowned theory (what exactly did it propose and who proposed it) and how this work is relevant to the research you are proposing. Without this information, the reviewer might well be at a total loss when attempting to follow the logic of your argument. And here, the deadly aspersions are "hand-waving" and "name-dropping." Once this happens, you can be assured that the reviewer's loss will not be your gain.

> *The theory I have promulgated has the potential to revolutionize the field of comparative psychology and the studies I have proposed in this application will profoundly change our views concerning species differentiation.*

Be humble, live to eat the pie. I expect that there are times and places in life where arrogance might be an effective aphrodisiac, but grant reviewers are not likely to be turned on by the grandiose. Asserting that yours is the most scintillating theory, the most sophisticated method, and the shiniest light is an invitation for ridicule and scorn (especially when you are relatively new at the grant game). A more measured approached pointing to advantages and disadvantages of your approach and treating other approaches with respect is more likely to influence reviewers positively and garner you shekels rather than chuckles.

Follow the Bill of Writes

At some time, each of us has probably entertained the thought of writing the great American novel, publishing a brilliant memoir, penning a book of poems that touch the soul, or writing the lyrics to a hit song. These are the dreams that stir the writer within us all. In this section, in contrast, the writing goal is much more pedestrian, simply to produce a grant application that can be understood easily and be appreciated by our peers. For this reason, some of these points may seem embarrassingly obvious. However, after having reviewed many, many applications that were replete with these kinds of mistakes and seeing these proposals fare poorly in review, it seems important to spend a moment going back over the basics.

Obfuscate at your own peril. There is no such thing as a paragraph in a grant application that is too clear. Perhaps in junior high school one gets points for covering up poor thinking with overly fancy prose, but not in the grant world. Instead, it's just the opposite. When your prose obscures the points you are trying to make, the reviewer is not going to spend time rereading your paragraphs, diagramming your sentences, and parsing your phrases.

Unclear writing is going to be equated with unclear thinking, and nobody wants to fund that. Thus, the goal for every section of every grant should be to achieve clarity and simplicity. This is the best way to convey your ideas so that they are understood and appreciated by your reader.

Jargon, be gone. The silo problem raises its ugly, peaked head again. When communicating with our intellectual soul mates, we can assume a commonality of technical language. But, this in-group knowledge is unlikely to be shared by outsiders. If a highly critical point in a grant proposal depends on the reader knowing the meaning of a specialized term that is presented without translation, it is an invitation for disaster. For this reason, it is best to avoid jargon completely, or, if you use technical language, make sure to define your terms.

Abbreviate sparingly. Abbreviations have the virtue of saving space, which can be particularly important when working against length limitations. However, it is important to know that the capacity of reviewers to store these abbreviations in memory is extremely limited under the best of circumstances. And, this is made worse by the reality that the average reviewer will read multiple applications (each possibly replete with its own set of abbreviations) in a relatively short period of time. For this reason, you are best off not using any abbreviations other than the most widely recognized ones. Or, if you feel absolutely compelled to "roll your own," limit them in number and try to use abbreviations that are highly evocative (e.g., RUN for the condition in which people engage in vigorous physical activity rather than C7). To do otherwise engenders the risk that the critical thread of your argument will become lost in a tangled knot of forgotten abbreviations.

Check your grammar and spelling. Reviewers are incipient trait theorists. Errors in your writing are often viewed as being indicative of personal failings (and this is made worse by the ready availability of word processors with quite sophisticated spell-checkers and grammar analyzers). Thus, once judged to be characterologically careless, you are not likely to be judged grant worthy.

Final Thoughts

It would be wonderful if there were a simple formula for successful grant writing. Unfortunately, the reality is that this is a highly complex algorithm, with some variables and operations that are knowable and many others that are not. What is known is that our grants are reviewed by our peers and that this process occurs in a highly social context. The reviewing process often unfolds over time, with the attendant waxing and waning of reviewers' attention, energy, and generosity of spirit. Despite the interpersonal context, the roadway that will hopefully connect your ideas with the desired funding is constructed from the written word. Although there are exceptions, you typically will not have an opportunity to present, refine, and defend your ideas in person. Thus, the words you write are your primary representative. For this reason, it is critically important that you craft them in ways that will best serve you, your ideas, and your research.

In this chapter, I have discussed a number of do's and don'ts for grant writers to consider. It is my hope that these comments will be helpful to those who are at various places along the path toward learning how to write effective grant applications. Good writing is not and should not be sufficient in itself for grant success. However, good writing does and should play a critical role in helping good science get the kind of positive reception and favorable outcome it deserves in the highly competitive grant world.

PART II

Applying for Grants From Specific Funding Agencies

4

It's Not Just the Science

Navigating the National Institutes of Health Application Process

Robin A. Barr

I do not like self-help books. How could some supposed expert know enough about me and my background to give advice that I can use on how to succeed in life, or to find inner peace, or even to get a grant? Doctoral training teaches research skills, and postdoctoral training gives real-world experience and a first chance to show an independent publication record. Surely, that fine training, the distinguished mentors and colleagues around me, and my own strengths are all I need?

But, the National Institutes of Health (NIH) offers an alphabet soup of grant opportunities, sets time limits on eligibility for some programs, waves single opportunities for research funding like a red flag to a harried researcher, insists on maddening changes to application length and review format or the number of amendments allowed, and goes through peaks and troughs in fund availability that seem to make the competition for funds a lottery. No doctoral course can teach the twists and turns of these paths. No single mentor can claim familiarity with all the territory.

Note: As I wrote this paper as part of my official duties as a U.S. government employee, the article is free of copyright restrictions.

So, here I go—offering advice, a partial guide to navigating that maze of grants and funding opportunities. Why do I think I am qualified? I have spent more than 20 years at NIH. Beyond years as a program administrator, I also was a Training Officer at the National Institute on Aging (NIA), and, in that capacity, worked with colleagues elsewhere at NIH, shaping programs for students and early-stage investigators to help them advance in science. Currently, as Director of the Division of Extramural Activities at NIA, I now work with staff here to improve their ability to help you and continue to advise applicants competing for funding. I have lectured many times about grant opportunities to groups of students and investigators around the country. Echoes of my lectures now litter the Web. Perhaps I can help.

Basic Rule 1: Apply for Funding

A typical comment: Why apply for funding when there's no chance that I will be successful?

A simple rule will always hold true in the grants world: If you do not apply for a grant, you do not receive one. NIH, other federal agencies, and private foundations have all experienced either very limited growth or a reduction in budgets in recent years. Success rates have fallen. Yet significant and important work is still being funded. Recently (2011), staff where I work, the NIA, had to confront a damaging rumor that—in one version—claimed that we had a 3 percent success rate and in another version claimed that our funding line was the third percentile. Neither version was true. Success rate is a simple measure of the chances that an application will be paid in a particular year. In 2010, our success rate was 14.5 percent. It was 16.1 percent in 2011. Funding line is a measure of how well an application must rank in peer review in order to be paid. We had different funding lines for different kinds of award and category of investigator in 2011, ranging from the 8th percentile to the 16th percentile (NIH ranks in reverse order compared with GREs, SATs, etc.). So the competition was tough, yes, but not impossible. Except, that is, if you did not apply!

Funding lines and success rates vary from year to year and sometimes in unexpected ways. For example, the success rate for 2011 was higher than for 2010, even though NIA's budget for 2011 was slightly smaller than for 2010. In this case, the reason is that we anticipated a smaller budget and announced stricter limits than previously on accepting expensive applications. Our budget for 2012 was almost identical to the 2011 budget. But, our success rate may be higher again! Perhaps some in the research community have given up applying to NIA or perhaps the fact that NIH now permits only one amendment of an application rather than two is reducing the total volume. In any case, the number of applications has declined somewhat and so success rates will likely rise. The general point is that there is no simple relationship between general funds availability and the likelihood of being funded. It is difficult even for us to estimate what our success rate will be more than a year from now. The only thing that we know with complete certainty is that if you do not apply, you will not be paid!

Basic Rule 2: Don't Let Stereotypes About NIH Hold You Back

Another typical comment: You only like the other guys' work.

A common complaint is that we at NIH give preference to trendy areas, or, alternatively, are unduly conservative in the awards we choose to pay. The "trendy" notion may come from the fact that we issue requests for applications (RFAs). These are single opportunity announcements—they have only one submission date—and they are in emerging areas of research that are perhaps too new to have a cadre of scientists already serving on peer-review committees who are capable of reviewing applications on these topics if they are submitted conventionally. Sometimes, we also use them to attract classes of investigators who would offer valuable additional science to our mission but whose numbers are not well-represented among our grantees.

Should you respond to an RFA? The announcement holds the allure of a definite pot of money. So, you are competing for "real" dollars. Also, the applications are reviewed together in a single meeting; under this special review, your application will not be disadvantaged relative to others that may be in more conventional areas of science. Money and special review are good reasons for considering an RFA. At the same time, however, most institutes at NIH put 10 percent or less of their available funds into RFAs. When you apply for a regular grant opportunity, you may be competing in a bigger pool of applications than if you apply for the RFA, but it is important to remember, too, that the pool of dollars for which you are competing is also much bigger than for the RFA. In reality, RFAs have varying success rates. Sometimes the rate is higher than for regular competition, and sometimes it is lower. When we issue an RFA, we have little idea what the success rate will be in advance of the competition. When does it make sense to apply for an RFA, then? Read the text carefully, and decide if your research or you fit the target topic or group well for the RFA. Get in touch with the named program contact and measure that person's enthusiasm for your work or you in relation to the RFA. Then, if the fit is good, apply for the RFA. If the fit is poor, there are plenty of other opportunities available, but—again—only if you apply!

Applicants often tell staff here that NIH is too conservative in its funding. This view has some traction. A recurring thought about NIH peer review is that it values safe science over risk-taking science. When a group of scientists is asked to advise on whether the government should invest $1 million or more in someone's research ideas, then it is not surprising that reviewers are likely to prefer research with a high likelihood of successful results over research proposing riskier hypotheses and strategies. When the investment is that large, it makes sense that reviewers be confident that the research will work before they assign it a good score. So, review is naturally conservative. At the same time, though, NIH works strongly against this bias. In the 1990s, we reshaped the review criteria. Now each application is evaluated on Significance, Approach, Investigators, Environment, and Innovation. In the last two years, reviewers have been required to assign individual scores to each of the five criteria. Applications that are discussed in a panel (usually the top half of applications reviewed) also receive a final impact rating that determines the application's percentile rank. Internal analyses of how criterion scores relate to impact ratings find that Innovation does matter—and not negatively!

NIH has also introduced the R21 research grant—an exploratory/developmental award that provides two years of funding and up to $275,000 for new methods, tests, animal models, or other new concepts for research. In short, it is the anticonservative activity code. It allows researchers who have not yet achieved the standard level of recognition for their methods, models, tests, and so on to gain that recognition. More recently, NIH encourages new thinking through our Transformative Research grant program, the NIH Director's Pioneer programs, and other smaller scale initiatives to shake up the research field, to bring in new talent, and to introduce new theory. Yes. There is a tendency for reviewers to be conservative. However, NIH offers many counterbalances. You can have truly new work funded by NIH. But, only if you apply!

Basic Rule 3: Find a Grant Opportunity That Matches You and Your Research

NIH has a broad array of training and grants programs for varying levels in your career. These include programs for undergraduates, even, in one case, high school students, doctoral students, faculty at less research-intensive schools, junior faculty, postdoctoral trainees, and those who want to convert from postdoctoral status to faculty status. NIH has several programs to diversify the research workforce, to allow people to reenter research careers, to redirect research careers, to gain research skills, to complete small projects, or to organize large projects. And, we even have loan repayment programs. We also have programs for small businesses. NIH's focus is health-related research, but that focus is broad. At NIA alone, we have supported work on economic history, on basic biology, and on clinical geriatrics, as well as considerable work on the brain and behavioral sciences. The Center for Scientific Review at NIH (which organizes peer review of most research applications submitted to NIH) has about 240 standing panels covering an enormous breadth of research areas. We support a lot of researchers, aspiring researchers, and research. Why not you?

Thinking your way to a particular program is an important part of applying. Do I need further training in the research area before I can be competitive for research grants? (Perhaps a postdoctoral fellowship is the best choice or a mentored career award if you are in a faculty position.) I am at the early stages of a research project but have insufficient funding to move on. Am I stuck? (Have a look at the exploratory/developmental [R21] award program, perhaps the small grant [R03] program.) Alternatively, the various NIH institutes and centers support Research Centers at many institutions and many of these institutes and centers offer pilot funding for studies that are not yet mature enough to compete for R01 funding. I am in a small business, and we need money to develop and evaluate our product. Is NIH any help to us? (Have a look at the small business research programs—R43 and R44. You can also collaborate with university-based scientists in a small business technology transfer application—R41 and R42.)

Matching the kind of application you submit—to your background, to your short- and medium-term goals, and to the stage of development of the project—is worth time and effort and increases your chances of success in competition.

Transitions Are Tough: Moving Up

The hardest transition in an academic setting is probably from postdoctoral status to faculty member, although faculty seeking tenure (when still available) or promotion can make some claims, too. NIH has recently focused on several transition points as a way to smooth career advancement in research. The Pathway to Independence (K99-R00) program was created around the postdoctoral-to-faculty transition point. Someone who is still in a postdoctoral or other limited term position, and who has completed fewer than five post-doctoral years in research, applies at one time for both the K99 phase—a continued one-year to two-year mentored activity in the current setting, and an up to three-year research phase (R00) when in a faculty appointment. The R00 phase requires administrative review by the awarding institute—mainly to make certain that the faculty appointment is one that will enable the scholar to pursue an independent research career and ensure that the scholar is receiving sufficient support from his or her department. The main transition advantage of the award is that it provides the scholar with a commitment to three years of research support at the point of looking for a first academic appointment. That is usually of interest to a selection committee at the desired institution!

NIH also has a program of mentored career awards for junior faculty members. The major programs are for clinically trained scientists, most often M.D.-trained but also including clinical Ph.D. specialties, including clinical and neuropsychology. These awards allow three to five years of mentored support to allow an individual to develop research skills through a career development plan and to accomplish independent research as a prelude to R01 or similar research grant support. The awards require a minimum of 75 percent effort (or nine person-months), and that can create a dilemma. Part of the value of such awards is that the sponsoring department has to respect the nine person-month commitment for the three-year to five-year period, and for the faculty member it is an extraordinary opportunity to build a strong research foundation. The downside is that the awards do not extend forever. So, another difficult transition is coming off a career award, obtaining a research grant, and continuing to negotiate release time sufficient to accomplish significant research.

About seven years ago, NIH responded to this problem transition by allowing a staged release from career development confinement. If a career development scholar obtains a federal research grant either as a sole principal investigator or as one of multiple principal investigators in the last two years of the career development award, then the scholar may reduce effort on the career development award to six person-months, provided that total research commitment remains at nine person-months. The idea is that the transition away from the career award is less abrupt this way and allows for continued research funding.

A particularly difficult transition is obtaining the first R01 research grant. NIH had seen an increasing age of its first-time R01 awardees over many years. Today, the average age at which a Ph.D. scientist obtains a first R01 is 42. For a physician-scientist (M.D.), the average age is 44. Though opinions may differ at what age scientists accomplish their greatest work, what is undeniable is that the later a scientist starts to receive substantial funding for that work, the less the scientist can accomplish. NIH has an interest in trying to bring researchers to full independence earlier than is now being achieved. For that reason, NIH centrally, as well as individual institutes and centers at NIH, are now giving advantage to R01 applications from new and early stage investigators for funding consideration. "New" investigators are individuals who have not received NIH R01 or similar funding previously. "Early stage investigators" are new investigators who are within 10 years of finishing research training. At NIA, for example, in 2011, although we funded most established investigator applications to the 11th percentile, we paid early stage investigator R01 applications to the 16th percentile.

Writing the Application

Imagine for the moment that you are a member of an NIH study section. You have been given 10 applications to review for the upcoming meeting. You have your own application to write. You have a Ph.D. student having a crisis, and when you arrive home, you remember it is your turn to walk the dog. When that is done and you have dealt with eight text messages and an anxious phone call from the same graduate student, and you have e-mailed the statistician who is collaborating on your own application, you can now settle down to read the ones you are supposed to review—except you are interrupted again by the now hysterical graduate student. Now imagine that you are writing for that study section member—because you are writing for that person.

An application to NIH is usually assigned to three reviewers who will in all probability be somewhat to very familiar with the topic of your application, who will be reading several other applications, and who will have many other things on their minds. So, you need to capture the reviewers early in the application. When you have a hook—a strong storyline—something that breaks through the background clutter from other applications, decompensating graduate students, and enthusiastic pets, then you have a chance. At this point, the reviewer wants your application to be good and though he or she will undoubtedly find flaws, with the enthusiasm stemming from the hook, the flaws will be cast as minor weaknesses on a strong application. Fail to hook the reviewer, and the same flaws will become significant weaknesses that affect the score.

Where do reviewers find weaknesses? Most often they find them in Approach. Often, reviewers (whose work is broadly in the same field as yours) will see the work as Significant. They are predisposed to find new work in their field Innovative to a degree. And, they will likely consider the investigators qualified if they have otherwise written a strong application. Mostly Environment matters little. Investigators know what resources they need to do the work. They can usually describe them successfully. But, Approach has many details that require careful setting out in the limited space of a grant application. The prominence of the Approach criterion helps explain why standard test instruments and methods tend to review better than new ones. With a standard test or method, much can be assumed safely. With a new test or method, everything can be questioned. (That was a large part of the reason why NIH developed the R21 award.)

Writing an application is an iterative, collaborative effort. Among your editors should be someone (maybe a tolerant spouse) who is not bound closely to the science you are describing. Remember that a study section has 20 to 30 members, sometimes more. Many of these research scientists' interests and work will be somewhat distal from your own. They will not be assigned to review your application. But, they all vote. It also makes sense to put your application through an internal (within institution) mock peer review. (Sometimes you can collaborate with investigators across institutions to set up a peer review network—but remember that none of these individuals can be true reviewers of your application when it is submitted to NIH. They would all be in conflict with you.)

Everyone who applies to NIH is a trained researcher and almost all (except some students) have published papers in peer-reviewed journals. The competition is tough. You need every advantage to succeed. Recognizing the task and devoting resources to shaping your application is a large part of how to succeed.

Learning From Success Stories

A short time ago, we at NIA were interested in looking at the paths recent early stage and new investigators had taken before obtaining R01 funding. The topic was of interest because we regularly evaluate our training programs to find out if—and how—they really help those who received such support to achieve research advances. (At NIH, that usually means obtaining another research grant!)

More than 70 percent of NIA's recent new investigator R01 recipients had received prior funding of one kind or another from NIH before their R01. As many of the very junior (four to seven years postdoctorate) as of the more mature R01 recipients (13 to 17 years postdoctorate) had had prior support. No single prior grant mechanism dominated. Many had been supported on training grants or fellowships. A good number also either had had a prior career development award or had held one when they obtained their R01. A similar percentage had received either small grant or exploratory/developmental grant support. Finally, a sizeable proportion of these new R01 recipients had received more than one prior award from NIH.

These data show that there are multiple roads to an R01. I hope this information counteracts some myths that have grown up about small grant or exploratory/developmental grant support. These are not must-have mechanisms in a stepwise progression to an R01. Yes. Some of our early stage R01 recipients had received prior R03 or R21 support. However, the majority had not received such support. Small grants and exploratory/developmental awards are useful mechanisms for particular circumstances. They are not a proving ground for investigators on their way to achieving R01 funding.

Career awards tell a slightly different story. In fact, in an earlier analysis we found that more than 70 percent of physician-investigators who held R01s from NIA had had a prior career development award. In other words, for physician-researchers, a career development award is normative as a stepping-stone to an R01, though not essential. For research-trained scientists (Ph.D. usually), prior career development awards were much less common. That difference is not surprising given the research focus of a Ph.D. scientist's doctoral training. Ph.D. scientists do occasionally obtain career development awards—most commonly when a scientist wishes to expand or change his or her research focus. More commonly, Ph.D. scientists have prior training grant, fellowship, or research grant support.

Making Sense of Success Rate Data

NIH publishes a treasure trove of success rate data on its RePORT site. The statistics could make a data analyst happy for many hours. Most researchers, though, are more interested in whether there are certain grant mechanisms that they should seek particularly because of high success rates, avoid because of low success rates, or are interested in going "institute-shopping" by finding out which institute has a generous success rate and which has a miserly one. This section tries to show both the uses and misuses of success rate data.

Success rate data are actuarial tables for grant applications. They have their uses and their limitations in the same way. As actuarial tables, they can tell you about outcomes yesterday. You can use them to forecast outcomes tomorrow, but if the environment changes significantly, their value diminishes.

It also makes sense to look at institute websites to find out if they have recently changed policies—such as giving a new advantage to a particular grant mechanism, a particular category of application, or of investigator. These are the kinds of environmental changes that can change future patterns of success rate. Similarly, they may make a meaningful difference in your choice of institute to aim your application at or in your choice of grant mechanism.

If you spend a little time with the success rate data, you will see that R03 (Small grant) and R21 (Exploratory/Developmental grants) have consistently lower success rates than R01s. That difference reinforces the earlier observation that R03 and R21 awards are occasional precursors to R01 awards but are by no means a major, let alone universal road, to an R01 award.

Should you apply for these mechanisms at all given their lower success rate? Why not aim at an R01? For early stage and other new investigators particularly, R01s have a distinctly higher success rate than R03s and R21s. Nevertheless, though the overall success rate data are possibly compelling, some qualifying considerations are necessary before you run away from R03s and R21s. First, some institutes have more generous funding lines for these smaller awards than for R01s and so have higher success rates for them than do other institutes. That means you need to check institute websites for their "funding line policies" to really interpret the success rate data well. Second, it is likely that the success rate for the R21 particularly has been lowered because of the misperception that it is a stepping-stone to an R01. Remember, the R21 was conceived as the "anticonservative" activity code meant to encourage new methods, tests, and such. If an R21 application is submitted whose goal is preliminary data for an R01, then, reviewers are likely to be disappointed if the application is not examining a new model, or method or test. Generally, reviewers are looking for an outcome from R03 and R21 applications, a publishable finding, an end result. When the application is couched in terms of a smaller scale version of a large project down the line, reviewers are going to be less positive about it, and so give it a score that puts it out of funding consideration. That likely contributes to the lower success rates for these mechanisms.

When you do have a small-scale project such as secondary data analysis, an R03 is a good mechanism. When you have a new test or model and two years of research will establish it, then an R21 is a good mechanism. Still, especially if you are a new or early stage investigator, really plan when you are submitting the R01 application. All other things being equal, you do have an increased chance of success with that mechanism.

A little browsing of the success rate tables will also tell you that resubmitted applications have higher success rates than new applications. Persistence does pay! For example, in 2010, new first-time R01 submissions at NIH had a miserable success rate at 11.5 percent. But, on resubmission, the success rate was 34.9 percent. The difference is so large that someone reading an overall success rate should treat that number with caution. Instead, an investigator who submits an application once and discovers that it will not be paid should read the critique carefully, consult others around her, ask the program staff contact whether she should resubmit or consider submitting the application elsewhere, and resubmit the application if the criticisms are addressable. The chances of success really are higher the second time around.

Nowhere is the disparity in success rate between new and resubmitted applications more severe than on mentored career award applications (K01, K08, K23, K25, K99). Peer reviewers are individuals and frequently have disagreements about the strengths of particular applications. However, I sometimes think they have made a pact to make every mentored career award applicant return with a resubmitted application! The difference is so marked that I do not even present overall career award success rates. They are misleading.

Although success rates give you some information about the competition for funding, other factors provide important context for them. Reading institute funding policies, looking to see which activity codes are favored—and which an institute funds at all—are all parts of increasing the odds of your own success when competing for funds. You believe in your research. You think it will make a difference. You need to give that work the best chance possible by knowing and using the materials that NIH provides to help.

Now I Have All the Answers and I Am Ready to Start

Not exactly! It bothers me that the NIH R01 award is seen by too many in the academic community as a mark of an investigator's independence. Before receiving the R01, the investigator needed the help and support of others. Now having the R01, she walks alone. No! Undoubtedly, the investigator obtained others' help in advancing to obtain an R01. Equally undoubtedly, she is continuing to receive help and cooperation while working on the R01. In fact, ask any senior investigator around you if she is independent. She will likely laugh. Of course not! She depends on junior colleagues and on students, and seeks the guidance of other senior colleagues. She very much is part of a team.

That's the point—you are part of a team. When you are taking leadership in an application, you are organizing the team. You can organize it well or organize it poorly. But, you cannot submit and succeed without a team.

Some of the players in the team are familiar to you—your collaborators, your students. Sometimes, you need to introduce yourself to someone at a meeting because that individual has some expertise or resource that you need. Another member of your team is the program officer at the institute where you are seeking funding. An early contact with this individual is a good idea in identifying both interest in the work you will be doing and sometimes advice on what reviewers in a field are looking for in applications. You also want others who will read and critique your application. Ideally, they should have an interest in the field but be a step removed from you. They should have no fear of threatening a relationship when giving critical advice.

Another use for the team is when you receive feedback from the peer-review committee who looked at your application. Again, only a little more than 10 percent of new applications are funded on initial submission. That means your application is likely to receive critical feedback from the panel. A team that shares the critique helps dilute the initial anger that you feel when confronted with seemingly unfair criticism of your best ideas. Instead, you can turn to the task at hand—looking to see whether your team can address the problems mentioned in the critique, sensing whether the panel members are expressing some enthusiasm for the application, and making the decision whether or not to resubmit the application.

Finding Funding in Hard Times

I cannot end this chapter without some reference to NIH's current budget situation. We are in an era of no growth, perhaps looking at real reductions in federal funding for behavioral and biomedical research. Though we may see occasional spikes in funding brought on either through a breakthrough that garners national attention or a legislator working particularly to secure funds for a specific cause, the general slope is flat or downwards for a few years. Yet constrained funding, for all its pain, means that we still do have funds available. We continue to solicit applications because we have funds to support some of the best behavioral and biomedical research in the country and we know that research has a strong track record of achieving health advances. And, we need more advances still.

Inside NIH, we are working hard to make the most efficient possible use of the funds we receive. We have gone beyond announcing our low staffing costs. They are low, but that is no longer enough. We have administratively cut the awards we make to try to spread the dollars among more awards, and we have put controls on the amounts that may be requested. But, these things, too, are not enough, and there are limits to how much we can control amounts requested or cut awards that have fared so well in review. We used to hold firm on the commitments we made in out years for funded projects. Now, we even trim these budgets, too. And, still, funding lines are too tight. We are now looking closely at the buildup of unobligated balances on awards for the simple reason that money sitting unused—even temporarily unused—is money that is not working for the cause of advancing research. We will continue to streamline our operation and maximize the dollars that go to competing research grants.

At the same time, we ask investigators to use all resources available to gain maximal benefit from them. At one level, that means searching to find out whether there are accessible data or resources already available that you can use to answer some if not all of your research questions. NIH makes available many sources of data suitable for advancing work in multiple fields. Conversely, it means honoring the responsibility to share data and resources once collected to maximize their value. At another level, it means looking to all funding sources to maximize their utility for your research. It can mean that funding for part of your research is an advance over funding for none of it, and so spreading the search for funds can move you forward further than the single big application to fund the whole project.

The truth is that in a difficult fiscal environment, the need for research does not diminish. The United States continues to face enormous health challenges. Disparities tend to rise in times of economic hardship. And, we have the extraordinary circumstance of an aging population, bringing with it a surge in chronic diseases that will require advances in biomedical research. We have made progress against several of the major causes of mortality— heart disease and cancer—but as we make that progress, we have learned that prevention and early treatment are key, and new research to address these critical problems is more critical than ever. We all need to pursue these goals with vigor even when funding is an issue. We owe it to our future to pursue research that matters today.

Final Thoughts

These reflections on seeking funding for your research carry a simple message. It takes skill and persistence to seek out funding for research just as it takes skill and persistence to advance our science. Learning how research funding works, and learning to use the resources that NIH or other funding agencies provide, are essential. They become even more important when funding opportunities diminish and competition tightens.

5

Navigating the Grant Process at the National Institutes of Health

William T. Riley, Tracy L. Waldeck,
and Lisa S. Onken

The National Institutes of Health (NIH) is one of the foremost funders of brain and behavioral science research. The NIH Office of Budget reports that in fiscal year 2010, nearly $31 billion was spent by the NIH to support biomedical and behavioral research, and more than $21 billion was awarded in research grants to nearly 45,000 grantees. Brain and behavioral science research is supported to some degree by all of the NIH institutes, and the four institutes that predominantly support brain and behavioral sciences (the National Institute of Neurological Diseases and Stroke, National Institute of Mental Health, National Institute on Drug Abuse, and National Institute of Alcohol Abuse and Alcoholism) awarded nearly 9,000 research grants totaling more than $4 billion in fiscal year 2010 (http://officeofbudget .od.nih.gov/spending_hist.html).

The purpose of this chapter is to provide brain and behavioral science researchers with guidance on developing, submitting, and managing an NIH grant. Even the best research ideas can fail to receive funding if researchers

---

Disclaimer: The content of this chapter represents the views of the authors based on their program and review experience at the National Institute of Health (NIH), and should not be considered as official NIH positions or policies.

do not understand the grant-application, review, award, and monitoring processes of the NIH. This chapter provides insights into these processes to help applicants maximize the likelihood of NIH grant funding. The chapter is organized by the three major steps in the grant research process: (1) developing and writing the grant application, (2) submitting the application for review and funding consideration, and (3) receiving the grant award and conducting/managing the project.

Developing and Writing the Grant Application

Generating the Grant Research Concept

Fundable research ideas are generated by an in-depth understanding of the current state of the science. Your next research idea typically emanates from recent work of your research team and other research teams doing similar work. Having a narrow and focused plan of research has numerous advantages, among which are allowing for deep expertise in the area of research, gaining extensive experience with unique study procedures, and developing substantive collaborations with colleagues doing similar work. The limitation of a narrow and focused approach, however, is that it sometimes can lead to small, incremental research ideas that may be the logical next step in a plan of research but may not produce bold and potentially riskier research ideas that could lead to more impactful findings. Given the lag from research idea to publication, it is important for grant applicants to be forward-thinking and to consider the impact they would like their project to have when it is published years later. Predicting the future is clearly an inexact science, but failing to consider the impact of your research at the time the results will be disseminated and published could diminish the reviewers' and funders' enthusiasm for the overall impact and significance of the application, and lessen the opportunity for funding. Even if funding is received, the impact on the science may be underwhelming when the results are eventually published.

To anticipate future advances, it is important to be aware not only of the published literature but also of research in progress. One excellent source of such information is the NIH RePORTER database, which provides a searchable list of NIH-funded research projects (http://projectreporter.nih.gov/reporter.cfm). RePORTER provides information on other actively funded projects, including the grant abstract and the investigators involved in the research. These investigators can be contacted to provide perspective on where they believe the field is going and what will be impactful research when the results of your study are published 5 to 10 years from now. From these contacts, collaborations can be developed that may further influence the reach and impact of your research project.

Another excellent source of information regarding where the field is heading is the NIH program official (PO) who manages the research portfolio or program in your area of research. His or her job is to understand not only the current state of the science but also to anticipate where the science is going, or needs to go. The PO also can provide information regarding the NIH institute's funding interests in your research area and how your research idea fits with similar research already funded by the institute.

With input from these important sources, it is possible to develop research ideas that will have a substantial impact on the field when the results are published. As you develop these research ideas, it is important to evaluate their potential impact. When the research is completed and if the hypotheses are supported, what will the scientific community learn that it does not already know? If the hypotheses are not supported, can the research be designed such that the findings will still be useful to the scientific community? What new methodologies or procedures will be developed that will advance the field? If you are proposing clinical research, will the study findings challenge current clinical practice patterns and guidelines? If as a result of answering these questions, you as the principal investigator (PI) are not excited about the potential of your research to make a substantial impact, then it will probably be difficult to get enthusiastic responses from the peer-review committee, a group of scientific experts tasked with rating the likelihood for the project to exert a sustained, powerful influence on the research field involved. Perhaps more importantly, if you are not excited about the potential impact of your proposed work, you may have difficulty sustaining your motivation to complete the project, should it receive funding.

Make Use of NIH Program Officials

Each NIH institute and center employs POs who are responsible for managing research portfolios in areas of research consistent with their expertise. Many of these POs have conducted research, and all are scientists who make it their responsibility to stay current on the state of the science that they are responsible for managing. One of their primary responsibilities is preapplication assistance (sometimes referred to as "technical assistance"). POs can help applicants navigate the application process and alert applicants to funding opportunities of which the applicant may not be aware or for which the applicant may not have realized their relevance to his or her research. When POs are unable to answer a question of a potential applicant, they can network with other POs to find the answer or refer the applicant to someone who can answer the question. Despite having this resource freely available to prospective grant applicants, many applicants fail to take advantage of this resource as they are developing their applications.

Once you have a research idea, contact the PO who is responsible for managing the portfolio of research that NIH funds in this area. If you do not know the PO for your research area, check the various NIH institute websites. Most institute sites include a detailed description of the organizational structure, including the science supported by each branch and the branch chief contact information. Some sites also provide the programs of research within each branch and the PO responsible for that program. Even if the only PO you know or can find is someone who works outside of your research area, this PO can help you by referring you to the most appropriate PO to provide preapplication assistance.

After identifying the appropriate PO with whom to discuss your research idea, the first step is to send a draft abstract or specific-aims page (a one-page description of project objectives) to orient him or her to your research goals. This is a critical step for a number of reasons. First, generating this draft abstract or a description of what you plan to accomplish will help you focus your research idea before discussing it. Second, after reviewing your specific-aims draft, the PO may decide that there is a more appropriate PO, either in the PO's institute or in another NIH institute, who is better able to provide technical assistance. Third, it is much more productive for you and the PO to discuss a concisely described research idea rather than preliminary thoughts you have about a research direction.

After providing the specific aims or an abstract draft to the PO, you can discuss the proposed research idea either through e-mail or by setting up a phone meeting. The questions you may want to ask during this discussion include the following:

- Is the research proposed relevant to the institute's mission or strategic plan? NIH institutes have their mission or strategic plans available through their Internet sites, but these are fairly broad descriptions of funding interests. It is almost always helpful to discuss the interest the institute has in funding the proposed research, if the institute is funding similar research currently or has funded similar research in the past, and if other institutes have interest in the proposed research. In some cases, the proposed research may be of interest to multiple NIH institutes. If this is the case, these discussions will be helpful in determining which institute you want for primary assignment, and which additional institute(s) you may want to request for secondary assignment. Secondary assignments facilitate transfers to or cofunding by the secondary institutes if the primary institute is unable to fully fund your grant for some reason. In a few cases, the proposed research may not be of interest to any NIH institute. This does not mean that the research is not important, but it does mean that you may need to modify your research idea if you want an NIH institute to fund it (or seek funding from another source). The PO may offer guidance on how the proposed research could be modified to be of greater interest to the institute, but this advice should be weighed against your interests and expertise to conduct research that may be a better fit with institute interests.

- Are there modifications to the proposed research that would increase institute funding interest and potentially have a greater impact on the field? POs spend considerable time and effort staying up-to-date on the current state of the science and reading applications in the areas of research that they are responsible for managing. They also listen to discussions by institute leadership and advisory councils on applications that generate considerable enthusiasm and applications that do not. As a result, they can provide suggestions for modifications to your draft-specific aims that may better align the goals of the research with the mission of the institute and may have a greater impact on the field. As noted earlier, you need to weigh this advice against your interests and expertise. Although POs may offer suggestions for reshaping the objectives of your study, you are the person who will be submitting the application and carrying out the research if funded, so it is critical that your study's objectives are congruent with your research interests and expertise.

- Which scientific review group (study section) might be most appropriate to review this application? POs are familiar with many of the study sections that review the research in their portfolio and can provide information on which study sections may be the most appropriate to review your grant application. (Assignment decisions will be discussed in more detail later in this chapter.)

- What issues should you be thinking about to improve the chances that your application will be reviewed favorably? POs often cover a wide range of research in their portfolio and are unlikely to have the depth of knowledge in your research that you do. They do, however, listen to reviews and read summary statements (review critiques) of many grant applications in their research portfolio. Over time, POs develop a sense of the common criticisms that reviewers have regarding similar research applications and can provide advice on particular issues that you want to be sure to address in your grant application.

There are many issues that you may want to discuss with your PO, but those listed here are the most common discussion points. After this initial consultation, you may have additional questions as you are preparing your application. POs cannot write the application for you or with you, but they can answer specific questions you may have as you consider different approaches to answering your research questions. Take advantage of the opportunity to get preapplication assistance from your PO. They will often provide advice with the caveat that they are not the reviewers, and therefore cannot guarantee that their advice will be viewed favorably by the reviewers; but providing preapplication technical assistance is an integral role of NIH POs, and many enjoy providing these consultations and "talking science" with prospective applicants. The websites of NIH institutes and centers also have resources to assist in developing a grant application, including sample applications (www.niaid.nih.gov/researchfunding/grant/pages/aag.aspx) and videos of study-section review meetings (http://cms.csr.nih.gov/ResourcesforApplicants).

Funding Opportunity Announcements

All NIH applications must be submitted in response to an active funding opportunity announcement (FOA). FOAs are published in the NIH Guide for Grants and Contracts, the publication in which NIH announces its interests in areas of science to stimulate grant-supported research. Most of the grant applications submitted to the NIH are "researcher-initiated," in which the PI and research team have generated the research idea. These unsolicited applications are typically submitted in response to an FOA termed a "parent announcement" (http://grants.nih.gov/grants/guide/parent_announcements.htm).

A smaller percentage of NIH grant applications, however, are submitted in response to request for applications (RFAs) or content-specific (i.e., non-parent) program announcements (PAs). A nonparent PA is an FOA that identifies specific areas of research interest that NIH institute(s) want to emphasize. An RFA is an FOA that identifies a more narrowly defined area of research interest for which one or more NIH institutes have set aside funds for awarding grants. The primary difference between a PA and an RFA is that an RFA is typically a one-time-only announcement designed to stimulate a fairly specific or narrow area of research that the NIH wants to encourage, for which the NIH has set aside funds to award grants from the applications received in response to the RFA. In contrast, a PA is typically active for three years, is more general in scope, and is designed to identify areas of research priority for an institute, but does not typically have specific set-aside funds. An exception to this is the PAS, or "PA with set-aside funds."

Researchers often overestimate their chances of funding from an RFA. There is set-aside funding for an RFA and your application is reviewed by a special review group convened specifically to review the RFA applications, but the chances of funding are still based on the amount of set-aside funds relative to the number of applications received. If, for example, an RFA has set-aside funds to award 5 to 10 grants, and the number of applications exceeds 50, the chances of funding from an RFA may be lower than for a researcher-initiated application. Therefore, it is critical to first evaluate how well you and your research team are able to respond to the research requested by the RFA. If you need to deviate substantially from what your research team has experience doing and has pilot data to support, it is probably better to submit a researcher-initiated application than to respond to an RFA. That said, an RFA is often only a one-time solicitation, so if your application does not receive funding from the RFA, you can take advantage of the review to improve your research application and submit it as a *new* researcher-initiated application.

If you are considering responding to an RFA, contact the PO listed on the RFA to discuss your research idea. RFAs are often written to accelerate research in a specific area, and applications that are not clearly consistent with the purpose of the RFA may be judged nonresponsive and be with-drawn before review. The PO contact for the RFA is often the person who developed, authored, and sought approval for the initiative at his or her institute. Therefore, the PO listed on the RFA has an intimate knowledge of the RFA and the type of research being sought by it, and she or he can pro-vide guidance to prospective applicants on the fit of their research idea to the purposes of the RFA.

In contrast to RFAs, PAs do not provide set-aside funds and indicate a broader area of research that the institute(s) wishes to encourage. Applications in response to a PA compete for funding with all the researcher-initiated grant applications received. So, what is the value of responding to a PA? First, it is important to understand that not all PAs are created equal. Although relatively uncommon, a PAS has set-aside funds, often with a spe-cific review group and multiple submission dates. A PAR (program announcement with review) does not have set-aside funds, but has review criteria or a specific review panel. Even for the garden-variety PA, there is a modest advantage in being able to indicate to reviewers that the NIH believes that the area of research encouraged by the PA is significant and relevant to the funding missions of the participating institutes. Also, PAs may convey a conceptual framework or define terms that facilitate communicat-ing your research ideas to reviewers.

How do you learn about these RFAs, PAs, and other FOAs? All of the grant-related FOAs are listed in the NIH Guide for Grants and Contracts (http://grants.nih.gov/grants/guide/index.html), which is located on the NIH Office of Extramural Research website (http://grants.nih.gov/grants/oer. htm). Researchers can sign up for weekly updates that provide information about recently released FOAs.

Because of the time frame required for the NIH to get an FOA approved, released, reviewed, and awarded within a fiscal year, the time from the FOA release date to the submission date may be as little as two months. There are ways, however, to anticipate FOAs before they are released. FOAs are often developed with input to the NIH from the research community. This input sometimes comes from the identification of research needs by other agencies (e.g., Institute of Medicine reports), but often comes from NIH-sponsored workshops that convene experts in a research area to assess the state of the science and research gaps. These workshops are announced on institute websites, and the institutes post summaries of these workshops. Institutes also may release requests for information (RFIs), asking researchers to submit feedback on the needs for a specific area of research. Requests for input by an institute, either through workshop or RFI, are often a good indication that the institute is interested in possibly pursuing an FOA depending on the results of this feedback from the research community. Proposed FOAs also are often presented to the institute's advisory council during the open session. As a result, council minutes, also posted on the institute's website, are an excellent source of information about potential FOAs. Since RFAs are one-time submissions with typically only two to four months from release to submission date, this advance information gives researchers an opportunity to do preliminary work, such as collecting pilot data, before the RFA is released.

Writing a Fundable Research Application

Once you have a research idea that you know is relevant to the funding interests and mission of one or more NIH institutes, you now need to write and submit your grant application. First, for any writing assignment—know your audience. In this case, your primary audience is the reviewers who will critique and score your application. Therefore, much of what constitutes good grantsmanship is based on thoroughly understanding the review process described later in this chapter. What follows in this section are tips for preparing each section of the grant application.

Specific Aims

If you have discussed your research application with a PO, you should already have a draft of your specific-aims section. The specific-aims section is often the first section that a reviewer reads, so his or her initial impression of your grant application is based on this one-page synopsis of your application. In this single page, you need to convey what your research questions are and why they are important to ask. Most specific aims include an introductory paragraph that addresses what led you to take on the research you are proposing and the specific aims of the research you are proposing, often with accompanying hypotheses. At the end of this section, the reviewer should have a clear idea of what you propose to do and why. Each specific aim should be sufficiently operationalized so that any research colleague can determine if you have achieved these aims by the end of the project period. Most grant applications have more than one but typically less than five specific aims. Having too many specific aims can raise feasibility concerns. Even if you have additional secondary aims for the research you propose, stay focused on the main goals of your research in your grant application.

Research Strategy

One of the major changes from the 2008 Enhancing Peer Review (EPR) initiative at the NIH (http://enhancing-peer-review.nih.gov) was a reduction in the page limit of the research plan (now called the Research Strategy) for an R01 application from 25 pages to 12 pages and the restructuring of the application to better align the structure and content of the application with the review criteria. The main purpose of the page reduction was to help reduce the administrative burden placed upon applicants, reviewers, and staff. This change sought to focus applicants and reviewers on the essentials of the science that are needed for a fair and comprehensive review of the application. Shorter applications may have additional benefits for reviewers, such as mitigating information overload, and/or enabling a larger number of reviewers to read each application and participate in review in a more informed manner.

In the research strategy section, most applicants usually use only a page or two to describe the significance of the research. Within this space, it is clearly impossible to show that you are aware of all of the research pertinent to the research you are proposing; thus, it is important to focus on the more seminal and salient research that supports why the field needs the research you are proposing and why it is needed now. Keep in mind that only a few of the reviewers will have the depth of scientific expertise in the area that you have, and do not assume that the significance of your research is obvious to all of the reviewers.

Innovation is often the shortest section of the research strategy section because there are only a few statements that can be made to support innovation, but it is a review criterion so you do not want to leave the reviewers unclear as to why the research is innovative. Innovation can be substantiated by noting the questions or study procedures that are novel to your research area. In many cases, a procedure may be novel not because you created it *de novo*, but because you borrowed and applied it in a novel way from another research area to your own area. Do not try to persuade the reviewers that something is innovative when it is not. If you are extending prior work and the research is more iterative than innovative, state this but make clear why it is important to do the research you propose even if it is not particularly innovative.

The *research design or approach* section of the research strategy section should fill the bulk of your page limit. Describe procedures in as much detail as space will allow. You can reference research procedures from the literature, but remember that reviewers are not required to read these additional articles, but only to review the information contained in the application as submitted. Be sure to add enough description to these cited procedures so that the reviewers understand what you are proposing to do. The description of measures is a good example of this balance. You want to describe each measure and its properties sufficiently but succinctly in a few sentences so that the reviewers understand which measures you are proposing and why, but then provide a citation for more details about the measures.

Investigators and Environment

In addition to significance, innovation, and approach, the standard review criteria also include investigators and environment. With the enhanced peer review changes, applicants can now include a paragraph in their biosketch that describes the expertise and experience that makes them competent to perform the research being proposed. This is an opportunity that should not be missed by simply cutting and pasting a standard biosketch. Instead, the biosketch, and particularly this paragraph describing your expertise, should be tailored to the specific research you are proposing in your application and should answer for the reviewers why you and your team are well suited to conduct this particular project. Document your experience and training, your record of accomplishments that have advanced the field, and note working relationships with the other investigators. Early stage investigators should make maximum use of this narrative portion of the biosketch to document their collaborations with more senior members of the research team and to describe their research experience that may not be evident from their publication record. After reading the investigator biosketches, including the synopsis of experience related to the proposed research and the description of the research environment, the reviewers should know why you and your research team are well positioned, perhaps uniquely positioned, to carry out the research proposed.

The environment criterion is often the easiest to address, especially for applications from established research institutions that have an extensive research infrastructure. The environment section should describe the common research infrastructure of the institution (e.g., library resources, information technology and data analysis resources, institutional review board, personnel and financial support) as well as the specific facilities (e.g., laboratory and/or office space) and existing equipment (e.g., magnetic resonance imaging or positron emission tomography scanner) that will be used for the proposed project. If some aspect of the environment puts you and your research team in a unique position to perform the research proposed, be sure to note this. Investigators from smaller institutions without an established research infrastructure (e.g., small colleges, small businesses) need to pay particular attention to the environment section and clearly document that the facilities and infrastructure are adequate to conduct the research proposed.

NIH Grant Application Review System

NIH receives approximately 80,000 grant applications each year (http://cms .csr.nih.gov/AboutCSR/Welcome+to+CSR). Some of these applications never make it to review but are instead rejected because the application is incomplete or fails to follow the submission instructions (e.g., page limits). The applicant should thoroughly understand the standard application process (http://grants.nih.gov/grants/funding/424) and the instructions of the FOA under which they are submitting. If your application is rejected for being incomplete or failing to follow instructions, you will need to wait until the next submission date to submit a corrected application.

Most of the applications that are accepted are reviewed by the Center for Scientific Review (CSR), which coordinates review across the various NIH funding institutes and centers. In addition to the CSR, each institute also has its own review groups or study sections. These institute-specific study sections review applications that use grant mechanisms or propose areas of research that are unique to that institute. It is important for grant applicants to recognize that both the CSR and the individual institutes have review groups where their application may be assigned.

Assignment of Grant Applications to a Study Section

The Division of Receipt and Referral within the CSR makes initial study-section assignments using referral guidelines developed by the various study sections, but the request of the PI in their grant application cover letter is considered in the assignment decision. As a result, it is important for the PI to understand review assignment and the specific study sections that are best able to review the application. The CSR website, as well as the individual institute websites, provide a list of the study sections, their areas of review, and membership rosters for chartered or standing review committees. Applicants should review this information to determine the study sections that appear to have the expertise to review their application. POs are familiar with many of the study sections that review applications assigned to their portfolios and also can provide advice on study sections for the PI to consider requesting for review.

After the grant application has been assigned to a study section, if the PI has concerns about the fit of the application to the study section, he or she can contact the scientific review officer (SRO) to discuss these concerns. SROs know well the expertise of their study section reviewers and are usually proactive in reassigning applications that do not fit that expertise, but there still may be occasions in which the PI has concerns about the study-section assignment. In most cases, the SRO will assure the PI that the expertise needed to review the application is represented on the study section, but if the application is determined not to be a good fit for the study section, the SRO can transfer it to a more appropriate study section. It is imperative, however, that this transfer be done early in the process, well before the reviewers have been assigned applications to review; so any discussion about reassignment should be initiated soon after the assignment is made, which is usually a few weeks after it is submitted.

Another option that the SRO has to ensure appropriate review expertise for a given application is to add *ad hoc* reviewers with specialized expertise to the standing study section. This is commonly done by SROs as they read applications and make reviewer assignments. Although the PI can discuss with the SRO the expertise that he or she believes is required to review his or her application, the PI cannot recommend a specific reviewer. Doing so automatically disqualifies the recommended reviewer from consideration. The SRO may consult with the PO assigned to the application for recommendations of *ad hoc* reviewers that can provide the expertise required to review the application, but the PI cannot recommend reviewers.

Grant Review Criteria and Scoring

Applications to NIH are reviewed based on five standard criteria that are described in each FOA:

- *Significance:* Does the project address an important problem or a critical barrier to progress in the field? If the aims of the project are achieved, how will scientific knowledge, technical capability, and/or clinical practice be improved? How will successful completion of the aims change the concepts, methods, technologies, treatments, services, or preventative interventions that drive this field?
- *Investigator(s):* Are the PI(s), collaborators, and other researchers well suited to the project? If early stage investigators or new investigators, or in the early stages of independent careers, do they have appropriate experience and training? If established, have they demonstrated an ongoing record of accomplishments that have advanced their field(s)? If the project is collaborative or multi-PI, do the investigators have complementary and integrated expertise; are their leadership approach, governance, and organizational structures appropriate for the project?
- *Innovation:* Does the application challenge and seek to shift current research or clinical practice paradigms by using novel theoretical concepts, approaches or methodologies, instrumentation, or interventions? Are the concepts, approaches or methodologies, instrumentation, or interventions novel to one field of research or novel in a broad sense? Is there a refinement, improvement, or new application of theoretical concepts, approaches or methodologies, instrumentation, or interventions proposed?
- *Approach:* Are the overall strategy, methodology, and analyses well-reasoned and appropriate to accomplish the specific aims of the project? Are potential problems, alternative strategies, and benchmarks for success presented? If the project is in the early stages of development, will the strategy establish feasibility and will particularly risky aspects be managed?
- *Environment:* Will the scientific environment in which the work will be done contribute to the probability of success? Are the institutional support, equipment, and other physical resources available to the investigators adequate for the project proposed? Will the project benefit from unique features of the scientific environment, subject populations, or collaborative arrangements?

In addition to these criteria, some FOAs, particularly RFAs, may have additional review criteria that are listed in the FOA. Applicants are strongly encouraged to read and fully understand the review criteria for the FOA under which the application is being submitted.

At the peer-review meeting, applications deemed to have the highest scientific and technical merit (generally the top half of applications under review) will be discussed and assigned an overall impact/priority score by the review committee members. The impact/priority score reflects the reviewers' assessment of the likelihood for the project to exert a sustained, powerful influence on the research field(s) involved, in consideration of the review criteria and any additional review criteria as applicable for the project proposed.

For each review criterion, the assigned reviewers describe strengths and weaknesses in a bulleted format, and rate the criteria from 1 (exceptional) to 9 (poor). The reviewers then score the overall application using the same 1 to 9 criteria to provide an impact/priority score. Because the reviewer may give different weight to the strengths and weaknesses of the application within each review criterion, the impact/priority score may not be consistent with an average of the individual criteria scores. For instance, if the reviewer considers the significance of the application weak, even if the other criteria are rated highly, the reviewer may rate the overall impact/priority in the moderate to low range as a result of the concerns about significance. The individual criterion scores, however, do give the PI and the NIH PO feedback on which review criteria are stronger and weaker for any given application.

Grant Review Process

Grant applications are assigned by the SRO to reviewers in the study section with the expertise to review the application. The SRO typically assigns the application to a primary, secondary, and discussant reviewer, but on occasion may assign a fourth reviewer or may be able to assign only two reviewers to an application. All of the study-section reviewers are expected to read and be familiar with all of the applications, but the assigned reviewers will review the application in depth, provide a written critique of the application, and lead the discussion of the application. As a result, the assigned reviewers, particularly the primary reviewer, have considerable influence over how the application will be evaluated by the members of the study section.

The assigned reviewers provide their draft critiques and preliminary criteria and impact/priority scores in advance of the study-section meeting. These initial scores are used by the SRO to determine which applications are deemed by the assigned reviewers to have the highest scientific and technical merit and therefore should be discussed at the study-section meeting. Typically, the grant applications in the lower half of scores are not discussed so that the study section can focus its work on the applications that have the most potential for funding. In setting the agenda for the meeting, the study-section chair will propose that the lower half of applications not be discussed, but will ask reviewers to nominate any applications in the lower half of applications that they feel require discussion. Any reviewer, not just an assigned reviewer, can nominate an application for discussion. Applications that are not discussed receive the critiques of the assigned reviewers, including their criteria ratings, but do not receive an impact/priority score. Also, since there was no discussion, there is no résumé or summary of discussion included in the summary statement.

Applications from early stage investigators (see http://grants.nih.gov/grants/new_investigators/investigator_policies_faqs.htm for a definition) are discussed first, followed by applications from established investigators. Within each group, the study section begins by discussing the best scoring application based on the preliminary impact/priority score of the assigned reviewers and continuing in order based on these scores. For each application, the assigned reviewers give their preliminary impact/priority score on a 1 to 9 scale. The primary reviewer briefly describes the proposed project and the strengths and weaknesses of the application following the review criteria outlined in the FOA. The secondary and discussant reviewers then add anything unique regarding the strengths and weaknesses of the application that were not mentioned by the primary reviewer. The more disparate the initial review scores are, the more the secondary and discussant reviewers will have comments to justify their differences with the other reviewers. A general discussion of the application will then ensue among all of the study section members. Finally, the primary reviewer will indicate if there are any issues regarding animal care or human subjects, or inclusion of children and minorities that should be addressed in the summary statement. Following this discussion, the assigned reviewers will provide their revised impact/priority scores based on the discussion, and all of the reviewers will score the application. If a reviewer wants to score an application outside the range of the assigned reviewers, he or she needs to declare that he or she is doing this. Following the scoring of the application, reviewers are asked for any comments on the budget. The entire discussion process takes about 10 to 15 minutes per application.

After the study-section meeting concludes, the assigned reviewers have the opportunity to revise their critiques as needed based on the discussion and submit their final critiques to the SRO. The text from the reviewers' critiques form the basis of the summary statement made available to the applicant. Prior to the release of the summary statement, the SRO responsible for the review meeting edits the reviewers' critiques for clarity and drafts the résumé and summary of discussion to complete the summary statement. The purpose of the résumé and summary of discussion is to highlight for the applicant the information that was deemed most important or relevant by the reviewers based on the discussion. The overall impact/priority scores of all the members of the study section are averaged and multiplied by 10, producing a final impact/priority score ranging from 10 to 90. These scores are then assigned percentiles based on the scores of all R01 applications reviewed in the study section over the past three rounds of reviews, including the current round, and rounded up to the nearest integer. For special emphasis panels and other smaller volume study sections, the denominator for the percentile is based on the scores of all R01 applications reviewed in CSR study sections, not just the individual study section. The goal of assigning percentiles is to adjust scores based on the scoring tendencies of the study section. Those study sections that provide better scores overall will have higher percentile scores for the same impact/priority score than those study sections that provide poorer scores overall.

Knowing the details of the grant-review process should influence the development of a grant application in a number of ways, including the following:

- Address the review criteria directly in your application. The reviewers need to know the following:

  o Why is this research question important to ask now? (significance)

  o Why are you and your research team the ones who should be doing this research? (investigators)

  o What is new or novel about your approach or research question? (innovation)

  o What approach do you plan to take to answer this question and why? (approach)

  o What resources are available to you to perform what you propose to do? (environment)

The reviewers should not need to look for or infer the answers to these questions from your application. These criteria should be addressed clearly in your application.

- Write a clear, well-organized and succinct grant application. Your assigned reviewers have full-time jobs and must squeeze in the review of your application among multiple work demands prior to the review meeting. Many of the unassigned reviewers will have time only to scan your application while traveling to or while listening during the review meeting. You want your application to be easy to read and your logic easy to follow. Sections should be short, well-delineated, and easy to find when a reviewer wants to reread a section. Don't waste the reviewers' time. Get to the point, get to it early, and give them the information they need to critique your application.

- Don't assume that the reviewers will know what you are talking about. Although the primary and secondary reviewers presumably will have the expertise to understand highly technical jargon, most of the reviewers in the study section may not. Be descriptive and explanatory. Using highly technical jargon may make you seem knowledgeable to some, but failing to explain your application in terms that most general scientists will understand may negatively affect the review.

- Give the primary reviewer a reason to argue for your application. Proposing iterative science that answers the next logical question in a plan of research may be easier and may feel safer, and might even be a necessary step, but if it does not excite the reviewers, the application may fare poorly. The reviewers, particularly the primary reviewer, need a compelling rationale for why the proposed research needs to be done.

Asking colleagues unfamiliar with your research, especially ones with NIH review experience, to read and critique your application before submission is one of the best ways to address these issues. They can point out where more explanation and description is needed for scientists who may not be as familiar with the research area as you are, give you feedback on how to make the proposal easier to read and follow, and tell you if they "got it" regarding the importance of the research to be performed.

Funding Decisions and Resubmissions

Within a few days of the study-section review, the PI should receive an overall impact/priority score ranging from 10 to 90 through his or her eRA (Electronic Research Administration) commons account. If the study section is large enough to have its own percentiles, then a percentile will also be included. If not, then the percentile may not get calculated and posted until all of the reviews for that round are complete. It is important to note that applications in response to RFAs or for some types of funding mechanisms are not percentiled. Each institute will have available on its website the percentile payline for the current fiscal year, or at least guidance on how they make funding decisions. In recent years, these paylines have been between the 10th and 20th percentile, but vary from year to year, institute to institute, and even by mechanism or investigator status (e.g., early stage investigator). If your percentile score is below (meaning better than) the payline percentile score, then there is a good chance, but no guarantee, that the grant will be funded. NIH institutes vary in the amount of discretion exercised around the payline. Some institute's do very few "select pays" of applications just above the payline while others will "select pay" well above the payline and will even skip a few below the payline that they consider to be less relevant to the institute's mission. Even if your percentile score is well below the payline, there are no guarantees that the institute will have the funds to pay up to that payline. There is no guarantee of funding until you actually receive a notice of grant award.

What should you do after you receive your overall impact/priority score? Nothing. One frustration of POs is when PIs contact them immediately after receiving their score to ask if their application will be funded or what the next steps should be. It is often months after review before all of the percentile scores are available and the institute has developed a preliminary pay plan. Until then, the program staff knows nothing more than the PI does, which is their percentile score and if it is under or over the payline, if indeed their institute has a defined payline.

Since many more applications are not funded than are funded, the discussion with the PO is primarily to discuss plans to revise and resubmit, but this should wait until the PI and PO receive the summary statement, which typically lags the impact/priority score by a few weeks. Even if your application was not discussed and did not receive an impact/priority score, the critiques of the assigned reviewers and their criteria ratings or scores will be provided in the summary statement. If the application was discussed by the study section and received an impact/priority score, then a summary of the discussion also will be provided. POs make every effort to attend study-section reviews, but their assigned grant applications are often scattered among various study sections, and study-section meetings may conflict with other obligations, including other study-sections meeting on the same day. As a result, the PO may not have had the opportunity to listen to the review of your application. Even if they do, the PO will want to wait to discuss the review until after the summary statement is released. Therefore, it is best to wait until your summary statement is available before contacting the PO to discuss the review.

In considering if and how to resubmit, some PIs focus almost exclusively on the percentile score and not enough on the critique. Even "not discussed" applications can be revised and have a chance, however small, of receiving a fundable score on the next submission if the weaknesses identified in the original application are addressed. Major weaknesses in approach, for example, can often be addressed if the investigators have the expertise to respond to these weaknesses in approach. In contrast, percentile scores that are close to fundable may not have much of a chance of being funded on resubmission if the weaknesses noted are concerns about the significance of the research or about the expertise of the investigators that cannot be easily addressed. Investigators should have a candid discussion with their PO concerning resubmission and how best to address the concerns of the reviewers.

Before moving on to the funding process, review these tips regarding resubmitted applications.

- Remember that in your resubmission, you usually have one page to respond to the previous review and your application is likely, although not guaranteed, to go back to the same reviewers who reviewed the application on the initial submission. Respond fully and completely to the reviewers' critiques. Do not ignore a criticism. Given the limited page constraints for the introduction to the resubmitted application, you can summarize and consolidate the weaknesses noted, but make sure you respond to all of the weaknesses noted.

- Disagree thoughtfully. It is easy on first read of the summary statement to be frustrated with some of the comments made by reviewers, especially if you think they were made in error. Take the time to consider the reviewer's comments fully. If you still disagree with a reviewer's concern, note this and justify your position without being antagonistic in your response.

- Make it easy for the reviewers to identify the revisions in the resubmission. Most applicants indicate changes from the original application by italicizing, bolding, and/or placing a left border on the sections that were revised. In the introduction to the resubmission application, cite page numbers where the changes occur, especially major changes. It is possible that the same reviewers will be assigned to your resubmission, and if so, they may focus on the changes you made in response to their comments.

- Take the time to make real, substantive changes to your resubmission. With the enhanced peer review changes, there is only one resubmission possible, not two. If the best way to respond to a reviewer's concern is to collect more pilot data, gain more expertise in a specific procedure, or do some other task that requires more effort than just rewriting the application, take the time to do it. You have only one chance at the resubmission, so take your time to do it right.

Institute Advisory Councils and Postcouncil Activities

Within a few months of the review, the institute advisory council will meet to advise the institute leadership and consider the reviewed applications. PIs are often confused about the purpose of the institute councils. Councils do not decide which grants will be funded. Their role is to provide a second level of review. Therefore, council members read the résumé summaries, and also sometimes the full summary statements and grant application for those applications that were reviewed and received an impact/priority score. Typically, councils concur with the study-section reviews, but on rare occasions, councils may take a different action on a specific grant application, such as not recommending funding. Some councils also identify applications that have high or low program priority.

Soon after council, most institutes generate a pay plan based on the merit of the applications, the projected funding available to the institute for new applications, and the relevance of the application to the institute mission. Prior to and following council, there are a few steps you can take to facilitate your application's being funded.

Respond to any funding bars as soon as possible. As a result of animal care or human research concerns identified during review, there may be a bar to funding of the application until these concerns are addressed. As soon as you identify these concerns on your summary statement and there is some reasonable possibility of funding, work with your PO to address these concerns. The process of lifting these bars takes considerable time, so the earlier these bars are lifted, the better. Concerns about inclusion of gender, minority-group members, or children should also be addressed promptly. Many institutes will not allow grant applications to be considered by council until these concerns are addressed and the bars are lifted.

Check with your PO about any further information the institute may need to make a funding decision. When an application is close to the payline, some institutes will ask PIs to respond to the remaining reviewer concerns. A letter to the PO that addresses how you will further improve the application based on feedback from the reviewers can be used by the PO to support a select pay request. If you write such a letter, it is important to address the reviewers' concerns in a clear and concise way. The more cogent and succinct the response, the easier it will be to make the case that you have successfully addressed reviewer concerns.

If your percentile score is just outside the payline of the primary institute, ask the PO if there is any advantage in transferring the grant to another institute, possibly with a better payline, or asking for cofunding from another institute. Transfers after review are often quite difficult to do, primarily because institutes prefer that a grant application be assigned based on relevance to the institute mission, not because they have a slightly better payline than that of another institute. However, if your grant application has secondary assignments, it may be worth the effort to inquire at the secondary institute about possible interest if the primary institute is not able to fund the application.

If your grant application is within or close to the payline, begin working on just-in-time (JIT) information such as documentation of other support, human-subjects ethics training, and institutional review board (IRB) submission and approval. Grants management will contact all PIs whose applications are eligible to be funded to request this information, but it is useful to be proactive and ready to provide these materials when asked. Some materials, like the documentation of other support and certification of human-subjects ethics training, are relatively easy to compile and send. Others, like IRB approval of the application, take time to obtain. The more responsive you are to grants management requests, the sooner you are likely to receive your notice of award (NOA).

Budget Adjustments

The award you request is unlikely to be the award you receive, and is often reduced from what was requested based on a number of factors. If budget concerns were raised by review, these concerns must be addressed and budget adjustments made. Regardless of review concerns, grants management specialists review the proposed budget and make administrative adjustments to correct for inappropriately budgeted items (e.g., nongrant-specific general office supplies that should be covered by indirect costs, personnel salaries that exceed the salary cap). Programmatic adjustments are less common than administrative adjustments, but POs also review the budget and may recommend reductions of budget items that do not appear to be adequately justified.

In recent years, to maintain the number of new grant awards during a time when funding for NIH has not kept pace with research costs and obligations, NIH institutes have made further reductions to most grant awards. Institutes have used a combination of percent reductions to new awards and/ or reductions in outyear obligations to preserve the number of new grant awards made each year. These grant budget adjustment policies are typically available on the institute's website, and the grants-management specialist can provide details on the budget adjustments that will be made to your grant award.

There is little recourse for these award reductions other than to refuse the award. What you can do is be proactive in determining the nature and extent of any award reductions before the award is made. When contacted by the grants management specialist for JIT information, inquire about possible award reductions. When you know what the reductions will be and have examined how these reductions will impact your project, contact your PO to discuss the impact of these reductions and how you plan to accommodate them. If the impact is substantial (e.g., reduced aims, smaller sample size), then these changes will require approval before the grant can be awarded.

Managing Your Grant Award

Receiving an NOA marks a start to the long effort to complete the work you proposed, and some preliminary work in anticipation of your grant award will facilitate starting the project when the funding arrives. Delays in initiating projects are a common problem among NIH grantees, and many of these delays could be avoided with some advance planning so that IRB approvals are in place, staff hiring can begin, and equipment and supplies can be ordered. The option exists to expend funds within 90 days of the grant start date, but your institution needs to approve this and may not since the institution is risking its own funds should the grant not be funded. Even without committing institution funds, some low-cost preliminary efforts before receiving the award will minimize delays. IRB approval is typically required before you receive grant funding, so getting IRB submissions started well before the anticipated start date is a critical step. Existing equipment and supplies can be inventoried, and purchase orders for supplies and equipment can be prepared and ready to submit when funding arrives. If your institution will allow you to post or advertise staff positions before receiving funding as long as nobody is hired until you receive funding, take advantage of this opportunity to accelerate staffing for your project. Most of the delays in NIH-supported projects are the result of slow starts to study initiation, and PIs can avoid many of these delays with some prudent planning in advance of receiving the grant award.

As a result of previous failures of grantees to complete the projects as proposed, particularly clinical trials that fail to meet their targeted enrollment, NIH has become increasingly vigilant about monitoring study progress. Some institutes request that selected projects provide more frequent reporting than the annual report. Even if you need to report progress only annually, it is important to remember that there are no guarantees that subsequent-year funding will be awarded, and failure to make adequate progress has been grounds for discontinuing funding. Therefore, it is imperative that PIs ensure that their projects get started promptly, make good progress, and ultimately meet their study aims.

NIH POs understand that unexpected events can slow progress, but you do not want your PO to be surprised by your annual report. (Note that the program official technically becomes your PO when assigned to your grant, but these are often the same person and "PO" is an interchangeable abbreviation for both roles.) If you run into difficulties with your project, let your PO know early. One role of the PO is to monitor progress on your grant and to assist you in resolving possible barriers to progress. With experience across a wide number of similar studies, the PO can often share ideas from other projects that have been successful in resolving the problem you are experiencing.

Under the current NIH policy of "expanded authority" (http://grants. nih.gov/grants/policy/nihgps_2003/nihgps_part7.htm) as the PI, you can adjust your budget to get the job done. If, for example, you do not need an additional research assistant and can apply these funds to additional recruitment efforts, you have the authority as the PI to do this. However, current policy requires that if you shift more than 25 percent of your budget from one area to another or have a change in key personnel, you need to report this immediately and receive approval before proceeding. Always make sure that budgetary actions are in accordance with current NIH policy.

Keep your PO informed of your progress, including your successes as well as your difficulties. POs are sometimes asked to highlight research in their portfolio, and if you have kept your PO informed, including sending any preprints of in-press articles related to your grant, the PO is more likely to highlight your work to NIH and Department of Health and Human Services leadership. Also, be sure to indicate grant support in the publication acknowledgments. If you are planning to attend a scientific meeting to present results of your grant project, let your PO know so if he or she is also planning on attending the meeting, the PO can attend your presentation. Even if you are not presenting on your grant-supported research, scientific meetings are an excellent opportunity to meet with your PO and discuss project progress, so let your PO know about the upcoming meetings that you plan to attend. A PO can have from less than 20 to more than 100 grants in his or her portfolio, depending on the institute, so your PO may not be able to monitor all of these grants as closely as he or she would like. Being proactive in letting your PO know about grant progress is always appreciated and helps to develop a working relationship that can be invaluable for your next grant application submission.

Completing a Grant Project

Despite your best efforts, there may be projects that cannot be completed by the end of the project period. If you have carryover funds from prior years remaining, your institution can request a one-year no-cost extension to complete the project. Although NIH prefers that the project be completed on time, if you can document the availability of adequate funds to perform the remaining work, these initial one-year extensions are usually automatic. Subsequent extensions, however, are difficult to obtain and are often granted only when events beyond your control have occurred.

If, in addition to running out of time, you also have run out of money to complete the project, the options are much more limited. In situations in which unforeseen costs have occurred, you can request an administrative supplement. In a tight budgetary climate, however, these supplement requests are rarely approved, and often only for relatively small amounts when they are approved. Clearly, the best solution is to be prudent with your budget so you can complete the project as proposed, but if unusual circumstances arise, contact your PO as soon as you realize that you have additional budget needs, not after you have already run out of funds, and discuss your options. In some cases, it may be preferable to reduce the scope of your project rather than to request administrative supplement funds, but there may be a compelling reason for requesting an administrative supplement.

At any time during the project period, you can submit a competitive supplement application. These applications are typically reviewed by the same study section that reviewed the parent grant, and are often submitted by PIs who want to capitalize on new findings, procedures, or equipment advances that were not budgeted for when the original application was submitted. You must have enough time remaining in the parent grant to conduct the supplement (i.e., a supplement cannot be used to extend the project period). But, if new innovations occur in your field that you want to take advantage of in your grant project, a competitive supplement is an excellent way to incorporate these innovations in your project.

At the end of your project, a final report is required. These reports do not need to be extensive, and you can cite the publications that have resulted from the grant project, but these final reports are important to file promptly. The grant is not officially closed out until the final budget report, invention report, and final progress report are obtained. Even if you have additional analyses and publications planned, a timely filing of the final report also gives NIH a record of accomplishments during the project period. In addition to these reports being reviewed and approved by the PO, these reports are sometimes requested by others in the government to determine how productive the NIH research investment has been. Providing final reports and other documentation of the productivity of your grant award helps NIH support its budget needs and requests.

Final Thoughts

Brain and behavioral researchers have a long history of successful grant support from NIH. By better understanding the process of grant submission, review, and award, researchers improve their chances of being funded by NIH. Researchers are encouraged to consider the perspective of reviewers as well as the mission and priorities of NIH institutes throughout the development of their application and to be sure that they submit an application that is clear, succinct, and easy for a reviewer to read and review. Researchers also are encouraged to contact NIH program staff early and often throughout the grant-application development and grant-management periods. Working closely with program staff can help grant applicants avoid common errors in the grant-submission and grant-management processes, and improve the applicant's chances of success with the NIH grant process.

6

Writing a Grant Proposal for the National Institutes of Health

Generalities and Specifics

Howard Eichenbaum

I have been successful in obtaining National Institutes of Health (NIH) grants. Indeed, I am proud to hold several at this time. And, I recently had one proposal that received the top score in a particular round of approvals at one NIH institute. But, I have also had many failed grant applications, albeit fewer these days than earlier in my career. Some of those proposals just missed being funded, some received a mediocre score, and some were not scored ("triaged"). In total, perhaps the number of failures is greater than the number of successes.

Let me also acknowledge at the outset that my research is in the area of behavioral and brain sciences, and more specifically in the analysis of brain systems that support memory. I have limited expertise in grant writing outside of this area, although I have reviewed grant applications in the broader fields of learning and memory and cognitive and systems neuroscience. I hope that some of the advice I am about to offer generalizes to a larger scope of research areas, experimental approaches, and levels of analysis.

Here I will first discuss generalities, including aspects of proposals that are largely successful and "red flags" that lead to failure, and these will be evaluated from the viewpoint of the review process. Then, I will get specific and describe and analyze that top-scored proposal of mine as an example of organizational strategies that led to success. My hope is that, between the generalities and specifics, you will find something useful in designing your own research proposal.

Generalities: What Matters Most?

My plan in this chapter will be to highlight insights that I believe lead to success against pitfalls that lead to failure. I will often use slogans to provide this advice, as if what I recommend is sure to lead to success or failure. But, nothing in this business is for sure. I have seen many proposals succeed despite their having ignored classic red flags, and I have heard about many perfectly written proposals that have failed. What succeeds, I believe, is a match between what you think is the best proposal and what the reviewers think. Since the latter is unknown, there is lots of room for guesswork in what to propose and in how to propose it. The best I can hope to do is to provide advice that may incrementally improve your chances of success.

What matters most is a really good idea. A really good idea is one that advances your field to a new level or in a new direction, involves a research design that distinguishes between possible, predictable outcomes that are important for advancing the field, and that describes an organized plan that is realistically doable in the time frame of the project. Most of what I write in this chapter is just an expansion on these points. Remember that hard work in addressing these points is better than good luck after ignoring them. I'd like to think that hard work in addressing these points begets good luck.

The Review Process

It is essential to understand the audience and review criteria for an NIH grant proposal. For a grant application, the primary audience is a large group of reviewers, the initial review group (IRG), whose job it is to distinguish your application as outstanding (or not) among a large number of competing proposals. The review criteria for NIH proposals are also highly specific and focused on the evaluation of the proposed research for taking the field to a new level. The sequence of events in review goes as follows: For each grant application, a member of the IRG is assigned as a primary, secondary, and tertiary reviewer, and prior to the IRG's meeting, each assigned reviewer writes a full critique based on the five main criteria for research grants: significance, investigator(s), innovation, approach, and environment. There are additional criteria for other types of grant applications (e.g., fellowship, career development, instrumentation), but I will not consider these here except to note that in fellowship and career development applications, the mentor and plans for training are as important as the research proposal itself; do not minimize these components of the proposal. The reviewers concentrate on strengths and weaknesses of the proposal on each of these criteria.

Reviews are organized specifically to address five criteria, and it is important that your proposal explicitly addresses each one. *Significance* refers to whether the proposed work will address a critical problem and, if the component studies are designed appropriately, whether the results will take us to a new level of understanding about the research problem. So significance is not about whether your experimental design is correct or whether you are using state-of-the-art or standard technical approaches. It asks how important the results are for the field. *Investigator(s)* refers to whether you are competent to pursue the project and what your track record is in publications in this area. *Innovation* refers to whether the approach involves new concepts, approaches, or tools. One would think that some difficult and important problems of high significance might be solved with conventional approaches. But, you would do well to describe what about your approach is new and innovative, such that the innovation is key to the significance. *Approach* refers to experimental design; this is the area that typically receives the most detailed attention. Can this project be done? Is your approach feasible? Will the results be unambiguous? *Environment* refers to the university, center, or department in which you will pursue the project. Does it have the facilities necessary to pursue first-rate research? Scores are given for each of these five criteria, and although the five scores are not arithmetically averaged, there is significant influence of the scores on each criterion that leads to the final score.

During the review meeting, the entire IRG will evaluate your proposal against 50 to 60 or more other proposals. Your review begins with an initial descriptor (e.g., exceptional, outstanding, satisfactory, or poor) provided by each of the assigned reviewers, and these descriptors are used to determine whether the application will receive a full review. Descriptors are verbal, but also are associated numerical scores. Thus, for example, the highest descriptor is "exceptional" and the associated score is 1, the lowest descriptor is "poor" and its associated score is 9, and other descriptors fall in between (outstanding = 2; excellent = 3; very good = 4; good = 5; satisfactory = 6; fair = 7; marginal = 8; and a score of 9 is reserved for proposals that have no merit or are deemed inappropriate as scientific studies or are unethical in some way). Usually, if the level of enthusiasm in the descriptor falls approximately in the top half of all of the applications being reviewed in that particular meeting, the application will receive a full review. On occasion, one of the reviewers will request a full review even if the initial descriptors are not enthusiastic. Otherwise, the proposal is not scored (that is, "triaged") and the investigator submitting the grant will receive the written critiques of the assigned reviewers without any summary of the discussion.

The starting point of the subsequent full review is the range of descriptor scores, and the aim of the review is to reduce that range and confirm the scores by a presentation and discussion of the application. The job of the assigned reviewers is to narrow the differences between their scores and to convince the entire IRG, which can number as many as 25 or more members, to assign the score the reviewers are proposing. To some extent, then, most of the IRG acts as a "jury" to consider the testimony of the assigned reviewers. Notably, the IRG members who are not assigned as reviewers are instructed that, if their score is to vary substantially outside the scores proposed by the reviewers, they must write an individual justification. So, generally the IRG votes consistent with the range of final scores of the assigned reviewers.

The review begins with the primary reviewer providing an overview of the application and his or her own critique, usually organized by, or at least touching on, each of the review criteria. Then, the secondary reviewer will confirm, expand on, or dispute the primary reviewer's critique as he sees fit. Tertiary reviewers often represent an area of specialty that is not covered by the primary or secondary reviewers, and their review centers on those aspects of the application. Then a discussion ensues in which other IRG members ask questions of the assigned reviewers, and the assigned reviewers discuss areas of disagreement. Through this discussion, common themes are identified and consensus is more or less reached. Usually, this is embodied in final descriptor scores that involve a narrower range than that of the initial descriptors. Then each IRG member assigns a final score somewhere within the final range. This last step is critical because a large number of applications receive scores between 2 and 3, so your final score reflects the number of IRG members who gave a final score closer to 2.1 as opposed to closer to 2.9, which under strong competition can make a very large difference in the funding outcome.

Faint Praise Versus Endorsement

When reading a review, it is good to keep in mind the jargon phrases that assign faint praise versus true endorsement of your proposal. Projects that are characterized as "descriptive" are being given faint praise, whereas projects that are "hypothesis driven" are being endorsed. Projects that are characterized as "incremental" are only faintly praised, whereas projects that are "transformative" are being endorsed. A "fishing expedition" is really bad, whereas "testing alternative hypotheses" is an endorsement. "Overly ambitious" is, of course, bad, but so is "replicative" (meaning the results are already known). These terms that endorse your plan, offer faint praise, or raise red flags are really important. As you write the proposal, you should ask whether any red flags could be applied to your plans and make sure to describe in your project the terms that readers can use in endorsing your project. That is, say how your project is hypothesis driven, how the findings will transform the field, and how the plan is new, builds on previous findings, and can be accomplished in the period of the grant.

More generally, following how the written reviews will be organized, consider the strengths and weakness of your proposal on each of the scoring criteria. Try to be self-critical and try hard to identify strengths and weaknesses in each section of the grant on each of the scoring criteria. Emphasize explicitly the strengths and address the potential weaknesses that reviewers are likely to identify. Ask your colleagues to read your proposal with these issues in mind and take their recommendations to heart.

Specifics: What Does a Successful Proposal Look Like?

These signs of praise and criticism can pop up in any of the sections of your proposal. But, it is useful to go through each component of a standard R01 proposal and think about how to solicit the praise and avoid the criticism. In the following sections, I will use fragments from my recent very successful proposal on memory and hippocampal neuronal activity that illustrate what I believe were successful strategic elements of the proposal. The proposal focused on the discovery of "time cells" in the hippocampus, principal neurons that fire at specific moments within temporally extended events, mapping out sequences of identifiable events and times between them. I use this proposal not so much to convince you about our research program in particular, but rather to demonstrate how we wrote sections of the application that were reviewed positively by the IRG. I will describe our approach and point out highlights for each section of the proposal as outlined in the NIH instructions to investigators.

Summary

One would think the Summary is an abstract of the application, and in some ways, it is. It is a place to emphasize the important and fundamental questions that will be pursued and the general approach to answering those questions. In other words, the Summary is a very good place to make the initial case for *Significance* of the proposed work. This is a very good opportunity to frame that significance in the terms you wish to use and hope the reviewers will adopt your description. Conversely, the Summary is not a good place to describe details of the design or expected results. There is just not enough space allotted to make the case on these issues.

We began the Summary to our "Time Cell" proposal as follows:

> Episodic memory is characterized by our ability to remember the spatial and temporal context in which events occur. There is substantial evidence that the hippocampal neuronal activity reflects a representation of space but, until recently, little was known about whether or how the hippocampal neurons encode time. However, recent studies by us have shown that hippocampal neuronal activity provides a temporal context signal that contributes to memory. In addition there is now evidence that hippocampal neurons—called time cells—fire during particular moments in a temporally extended experience, similar to hippocampal place cells that fire associated with particular locations in a spatially extended environment. The proposed studies will explore the nature of temporal representation by the hippocampal system and prefrontal cortex.

Notice that the first line states the "big-picture" question that we propose to address: Memory is characterized by spatial and temporal organization. An answer to how spatial and temporal organization of memories is accomplished by the hippocampus would be significant indeed. Then we state what we already know of relevance—we know lots about spatial representations in the hippocampus—and we state what is not known—much of anything about time. The remainder of the Summary states our approach, framed as a series of hypothesis-driven questions and predicted results that, if confirmed, would transform our understanding of how the hippocampus organizes information in time. So, I think we succeeded because we began with a major question in the field that any neuroscientist can appreciate, and we provided a basic framework for what would constitute an answer to that question. If we can convince the reviewers on these points, we have earned a high score in *Significance*.

Specific Aims

The Specific Aims section is the important version of the abstract for the reviewers. This section should provide enough information for them to begin to judge not only the significance of the proposal but also the innovation and approach. Here you have enough space to outline both the rationale and scope of the work. And you should introduce the organization of the proposed studies, what they hope to show, and what each result would mean.

In my "Time Cell" proposal, I wrote:

Specific aims. This proposal aims to continue progress . . . towards understanding how the hippocampus and related cortical areas support the temporal organization of memory.

I began by repeating the big-picture goal as a natural continuation of my own previous work, then, following some background, I elaborated more specifically my overall goals:

The overall goals of this project are to identify how hippocampal time cells represent events and temporal gaps between key events in both non-spatial and spatial experiences, how they disambiguate overlapping sequential experiences, and how they are generated and controlled within hippocampal and cortical circuitry.

In beginning with the overall goals, the initial paragraph prepares the reader for a summary of the specific aims in terms of key questions, hypotheses generated by those questions, and how those hypotheses will be tested:

Specific Aim 1. Do hippocampal time cells have properties analogous to place cells and is their activity related to memory performance? Fundamental properties of place cells are their persistence in familiar environments, their "re-mapping" when a salient spatial cue is modified, their distinct representations of overlapping spatial trajectories, their replay of sequential activity in sleep, and attractor state dynamics in CA3 versus continuous dynamics in CA1. To examine the hypothesis that time cells have parallel properties in the temporal dimension, we will explore how these cells respond to modifications of the critical temporal features of spatial and non-spatial tasks, and we will study the relationship between time cell firing patterns and memory performance in tasks that require disambiguation and memory for previous events within an episode.

The same basic format was then used for Specific Aims 2 and 3.

Note, first, that the Specific Aims section is brief although it should introduce all the key elements of the plans. Never let it run over one page. You want the reviewers to see the core points of the entire proposal at once, and that can only be accomplished if you limit it to one page. If your Specific Aims section runs longer, then remove details. Even the most complex or long series of studies can be explained in one page. If not, your proposal is likely to be evaluated as "overly ambitious"—one of those red flags you want to avoid.

Second, the initial paragraph begins where the Summary left off. The Summary frames the big picture—we need to understand how the hippocampus organizes memories in space and time, and we know about space, so this proposal is to improve our understanding about time. Here we begin by re-stating the overall goal of understanding temporal organization (repetition of where the previous section left off at the outset of a new section is a good thing). Then we provide further background outlining the initial discovery of time cells and defining them, and we make explicit in the last sentence the overall goal of the project that the specific aims will address.

Third, the specific aims are organized as a list of aims, each of which begins by asking an interesting and important specific question. Then each introduces what would constitute an answer to that question, in the form of a strategy and a hypothesis or a prediction that will be tested to provide the empirical evidence for the answer.

Although details necessarily cannot fit in this small space, all major take-home points about the proposal should be included here. You should write these specific aims in a simple fashion, making it easy for the primary reviewer to describe your proposal accurately and favorably when he or she presents your proposal in the written review and orally to the IRG.

Research Strategy

The Research Strategy section is, of course, the main body of the proposal. It is organized to ask you to address the main criteria for scoring in the following order. First, in the context of the existing knowledge about your research area, what is the significance of the proposed work? Second, what is innovative about your approach, compared with the state-of-the-art ideas and methods? Third, what are the details of your approach in terms of the specific aims introduced above? Fourth, what preliminary data can you offer to support your expertise and experience in the proposed studies? These are the questions the reviewers will be asking as they read the proposal, and the questions on which the IRG will score the proposal. So, it would be wise to ensure that you answer each of these questions explicitly in those sections.

Significance

The Significance section used to be called "Background," and surely providing a background for your proposed work should be one of the main goals for this section. At the same time, the new title emphasizes that the aim of this background section is not just to show that you are aware of the relevant literature. And this section is not meant to be a comprehensive review and critique of all of the important studies in the relevant area. It could hardly serve those purposes, because the maximum length should be restricted to three pages at most. Furthermore, this is not the best location for discussing details about previous studies—that is better accomplished within the introductions to the specific proposed experiments.

Instead, the Significance section should provide an overview that would interest a broad scientific audience, including readers who may work outside your research area. This is your chance to introduce in modest detail your overall goal, your big-picture research question, and explain why it is important. And your aims for this section should be to expand on that goal in a sequence of three closely related take-home points: (1) to state explicitly the big-picture question, and provide an overview of the state of our knowledge on that question; (2) to express where the state of our knowledge falls short; and (3) to state how the proposed studies will advance our understanding in a highly significant, "transformative" way. A major difference between a Significance section and a review of the literature is that you do not want to end with answers to the "big question"; instead you want to end with major limitations to what we know and how your proposed work will answer those questions through a natural and important new extension of your work to date.

In the Significance section of my "Time Cell" proposal, I introduced my big-picture question as follows:

Significance. "Acts of recollection, as they occur in experience, are due to the fact that one thought has by nature another that succeeds it in regular order." (Aristotle, 350 B.C.E.)

Aristotle may have been the first to emphasize the temporal organization of recollective experiences. In modern times, Tulving (1972) defined episodic memory as our capacity to mentally "replay" unique personal experiences and emphasized that episodic memories are characterized by their temporal organization. But what brain mechanisms support temporal organization and mental replay of episodic memories? Despite its importance as a fundamental feature of episodic memory, relatively few studies have examined the neurobiological basis for the ability to remember the order of events in unique experiences. Some years ago my colleagues and I at Boston University began studies on the hippocampus and memory for order . . . [and I go on to briefly outline the main findings in our previous work].

Note that the introductory paragraph is written to introduce all three aims listed earlier. I began with a historical quote from Aristotle, hoping to raise to the top of the reviewers' minds that my big-picture research question is based on a long-standing view about the organization of memory. Then, I grounded this perspective in modern cognitive science by referring to the pioneer in memory research who adopted the same view in defining the kind of memory (episodic memory) that this proposal is aimed to examine. This, then, was followed by an explicit statement of the big-picture question, "What brain mechanisms support temporal organization and mental replay of episodic memories?" Next, I assert that actually this is a much understudied question; then I begin to outline in greater detail our own initial attempts to address the question. In subsequent paragraphs, I outlined the existing literature on the topic, covering studies from various approaches, including experiments on the effects of selective brain damage in animals' ability to remember the order of events in experiences, and functional imaging studies on humans and memory for temporal order. Then, because the proposal will focus on neurophysiological studies on how neuronal activity in the hippocampus represents temporal information, I provide an overview of what we know about temporal firing patterns in hippocampal neurons. I began by introducing findings generated by other investigators:

> Single neuron recording studies in animals also indicate that hippocampal ensembles encode and replay sequential information. The most prominent of these are studies showing that hippocampal place cells that fire sequentially as rats repeatedly traverse a route also replay in the same order when rats subsequently sleep . . . (followed by the main findings of several studies). . . . Thus, the firing patterns of hippocampal neurons associated with repeated routes traversed by rats appear to encode spatial memories as temporally sequenced place representations (for review see Buzsaki, 2010).

Then, I focused on more recent previous studies where we have made major contributions:

> Sequential spatial firing patterns of hippocampal neurons also reflect the disambiguation of spatial memories . . . (followed by brief summaries of

several studies, ultimately focusing on the findings most relevant to this proposal).... [T]he temporal organization of hippocampal neuronal activity was highlighted in a study where rats ran in a running wheel in between each trial in a T-maze alternation task (Pastalkova et al., 2008). The major findings were that some hippocampal neurons fired at specific brief periods during the 10 sec wheel running, and the firing rates of some cells distinguished subsequent left and right turns. Pastalkova et al. called these neurons "episode cells" because each one fired at a particular time in each of the two types of trial episodes (routes). We have replicated this finding, using a treadmill that strongly maintains the animal's head and body location (Figure 1 left; Kraus et al., 2010; see Preliminary Data), as well as in animals performing a non-spatial task where we have directly compared temporal and spatial influences over firing, showing that hippocampal neurons encode time even when location is held constant (MacDonald et al., 2010; see below).

Note that I began with the prevalent finding in the place cell literature, showing that hippocampal neurons fire in order as animals move through sequences of locations, and that these temporal patterns replay in sleep and other off-line states. Then I bring these findings into the domain of memory by discussing how these temporally organized spatial firing patterns differ, even when animals traverse the same series of locations, when the paths reflect different memories. Furthermore, I introduce in this section the key new discovery of "time cells," first observed by Pastalkova et al. (2008) and subsequently reported by my colleagues and me in different behavioral paradigms. In reporting those results, I provided a picture, definitely worth a thousand words, showing how ensembles of neurons fire in a temporal sequence. The use of pictorial illustrations that provide simple and compelling evidence for your proposed direction is highly encouraged.

Next, I want to expand on these initial findings and introduce the questions that will be pursued in the proposed work. I begin that direction by asking a question:

The sequential firing of place cells that represent adjacent locations in a path is readily viewed as a code for spatial memories. But how does the hippocampus organize the sequential firing patterns of hippocampal neurons when the animal is not traversing space, and how does the hippocampus temporally organize non-spatial sequences? Our initial exploration of these questions involved recording from hippocampal ensembles as rats had to remember unique sequences of odors (Fortin et al., 2002) ... [and then I go on to summarize details of our published experiments to date on the firing properties of hippocampal neurons in animals performing tasks where they must remember the order of events].

So, this section begins to question how these temporal sequences for spatial memories might apply in general to memory, and specifically to sequences of non-spatial events. I finish this part with an initial experiment aimed at this question and use a picture to illustrate that result. But, now I want to make the point that this study does not provide a full answer to how temporal organization works, and instead discuss how pursuing the discovery of time cells can provide greater understanding:

> Because sequences were unique to each trial in that study, a major limitation of Manns et al. (2007) findings is that we could not determine whether the temporal organization of neural activity encoded specific events. Therefore, in a subsequent study, we recorded hippocampal neural activity in rats performing the task developed by Kesner et al. (2005) to examine patterns of hippocampal neural activity as rats learn to disambiguate two overlapping object-delay-odor sequences. In this task, each trial begins with one of two objects, followed by a 10 sec empty delay, and finishes with presentation of one of two odors, which is rewarded or not depending on which object began the sequence. Thus, even though the sequences repeat many times, on each trial the rat must remember the initial object presented in order to respond to the correct odor at the end. We observed substantial numbers of CA1 cells that fired at each stage of the task (object, delay, odor) and in each stage, different cells fired sequentially. The neurons that fired during the delay were active only at specific periods (MacDonald et al., 2010), similar to the cells that fired at specific times when the rat was in a running wheel or treadmill in spatial memory tasks (Pastalkova et al., 2008; Kraus et al., 2010). Furthermore, many of these "time cells" fired differentially depending on which object began the trial, and the timing of their activity could not be accounted for by differential locations of the rat (see Preliminary Data). These firing patterns likely underlie the gradually changing temporal context representation observed in Manns et al. (2007) and show that hippocampal firing sequences occur reliably during repeated sequences of events in a non-spatial task.

So, I argue, time cells hold the key to understanding temporal organization of memories. I now finish the Significance by summarizing the existing findings, asserting their significance, and most importantly, raise more critical questions that the proposed work will address:

The data described above indicate that the hippocampus supports the temporal organization of episodic memories. The hippocampus is critical to memory for the order of unique sequences of events, and hippocampal (and parahippocampal) neural activity in humans and animals reflects the temporal organization of events in spatial and nonspatial memory. Furthermore, the hippocampus contains a temporal context signal that is associated with memory and may be based on time cells whose activity reflects successive moments in a temporally extended episode even when behavior and location are held constant. These findings challenge the prevalent view that hippocampal neurons fundamentally encode space, suggesting that time may be equally represented, and raise basic questions about the nature of memory representation within the hippocampus. Are time cells fundamentally the same as place cells, in that both reflect elements of the contextual framework in which events are represented in temporal and spatial dimensions, respectively? Are the activity patterns of time cells directly related to memory performance? How are time cells generated and what supports their disambiguation of distinct experiences? The answers to these questions bear high significance in understanding how episodic memories are organized by the hippocampus.

You want to end by introducing the questions that your studies will address, and do so in the form of stating the specific aims of the experiments that will be described in the subsequent sections.

Innovation

Before describing the experiments, there is a brief divergence. In this section, you need to convince the reviewers, and ultimately the IRG, that the proposal has innovative features that will bring a new direction to the area of study. The instructions to proposals emphasize that innovation can be theoretical or methodological, but there is strong temptation for reviewers to focus on the latter—new techniques—rather than new insights or approaches. My best advice is that it is important that you include some of both. In this proposal I tried to accomplish that:

Innovation. The proposed research is innovative in providing an alternative to the prevalent view that the hippocampus creates spatial maps that support navigation and path integration, arguing instead that hippocampal representations serve to bind both spatially and temporally discontinuous events to support the organization of events in memory.

We believe that knowledge about the temporal coding properties of hippocampal neurons, and comparison of these properties with the literature on place cells, can provide breakthrough insights into the fundamental information processing functions of the hippocampus in memory.

In addition to the innovative approach to understanding hippocampal function, some of our experiments will employ innovative techniques. Some studies will involve a novel head-fixed preparation for rats that will allow us to fully eliminate the possibility that time cell activity is secondary to movements or head location. In addition, some studies will use an innovative methodology for reversible neural silencing by optical control, which promises the ability to examine the effects of millisecond resolution inactivation of one brain structure while recording from another.

This section is typically brief, but do not overlook its importance. The issue of innovation will specifically be discussed in the review, and it is explicitly scored by the reviewers. You need to convince the IRG that your innovations will result in breakthroughs toward a qualitatively higher level of understanding of your big-picture question.

Approach

This section is the real "meat" of the proposal, where you need to be specific about what experimental questions are being addressed, how you will address them, and how the answers will improve our fundamental understanding of the big-picture question. Hopefully, the reviewers have bought into your argument about the importance of the big-picture question and that your general approach can provide breakthroughs. Now, you need to convince the reviewers that your experiments will address key issues and provide definitive answers on the big question.

In my "Time Cell" proposal, I began this section by introducing a major strength of our approach and reminded reviewers about my specific aims, each framed as a question:

Approach. A major advantage to the study of time cells over place cells is that experiments in the temporal domain naturally identify the onsets and offsets of specific events and behavioral actions within the relevant parameter (time) that organizes episodic memories. By contrast, it is impossible to identify with certainty which environmental cues define a space, how those cues define the relevant spatial dimensions, or when information about spatial cues reaches the brain. We aim here to exploit the advantages of the temporal domain to examine how temporal coding and disambiguation of overlapping sequences is accomplished in the hippocampal-cortical system. Our research plan is organized to address three main questions: What are the properties of time cells? Is their activity related to memory? How are they generated and controlled to distinguish experiences? We believe the answers to these questions will provide important and fundamental insights into how the hippocampus encodes episodic memories.

Next, the details of your proposed studies should follow the organization of Specific Aims that were introduced at the outset of the proposal. Here is how I began the first section of this part of the "Time Cell" proposal:

Specific Aim 1. Do hippocampal time cells have properties analogous to those of place cells? To address this question we will examine the responses of time cells to manipulations of the temporal dimension in ways analogous to the manipulations of spatial cues that revealed the properties of place cells (reviewed in Muller, 1996; Leutgeb et al., 2005b; Colgin et al., 2008). Our hypothesis is that time cells will respond to temporal manipulations similar to the responses of place cells to manipulations of salient spatial cues. These results would support the view that the hippocampus creates a "memory space," a network of memories that is organized by relevant dimensions of experience, including space, time, and more (Eichenbaum et al., 1999).

And, then I go on to describe basic properties of place cells and how I would test the hypothesis that time cells have parallel properties.

Note that this section is titled the same as one of the Specific Aims listed earlier and begins with a very specific version of the aim in the form of a question that the design of the experiment will answer. This is followed by a brief outline of additional key details that explain what would constitute an answer to this question, including an introduction to how the experiment is designed to address the question. Next, I become more specific yet, by outlining the experiments in some detail. Here are elements of one of the proposed experiments:

Properties of time cells in rats performing a spatial alternation task. The task will be T-maze alternation with a treadmill located in the central stem of the maze. Rats will be shaped to run in the treadmill for a water reward, then alternate turns at the choice point in order to obtain another reward. This is the same situation in which we first observed time cells (Kraus et al., 2010). We will systematically vary treadmill speed, duration, and distance to determine the parameters controlling time cell activity. Then, to address the questions introduced above, we will vary the task demands; most of the following manipulations can be examined in the same animals on different recording sessions.

- In order to examine the nature of time cell representations, . . . [here I outline the experimental design]. . . . The expected results would show that time cells parse the reliable organizational parameter, rather than time *per se,* supporting the memory space hypothesis (Eichenbaum et al., 1999). Our preliminary data (Kraus et al., 2010) are consistent with this prediction (see Preliminary Data).
- We will examine the stability of temporal firing patterns by . . . [here I outline the experimental design]. . . . We expect strong consistency of temporal firing patterns with repetition of the same temporal parameters. Furthermore, we expect to observe time cell sequential replay during sleep following the initial treadmill running experience.
- To examine the formation of new representations when the salient temporal dimension has two consistent conditions, we will . . . [here I outline the experimental design]. . . . We expect that time cells will . . . [here I outline the predicted results]. Alternatively, time cells that fire near the onset may fire at a fixed time in both durations, or shift in firing time relative to the change in duration.
- To examine the development of distinct representations of overlapping segments in different routes, we will . . . [here I outline the experimental design] . . . we expect place cells to remap when the alternation is introduced and that time cells will also remap and fire differently on left turn and right turn trials. To examine whether time cells are retrospective or prospective, and whether their activity predicts accurate memory, we will . . . [here I outline the experimental design]. . . . We predict that time cells will variously code retrospective and prospective information (Ferbinteanu & Shapiro, 2003).
- To examine the dynamics of CA1 and CA3 responses to changes in the temporal parameter, we will . . . [here I outline the experimental design]. . . . We predict CA3 time cells will have an attractor dynamic such that their patterns will be the same as those on either the 10 sec or the 20 sec duration, but CA1 time cells will gradually

change between patterns observed on the 10 sec and 20 sec durations for the intermediate durations. These findings would show that . . . [here I outline the predicted results].

Note that I begin by describing just enough detail so the reviewers can understand the basic protocol. Then, I provided a numbered list of very specific experimental questions. For each one, I state the question that will be explored, the experimental protocol and manipulations that will be implemented to address the question, then the predicted outcome and something about its significance. These descriptions are purposely brief, providing enough detail so an expert in the field can understand clearly what is being done and what we hope to show. This section is written specifically for the assigned reviewers and so assumes considerable knowledge of the relevant literature and an easy understanding of the experimental details, which are scantly provided. This list, however, leaves out one more critical component, a consideration of alternative outcomes and interpretations. This comes next:

Alternative outcomes: It is possible that time cells behave differently than place cells, refuting our hypothesis. More subtly, providing a reward at the end of the treadmill phase may eliminate the "splitting" or dissociation of firing patterns that distinguish left and right turn trials, as observed previously (Bower et al., 2005), or it might delay splitting of firing patterns until after the treadmill phase. It is likely that repeated exposure to varying treadmill durations will cause time cells to develop a continuous dynamic even in CA3 (Leutgeb et al., 2005a). Also, CA1 cells may be more involved in temporal coding than CA3 cells, as predicted by findings showing that CA1, but not CA3, is essential for associations across a delay (Kesner et al., 2005; Farovik et al., 2010).

It is key that you acknowledge that the experiment has at least two outcomes, the one you predict and either a failure of that outcome or an explicit alternative outcome. If there is no alternate outcome, why do the study? And if there is the possibility that the predicted result does not occur, or there are explicit alternative outcomes, then what would be your interpretation and how would you follow up with additional studies?

This process is repeated for additional experiments. In my "Time Cell" proposal, I included another experiment using nonspatial sequences. Then this set of experiments under Specific Aim 1 ended with an overall statement about the significance of the expected results:

The predicted findings of these experiments would show the properties of time cells are analogous to standard features of place cells, and that these properties extend to non-spatial as well as spatial tasks. Furthermore, these findings, including the expectations that hippocampal firing patterns can be organized by distance traveled when distance is fixed in the spatial task, would strongly support the hypothesis that the hippocampus organizes events according to the relevant continuous dimensions in any situation (Eichenbaum et al., 1999).

I felt it was really important to repetitively return to the big-picture question and explicitly state how the results under each specific aim would advance our understanding.

My "Time Cell" proposal then went on to describe two more Specific Aims, using the same organization of introduction and review of key aspects of the literature leading to what would constitute an answer to the specific question, a general description of the paradigm, a list of specific manipulations and expected outcomes, and alternative outcomes. Some of the alternative outcomes raised potential technical challenges and described how they would be addressed. It is critical that you acknowledge limitations of your study and places where you might fail to obtain a clear result, and then describe how you will confront these alternative outcomes. You will not have an opportunity to exchange questions and answers with the reviewers, except in a revision of the proposal—to be avoided—so it is much better to pre-empt every possible issue.

Preliminary Data

There is one more critical section, which serves to support a positive evaluation of you as an expert in the area of proposed research, and at the same time, demonstrate the feasibility of the proposed work from a technical standpoint. In the Preliminary Data section, you want to, first, establish that you are an expert by describing aspects of your experience that are generally along the lines of the proposed work, both in the questions your previous research has addressed and in the research techniques that will be used in the proposed studies. Then, second, you want to provide specific preliminary findings that demonstrate this expertise and show that the proposed studies will succeed in producing interpretable results. In my "Time Cell" proposal, I introduced this section as follows:

Preliminary Data. Approximately 4 years ago, a group of investigators at Boston University established a Conte Center for Neuroscience

Research focused on this problem. We have had substantial success in demonstrating . . . [here I outline the specifics of our earlier findings].

Now, this introduction is unique because the proposal followed on a previous grant where multiple investigators began to ask similar questions about temporal organization of memories. Still, my main point here is that you begin with an outline of your general experience in the relevant area before providing specific preliminary data. I provided several forms of preliminary data and will outline two here briefly. First, here are preliminary data I provided for the time cell firing patterns observed in the non-spatial task:

Non-spatial sequence memory. In this task rats must remember one of two objects over a 10s delay in order to identify the correct associated odor. We have collected data from 298 cells (4 rats), many of which fire during specific phases of the task and at particular times during each phase (MacDonald et al., 2010). We found . . . [here I outline the findings reported in that paper].

As mentioned earlier, in the grant application I employed a few simple but compelling figures to illustrate the main findings, and I used the text in the Preliminary Results to further describe the main results and use the figure captions to provide sufficient detail to understand the results. These data demonstrated the feasibility of the study in the form of substantial findings that were replicated in the complete experiment funded by the grant. A main point here is that you want the readers to understand that the proposed work is a natural extension of your previous work and expertise and is directed to make new and important breakthroughs. So, it's both important that the proposed work is based on your past experience and evidence of feasibility, and at the same time that the proposed studies are more than "incremental" and will provide a new level or direction of understanding.

In addition, the Preliminary Results section is an opportunity to present evidence of the feasibility of novel techniques. In my "Time Cell" application, I proposed to employ optogentic inactivation to silence hippocampal neuronal activity. I also included as consultants experts in optogenetics to bolster the feasibility of the use of this new technique. For techniques where you do not have a track record in the form of publications using the approach, the inclusion of a consultant who does have demonstrated expertise is essential. Be sure to obtain a written letter of support and agreement to assist you from the consultant. As you include consultants, be sure that it is clear that the project is yours and the assistance will improve the likelihood of success of your project, and that eventually you will no longer depend on the consultant when you, too, are an expert in that approach. You want to balance evidence for maximizing feasibility of the proposed work against the liability of dependence on others for success of the project.

Finally, the last issue of feasibility concerns whether the proposed work can be accomplished within the time period of the requested grant. Therefore, you must include a timeline that describes the sequence of experiments and provides a realistic appraisal of when they will be executed and completed:

> *Timeline:* Given our considerable preliminary data, we expect to complete Aim 1 experiments in the first year. Then we expect to readily expand to recording from multiple areas quickly, allowing us to complete Aim 2 in the succeeding 1.5–2 years. We have begun exploring the use of optical inactivation (see above) and fluorescent muscimol (Navawongse et al., 2010) and will continue preparing to use these, and expect to complete Aim 3 in the final 2.5 years.

My "Time Cell" proposal received high scores in all categories, particularly in both the use of an innovative idea about the hippocampus encoding time similarly to its representation of space, to the use of new behavioral protocols that would address the main predictions, and to the use of optogenetics techniques. There were some criticisms, but they were relatively minor and useful as advice in the final design of the experiments and interpretation of the data.

Final Thoughts

I realize that I have focused heavily on one proposal that I know exceptionally well, and that yours may involve different questions, approaches, techniques, and levels of analysis that have distinct issues. Nevertheless, I believe that this present description and analysis of this proposal can be useful as a model for designing and combining the pieces of your proposal into one that is successfully funded. Think about both the generalities discussed early in this chapter and about how they apply to the specifics of the example proposal described here. Then, apply your results of this analysis to your own plans, and I surely hope you find the exercise valuable.

References

Aristotle. (ca. 350 BC). *On memory and reminiscence* (J. I. Beare, Trans.). Originally published in Ross, W. D. (Ed.). (1930). *The works of Aristotle* (Vol. 3). Oxford: Clarendon Press.

Bower, M. R., Euston, D. R., & McNaughton, B. L. (2005). Sequential-context-dependent hippocampal activity is not necessary to learn sequences with repeated elements. *Journal of Neuroscience, 25,* 1313–1323.

Buzsaki, G. (2010). Neural syntax: Cell assemblies, syapsembles, and readers. *Neuron, 68,* 362–385.

Colgin, L. L., Moser, E. I., & Moser, M. B. (2008). Understanding memory through hippocampal remapping. *Trends in Neuroscience, 31*(9), 469–477.

Eichenbaum, H., Dudchencko, P., Wood, E., Shapiro, M., & Tanila, H. (1999). The hippocampus, memory, and place cells: Is it spatial memory or a memory space? *Neuron, 23,* 209–226.

Farovik, A., Dupont, L. M., & Eichenbaum, H. (2010). Distinct roles for dorsal CA3 and CA1 in memory for nonspatial sequential events. *Learning and Memory, 17,* 801–806.

Ferbinteanu, J., & Shapiro, M. L. (2003). Prospective and retrospective memory coding in the hippocampus. *Neuron, 40,* 1227–1239.

Fortin, N. J., Agster, K. L., & Eichenbaum, H. (2002). Critical role of the hippocampus in memory for sequences of events. *Nature Neuroscience, 5,* 458–462.

Kesner, R. P., Hunsaker, M. R., & Gilbert, P. E. (2005). The role of CA1 in the acquisition of an object-trace-odor paired associate task. *Behavioral Neuroscience, 119,* 781–786.

Kraus, B. J., Robinson, R. J., Hasselmo, M. E., & Eichenbaum, H. (2010). Time and distance dependence of rat hippocampal neuron responses. *Society for Neuroscience Abstract* #100.16.

Leutgeb, J. K., Leutgeb, S., Treves, A., Meyer, R., Barnes, C. A., McNaughton, B. L., . . . Moser, E. I. (2005b). Progressive transformation of hippocampal neuronal representations in "morphed" environments. *Neuron, 48,* 345–358.

Leutgeb, S., Leutgeb, J. K., Moser, M. B., & Moser, E. I. (2005a). Place cells, spatial maps and the population code for memory. *Current Opinion in Neurobiology, 15,* 738–746.

Manns, J. R., Howard, M., & Eichenbaum, H. (2007). Gradual changes in hippocampal activity support remembering the order of events. *Neuron, 56,* 530–540.

MacDonald, C., LePage, K., Eden, U., & Eichenbaum, H. (2010). Hippocampal neurons encode the temporal organization of non-spatial event sequences. *Society for Neuroscience Abstract* #100.15.

Muller, R. (1996). A quarter of a century of place cells. *Neuron, 17,* 813–822.

Navawongse, R., Octeau, C., Lai, J., & Eichenbaum, H. (2010). Responses of CA1 neurons during inactivation of the medial entorhinal cortex in rats performing an object-context association task. *Society for Neuroscience Abstract* #708.10.

Pastalkova, E., Itskov, V., Amarasingham, A., & Buzsaki, G. (2008). Internally generated cell assembly sequences in the rat hippocampus. *Science, 321*(5894),
1322–1327.

Tulving, E. (1972). Episodic and semantic memory. In E. Tulving & W. Donaldson
(Eds.), *Organization of memory* (pp. 381–402). New York: Academic Press.

7

Applying for a Research Grant From the National Institutes of Health

A Primer

Nathan A. Fox

F unding for research is an important element in one's academic career. The money received to support one's research provides an opportunity to hire personnel who can assist in data collection or coding, support graduate and postdoctoral fellows who can collaboratively work with you on the research, compensate subjects for their time, purchase equipment and supplies that are necessary for the research, and contribute to your university salary (summer or academic). Universities and research institutions also value individuals who generate grant funding. In part, this is because the university receives additional dollars beyond the funds generated by the investigator for his or her research. In addition, departments, colleges, universities, and research institutions understand that receipt of funds for research support is a sign that an individual's work is recognized as important and of interest.

This chapter addresses just one type of research funding, that awarded by the National Institutes of Health (NIH). The chapter is divided into four parts. In the first part, there is a brief discussion of the types of research that NIH funds. The second part describes the different mechanisms that are available for funding. The third part describes the process and sequence of steps from application to funding, and the fourth section outlines the general structure of the NIH grant application with some suggestions on how to craft these sections.

This brief overview comes at a time of economic uncertainty in the United States and with that, debate over the priorities for spending of the federal budget. These issues directly impact the number of new grants that can be funded by NIH and have increased the level of competition (both direct and indirect) for grants. As of mid-2012, it is not clear how this would work out. Nevertheless, it is important that investigators have the information and knowledge of the system and how to write the grant that has the best chance of funding, as these skills are crucial now more than ever.

Funding at NIH

NIH is situated in the U.S. Department of Health and Human Services and is the largest source of funding for medical research in the world (www.nih. gov/about). There are 27 institutes and centers, 24 that support research, and each focuses on a different area of research, disease/disorder, or organ system. For example, among the institutes are the National Cancer Institute; the National Heart, Lung, and Blood Institute; and the National Institute for Alcohol Abuse and Alcoholism. Each institute sets its research priorities, providing the researcher with an overview of the areas that a particular institute is interested in funding. For example, the National Institute of Mental Health (NIMH) lists on its website as strategic priorities to "Promote discovery in the brain and behavioral sciences to fuel research on the causes of mental disorders" and "Chart mental illness trajectories to determine when, where, and how to intervene." Each institute usually also provides program announcements that guide applicants with an overview of the particular kinds of research that the institute is interested in funding.

In addition, there is an important administrative structure within each institute to develop funding priorities and inform researchers about specific areas. For example, within NIMH, a branch is interested in the development of anxiety disorders. This branch, currently called the Developmental Trajectories of Mental Disorders Branch, sits within the Division of Developmental Translational Research. The people who work in these areas are usually Ph.D.-level scientists who themselves are informed about the latest research in a particular area as well as about what the current priorities are of their division and the overall institute. These individuals, called program officers, can be quite helpful to investigators in navigating through the administrative issues of grant funding. They also can play, as we shall see later, a critical role in the funding process of a grant.

It is important to note that many of the institutes have a broad research agenda that can extend to research in many areas of psychology and the behavioral sciences. For example, the National Institute of Deafness and other Communicative Disorders focuses on research in both normal language development as well as disorders of language and speech. The National Institute of Diabetes and Digestive and Kidney Diseases is also interested in childhood obesity. The funding for different research areas varies. For example, research on attention deficit-hyperactivity disorder received $55 million in 2011, and research on childhood abuse and neglect received $30 million during that same year. These figures can be found at www .report.nih.gov/categorical_spending.aspx. In general, research funding from NIH is designated for basic and clinical biomedical studies and not necessarily for basic research. There are often multiple options for research with an applied emphasis, particularly as it is related to the origins, treatment, and prevention of physical or mental disorders. In general, NIH funds both basic and clinical work across a broad spectrum of areas.

Funding Mechanisms at NIH

NIH has a number of mechanisms for funding research. There are both grant and cooperative agreement mechanisms, and within both some are individual-investigator initiated while others are multi-investigator (for example, a center-based initiative). Among the individual-investigator–initiated grants, a subset is specifically designated as training grants (e.g., F31/predoctoral, F32/postdoctoral, and K [career development awards]).

There are three different individual-initiated grant mechanisms. The R03 is a grant for two years and $50,000 each year. This grant was initially called a "small grant" (because of the small amount of funds that could be requested) and thought to be for first-time investigators. It is still a good mechanism for newer investigators. For example, institutes may convene separate review committees for the R03 mechanism (along with other training mechanisms). Thus, these grants will not be reviewed with (and hence often compared to) the larger and more detailed R01 grants. R03's are only six pages in length and technically do not require preliminary or pilot data for submission or review. These grants cannot be renewed. These grants, however, are no longer just for young investigators, as their scope now includes pilot or feasibility studies, secondary data analysis, and development of research methods or technology. It is important to note that some institutes do not accept investigator-initiated R03s except in response to specific topical funding opportunity announcements (for example, the National Cancer Institute).

The workhorse of the individual-investigator awards is the R01. With this mechanism, individuals can request up to $500,000 in annual direct costs per year for up to five years. The R01, according to the NIH website, is the original and historically oldest grant mechanism used by NIH. Individuals are allowed two submissions, and there is a 12-page limit. The R01 is considered a significant grant application, requesting funds for a detailed set of experiments or a large study. It is thought to be all-encompassing and definitely not for research that does not have pilot data attached to it.

Numerous other funding mechanisms are available to investigators. There are specific mechanisms for high-risk and innovative research (the R21) and for research developing interventions or prevention strategies (R13). There may also be different pots of money that are involved in the funding of these mechanisms. In general, funds for particular mechanisms (like the investigator-initiated R01 or R03) are allocated by the institute director for all grants that have been identified as being meritorious by the grant review system (more on this in the next section). There is a "pay line" above which grants with a particular score will (with institute council consent and institute director agreement) be funded.

In addition, a second pot of money may be set aside for a particular initiative. This is often known as a request for applications (RFA). For example, NIMH may decide that it wishes to solicit and fund proposals in the area of novel interventions for childhood psychiatric disorders. NIMH can issue a specific RFA, which provides an overview of the area of interest that it wishes to fund, the date by which these grants should be received, the type of funding mechanism (R01, R03, etc.), and whether the RFA is a one-time or repeated offer. The institute may decide to set aside a certain amount of money for this RFA with the idea that it will fund a certain number of grants from the applicant pool. Although these grants will be in the specific format (R01, R03), they will obviously have to address the area of the RFA. Review decisions about their funding priority may be completed in a manner different from the decisions on regular R01s. For example, grants reviewed for an RFA may be rank-ordered and funded in order of their rank, rather than percentiled, as is the case for R01s reviewed in standing study sections. This happens more often if these RFAs are usually one- or two-time announcements and are not subject to the same funding principles as regular mechanisms.

The Grant Process

This section details the grant submission, review, and funding process. It starts with the research ideas and the background work, and then focuses on writing the proposal. It is common for individuals to have an NIH institute targeted for their application. The next step may be to make contact with a program officer, who can discuss their research ideas with the investigator. It is not unusual to find program people who would be willing to read the specific aims of a proposal and provide feedback. Program officers can also be quite helpful with issues pertaining to structure of the budget, human or animal subject research issues, and the relevance of a particular topic for their branch or institute. This may be particularly useful in the case of a specific RFA. Thus, it is a good idea to contact a program officer and discuss a grant prior to submission.

One of the first decisions that investigators can make with regard to their grant submission is which review panel they would like to have review the work. This is a critical option. Review panels are organized by the Center for Scientific Review (CSR). CSR is an independent entity within NIH that reviews applications for all NIH institutes. Its independence is important as part of the peer-review process. CSR sets up standing review committees that cover all of the areas of science of the NIH. If an investigator were not to request a particular study section, CSR would decide the appropriate study section based upon a review of the grant abstract and key words. This can work, but your application might be assigned to a study section with expertise that does not overlap with the topic being presented in the grant. So, it is important that investigators examine the list of regular standing study sections and then request in a cover letter to CSR that their grant be assigned to a particular one. You can find a list of the standing study sections, their acronyms, and the scientific review officer (SRO) at www.csr.nih.gov/roster_proto/sectionI.asp. In addition, program officers in areas related to your research can advise you regarding the best match between your grant and a study section. You can then write a letter requesting a particular study section (at the time of submission) and mention who advised you of this choice.

What Are Study Sections?

Study sections are organized by CSR to review submitted grant applications. In general, an SRO is placed in charge of a study section and given a mandate to oversee the range and types of grants that are to be reviewed by that panel. The SRO selects scientists who she believes would be good reviewers, are knowledgeable in certain fields of expertise, and who can provide a timely and thorough review of a set of proposals. Anyone who is named on an application under review may not serve on that panel. The usual term for a member is five years. Committees meet three times a year. The review panel is formed in a staggered way so that people rotate on and off the committee at different times.

How Does a Study Section Operate?

There are a number of pieces to the puzzle of how grants are reviewed in study section. First, at its assignment in CSR to a study section, a particular grant is also linked to an NIH institute. Assuming that a particular grant is going to get a good score from a study section (more on that in a later section), there must be an institute that is interested in funding the work, and the work must be relevant to a particular institute's priorities. Thus, each grant is linked to an institute and possibly to more than one.

The SRO first reviews the grants that are submitted for a particular round in her study section. The SRO may then identify outside reviewers—that is, reviewers who are not regular members of a study section—who are brought in either to review a number of proposals or just a subset in a particular specialty. The SRO typically assigns three study section members to each grant: primary, secondary, and tertiary reviewers. The reviewers are provided the grant material a number of months prior to the study-section meeting. They review the grant, providing an overall critique, and then comment on the different sections of the proposal. Reviewers typically use a template that contains a number of sections.

The first is titled overall impact and the reviewer provides a paragraph summarizing the factors that led to the overall score. Overall scores range from 1.0 to 9.0, with 1.0 being absolutely excellent to 9.0 being not worthy of consideration. The reviewer then completes the remaining sections with the strengths and weaknesses for Significance, Investigators, Innovation, Approach, and Environment. There are also sections dealing with issues of human subjects, care of vertebrate animals, and diversity of sample, which will not be addressed in this chapter. Each of these subsections is given a score by the reviewer on his or her score sheet, but it is the overall score that is most important.

The Study-Section Meeting

Study sections usually meet three times a year. The roster and dates of the meetings are posted on the CSR website. So what happens at a meeting? First, there is usually an order of review. This order is determined in part by the availability and schedule of the program officers, who are asked to be present when a grant for a particular institute is reviewed. The order is also determined by the availability of phone reviewers, who may or may not be available for the entire section meeting. Order of review is often determined by the mechanism. Usually, SROs would like all the grants of a particular mechanism to be reviewed together. For example, if a study section is to review R03, training grants, and R01s, the SRO may try to schedule all grants of a similar mechanism together. And, finally, order of review is determined by whether the grant will be discussed or not. NIH and any given study section receive many grants, and the range of quality is wide. Generally, SROs rank-order the grants by the average of the three reviewers' overall scores. They then identify the median, and those grants below the median are recommended for nondiscussion (also known as triage). Triage may not happen to a grant with wide variability among the reviewers (i.e., one reviewer really likes it, another reviewer does not), in which case such a grant might be reviewed. But, in general, grant applications with an average score below the median are not discussed. Grant applications above the median are usually discussed.

What Does It Mean for a Grant to Not Be Discussed?

There are two implications to grants that are not discussed. First, they do not receive a percentiled score. Second, they are literally not discussed by the full panel at the study-section meeting. Thus, the feedback that an applicant gets includes the three critiques with no summary of discussion or feedback from the panel. Receiving a nondiscussed score means that a particular grant will not be considered by a particular institute's council and program officers for funding. It is important to note that grants below the median can be "saved" from triage. Before proceeding to discussion, the study-section chair will call out the name and title of each of these grants and ask if anyone, particularly anyone of the three reviewers, objects to that particular grant's being triaged. If anyone does, then the grant will be discussed. Getting a grant triaged (not discussed) is not great, but you are entitled to resubmit it.

For Grants That Are Discussed, What Happens During a Meeting?

Every study section has a chair who is one of the members of the study section and runs the meeting. Here is a typical procedure for grant review. (Note that study sections may vary as a function of their chair, SRO, number of grants needed to review, time allocated for review, etc.) The chair of the study section will ask each of the three reviewers for their initial score (total overall score on an application). After each of the three reviewers has given that score, the primary reviewer presents a brief description followed by his or her critique, providing key strengths and weaknesses in innovation, approach, methods, and significance of the question. The secondary and tertiary reviewers are then asked, in order, to add their comments. After that, the chair will usually open the floor for discussion and any panel member not in conflict can ask questions, make comments, and critique the grant. Usually, it is the reviewers' job to answer questions that other panel members may raise, though they need not defend the grant if they do not think it is worth defending. There is no doubt that a grant benefits from an advocate if it is to get the attention and positive scores of a panel. If the assigned reviewers are not advocating for the grant, then it is highly unlikely that a grant will be successful in a particular round of review.

Once the panel has discussed the grant application and questions from the panel have been answered, the chair of the study section will again ask each of the reviewers to state their final scores. The three reviewers (primary, secondary, and tertiary) each give their scores and that sequence establishes a range of scores for the panel (for example, if the scores are 2.0, 2.5, 1.8, the range is 1.8–2.5). The chair will then ask if anyone on the study section will be voting outside this range. Each individual panel member has the right to vote according to his or her conscience and may give a higher/better or lower/worse score to a particular grant. However, if a panel member says he or she is going to vote outside the range, the panel member must provide the SRO (and the panel) a reason for why. After voting, issues about the budget are discussed.

The mean overall score of a grant from a study section is reported to the program officer. As well, the NIH grant system computes a percentile score based either on the grants reviewed in that study section or based upon an average of scores from the past three study sections. That percentile score is critical for decisions about funding.

The next steps toward funding have to do with decisions by the council for the particular institute your grant has been assigned to and the director of that institute. Each institute has a panel called its council, which is advisory to the director on issues of policy, areas of research, and review of grant funding. The councils meet three times a year, and grants that are reviewed and scored at a particular study section usually are reviewed at the next council date. Once council has considered and approved a grant, it must then be signed off by the institute director before a notice of grant award starts to be processed.

Structure of the R01

The R01, as mentioned earlier, is the workhorse of the NIH grant mechanisms. The current maximum page length is 13. The sections are as follows: one page of Specific Aims. The Research Strategy, which includes *Significance, Innovation, and Approach*, is 12 pages. What are the goals of each section? *Specific Aims* is meant to present the reader with the goal of the proposed research, the reasons for the importance and need for the research, the relevance of the research for the particular targeted institute, and the research methods that are going to be used to achieve the goals. In addition, the *Specific Aims* section should provide the reader with the actual aims of the proposal (enumerated as in Aim 1, Aim 2...) and how these aims will be achieved.

This is quite a bit to squeeze into one page, so there cannot be a great deal of detail. However, the critical goals of the project, and the aims and hypotheses should (indeed, must) be presented. This one page should stand on its own. A reader should be able to tell what the proposed research will accomplish and how the scientist is going to accomplish it. The aims should be clearly stated and should then be linked throughout the other sections of the grant. For example, in the significance section, the proposal might highlight the lack of work in a particular area. The grant text could then link back and say that Aim 1 of the current proposal will fill that void. Similarly, in the data-analysis section of the grant, each of the hypotheses stated in *Specific Aims* should be addressed with a particular data-analytic approach.

The remaining 12 pages of the R01 constitute what is called *Research Strategy*. There are four major subsections. The first is called *Significance*, and it is the section where the problem to be studied is introduced and framed within the context of previous research. The goal of this section is to tell the reader what is already known, what theoretical or conceptual model or approach the current grant is taking, and how this will advance knowledge in the field. It is a selective review of the literature that highlights why your study or project is important.

This section is followed by a section called *Innovation*. NIH is interested in funding the best cutting-edge research that is of the highest scientific quality. It asks applicants to explicitly provide a section on why their project is unique, cutting edge, and important for the field. In addition, there is an explicit request to provide a rationale as to why this particular research is innovative—not just more of the same.

The *Innovation* section is followed by a large section called *Approach*. The *Approach* section itself can be subdivided into a number of different subsections: preliminary data, methods (and this subsection can be further subdivided into participants, experimental design, measures, data analysis, power analysis, and work plan). Obviously, in terms of providing detail to the reviewer about what you propose to do and how you are going to do it, these sections are critical. These sections must be detailed and well structured if they are going to be reviewed favorably.

Six Top Things to Think About When Writing a Grant Proposal

1. *Anticipate criticism, raise the critical issues, and respond.* It is now common to have a section at the end of an empirical paper that is called "Limitations." In that section, the authors raise the problems with their study that cannot be directly addressed but are not fatal flaws to interpretation of their data. For example, perhaps a study examined only female participants and wants to claim generalization to both males and females. The authors might raise this issue in the limitation section and suggest that future work will address both male and female participants. Such an approach is critical in writing a grant proposal. If there is an issue that cannot be easily addressed but that is not a fatal flaw to the studies proposed, it should be raised in the body of the grant. Acknowledging these problems allows the reviewers to appreciate the writer's knowledge of the issues. They may or may not accept the explanations, but at the least the reviewers cannot claim that they were not raised as issues.

2. *Link each of the specific aims to a hypothesis and data-analytic strategy in the Approach.* It is important that the grant be a coherent whole. One way that can happen is by providing the reader with connectivity between the specific aims and the methods and data analysis. Note the goals as outlined in the Specific Aims, and then explicitly state how they are going to be tested and the data-analytic strategy that will be involved.

3. *Remember to provide alternatives for sequential experiments.* Many proposals list a set of experiments that follow one on the other. However, too often grant writers forget to ask the question—what happens if the results of Experiment 1 do not come out as predicted? If subsequent experiments are based on the success of earlier ones, then the writer must provide alternative routes or thinking about subsequent studies so that all does not rise or fall on the success of one experiment.

4. *Include pilot data.* The guidelines for some mechanisms (R03, R21) explicitly state that pilot or preliminary data are not necessary to submit a

grant. However, consider a comparison between two applications: one has no pilot or preliminary data while the second provides data demonstrating feasibility and perhaps even a pattern of data that suggest success for the proposed experiments. All things being equal, the application with the pilot data will be judged higher (in this author's opinion). R01 mechanisms definitely require extensive pilot data as they are the largest and most complex of the types of proposals.

5. *Keep the application sharp and focused.* It is hard to provide a reader with experimental methods and detail in 12 pages of text. It is even more difficult if the experiments and/or studies are complex, multivariate, and multimethod. Reviewers like grants that are clearly written, sharp, and focused. It is obviously impossible to answer every burning and important question about a particular issue or area in one study or set of studies. Clear and concise language is appreciated. Tables with lists of measures and variables, and in the case of longitudinal or cross-sectional studies, listing of the age points of assessment are welcome. In addition, figures that illustrate a conceptual model or statistical links between measures or ages help greatly.

6. *It hard to do most research alone these days.* Most research is no longer completed by a single individual toiling in her laboratory by herself. Particularly for the type of biomedical research that NIH values, collaboration and expertise across multiple areas is the norm rather than the exception. This can be accomplished at both the junior and senior levels in multiple ways. First, and easiest, is the inclusion of consultants who can work with the investigator to frame the grant correctly, to choose the best measures, and to help ensure data quality. As well, statistical expertise is always welcomed and valued. A second way is to directly involve individuals with particular expertise in the work, having them on as coinvestigators for one's work. There are multiple methods for this kind of collaboration, from subcontracts to different institutions to pay for an individual's time, to a mechanism that the NIH has called multiple R01s. The point is that one strength of an application is in the quality of the group that is involved in the research—indeed, the investigative team itself receives a separate score on the 1 to 9 scale.

Final Thoughts

This brief overview provides the reader with the different funding opportunities and mechanisms for application with NIH. Grant applications are hard work, requiring attention to detail, thought, planning, preliminary data suggesting success, and a bit of luck for their funding. Many universities now provide training courses for faculty on grant submission and program offi-cers from NIH institutes are helpful in the assembly of grants. Success at getting funded depends not only on writing an excellent grant and on being successful in the review process but also on the level of funding that NIH receives from the federal government. And, that level funding is, in part, a reflection of the success of our science and scientists in demonstrating the translation of their work to solving the real health problems of our society.

The grant enterprise is an important aspect of scientific life, particularly when experiments involve expensive equipment, technology, and the col-laboration of multiple individuals. They provide the researcher with the means to undertake work, that at least in regards to funding from NIH, should ultimately address important public health issues. Navigating through the different options available may seem difficult, but the rewards for successful grant funding are significant. There are two final thoughts to offer: first, you cannot get funded unless you apply. It is probably the case that every successful grant-funded scientist has at one time received an unfunded score. Like the publication process, one must experience the review process for NIH grants and become familiar with what a successful grant looks like to have one's own success. So, for those who have never applied, it is important to take the first steps and apply. For those who have applied and have been turned down, it is important to learn from feedback and reapply. Second, one critical point in the grant funding process is review. Review panels need to have individuals from a range of backgrounds who are familiar with biomedical and psychological research and can provide thoughtful critiques. Serving on these review panels takes time and work, but it is critically important that researchers give their time and effort to this endeavor. Without the participation of knowledgeable scientists on review committees, grants will not get the hearing that they deserve no matter how well they are written. So, the next time an SRO contacts you to serve on a panel, please consider that request carefully.

8

While You're Up, Get Me a Grant!

Grantsmanship From the Perspective of a Retired National Science Foundation Grant Giver

Joseph L. Young

Wouldn't it be terrific if one really could get a grant for scientific research the way one can get a glass of Grant's Scotch; just belly up to the bar (or have a friend do that) and ask for one? But, alas, it doesn't work that way, and it takes a great deal more work to get a grant than to get a Grant's. The purpose of this chapter is to provide an idiosyncratic view of the best way to go about doing that. It comes from someone who spent the better part of his career in the business of evaluating grant proposals and, in most cases, making funding decisions. My view is by no means comprehensive, but it is based on a long, relevant career, the majority of it at the National Science Foundation (NSF), the focus of this chapter.

The landscape of grantsmanship has changed markedly since I began my post-Ph.D. career as an assistant professor in an academic psychology department. I recall applying to both the NSF and the National Institutes of Health (NIH) for a grant for some research that followed up on my dissertation results. I had no guidance whatsoever on that process, no book like this one, no examples of successful grant proposals, no talks on how to write proposals, and no mentoring. I found myself quickly turned down by NSF, but, after an inordinately long hiatus, I was awarded a grant by NIH. To this day, I have no idea what the grounds were for my rejection or for my award, since, in those days, neither reviews nor summary statements were released, and I received no written materials that could have helped me prepare a better proposal if I hadn't been awarded a grant. I certainly couldn't have given anyone the slightest assistance in preparing a grant application.

My mentorship in grantsmanship didn't occur until I left academia to come to Washington to work at the Office of Naval Research (ONR) and, after four years, the NSF. There I learned about what makes a good proposal and, as well, what manner of presentation of a good idea is likely to capture the attention and approbation of peer reviewers. Since my retirement more than a decade ago from NSF, I have been privileged to have a number of part-time and consulting jobs (and even a brief full-time job). The greater part of my work since retirement has been as a scientific review officer in a firm managing peer review for government (and even some private) research organizations lacking internal peer-review management capabilities, thereby gaining additional experience in how peer review works in different agencies. Therefore, although my experience is relatively broad, it is far from universal, and what I say in the remainder of this chapter must be viewed in that context and added to insights from other chapters in this book.

General Requirements for a Good Proposal

I cannot overemphasize the two main requirements for a good proposal; these hold for every funding agency and are paramount for NSF proposals. They are a good idea and an effective presentation of that idea. Both are necessary, and proposals that fail to meet both of these requirements are extremely unlikely to be funded at NSF or any other agency using peer review. Proposals that are beautifully presented but have an undeveloped, incomplete, or pedestrian idea behind them will almost certainly fail to impress peer reviewers, and proposals that are lacking in effectiveness of presentation are likely to obscure the quality of even an outstanding idea. In many ways, the rest of this chapter is an elaboration of these two requirements.

What to Do First

You think you have a good idea, and applying to NSF to carry out that idea is something you'd like to do. The first thing you need to do is to go online to the NSF website, www.nsf.gov/, and do a lot of reading. The NSF website, like most websites, is ever changing, and it may look different when you access it than it does today; as I write these words, it surely looks different than it did a decade ago. So, anything I say about it may be different when you look at it. However the website is organized, the first thing you want to do is to look through the various funding opportunities to see where your idea would best be reviewed. In many cases, this is extremely simple. So, for instance, if you are a cognitive psychologist, you probably will look first at the Perception, Action, and Cognition (PAC) Program; if you are a social psychologist, you probably will look first at the Social Psychology Program, and so forth. It is likely that you will find that your idea does fit in the "obvious" program. But, don't neglect the other programs in the Directorate for Social, Behavioral, and Economic Sciences and even those in other Directorates. And, certainly don't neglect various cross-cutting funding opportunities. You may find that the idea you already have fits better elsewhere, and in addition, you might find inspiration to consider some funding opportunity or opportunities you might not even have known about.

Applying to Standard NSF Programs

Let's focus on the most likely scenario: You find a standard NSF program where your idea fits. The first thing you need to do is to read everything you can about that program. How is it described? What are the scientific areas it covers? Yours is certainly one, but what are the others? Are there recurring target dates? There typically are, and you need to note the next date, as well as the one after that.

Once you have learned about the program to which you are applying, you need to read the Grant Proposal Guide (GPG), a well-written 71-page explanation of requirements, assumptions, and procedures that pertain to proposals to all NSF programs and special competitions. The GPG changes periodically, but as I write, it can be accessed at www.nsf.gov/publications/pub_summ.jsp?ods_key=gpg. There is a huge amount of information in the GPG. It is important information, and you need to read it carefully. It is critical that you understand this material, as well as material specifically pertaining to the program to which you intend to apply, BEFORE you start writing. It may even require more than one reading, but you still need to read it carefully. If you don't, you may spend a good deal of time in writing a proposal that is withdrawn administratively before being reviewed.

Another online tool that may be helpful is the link on the website under each program to research already funded by that program. You can get the identity of the researcher, the title, and by clicking on the title, you can get the abstract of the research. This will give you a sense of the kind of research that has been funded by the program in recent years. Surfing the various parts of the website relating to the program, which differ from program to program, can also be helpful in telling you what items are of particular interest to the program. So, for instance, today, as I surf through the items under the PAC program, I find URLs for a European Science Foundation Program and for a book of tutorials.

Now that you've read everything online, there are a few other things that make sense to do. First, learn about the review process. Here's the place where the GPG starts not to be as helpful as you would like. The reason for that is simple: What NSF calls Merit Review, a general concept, is applied differently in different parts of NSF. As noted in the GPG, all proposals are reviewed by 3 to 10 scientists with respect to "Intellectual Merit" and "Broader Impacts." However, how that review is conducted varies widely, with some parts of NSF using convened panels of reviewers, and others using what I will call "outside" review, that is, reviews of a specific proposal accessed electronically and submitted online from the reviewer's institution. Some parts of NSF, in particular, most programs in the Directorate for Social, Behavioral, and Economic Sciences, use both. I know of no other funding agency that does this routinely.

Thus, for your "standard" NSF proposal, panel review is aided by outside review. In this case, program officers send each proposal electronically to several outside reviewers who review online and whose reviews are considered by the standing panel in their deliberations and by the program officer in decision making. Applicants are given the opportunity to suggest reviewers and to give a list of individuals they do not want to review their proposal. This can be a useful tool for you, but it needs to be used wisely. If you suggest reviewers, be sure they do not have a conflict of interest; don't use colleagues at your institution or people with whom you have worked. And, if you suggest individuals you don't want to review, keep it to a relatively small number. Listing more than four or five tends to lead to the suspicion that you have lots of scientific enemies.

At NSF, it is important to know the identity of the program officer who is in charge of the program to which you are submitting, because that individual chooses the review panel and outside reviewers and will make the final decision about funding or not funding your proposal. There are two kinds of program officers: permanent and visiting scientists. I was a permanent program officer, and the scientific community had a good idea of how I operated, as I'd been around for quite a while. Visiting scientists are at NSF for one to three years and often arrive with an agenda to foster, in the program they are to administer, research in specific areas of the program of particular interest to them. Of course, no visiting scientist will stop funding proposals in other areas within the purview of the program, but their scientific interests are likely to influence their choice of panel members and outside reviewers, as well as their funding decisions. Thus, it is useful, if the program officer is a visiting scientist, to research his or her background and consider it in writing your proposal.

Applying to Other NSF Programs

But, what if you find a funding opportunity that is not a "standard" NSF program? In this case, the funding opportunity may be described with the same sort of program description as for a "standard" program. Another possible descriptor is a program announcement, which is a somewhat more formal description of a funding opportunity. There are also other ways in which the funding opportunity may be described. In all cases, whatever sort of documentation is provided outlines the scientific areas under consideration, as well as all the administrative requirements, dates, and the like that pertain to the competition to which you plan to apply. These need a bit of decoding. Some of these are essentially special emphasis parts of regular programs. Others cut across different programs, divisions, and even directorates. The easiest way to start the decoding is to look at the personnel involved with the funding opportunity and the dates associated with the funding opportunity. Are the dates given target dates, as used for regular programs, or are they deadlines? The latter are more commonly associated with funding opportunities that cut across various parts of NSF. Often they have a formally constituted group of program officers from different parts of NSF who work together (typically in addition to their work in standard programs) to run this funding opportunity. Thus, you should look at the personnel associated with the funding opportunity; as you click on each of them, you will see what their standard program assignment is, if any.

Another aspect of these funding opportunities that you should note is whether the deadline or target date is one-time only or continuing from year to year. If the funding opportunity has been around for a while, you can find what has been funded before, as with standard programs, but if it is new, that will not be possible.

Should I Apply, and If So, When?

Now that you know everything about the funding opportunity to which you are thinking of applying, you need to make the final decision about whether or not to apply, and, if so, when. In the standard program case, the decision is certainly likely to be to apply, but the decision about when to apply is a bit tricky. There are typically two target dates per year. Should you apply for the next one or the one after that? The answer depends on whether you can be ready for the next target date, and you really don't know that yet. My advice is to start working on your proposal, taking into account all the information you have gleaned, and taking into account some guidance below, and submit it for the next target date only if it is ready. Otherwise, keep working on it until the following target date. I discuss below the way to decide whether it is ready to submit.

In some cases of nonstandard funding opportunities, the decision process may be more complex. In cases in which there are at least two future target dates or deadlines, you can operate as discussed earlier, but there will be cases in which it is a "one-time" opportunity, with only one deadline coming up, with no assurance that there will be another one. In that case, you need to assess whether you can get something competitive together by the deadline. Unless the deadline is far off, you probably won't be able to do that unless you've already been thinking about the area in some detail. Try to be realistic about what you can do by that date; we always seem to assume that we will be able to accomplish more in a given amount of time than we can, as anyone who has promised to produce an article or book chapter by a given date can attest.

The Writing Process

You've decided to apply, and you have noted all the special requirements, such as page limitations, sections of the proposal, and the like, as well as the general requirements of the GPG. You are keeping all the relevant documents handy so that you can refer to them as often as needed as you write. You are finally sitting down to write.

The most important thing to realize when you write a proposal is that you know more about the specific topic than anyone else, in particular, anyone who might review it. You may well have conducted some preliminary research that you are discussing in the proposal for the first time outside your institution and close circle of colleagues. If you don't know more than anyone else about the specific topic, you have no business writing a proposal on it; the person who knows more about it should be writing one. So, you need to overexplain rather than assume that the individual who is reading the proposal knows as much as or more than you do. This means that you want the reader to be eager to see the next points of your argument when she reads each section. Introduce the problem in such a way that the reader wants to see your approach to it, and then show the reader how your approach illuminates the issue you introduced.

I cannot overemphasize that last sentence. I can't tell you how many proposals I've seen in which the applicant does an extremely good job of introducing a problem followed by a comprehensive description of an experimental program, but without any serious attempt to explain how the experimental program attacks the problem. So, make sure there's a logical flow from an important problem to an experimental program that will attack the problem appropriately. Make sure you explain why the experiments put us on the track of solving the problem; don't leave it to the reader to figure it out. Remember that it might be obvious to you, because you know more about the topic than the reader, but not obvious to him or her.

To recapitulate, the narrative portion of a good proposal contains the following parts:

1. An introduction that explains the problem and its scientific and/or societal importance. This will include background, brief review of the literature and your preliminary data, and it needs to make the reviewer care about the problem. Ideally, after reading this section, the reader should be captivated by the problem and be eager to see how you will address it.

2. A section that connects the introduction to the experiments that you propose conducting in a way that readies the reader for the experiments.

3. A clear description of the experiments that you plan to conduct. Ideally, the reader should be able to see immediately, based on the first two sections, that these are the right experiments to do to address the problem. For NSF (and this might not apply to other agencies), it is NOT essential that every experiment you plan to conduct be described in full detail. My usual advice is to be very complete about the experimental plan for the first year and provide an outline of the rest of the research plan.

4. A section that explains where you expect to be at the end of the funding period with regard to addressing the problem you discussed initially.

Give yourself enough time for the next step, which is to give a draft to colleagues, mentors, students, and people in related areas to read and critique. These are people who won't be asked to review, as they have a conflict of interest, but are in other ways similar to the reviewers. They should be able to tell you places where they can't follow your logic, where there is a lack of clarity, or many other easily remedied flaws in your draft. Then make changes and return it to these readers. Resist the urge to explain orally the things they don't get; you need to make it clear in writing, as you will not have the opportunity to explain yourself orally to the reviewers. Be sure that all is in readiness before submitting; if you are not ready by the next target date, then keep on working and aim for the following target date.

Specific NSF Writing Guidance

The writing guidance above is applicable to any funding agency, not just NSF. Funding agencies differ in many ways, and it is not possible to provide "micro-guidance" that will work for every proposal-writing effort. However, there are some specifics that are, in general, appropriate for "standard" NSF programs.

The two most important things to remember about NSF, particularly in its "standard" programs, are that its primary mission is the health of the scientific endeavor in America and that its secondary mission is societal benefit. The GPG describes the review criteria that address these missions as "Intellectual Merit" and "Broader Impacts," respectively. That means that every "standard" NSF proposal, in conveying its "Intellectual Merit," needs to explain how the work would advance the science, and in most cases, that means how the work would advance theory, since theoretical advancement is what advances science. The review criterion of "Broader Impacts" is a more recent addition, although it has been around since well before I retired. "Broader Impacts" translate to the societal benefit of the research. The latter may be long term, for instance, the beginning of a chain of research that will ultimately (but not necessarily very soon) be of immense societal benefit, but it must be there. It really doesn't even have to be the research itself; it might be something as simple as providing training to the next generation of scientists, although that's typically not quite enough. Oddly enough, although applicants often complain about the need to explain societal benefit, it's fairly easy to do in almost all cases, and we all benefit by doing it, since that is the means by which support of science is "sold" to the public and the Congress. And, if we communicate outside the bubble of the scientific community, as most of us do, we probably already attempt to do this with friends, relatives, and even nonscientific business associates.

What to Do While You Wait

There's often a considerable length of time between the deadline (or target date) for your proposal and the date you find out its fate. Although there's a temptation to breathe a sigh of relief and take it easy, that's not the best idea. There's one mandatory activity, in my view, and one highly desirable one. The mandatory one is to keep thinking about the problem. It is very unlikely that your proposal was truly the last word on the subject. It could have been better, and in particular, it could have benefited from additional thinking about the topic. So, give it that level of attention; you'll thank yourself when the "verdict" comes in. The highly desirable one is to do some preliminary research on the topic, in addition to whatever preliminary research you included in the proposal, if possible. If you have sufficient resources, you may even be able to do the first experiment or two that you suggested in your proposal. If you have some resources, you may at least be able to do some preliminary or pilot research. Only if you have absolutely no resources or if your research requires resources unattainable without the funding for which you applied should you forego the research. But, even in that case, keep thinking!

What to Do When the Decision Arrives

When the decision arrives from NSF, either you were funded or you weren't. If you got funded, celebrate! When you are done celebrating, you should be happy that you kept thinking about the research during the waiting period, because you should be ready to take a "running start" into the research, without having to reconstruct the thinking that went into the proposal. The research itself will benefit from your thinking, as well as from the review feedback. But, what if, like the majority of applicants, you don't get funded? With any proposal, you will almost certainly get some sort of summary statement, and especially in the case of NSF, a summary accompanied by the verbatim reviews of your application. You'll probably want to read them right away, even though it's probably not a good idea. You're probably distraught! Why didn't those dumb reviewers love my proposal? Stupid people! They couldn't understand my brilliant work! That's understandable, but it's not a good frame of mind to be in to get something out of these documents. Better to wait until you've cooled down a bit.

So, assume you have cooled down and read what was sent, probably for the second time (since you didn't heed my advice and went ahead and read immediately anyway). You probably still are not feeling good about things. What you want to do is give those ignorant reviewers a piece of your mind, tell them how wrong they were, explain things they didn't seem to understand. In short, you want to resubmit, and, particularly at NSF, that's often an option, typically with a very short turn around time, at least for the next deadline or target date. But, immediate resubmission is typically NOT a good option. You're very angry, very defensive, and an immediate turn-around resubmission is likely to show that and, in addition, to be very superficial and without much substantive change, which is something that NSF specifically requires.

But, When Is an Immediate Resubmission All Right?

There is one set of circumstances in which an instant resubmission makes sense. Suppose you followed my advice, kept thinking about the problem, even did some preliminary research. And then, the negative decision arrives with all the feedback. But, amazingly, the feedback is right in line with what you've been thinking during the waiting interval. It's telling you that there are problems in the proposal, and those are actually the same problems you have identified yourself. And, moreover, you have already come up with a way to remedy those problems. In this case, which happens rarely but does indeed happen, you are in a position to write a revised proposal immediately.

What to Do Before Resubmission

Whether you resubmit immediately (for the next target date) or wait until later, there is one really important thing to do. You need to show the feedback to one or more people you trust, a colleague, a mentor, even a student, and get feedback. These need to be people who won't be judgmental, but who will be honest with you. Under certain circumstances, it might even be a paid consultant (full disclosure: I do this kind of work when asked), but this is rarely essential. The important thing is that this person be one who can help you interpret the feedback and help you to decide how to handle it. One important thing that an objective individual can help you understand is whether the problem with your submission is a deficient idea, perhaps even with an effective presentation, or a poor presentation of a good idea.

Writing the Resubmission

Unless the funding opportunity has a formal resubmission process where it is a required part of the process, and this is virtually never the case at NSF, you do NOT want to give a point-by-point refutation of the criticisms or a point-by-point discussion of how this new submission avoids the problems that were pointed out in the feedback. It is important, of course, that the resubmitted proposal do all those things. One goal is for the resubmission to convince someone who criticized the original submission that you understood the criticism and that the new submission avoids the problems noted. But, the new submission almost certainly will be reviewed by some people who didn't see the original submission, and you need them to be convinced that this proposal is a good one; any sense that you convey in your writing that this was submitted before and not funded certainly can't be helpful.

In writing a resubmission (and in the original submission, as well), it is important not to write about completed research as though it is planned for the future as a part of the proposed work. Not only is this dishonest and an instance of academic misconduct, but it almost always backfires on the applicant. People in your field know what you have and have not done already, and you will be found out and, at least, marked down for engaging in this deceptive practice. The thing to do, if you have completed some research between submissions, is to discuss the completed work as part of the background section of your resubmission, thereby strengthening it.

What If You Are Not Funded a Second Time?

During my time at the NSF, it was not uncommon for a proposal to be submitted multiple times before finally being funded. Particularly if the review seems more positive the second time but the proposal still wasn't funded, a third submission, going through the process again, might be helpful. But, suppose the second review is not more positive? In my experience, there are two possible reasons for that. The first typically occurs in the case of immediate resubmission. Since these immediate resubmissions often come across as superficial, defensive, or both, reviewers spot that and don't respond very positively. In that case, you might want to consider going back and taking my advice (earlier) about how to prepare for a resubmission.

The second reason that a second review may not be more positive is that the substance was weak the first time and has not been improved. Maybe the presentation was actually very good the first time around, but the idea just wasn't terribly good. In that case, fixing the presentation would not be the remedy; the remedy would be improving on the substantive idea. Sometimes, the substance was weak and the presentation was relatively poor; in that case, improving the presentation can clarify the idea and make it clearer to the reviewers that the idea was in fact weak.

Proposals to Funding Agencies Other Than NSF

This chapter has focused on proposals to NSF, with occasional asides about other agencies. Most of what I've said that is not NSF-specific is broadly applicable to every proposal to all federal (and even some nonfederal) funding agencies. Paying attention to the documents laying out the specific funding agency to which you are applying, as well as general documents about submissions to the agency, having a good idea, and presenting it well are all necessary in submitting proposals to any funding agency.

Final Thoughts

Funding in all government agencies, especially NSF, is extremely competitive, and many good ideas don't get funded. Some don't get funded because the idea, while perhaps worthy of funding in absolute terms, simply was not as good an idea as those that did get funding. Other proposals with good ideas don't get funded because those proposals don't present the ideas sufficiently well. This chapter can't do much about the former, because the process of coming up with good ideas is beyond its scope. But, it is my hope that I've given you a short orientation to the necessity for presenting your ideas well. The ideal situation from the standpoint of a grant giver is for everyone to make the most effective presentation possible of their ideas, so that the decision process depends only on the quality of the ideas and not on the quality of their presentation. That way, the limited funding available will fund those ideas found best by peer review, admittedly an imperfect process, but still the best available way to make informed scientific decisions.

9

Writing a Grant Proposal for the National Science Foundation

John F. Dovidio, Louis A. Penner, and Terrance L. Albrecht

Obtaining external support for research has become increasingly important for faculty members over the past decade as institutions have faced significant economic challenges (Blumenstyk & Brainard, 2011). Grants have also become a marker of institutional prestige. Grants received by faculty members were used by the National Research Council as a criterion in its 2010 assessment of the more than 5,000 doctoral programs in 212 universities across the United States (The National Academies, 2010). The emphasis on faculty grants is likely to continue. Just a few years ago, many institutions expected new faculty to *pursue* outside funding; now many expect faculty to *obtain* funding by the time they stand for tenure.

Note: The preparation of this chapter was partially supported by grants to the first author from NIH (RO1HL 0856331–0182 and 1R01DA029888–01) and to the second and third authors from the National Cancer Institute (U01CA114583, 1U54CA154606–01, and 1R01CA138981–01). The contents of this chapter reflect the views of the three authors and have not been reviewed or endorsed by any official of NSF.

Correspondence regarding this chapter should be addressed to the first author at the Department of Psychology, Yale University, P.O. Box 208205, New Haven CT, 06520–8205, e-mail: john.dovidio@yale.edu.

This chapter is about writing proposals and obtaining research grants from one of the federal agencies that funds basic research in the behavioral and brain sciences, the National Science Foundation (NSF). Funding from NSF is highly competitive, especially in the last few years. Thus, proposals for funding not only have to be scientifically rigorous and highly innovative, but they also have to be tailored to fit the mission of NSF. In this chapter, we first briefly describe NSF and its mission. Then we identify research-funding programs most relevant for work in behavioral and brain sciences. After that, we discuss the proposal review process, including the criteria for funding, at NSF. Although these sections provide a foundation for understanding what kinds of proposals are best suited for NSF, we devote the major portion of this chapter offering concrete guidance about how to write effective research proposals—from finding an appropriate idea to writing the narrative to developing supporting documentation.

Mission and Structure of NSF

NSF, created by Congress in 1950, is the second largest U.S. government research-funding agency, after the National Institutes of Health (NIH). The stated mission of NSF is "to promote the progress of science; to advance the national health, prosperity, and welfare; to secure the national defense." Whereas the various institutes within NIH often have specific applied health-related missions, NSF emphasizes basic research—research that addresses fundamental theoretical issues but that may not have an immediate practical impact. NSF is a major source of funding in mathematics, computer science, and the behavioral sciences. It also supports "'high risk, high pay-off' ideas, novel collaborations, and numerous projects that may seem like science fiction today, but which the public will take for granted tomorrow" (NSF, 2009). The mandate of NSF does not include medical fields of research directly, but it does encompass basic research in the physical, natural, and behavioral sciences that are relevant to health and medicine. NSF funds about 20 percent of all federally supported basic research conducted by America's colleges and universities. It receives more than 42,000 proposals per year, funds a little less than 20 percent of them, and annually supports approximately 200,000 scientists, engineers, educators, and students in the United States and throughout the world. In 2012, the president and Congress allocated NSF $7.033 billion, a 2.5 percent increase ($173.18 million) beyond the 2011 level. Thus, NSF is a major funding source for research scientists.

NSF includes seven directorates that represent several different disciplines. These directorates are (a) Biological Sciences (molecular, cellular, and organismal biology, environmental science); (b) Computer and Information Science and Engineering (fundamental computer science, computer and networking systems, and artificial intelligence); (c) Engineering (bioengineering, environmental systems, civil and mechanical systems, chemical and transport systems, electrical and communications systems, and design and manufacturing); (d) Geosciences (geological, atmospheric, and ocean sciences); (e) Mathematical and Physical Sciences (mathematics, astronomy, physics, chemistry, and materials science); (f) Education and Human Resources (science, technology, engineering, and mathematics education at every level); and (g) Social, Behavioral and Economic Sciences (neuroscience, management, psychology, sociology, anthropology, linguistics, and economics).

NSF's budget includes $247.3 million for projects related to the behavioral sciences, and the Social, Behavioral, and Economic Sciences (SBE) directorate is most directly relevant for researchers in the behavioral and brain sciences. Unfortunately, behavioral science (and thus this directorate) frequently receives political challenges. Starting in the mid-1970s and continuing for over a decade, the late Senator William Proxmire attracted national headlines with his Golden Fleece Awards that identified (and ridiculed) federally funded research he believed was trivial or pointless and, thus, wasted taxpayer money. Proxmire's "award" seemed to disproportionately target social and behavioral research. In the early 1980s, because of "pressure from the Reagan administration, Federal agencies [began] to weed out or drastically scale down their support for basic research in economics, sociology, psychology, and other social and behavioral sciences" (Reinhold, 1981, para. 1). The Senate later voted to restore NSF funding for behavioral sciences, but in the early 1990s, Senator Robert Byrd proposed that 32 NSF grants, mainly in the behavioral sciences, be rescinded (Breckler, 2005). Recently, funding for the SBE directorate has again come under scrutiny by Congress. In May 2012, the House of Representatives passed an amendment prohibiting NSF from funding political science research (Lane, 2012). Social and behavioral science research for NSF is thus often targeted by legislators (as articulated in the Golden Fleece Awards) and the media as, on the one hand, not being relevant to practical problems, and, on the other hand, as not being sufficiently "scientific" to merit funding by the National *Science* Foundation.

Although these macro-level political struggles seem distant from the immediate challenges of preparing an NSF proposal, as we discuss later, they are important to consider as researchers craft their proposals. In the next section, though, we consider the more technical issues for writing an NSF proposal, identifying an appropriate program within NSF.

NSF Funding Programs and Criteria

One can electronically search for the kinds of projects that NSF is interested in supporting by using *The Find Funding* function on the NSF website (www.nsf.gov). In addition, NSF often has Program Solicitations that encourage the submission of proposals in specific topics of interest. Solicitations are usually more focused than program announcements, and they normally apply for a limited period.

Researchers most commonly seek support from NSF for specific research projects rather than broad research programs. In general, NSF awards are often smaller than awards from other federal granting agencies, such as NIH in scope, total funding, the number of years of support, and the kind of support provided (e.g., teaching release in some programs). While acknowledging the great variety of funding opportunities offered by NSF, we describe a subset of research programs that are most relevant to behavioral and brain science researchers and that require similar types of proposals.

The *CAREER Program* at NSF supports basic research activities among researchers at various stages of their career and in a range of professional contexts. The CAREER program supports the early development of academic faculty as both educators and researchers and is intended to foster the integration of research and education components of a faculty career.

In addition, NSF has a specific program for supporting research among faculty who teach at "predominantly undergraduate" colleges. Research in Undergraduate Institutions (RUI) grants support (a) individual and collaborative research projects, (b) the purchase of shared-use research instrumentation, and (c) opportunities for faculty at these colleges to work with NSF-supported researchers at other institutions. Each of the NSF directorates supports RUI activities.

NSF also supports undergraduate and graduate education directly. The Research Experience for Undergraduates (REU) program supports active and meaningful involvement in research by undergraduate students in any of the areas normally funded by NSF. REU grants are awarded to initiate and conduct projects that engage a number of students in research from the host institutions as well as other colleges. NSF also provides Graduate Research Fellowships for outstanding graduate students and the directorate for SBE offers Minority Postdoctoral Research Fellowships.

All funding opportunities within NSF are announced on the NSF website (www.nsf.gov) and at www.grants.gov. Proposals to NSF must conform to the procedures and format outlined in the *National Science Foundation Proposal and Award Policies and Procedure Guide* (NSF, 2010). Contact with NSF program personnel prior to proposal preparation and submission is permitted and encouraged. Proposals are submitted electronically through the Fastlane system.

NSF Review Process

NSF greatly values the peer review process, and peer evaluation that involves outside evaluators and panel deliberations is central in the proposal assessment process. The NSF staff screens proposals to determine whether they conform to the program guidelines, but even though program directors and key administrators have solid research backgrounds, assessments are made through full merit review. Understanding this process can help investigators prepare their proposals in the most effective way.

Grant proposals are sent to outside reviewers who have relevant expertise on the topic. Each reviewer (normally three) makes a summary rating on a 5-point (1 = excellent, 2 = very good, 3 = good, 4 = fair, 5 = poor) scale. Reviewers are asked to evaluate the proposal on two criteria, intellectual merit and broader impacts. *Intellectual merit* is an evaluation of the importance of the proposed activity "to advancing knowledge and understanding within its own field or across different fields," and judgments of the extent to which the project is "well conceived and organized" and explores "creative, original, or potentially transformative concepts" (NSF, 2002). Intellectual merit also incorporates an assessment of the investigator's qualifications for successfully conducting the research. The second criterion, *broader impacts*, is the extent to which the project promotes teaching, training, and learning; enhances the participation of underrepresented groups; and benefits society (NSF, 2002).

Although not yet a formal criterion for reviewer evaluation, NSF submission guidelines now also require investigators to provide plans for data management and the sharing of products of the research. NSF specifies that this *Data Management Plan*, which we describe in a later section, will be reviewed as part of the intellectual merit or broader impacts of the proposal or both.

Following the initial reviews, proposals are evaluated by standing NSF panels, which are composed of scholars who, as a group, have the expertise necessary to evaluate the projects submitted to a particular program. Neither the membership of the panel nor the dates the panel meets are publicly available. The panel reads the external reviewers' comments on an application before it begins its review process. One panel member with highly relevant expertise is assigned to be the primary panel reviewer, who submits an individual assessment before the panel meets; another is asked to be the secondary panel reviewer. For the panel meetings, the primary reviewer prepares a brief synopsis and recommendation for the proposal. The secondary reviewer provides supplementary remarks. Proposals that receive a rating of "very good" or higher from at least one reviewer—an outside evaluator or a panel member—are discussed by the entire panel. Even if a proposal does not receive a rating of "very good" or better, it will be reviewed for mentoring purposes if submitted by a "new investigator" (someone who has not previously received NSF funding) or researchers from undergraduate institutions.

At the end of the panel discussion of a proposal, the primary and secondary reviewers propose a classification for funding (high, moderate, or low) or do not recommend funding. One panel member is assigned the role of recording and summarizing key elements of the panel evaluation and feedback to the investigator. When all of the proposals have been discussed, panel members are given the opportunity to propose a reclassification of any proposal and to prioritize projects within each category of support. The comments and rankings of the review panel are recommendations to the program officer; the panel does not make the funding decisions.

It is rare that investigators receive a grant on their first submission of a proposal. The panel letter indicates whether a proposal was evaluated as highly competitive, competitive, or not competitive. Only a small percentage of the proposals are judged to be highly competitive, and not all of them are able to be funded. Thus, like a research article, revision of a proposal is typically needed. NSF (unlike NIH) does not limit the number of times an investigator can resubmit, but it does require that the proposal be substantially revised for reconsideration. In our experience, when a proposal is judged to be not competitive, researchers should pursue a different topic or a substantially different direction for their next proposal. For revised proposals, the NSF staff tries to involve the same reviewers and panel members in the second review. However, about a third of a grant panel turns over each year, and thus the chances of getting exactly the same reviewers is less than for a manuscript that has received a "revise and resubmit" for a journal. Nevertheless, like a journal submission, it is very important to be responsive to the feedback of scholars who have devoted significant time and energy to comment on your work.

The program officer for NSF considers the recommendation and discussions of the review panel, but may also include other factors, such as the transformative potential of the project or particular program objectives, in making funding decisions. The program officer evaluates projects in light of previously funded projects. Whereas the panel review focuses on the merits of each proposal individually, the program officer adopts a broader perspective on how a specific project is related to other projects that are currently funded. After scientific, technical, and program review, and after consideration of appropriate factors, the program officer makes a funding recommendation to the division director. If the division director concurs, the recommendation is submitted to the Division of Grants and Agreements for award processing.

NSF grants include both direct costs for carrying out the research and indirect costs, which is the amount paid to the institution for providing the infrastructure to support the research; these are based on an existing agreement between the principal investigator's institution and the government. Although the size of the budget is not a formal criterion in the review, panel members cannot help but notice when a proposal requests a disproportionate amount of available funds. In addition, budgets are reviewed by NSF staff for appropriateness at later stages of the process. Million- or multimillion-dollar grants are much rarer at NSF than at NIH. NSF appears to try to "spread the money around," reducing the cost of specific grants by asking the investigators, based on panel and reviewer input, to limit funded research to the most promising aspects of the proposal. In addition, NSF tries to support new investigators and investigators from undergraduate institutions, often providing a smaller grant (in the range of $50,000 to $75,000) for initial work on a promising larger proposal that was submitted. In general, successful applications are awarded less money than the amount initially requested—but funded at a level that is sufficient (and often more appropriate) for the key elements of the project to be conducted successfully.

In the next two sections, we discuss how to write a strong NSF proposal. First, we review the basic structure of a proposal. After that, we present an extended section on suggestions for writing the narrative of the grant proposal—the section describing the proposed project and the case for the potential contribution of the work—effectively. However, we caution that, like writing a strong research article, there is no single recipe for success. And, there is no substitute for an original idea. Nevertheless, based on our personal experience as reviewers and recipients of grants, we do present specific suggestions about what to do and what not to do in a grant proposal.

Elements and Structure of the Grant Narrative

Because detailed information on the formal elements of an NSF proposal is available in the *National Science Foundation Proposal and Award Policies and Procedure Guide* (NSF, 2010), we offer only a brief overview of the structure of the proposal. Our focus is on the most central aspects of the narrative and supplementary materials, except for the budget. We do not discuss how to prepare a budget for an NSF application or related administrative issues, because these issues are beyond our expertise and because institutions vary greatly in how they prepare budgets and the level of support they provide for grant applications. These aspects of a grant application are extremely important and often require knowledge and expertise not possessed by the typical academic researcher. Thus, we urge researchers who are preparing applications to establish contact very early in the process with their institution's Office of Sponsored Research, Grants Specialists, or some other department that deals with preparing and managing grant applications.

Researchers should also note that applications are not submitted by individual investigators, but by their institutions, and grant awards are made to the institution, not the investigator. Several stages of institutional approval are typically required before an application will be submitted by the institution, so researchers should allow ample time before the NSF submission deadline (typically in the summer and winter) for institutional review and approval. Also, we do not consider issues of institutional and investigator compliance, if a proposal is funded, but these are important issues, and investigators should work closely with their institution and NSF to be sure that funds are spent and accounted for appropriately.

NSF proposals have strict page limits, so investigators have to be economical and precise in their presentation. In addition, NSF has a number of specific formatting requirements. For example, the proposal must use one of the following fonts: Arial, Courier New, or Palatino Linotype with a font size of 10 points or larger; Times New Roman at a font size of 11 points or larger; or Computer Modern family of fonts at a font size of 11 points or larger. Researchers should, obviously, read the submission guidelines closely.

An NSF proposal begins with a one-page Project Summary. The Project Summary is not simply an abstract of the proposal; it outlines the specific aims of the proposed project and the methods to be employed to achieve that goal. The Project Summary must explicitly speak to the two NSF merit review criteria—intellectual merit of the proposed activity and broader impacts.

The other major portion of the proposal is the Project Description, which can be up to 15 single-spaced pages in length (although brevity is encouraged). In the Project Description, the investigator needs to clearly explain what the proposed research is, its significance, and how the research will be conducted. Like a research article, the narrative should develop a theoretical rationale for the research, evidence of the promise of the proposed line of work, and an integrated view of the progression— methods, analyses, and expected outcomes—of proposed studies. Within the space constraints, the investigator needs to provide enough detail for reviewers to evaluate the appropriateness of the designs and procedures and the scientific rigor of the research. It is also useful to provide a timeline indicating what aspects of the project will be completed when, which will also help to illustrate the feasibility of the project.

It is important to include explicit consideration of broader impacts, either integrated in clear and appropriate ways in the narrative or in a subsection of the Project Description. As the NSF proposal guide and website explain, broader impacts include:

> how the project will integrate research and education by advancing discovery and understanding while at the same time promoting teaching, training, and learning; ways in which the proposed activity will broaden the participation of underrepresented groups (e.g., gender, ethnicity, disability, geographic, etc.); how the project will enhance the infrastructure for research and/or education, such as facilities, instrumentation, networks, and partnerships; how the results of the project will be disseminated broadly to enhance scientific and technological understanding; and potential benefits of the proposed activity to society at large. (NSF, 2010, p. II-8)

Examples of broader impact statements are available on the NSF website (NSF, 2007).

A number of other key elements of the proposal are included as supplementary material. The budget and budget justification are obviously critical. The application must include biographical sketches of major research personnel. NSF grants fund a person as well as the research, so biographical sketches should be prepared carefully.

As mentioned earlier, NSF has started requiring Data Management Plans. According to the NSF guidelines, proposals must indicate "plans for data management and sharing of the products of research, including preservation, documentation, and sharing of data, samples, physical collections, curriculum materials and other related research and education products" (NSF, 2010, p. II-8). Information describing the results of prior NSF funding received within the past five years, if applicable, is also part of the supplementary materials.

Because NSF guidelines regularly evolve, investigators should consult the NSF Web page (www.nsf.gov) and staff in their institution's Office of Sponsored Programs before preparing a proposal. Despite frequent "tweaks" of proposal formats, the core expectations of the substantive content of competitive NSF proposals have remained consistent over the years. We consider these expectations and offer specific advice in the next section.

Developing the Narrative

In this section, we describe some "do's and don'ts" of writing grant proposals for NSF. This part of the chapter is largely subjective—it is based largely on the interpretations we have of our collective experiences as investigators, reviewers, and panel members. Much of this advice will apply to proposals to other government agencies, such as NIH, but we also emphasize how some of the points we make are especially appropriate for NSF proposals. We offer concrete examples to illustrate our points, but because NSF proposals are confidential documents, we alter our descriptions to make the essential point while protecting the confidentiality of the investigator and the project. We organize our observations and suggestions generally chronologically, beginning with the identification of the topic, to identifying the appropriate program to submit to, to writing various parts of the actual narrative.

Coming Up With the Idea

Although NSF often has specially targeted programs (e.g., to promote nanotechnology undergraduate education and increasing the participation and advancement of women in science), one of its unique appeals for researchers is that it is broadly interested in scientific innovation. The foundation takes great pride in being "a bastion for basic research." Most programs are organized around general areas, such as economics, sociology, cognitive neuroscience, and cultural anthropology. Thus, unlike many other foundations or institutes, for most NSF programs researchers do not have to tailor proposals around requests for research on specific topics. In this respect, writing a proposal for NSF is like writing a research article for a top journal. Researchers should start with a novel and promising idea, and then work from that.

We understand the challenge of coming up with a significant new idea, and we cannot offer specific advice about how to generate one. But, we can suggest some ways to think about this and evaluate how appropriate an idea is for a grant proposal. Although investigators should aim for a guiding idea in a proposal that would be equivalent to one worthy of publication in a top professional journal, it is important to keep in mind that a grant proposal is evaluated on its promise while a journal article is assessed based on a review of what was done. Thus, for an NSF grant proposal, investigators need to convince reviewers that an idea is both original and feasible.

One major distinction between a grant review and a journal review is that in the former the investigator's previous accomplishments and potential for conducting the proposed research are evaluated. This criterion does not mean that junior investigators are unable to get grants. Reviewers, panel members, and program officers are, in fact, quite interested in supporting junior faculty members. What it does mean, though, is that investigators who have a demonstrable track record for successfully conducting and publishing research related to the proposed research will have an advantage over those who do not.

The desired balance between innovativeness of an idea and feasibility of successful completion of the project also suggests theoretical "bookends" for a proposal. Even if a grant proposal outlines research that is quite *feasible*, it must also be sufficiently *innovative* to draw the interest of the reviewers. Thus, a proposal is not likely to be competitive if it represents relatively minor parametric variations on a result the author has already demonstrated— even if the original finding was quite novel. What makes a variation major or minor often depends, of course, upon perspective. What may seem major to an investigator, who is close to the problem, may seem minor to a more distant reviewer. Investigators should understand the perspective of people who will view the conceptual issues from the more distant vantage point. They need to propose work that represents a significant advance or new direction—and is theoretically and empirically linked to the investigator's interests and previous accomplishments. But, the investigator must also show that the project is feasible; any uncertainty among reviewers about the feasibility of a project weakens the proposal.

One strategy to help balance innovation and feasibility is to have coinvestigators, with complementary expertise or different levels of experience, for the proposal. For example, a grant proposal on the responses of minority-group members' reactions to discrimination might be cowritten by one researcher who has studied intergroup relations and another scholar who uses psychophysiological measures (e.g., of threat and challenge) or studies hormonal influences on behavior (e.g., of testosterone levels). Panels we have been on have also favorably evaluated applications cowritten by a junior faculty member at a liberal arts college and a senior faculty member at a research-intensive university. Although having coinvestigators can drive up the amount of funds requested quite significantly (something the coinvestigators should be mindful of), the balance between novelty and feasibility may significantly increase the quality of the proposal and thus its chances for funding.

Identifying the Right NSF Program

For many innovative proposals, it may not be clear which directorate or program an idea best fits. And, "fit" matters. For example, an ethnographic study of social influence as indigenous tribes in New Guinea encounter urban expansion could be construed as important social psychological research, but there are disciplinary biases. Just as this line of research would probably not be well received in a mainstream social psychology journal, it would be unlikely to be rated among the most competitive proposals by a social psychology panel at NSF. Although the panel is open to different methodologies and ideas, proposals that deviate too much from the culture of a subdiscipline (e.g., social psychology) are less likely to generate enthusiasm for funding among panel members from that discipline. The ideas may be recognized as fascinating and valuable, but the proposal will likely be viewed as just "not quite right" when contrasted with more conventional proposals.

Although the example of social influence and cultural contact may obviously be seen as not a strong fit for a social psychology panel, many more "mainstream" proposals may seem either to be appropriate for multiple panels (e.g., cognitive neuroscience and social psychology panels) or sit at the intersection of panels. Program officers at NSF can be helpful in directing researchers to the most appropriate program for a proposal. The NSF directorate for SBE currently lists 75 different programs and panels (www.nsf .gov/funding/pgm_list.jsp?org=SBE). Some relevant topical programs for brain and behavioral science researchers are Cognitive Neuroscience; Decision, Risk, and Management Sciences; Developmental and Learning Sciences; Law and Social Sciences; Linguistics; Perception, Action, and Cognition; and Science of Learning Centers, Science of Organizations, and Social Psychology. In fact, investigators might want to have their proposal reviewed by more than one NSF panel, and this is possible and, in fact, not uncommon at NSF.

When in doubt about which panel to choose, the researcher should contact the appropriate program officers at NSF. The goal of NSF is to fund worthy projects, and it is in everyone's best interest that proposals present the strongest case possible and are reviewed most fairly. Program officers will not give specific feedback on the details of a proposal; it is not their job to provide a preview. However, program officers can, and typically will, guide investigators to appropriate programs within SBE and instruct investigators about how to submit to one or more programs. We have found that program officers are especially helpful in telling you that their program is not interested in the kind of research you want to do. This information can save researchers considerable time and effort. Thus, some guidance on the kinds of research a program is looking for is quite useful. The best way to determine this is to have an initial dialogue with a program officer or director prior to the submission of an application. We caution, however, that making contact with a program officer, who is responsible for many different activities daily, is best done only when an investigator has specific questions and concrete issues to discuss.

Deciding on a Title and Writing the Project Summary

Given how competitive NSF grants are, no detail is too small to attend to. Thus, we begin our advice at the very beginning of the proposal, the title and the Project Summary. As we noted earlier in this chapter, NSF funding for the behavioral sciences regularly comes under close scrutiny by politicians, the media, and the general public. The title of the project and the summary of the proposal are the most easily accessible parts of a proposal and are thus most readily scanned by people who might be skeptical of the value of research in the brain and behavioral sciences. Thus, it is important not only for the investigator, but also for NSF and the field, that the title and Project Summary convey the importance of the work clearly and broadly. In doing this, the researcher should avoid "clever" phrases that may be taken out of context and used by critics to argue for the esoteric or frivolous nature of social and behavioral research. In 2011, Senator Tom Coburn, in the report *National Science Foundation: Under the Microscope* (Coburn, 2011), argued that NSF used its funds wastefully, citing summaries of research that NSF supported. For example, he cited a project examining how and why the same leading (and winning) college basketball programs keep attracting the best recruits. Coburn wrote, "It seems obvious to most, but the mystery kept this team of researchers busy studying the phenomenon with the taxpayer support" (p. 27). In reality, the researcher used this situation mainly to test a larger theory about general forces that shape the way biological, physical, and psychological systems develop. Thus, researchers should carefully consider what they choose for a title and how they describe their proposed research in the Project Summary.

Writing the Project Description

External reviewers and panel members are instructed to attend to the scientific merit and broader impacts of the proposal, which are presented in the Project Description. Scientific merit is the primary criterion that reviewers focus on, and it is prerequisite to consideration of broader impacts.

As we noted earlier, the Project Description is strictly limited to 15 pages. The presentation thus has to be economical and persuasive. The concentration of information that is required in the Project Summary leads our main, overriding piece of advice: understand that everything counts. By everything we mean style as well as content, and supplementary as well as primary materials. Being a panel member puts extra demands on people's time and resources not only during the intensive two- to three-day meeting period but in the weeks leading up to it. Panel members are assigned several proposals as primary and secondary panel reviewers and read other proposals as well. The quality of the proposals is generally high, so their task is to separate the great from the near great.

Under such conditions, we, as psychologists, know that heuristics matter. Thus, it is important that proposals conform to the guidelines in format and be written carefully and in a fluent way. Before being submitted, an application needs to be closely read by as many people as possible and carefully proofread. As one fellow reviewer said about a typo-filled application, "If they are this sloppy with the application, how will they carry out the actual research?" Write the proposal for a scholarly audience, but try to avoid terms, acronyms, and jargon that apply to a narrow subfield. Even for many abbreviations (such a PFC for prefrontal cortex) that are widely recognized, be sure to define key terms as they are introduced. In addition, references need to be very current. Citing older references instead of relevant new work will raise questions about how up-to-date the investigator is and undermine any case that the proposed work is cutting edge.

A challenge that NSF staff perennially faces is trying to get established researchers to submit reviews for panel deliberations. One way investigators can help NSF and themselves is by citing the research of scholars who would be appropriate reviewers for the proposal. Although NSF program staff members have research training, the staffing is limited, and staff members do not have expertise in the vast variety of different topics eligible within even a single program. Our advice is to cite early and often scholars you would like to review your proposal. When there is an opportunity in the submission process to suggest the names of reviewers, do not be shy: suggest names. It is in NSF's best interest, as well as yours, that you identify the most qualified people to review your grant proposal. In addition, junior investigators can contact NSF about their availability to be reviewers, which will help them understand more about what an effective or ineffective proposal looks like.

Review panels are selected to represent diverse areas of expertise in the program area. It is thus critical to recognize that it is unlikely that you will get two panel members who have intimate knowledge of the particular avenue of your research. Therefore, your proposal needs to stand on its own. By this, we mean that an applicant should not assume that the reviewers will know who they are or, more importantly, be familiar with the problem of interest, the research approach one is taking, or the way in which data will be analyzed.

We have been extremely impressed with the care and thought displayed by reviewers and members of review panels, but the fact is that the assigned reviewers, although they are accomplished researchers, may not be accomplished in the specific area of your application. Like everyone else who has submitted an application, we have railed about the ignorance and biases of our reviewers, but the truth is that if a reviewer is confused about the importance of a project or does not understand the research approach an applicant has taken, that is the applicant's problem, not the reviewer's.

One strategy that we suggest using to address this problem, which is also recommended for proposals to other granting agencies, is to present a theoretical or conceptual model very early in the application, and, when possible, provide a diagram of the model (Jeffrey, 2009; Reid & Kobrin, 2009). A conceptual model helps readers understand the "big picture" of the proposed research, links the specific topic to reviewers' areas of expertise, foreshadows the organization of theoretical arguments, and creates a foundation for the progression of proposed studies. The conceptual model has to be simple and clear enough for readers who may not be familiar with the specific topic to comprehend it—too much complexity (e.g., too many arrows) will confuse readers—but be comprehensive enough to preview the main independent variables, processes and mechanisms, and outcomes studied, as well as the major proposed interrelationships. One question that panel members have to answer about the proposals they review is whether the work is potentially transformational. If you feel that your proposal is transformational methodologically and theoretically, you should make your case as you present your conceptual model. Do not be modest about pointing this out.

Like a multistudy research paper, researchers need to develop a tight, logical rationale for the proposed program of work. Some researchers invest too much time in presenting the reasoning behind the first study in the sequence, but, because of limited space and time, fail to adequately develop the chain of logic that ties the full set of studies together. Grant reviewers, including panel members, evaluate proposals like they review articles. The overall evaluation is a weighted average of the individual components and separate studies, with the weakest elements weighed most heavily. Sometimes researchers try to emphasize the relevance of the proposed research and tack on a brief concluding study, sketchy in methodology and contribution, that represents an intervention or other practical application of the ideas in the proposal. These are valuable endeavors, but when the investigator introduces a study with a vague description of how he or she will apply the findings from the first seven studies to create an intervention (e.g., to increase women's motivation to pursue a career in science), it weakens the proposal. Reviewers should not have to, and will not, take anything "on faith"; it is the investigator's responsibility to fully and explicitly develop all of the ideas and the tests of them explicitly. It is better to omit a study than to include one that is not well developed. More, in this case, does not mean better.

Methods, procedures, data-analytic procedures, and expected results have to be clearly but economically stated. One way to accomplish this is to include a section before the specific studies that describes specialized techniques and/or the operationalizations of independent and dependent variables that will be used across several of the proposed studies. Also, investigators should be sure that the analytic procedures described in the proposal are up-to-date and are explained well for reviewers unfamiliar with the procedures. Some consideration of power and anticipated effect sizes can be helpful for determining appropriate samples and justifying them for reviewers.

One critical feature of an NSF proposal is evidence of the feasibility and promise of the proposed line of research in terms of a pilot study or a recently published work that forms the basis of the proposal. In the former case, the data do not have to be perfect, but the pilot work has to illustrate that the methods and procedure are appropriate and produce interesting results. In the latter case, the feasibility of the work is strongly implicated, but the challenge will be to make a persuasive argument that the incremental knowledge that will be gained beyond the initially established evidence is sufficient for funding. From our experience, it is exceedingly rare for an NSF proposal to be funded without preliminary supporting data. Panel letters to investigators who have not been awarded a grant frequently ask for more pilot data.

One question we are commonly asked by colleagues who plan on submitting a grant proposal to NSF is about how many proposed studies should be included in the document. Of course, this is impossible to answer in the abstract. The time, expense, depth of investigator involvement varies dramatically across subdisciplines with various techniques and paradigms. Nevertheless, we offer some guidance about the length of the proposed research and the nature of the program of research described to help researchers think about what is right for them.

The maximum duration of a grant that NSF will fund is five years. CAREER grants, which involve support for professional development, *have* to be five years long. Because of their length and expense, very few CAREER grants get funded, despite NSF's efforts to have these in their grant portfolio. In our experience, other proposals for four to five years rarely get funded for that period. One of the main reasons is that all of the studies proposed are not sufficiently strong to merit full funding. The farther into a series of proposed studies an investigator goes, the more likely that studies will appear more speculative than solidly theoretically grounded. If there is enthusiasm for a four- to five-year proposal among reviewers, the panel often identifies the most promising ideas and studies, which gives the NSF staff guidance for making an award for a shorter period. This approach enables NSF to distribute its funds to support more researchers.

With respect to the right number of studies in a proposal, the norm is probably two per year, but reviewers understand that, depending on the problem and approach, there may be more or fewer studies in a given year. In terms of the lower limit, we have never seen a grant proposal—even one involving longitudinal designs—that has failed to promise sufficient data collection for analysis within one year.

What is more important than the number of studies is the progression. Proposed studies should show a clear, logical progression—avoiding redundancy while also avoiding overly complex designs. One grant proposal, for example, presented an initial study and then followed it with a second to address a potential confound. In this case, if there was a confound in the first study, then only the second study should have been proposed in the grant application. Another application was much too complex. The critical finding in the first study was an expected four-way interaction, and then subsequent studies were designed to show further moderation. Predicting a four-way interaction may be appropriate for understanding some questions, but it is risky. It is exceptionally hard to obtain such an interaction, particularly in a way that conforms to the hypothesized pattern. In the absence of a strong rationale for why it was necessary to begin the proposed research with such a complex design, reviewers had serious concerns about the feasibility of the project.

Even more common is the problem of redundancy. Another grant proposal was organized into three phases. The first set established a finding, the second set included potential mediators for the finding, and the third set looked at potential moderators. Further, within each phase, three studies used different operationalizations of the main independent variable. Although the programmatic nature of the proposal and the multioperational approach were careful and commendable, this was not a strong proposal. The reason is that many of the elements of the proposal—the primary hypothesized mediator and moderator—could have been incorporated into the design of the early studies, and once the convergent effects of different operationalizations were established, repeating three studies to make the same point was not economical. Our advice is to avoid proposing "experiments about experiments"—experiments to address a confound or limitation in another study that could have been readily addressed in the first place. And, make sure that there is a strong theoretical (not just methodological) progression across the suite of studies proposed.

One surprisingly frequent mistake investigators make in their proposal is failing to articulate its broader impacts. NSF's guidelines, which we reviewed earlier, directly state what qualifies for broader impacts, including educational or training benefits, the participation of underrepresented groups, and positive impact on society. If funding is requested for graduate research assistants or postdoctoral students, the training benefits for these students should be articulated. For requests for postdoctoral fellows, a separate mentoring plan is also required. The proposal should also explain how the experiences of undergraduate research assistants, if requested, will contribute to their education (e.g., giving them a broader perspective of the research process and a deeper understanding of methodological and technical aspects of research). For example, investigators could have these students participate in weekly laboratory meetings or keep a diary reflecting on their experiences. If the graduate or undergraduate assistants or study participants represent a racially and ethnically diverse student body, investigators might comment on this with respect to broader impacts in their proposal. In addition, it is valuable for researchers to explain why their work is valuable for society in general. Describing the practical implications of the research is not only helpful for making the case for the value of basic research to a general audience, but also it helps researchers develop skills for communicating to a broad audience.

NSF panels are particularly impressed when the presentation of broader impacts goes well beyond "boilerplate" text and minimal activities. For instance, researchers can develop a project-related webpage that makes links and other resources, study materials, and summaries of new findings available in ways that will appeal to other researchers and the general public. Other researchers have emphasized their relationships with local science museums and explained how the research can contribute to activities and displays at the museum, either as the studies are being conducted or after the data are collected. While not as important as the scientific merit in reviewers' evaluations, a strong and innovative explanation of broader impacts makes a proposal more compelling. As we have said, everything counts in NSF proposals.

Including Other Documentation and Supplementary Materials

As outlined in the proposal guidelines, NSF requires a lengthy list of materials and requests supplementary explanations about information in the narrative or budget. We highlight just a few types of materials here.

The budget and its justification obviously are important parts of the proposal. They are not part of the formal criteria used by reviewers (assessing and potentially revising the budget is the responsibility of NSF staff), but, informally, budget considerations may influence the overall evaluation of an application. Reviewers and panel members are a curious bunch, and we find it hard to resist looking through the budget. We are painfully aware that funds are limited at NSF, particularly given the increasing number of people applying each year. As a consequence, when we see a bloated budget, it creates a negative frame that may color other aspects of our assessment. For instance, in one proposal an investigator asked for more than $10,000 a year in travel funds to present at professional meetings. This amount is unrealistic. It leaves an impression of a scholar who is either naïve or greedy—either of which erodes a reviewer's confidence in the investigator and proposal. Researchers should also resist the urge to pad their budgets in anticipation that NSF will reduce the amount if the grant proposal is funded. An inflated budget can negatively bias reviewers, even when they try to prevent it from affecting their judgment of how well the proposal meets the stated criteria for scientific merit and broader impacts.

As we mentioned earlier, investigator biographical sketches of senior personnel also need to be included. A biographical sketch presents the person's professional preparation and appointments, up to five publications most closely related to the proposed project, and up to five examples of synergistic activities that demonstrate the impact that the individual has had in the creation, integration, and transfer of knowledge (e.g., curricular developments or pedagogical innovation). This biographical information is important for establishing credibility with reviewers, who may not be familiar with the investigator's relevant background and achievements.

A Data Management Plan is now required for NSF proposals. The primary presenter at the panel meeting describes the plan to the rest of the panel and comments on its adequacy. However, an assessment of the strength of the plan is not part of the formal evaluation of the merits of the proposal; the plan just has to be there. A minimal Data Management Plan states that the anonymity of participants will be protected and data will be securely stored (as institutional review boards normally require) and that data will be made available to other researchers after the data are published (a current requirement of the American Psychological Association). This is adequate for NSF. Nevertheless, a good plan leaves a good impression for reviewers. Some successful researchers, for example, offer to make their stimuli, measures, and procedures immediately available to other researchers (e.g., on a website). Others mention that they will consider requests for data even before the data are fully mined for publication. Investigators are not penalized for being protective, but hearing a panel presenter describe a generous and imaginative data-sharing plan generally creates a positive frame in the discussion of a proposal.

Also, as we noted previously, if a postdoctoral scholar is requested in the funding, investigators must include a mentoring plan (with a one-page limit). According to the NSF guidelines, "Mentoring activities include, but are not limited to: career counseling; training in preparation of grant proposals, publications and presentations; guidance on ways to improve teaching and mentoring skills; . . . and training in responsible professional practices" (NSF, 2010, p. II-19). Mentoring a postdoctoral scholar is a training activity, and thus evaluation of the mentoring plan is associated with the assessment of the broader impacts of the work.

Final Thoughts

Writing a proposal to NSF for a grant is extremely challenging. It requires the skill and knowledge that are needed to publish multistudy papers in leading professional journals. It also demands the creative vision to look beyond a current finding or immediate interest to devise and describe a plan of study for several years into the future. And, the proposal has to be written in a succinct scholarly way to impress distinguished experts in the field and be clear and accessible to scholars in different areas. In this chapter, we have provided basic information about the mission and structure of NSF, the review process, and the organization of NSF proposals in a way that will help readers understand what is needed for writing an effective proposal. We have supplemented this information with advice based on experiences in applying for grants and serving as reviewers and on grant panels.

One point that should be clear from our discussion is that you cannot start preparing a grant application too early. For most programs, NSF has fixed submission dates and will not consider proposals that come in late for that round of reviews. Besides the effort that has to be devoted to writing the grant proposal and the number of supplementary materials that have to be provided with the application, a proposal needs various types of review and approval at your institution. Listen carefully, and you will frequently hear frazzled colleagues respond when asked to do service for the institution or profession say, "I can't. I have a grant proposal due soon." After you write your first grant, you will immediately understand; it is difficult to comprehend the intensity of the enterprise without personally experiencing it.

Because of the number of proposals submitted and the high standards of reviewers, it is very difficult to receive NSF funding. However, the odds are no worse than getting a manuscript published in a top journal. As with the journal process, it is rare that a proposal gets funded on the first try, and responsiveness to reviewer comments and perseverance are critical. However, even if a grant application is not funded, the preparation of a proposal allows a researcher to step back from the day-to-day demands on their time to envision a coherent program of research for several years to come—an exercise valuable for scholars at any stage of their career.

References

Blumenstyk, G., & Brainard, J. (2011, July 6). Few finance chiefs are optimistic in face of slow recovery. *Chronicle of Higher Education*. Retrieved from http://chronicle.com/article/Few-Finance-Chiefs-Are/128134/.

Breckler, S. (2005, July). *Again the target: The National Science Foundation faces funding challenges.* Retrieved from http://www.apa.org/science/about/psa/2005/07/ed-column.aspx.

Coburn, T. (2011, April). *National Science Foundation: Under the microscope.* Retrieved from http://www.coburn.senate.gov/public/index.cfm?a=Files.serve&File_id=2dccf06d-65fe-4087-b58d-b43ff68987fa.

Jeffrey, D. (2009, May). *Writing a seamless grant application.* Presentation at the New Investigator Workshop, National Cancer Institute, Washington, D.C.

Lane, C. (2012, June 4). Congress should cut funding for political science research. *Washington Post Opinions*. Retrieved from http://www.washingtonpost.com/opinions/congress-should-cut-funding-for-political-science-research/2012/06/04/gJQAuAJMEV_story.html.

The National Academies. (2010). *Research doctorate programs: Board of higher education and workforce.* Retrieved from http://sites.nationalacademies.org/pga/Resdoc/index.htm.

National Science Foundation (NSF). (2002). *NSF proposal processing and review.* Retrieved from http://www.nsf.gov/pubs/2002/nsf022/nsf0202_3.html.

National Science Foundation (NSF). (2007). *Merit review broader impacts criterion: Representative activities.* Retrieved from http://www.nsf.gov/pubs/gpg/broaderimpacts.pdf.

National Science Foundation (NSF). (2009). *What we do.* Retrieved from www.nsf.gov/about/what.jsp.

National Science Foundation (NSF). (2010). *National Science Foundation proposal and award policies and procedure guide.* Retrieved from http://www.nsf.gov/pubs/policydocs/pappguide/nsf11001/nsf11_1.pdf.

Reid, B., & Kobrin, S. (2009, May). *Common flaws in initial applications.* Presentation at the New Investigator Workshop, National Cancer Institute, Washington, D.C.

Reinhold, R. (1981, April 21). U.S. states to withdraw all support for social research. *New York Times.* Retrieved from http://www.nytimes.com/1981/04/21/science/us-states-to-withdraw-all-support-for-social-research.html.

Russell, S. W., & Morrison, D. C. (2010). *The grant application writer's workbook.* Paper presented at Grant Writers' Seminars & Workshops, LLC, Los Olivos, CA.

10

Obtaining Department of Defense Funding for Research in the Behavioral Sciences

Susan E. F. Chipman

The various agencies of the U.S. Department of Defense (DOD) have long been a major source of funding for behavioral science research. The early development of the Army Alpha test of mental abilities during World War I is well known, but it was during World War II that behavioral science research, like many other kinds of scientific research came to play an important role in the war effort. In 1946, the Office of Naval Research (ONR), the agency with which I am most familiar, was founded to continue the relationships with the university research community that had proved so useful during the war. Behavioral science was included in the research program from the beginning, although social science fields such as sociology and economics were not. ONR preceded the National Science Foundation; a couple of years later, some employees of ONR were assigned to work on the creation of NSF. The DOD agencies are, of course, *mission-oriented* research agencies; they exist to foster the development of scientific research in areas that are relevant to the military. What this means may not be immediately obvious to many. One thing it has meant is a major emphasis on normal psychology, as opposed to the psychology of mental illness that tends to be emphasized in the National Institutes of Health (NIH).

The military services are very large organizations with large numbers of employees. Thus, they have been concerned with improving the approach to selecting employees and assigning them to appropriate jobs. A recent example of DOD-supported psychometric research was the development of the underlying technology needed for computerized adaptive testing, which is faster and more efficient than traditional testing. This was done to create a computerized adaptive version of the Armed Services Vocational Aptitude Battery (ASVAB), but its first implementation was to an Educational Testing Service (ETS) placement battery for postsecondary use, and a computerized adaptive Graduate Record Examination (GRE) came soon afterwards. Training people efficiently for a wide array of sometimes exotic jobs has always been a major concern. The annual cost of training in the Navy alone has typically been estimated as $15 billion. The viewgraph machine was invented by a Navy training laboratory during World War II as a method for standardizing the content of training courses, providing standard sets of transparencies to course instructors. The technology of instructional systems design, which has by now migrated into civilian curriculum development, was also a creation of DOD funding. Flying is an example of military job training that comes readily to mind, but the maintenance of all kinds of very sophisticated and specialized equipment is a major concern. For many of those jobs, substantial initial training in basic electricity and electronics is a prerequisite. This training is the largest single "course" in the Navy and is also very big in both the Army and Air Force. Officer training can range from relatively straightforward skills like flying and ship driving to military tactics and strategies—such as in tank warfare—and efforts to develop sophisticated decision-making skills and leadership skills. General management skills, such as are taught in civilian master of business administration programs, are another major area for officer training. Many people in civilian employment actually receive their training in the military before going on to civilian employment as pilots, electronics technicians, or cooks. The military services also provide society with large numbers of people trained in the elements of fire-fighting and basic first aid, as well as trained medics. Training in specific warfighting skills also exists, of course, especially in the Army and Marine Corps, but it represents only a small fraction of military training.

Some military jobs push the limits of what people can do—in high-speed operations such as flying military jets, enormous amounts of information must be processed and considered in time-pressured decision making while multitasking. Consequently, human performance capabilities are another major focus of DOD behavioral science research. This is beginning to extend into modern human factors approaches to the design of equipment and computer systems to be as usable and helpful to human operators as is possible.

It is particularly important to avoid designing equipment that makes demands exceeding what the human operator will be able to do. That has happened.

Of course, especially during times of actual war, the DOD also has a special concern for ameliorating the human consequences of war: cognitive and other kinds of rehabilitation, the design of better prostheses, and the treatment of posttraumatic stress disorder. Programs supporting this type of work would typically be found under military medical programs or agencies.

Finding a Home for Your Research Interests in DOD

Obviously, a large percentage of behavioral science researchers will be able to find some relationship between their research interests and the interests of DOD. However, the single most important thing to understand about DOD is that the actual current interests of DOD agencies are constantly changing, as are the funds currently available for making new grant awards. It is *extremely important,* even if sometimes difficult, to make contact with DOD program officers to find out what the current interests and prospects for funding actually are. As I write in the fall of 2012, the situation is particularly uncertain because of the failure of Congress to pass a budget and the likelihood of severe budget cuts. Agency websites are typically outdated and state interests in terms that are broader and more abstract than the actual funding actions at a particular time. There is no substitute for current personal contact, which can save researchers a great deal of wasted effort and can significantly increase the probability of funding. A conversation between the funds-seeking researcher and a program officer can bridge the gap between the researcher's interest and the agency's interests. For example, I would often suggest that a researcher interested in basic research on problem solving choose to explore those issues in the context of basic electricity and electronics, a topic of obvious potential application to military training. If the research questions are truly basic, it should be possible to explore them in a variety of contexts. Certainly, I would counsel a researcher away from toy problems or other types of problems that might be open to Congressional ridicule. Although the choice of such research topics may be justifiable from a purely scientific point of view, they can jeopardize the funding of entire research programs and damage the interests of the entire research community, as periodic Congressional attacks on behavioral science programs at the National Science Foundation (NSF) illustrate. Researchers themselves are not always very good at recognizing and explaining the relevance of their work to agency research priorities. I have read many a silly claim in that section of the standard NIH application form. Knowing how typical research projects relate to big important questions is part of the job of the program officer, and good program officers serve as brokers between the interests of the researcher and the interests of the agency.

A vague relation between the researcher's interests and the interests of the agency is not enough. This is well illustrated by what typically happens when an agency issues an RFP (request for proposals) for some specific, quite well-defined piece of research. The bottom-ranking half of the proposals will be distinguished from the top half by whether or not the person proposing carefully read the RFP and seriously tried to address what the agency was asking for. The bottom half will have been submitted by people who perceived some vague relation between the topic of the RFP and their research. They will have wasted their time. The same point applies to broader and more open competitions, but in a more subtle way. RFPs for specific research studies are usually well publicized because the agency is very interested in having the specific research done. Sometimes many proposals will be submitted, but an RFP is likely to be issued because the agency is not receiving proposals for the type of research desired. In that case, very few proposals may come in because no one is currently doing closely related research. This situation can be a good opportunity for someone who is qualified to do the research and willing to adapt his or her research interests to what the agency is asking for. Sometimes no award will be made if no proposal adequately addresses what is asked for, and there may be a recompetition aiming for a better proposal.

The Typical, Traditional Interests of the Various DOD Research Agencies

Despite the picture of constant change, some traditional interest areas characterize each of the agencies. Some topics are more relevant for one service than for another. Furthermore, it is always politically important to avoid the perception of "overlap" in agency programs. Although perceived overlap may be very superficial, it can lead to Congressional perceptions that too much money is going to the topic of overlap and thus to budget cuts. Consequently, the agencies adjust their programs to the larger context of research funding, which may include attention to what agencies outside of DOD, such as the National Institutes of Health, are doing. In the following sections, I attempt to summarize the long-term interests of the various DOD agencies as well as some significant changes that have happened over time. Because I worked for the ONR for 22 years managing programs related to cognitive science, I obviously know most about ONR and will begin with that agency.

The Office of Naval Research

As noted earlier, ONR was founded immediately after World War II, and has always had more of a basic research character than the other DOD agencies, although the pendulum has swung along the basic to applied continuum from time to time. DOD actually has a legal definition of basic research funds (also known as 6.1 funds) but that definition is obviously subjective and can vary quite a bit in practice. Some 6.2 funds (applied research) have also been spent through ONR. One reason ONR tended to more basic research was that it reported directly to the Secretary of the Navy until recent years, rather than to high level operational military officers who tend to have rather short-term interests and goals.

ONR's target application areas for the results that may be achieved in basic research have always included training and they continue to do so. Although psychometrics was once a significant area of activity (ONR had the lead role in developing the technology to support the computerized adaptive ASVAB), psychometric research is no longer supported. In recent years, human factors—the design of more effective human-system interaction—has emerged as a more significant target application for ONR. Like psychometrics, however, more traditional human factors research is no longer supported in the program. There was once a large social psychology program at ONR, but it is no more. As I pointed out earlier, the military services are very large organizations, so the questions of social and organizational psychology are very relevant to them. However, there are often issues of quality in the way those questions are addressed. In ONR, an organization dominated by physical scientists and engineers, perceived lack of rigor was a particularly severe problem. It was exacerbated by the fact that the program officers responsible for presenting and defending the program were not very good. Even I, a psychologist, did not find them very convincing. Unfortunately, a major emphasis of the social psychology program was studying small-group processes, typically in randomly assembled groups of college students from the subject pool. This had little perceived relevance to military organizations or even small teams, where there are organizationally defined and important authority relationships, relatively long-term working relationships, and so on. Currently, there is a small program dealing with social networks, seen as relevant to the problems posed by terrorism. This was initiated by a program officer with a background in anthropology. It has attracted much interest from other agencies and even some contributions to the funding of the program.

The money that had been supporting social psychology was redirected to neuroscience of a quite basic character. Several factors contributed to that decision. ONR's pendulum was then at the extreme basic end of its periodic swings, making neuroscience an attractive choice, even though its possible applications for the Navy were very distant. The department head at the time was a neuroscientist and came to the job thinking (incorrectly, I must say) that neuroscience was generally underfunded. Needless to say, neuroscience was then, as now, a fashionable area of research. As the pendulum began to swing back in the applied direction—largely as a consequence of the fall of the Soviet Union, the neuroscience program began to be seen as a source of ideas for reverse engineering of artificial systems of sensors and effectors. Today the relevant department is named the *Warfighter Performance Department* and the relevant Division is called *Human and Bioengineered Systems.* The other medically oriented division in the department is called *Warfighter Protection and Applications.* (The term *warfighter* was never heard at ONR until after the fall of the Soviet Union.)

Armed with this terminology, a funds-seeking researcher can go to the main ONR website: www.onr.navy.mil. As of this writing, the following describes the appearance and behavior of the website. It may change. On the opening page, you want to click on 34 (also known in some places as Code 34). A picture of a robot illustrates this department currently, even though this is where you will find the research programs concerned with humans. There is a somewhat random list of program names on this page. If one of these programs strikes your interest, clicking on it will get you to a program description and the name of the responsible program officer. Asking to see all programs will get you to a page, including the two divisions in the department. Underneath the divisions, you will find various program names. Clicking on those will lead you to the names of individual program officers, with their contact information. These are the people you need to talk to, although you may well find that the specific programs and funding opportunities have changed since the site was last updated.

The fact that a program is listed does not necessarily mean that the named program is a continuing interest with dedicated funds. It may have been a special event with short-term funding that has been completely spent, although the funded research projects are still active. It may simply be an emphasized theme within one of the major continuing programs that does have dedicated funding. For example, I had such a theme called *Tutorial Discourse*—aiming at true natural language interaction capability for artificially intelligent tutoring systems. That theme lasted for 15 years but was simply part of the larger Cognitive Science program and had no dedicated funds of its own. These examples illustrate the importance, once again, of contacting the particular program officers.

Another path you might be tempted to take from the main page of the ONR site that appears under "Quick Links" is called, "Explore Research Opportunities." Unfortunately, this path will not get you to information about the program officers you need to talk to or to descriptions of funding opportunities in the behavior sciences. One thing you will find there is the list of current broad agency announcements (BAAs). The legal basis of nearly all awards from ONR is a very broad annual BAA saying that ONR is interested in virtually all of science and technology. Generally, grants are made to universities and other eligible nonprofit organizations. Contracts are made to for-profit organizations, although on occasion ONR might enter into a contract with a university to have tighter control on the work that is done and the products delivered. ONR is now using the governmentwide application form to be found on grants.gov.

Obviously, anything I currently say about how to find things on the ONR website could change tomorrow. This is particularly true because I have pointed out some of the current shortcomings to current staff members, in the hopes that there will be changes. The primary message is that you should be persistent in finding the information you need to find—program descriptions and the names and contact information for program officers. Don't give up when an apparently obvious link, like "Exploring research opportunities" does not work for you.

Younger researchers will be tempted to rely on Web information, but that is not a good idea. Agency websites are almost always outdated because administrative support services for these agencies are always underfunded.

The Importance of Program Officers

As noted earlier, it is very important to contact program officers to get up-to-date information about programs and the availability of funds for new grants. Sometimes the programs have large existing grant commitments and tight budgets or budget cuts can result in situations where there is little or no money for new grants. In such circumstances, you do not want to waste your time writing proposals that have no chance of funding, and the program officer will let you know. ONR has never encouraged the submission of excessive numbers of proposals as an approach to arguing that more funding is needed. If the research you want to do is not suited to current program interests, the program officer will let you know. This will save you the effort of writing and submitting a proposal that has very little chance of getting funded. If the program officer sees some promise in your research interests, the program officer may make suggestions about how to modify what you are proposing in a way that will make it more fundable. Typically, this might involve changing the context in which you are addressing your general question to one that has more face validity or relates to a current emphasis in more applied ONR projects, such as shipboard fire-fighting.

Within a very broad program area like *Cognitive Science*, the program officer will typically be emphasizing just a few topics at any given time. This happens for several reasons. Obviously, there is never enough money to support everything good in a broad area like cognitive science. Program officers at ONR are responsible for doing periodic reviews of the work in their programs, pointing to research accomplishments that may be accumulating to the point where one can hope for meaningful applications. Program officers are also expected to promote those applications, to try to make them happen. These responsibilities shape the programs in ways that are different from similar programs at NSF or NIH They mean that it is important to have a coherent program that one can talk about. The ideal standard for program officers at ONR was always to define a focus with exactly the right breadth to match the money available. I tried to do that but I also thought it would be nice to have more money, and I constantly tried to get it. A consequence of the defined, coherent focus is that occasionally proposals that are merely okay but not great may be funded because they fill an important gap in such a program focus, something that must be done before applications are feasible. In a few cases, I even worked with young, inexperienced researchers to improve their research approach to addressing such a high priority gap. At times other, higher quality proposals or research ideas within the broad topic area of the program may not be funded if they do not contribute to such a focus.

By the time a program officer encourages a researcher to submit a proposal to ONR, the probability of funding is high. Sometimes the quality of the actual proposal is disappointing, so it will not get funded. Sometimes there may be unexpected budget cuts so that money is no longer available. In addition to telephone conversations, these all-important conversations with program officers may take place at scientific meetings. ONR program officers typically attend the annual meetings of scientific societies relevant to their programs. If asked by the meeting organizers to appear on a panel of funding agency representatives, ONR program officers will typically agree—it is part of the job. Sometimes organizations do not bother to organize such panels. And, when they do, the audiences tend to be small. I have never forgotten a regional meeting of the Society for Research in Child Development that took place in Alexandria, Virginia. Because of the location of the meeting, a panel of agency representatives included several very high-ranking people from the National Institute of Child Health and Human Development. I was there as a representative of the National Institute of Education. Our audience was tiny because there was a competing cocktail party, where no doubt people were complaining about the difficulty of obtaining funding!

Another reason it is important to talk to the ONR program officer is that the program officer will likely be the reviewer who decides whether to fund your proposal. The program officer may ask other researchers, inside or outside the agency, to review the proposal and offer an opinion, but that is quite rare. This is very different from the typical review processes of agencies like NSF or NIH. At ONR, you will usually know the audience for your proposal. A few special competitions are exceptions to this rule. Also, for some reason, the biologists at ONR typically used panels of paid reviewers, organized by a professional society, to review their proposals. Because reviewing proposals is a large fraction of program officers' workload, if you submit a proposal without any prior conversations, especially if you let the grants.gov operation tempt you into submitting a proposal to ONR that was intended for the National Institute of Mental Health, you will just overburden and alienate the program officer. Individual program officer funding decisions are reviewed and approved (or rarely disapproved) by their superiors, but this is usually a cursory review based on what is written about the project in the document recommending funding that goes to the contracts office. This situation makes ONR program officer jobs much more interesting than most. ONR program officers have real power of decision.

In addition, program officers usually determine what the actual program foci within the general program area will be. Consequently, it makes a great deal of difference who the program officer is, what the program officer's personal interests are, and how good the program officer is. When I joined ONR, I was quite familiar with the cognitive science program (then still called Personnel and Training Research) and admired the program a great deal. Therefore, I did not make any radical changes in the program. However, when I was soon required to conduct a major program review, I found that developing a coherent organization for the entire program was quite a challenge. The program had broad and spotty coverage. Also, a large proportion of the total program was in a temporary funding line destined to end soon. For that reason, I began to refine the program, emphasizing what I perceived to be unique about the ONR program in the context of the overall federal funding scene. In part, I wanted to avoid the appearance of overlap with other agency programs. There were quite a few other sources of support for cognitive experimental psychology: NIMH, NSF, the Air Force Office of

Scientific Research, and the Army Research Institute. ONR was already known for an emphasis on computational modeling of cognition. Therefore, I gradually made that the primary focus of the Cognitive Science program at ONR, eventually refining that emphasis to computational cognitive architectures. Another major emphasis of the ONR program had been artificially intelligent tutoring, largely an artificial intelligence activity but with important components of the psychology of learning and instruction. In fact, a large finite life program with that focus had just begun. Most of that money was unspent when I joined ONR in 1984. By the time that special program ended, there had been so much progress that artificially intelligent tutoring was becoming an applied enterprise. So, I turned my emphasis for this ONR tradition to the basic unsolved research problem of true natural language interaction capability for such systems, an effort I funded out of the regular core Cognitive Science funds. Initially, it was hard to find anyone to do this work, so funds were not a problem.

Interestingly, ONR's first award for research on artificially intelligent tutoring was made in 1966. The first practical tutor for a Navy training application appeared 30 years later. Perhaps this is a typical time span from initial basic research investments to application. The lithium battery, one of ONR's proudest accomplishments, also took 30 years.

Although I did not make radical program changes, the retirement or departure of a program officer, or the hiring of a new program officer often means a radical change in the program. When my primary predecessor was hired at ONR, he was ordered to terminate the funding of all the famous verbal learning researchers who had been supported by ONR for a long time. When the program officer who had managed the psychometric research at ONR left, that meant the end of psychometric research at ONR. The money was reallocated to neuroscience research, not to the cognitive program. If the psychometric program officer had remained at ONR, the money probably would have been used for research bridging the gap between psychometrics and modern cognitive theory—our managers had already been pushing that new emphasis. Special funding was allocated for an initial set of grants (Nichols, Chipman, & Brennan, 1995), and there had been a couple of related conferences previously. My own primary successor as a cognitive science program officer came from a background in artificial intelligence and philosophy, not cognitive psychology. Therefore, he is less concerned about the psychological validity of cognitive models than I was. Also, he is less concerned about the potential applications in training than I was, even though training remains a huge issue for the Navy. This may be explained by the fact that, unlike me, he was not hired into a program that was called Personnel and Training Research. He is interested in natural language interaction, but not particularly in the focus on tutorial dialog for training applications. These examples illustrate the importance of communicating with program officers and understanding the social organization of the personnel who make funding decisions.

Another way in which program officers are very important is their role in maintaining program funding and obtaining new program funding. As mentioned earlier, a less than excellent program officer can result in the demise of a program. This happened to the social psychology program at ONR, which had been one of the relatively stable so-called core programs with a relatively large budget. The chief program officer did not make the program sound good when he reviewed it. Before our department head was permitted to terminate the program and reallocate the funds to his preferred field of neuroscience, his superiors required him to conduct an external review of the program. Unfortunately, the chairman of the review committee recommended that all the funds be dedicated to research of the type done by the chairman and his students. A grant competition with that focus was conducted, demonstrating that the program had far too much money for that narrow and not particularly military relevant focus. There are two lessons here for members of research communities: individuals with broad interests and good presentation skills may want to consider a career as a program officer as a way of making an important contribution to the field. Second, if asked to serve on an advisory committee, you should behave in a statesman-like manner, considering the interests of the field as a whole, not just your own interests.

Another somewhat similar event occurred during my time at ONR. Decision-making research (so-called) had been supported by ONR for many years, notably including the famous research of Kahneman and Tversky but also much more similar research. Shortly after I joined ONR, a workshop was convened at the National Academy of Sciences to inform ONR's own decision making. The decision-making researchers supported by ONR participated but so did people who were more concerned with actual military decision making in the field. As a relatively neutral observer, my own conclusion after this workshop was, "Never the twain shall meet." Somebody should have been working on bridging the gap for years. ONR ceased supporting that kind of research. In contrast, during a short period of service in the Army Research Institute basic research office, Dr. Judith Orasanu did initiate a new research direction, Naturalistic Decision Making, that did tend to close that gap.

Program officers contribute in a more positive way by competing for additional money that they will then be able to give away in grants. During much of the time I was at ONR, there were formal contests for money in which program officers could compete for money by proposing new program ideas. Although there were some short written documents associated with these competitions, they were primarily based on oral presentations with a short time limit—very challenging and nerve-racking. It isn't that often that one gives a 15-minute talk on which $5 million depends. The source of funds for these competitions was other finite life programs that were ending and funds shaved out of the relatively stable so-called core programs. So, it was necessary to compete to maintain or perhaps increase the funds for one's programs. Success was by no means certain. One of my notable successes was a very early (before functional magnetic resonance imaging) neurocognitive science program called Neural Constraints on Cognitive Architecture. It was partially inspired by interesting results that existing ONR grantees Posner and Kosslyn had obtained with positron emission tomography scanning and more importantly by the fact that the first hurdle on the way to success was my department head, a neuroscientist. I was able to make this proposal because, as a graduate student in psychology at Harvard, I had been required to study physiological psychology and take a preliminary exam on that topic. So I knew much more about the brain than did most cognitive psychologists at that time.

There were two other ways in which program officers could compete for money. One was competitions for multidisciplinary university research initiatives (MURIs), which are conducted at the DOD level, with the Assistant Secretary of Defense for Research and Engineering being the decision maker, after initial competitions within the various agencies. These competitions came into existence about halfway through my ONR career. These MURIs were for a single (usually) very large grant on the topic proposed by the program officer(s), initially for three years, with a two-year renewal likely. I had two successes in the MURI competitions. After several years of investment in research on tutorial discourse and much research progress, I obtained a MURI topic called Tutorial Dialog. In this case, two awards were made. Another was called Automated Skills for Cognitive Readiness and specifically called for the use of fMRI imaging. In these competitions, the internal proposal was a short written document. Once a MURI topic was selected for funding, the opportunity was widely announced, and the proposals, unlike others at ONR, were reviewed by an ad hoc review committee that had to include at least some representatives from all three services.

Another way in which program officers could make specific proposals for money was in the small business innovation research (SBIR) programs, either within the agency or service or at the level of the Office of the Secretary of Defense (OSD). The small business lobby has been very successful in having Congress set aside an increasing proportion of each research agency's funding for small business contractors. Different agencies run small business programs in different ways. In some agencies, the research topics are unrestricted, but in DOD, a set of specific research topics is announced each year, selected from topics submitted by program officers. Some guidance as to the character of desired topics is provided each year by the Office of the Secretary of Defense. Although the money that is used for SBIR competitions may be officially designated as basic research money, few small businesses have basic research capability so the topics tend to be somewhat applied in character. For program officers, the SBIR program can be a way to move promising basic research results toward application. There were also some cases in which the OSD guidance encouraged topics that were not of great interest to my program but were topics for which there were appropriately qualified companies working in psychology, so I made SBIR proposals to create opportunities for them. A few good researchers who know how to write very good proposals have made a very successful business by competing in the sheltered SBIR world. For example, after the breakup of Bell Labs, Tom Landauer and his wife Lynn Streeter founded a company called Knowledge Acquisition Technologies and won many SBIR awards from various agencies because they wrote excellent proposals. Similarly, Alan Gevins won many SBIR awards for his company, mostly from NIH. To compete for SBIR awards, researchers need to form a legitimate small business and get it certified as eligible. Many such small businesses are tiny, but they must have at least one person for whom the small business is primary employment. In other words, a university faculty member alone cannot constitute an eligible small business.

These stories may have provided some insight into the many factors that influence the research funding opportunities that are actually available at any given time.

The Air Force Office of Scientific Research

The history of the Air Force Office of Scientific Research (AFOSR) is very similar to that of ONR. It was founded a few years later than ONR (1950) with similar purposes. It is a basic research agency making grants to external researchers, like ONR, and has always been smaller than ONR. For behavioral scientists, the relevant department at AFOSR is called Mathematics, Information and Life Sciences. The relevant programs currently listed include Sensory Information Systems, which addresses audition as well as vision; Mathematical Modeling of Cognition and Decision Making; and Collective Behavior and Social Modeling. There is also a program called Information Fusion, which is primarily a computer science program. Traditionally, visual perception has been a major interest area of AFOSR for obvious reasons. Although ONR invested a great deal of research money into both visual and auditory perception in the past, these areas are no longer emphasized at ONR, so AFOSR represents better opportunities for perception researchers. Also, the mathematical psychology of decision making, which was dropped by ONR, remains a current interest of AFOSR, as does more general mathematical modeling of cognition, as opposed to the computational modeling approaches emphasized by ONR. Although not mentioned in the current language, circadian rhythms have also been of interest to AFOSR, again for rather obvious reasons. At one point, I referred a friend who is a physiological psychologist/ neuroscientist to AFOSR because she was concerned that her longtime NIH grant might not be renewed because of a budget crunch at NIH. She did receive a grant from AFOSR, and her NIH grant was renewed as well. This research used animal subjects, not humans, illustrating the basic research orientation of AFOSR. Collective Behavior and Social Modeling is a new direction for AFOSR, reflecting the realities of modern warfare that require collaboration with countries that have very different cultures from our own. Funding for this new direction was obtained by one of the program officers.

This has been a time of great turnover in the program officers at AFOSR. Before writing this chapter, when I was doing research to update my knowledge of AFOSR, I found that most of the listed program officers were no longer there. One longtime program officer who remains is Dr. Willard Larkin (willard.larkin@afosr.af.mil), whose primary responsibility is the Sensory Information Systems program. It appears that AFOSR has been using short-timers on leave from university jobs as program officers in recent years, rather like NSF.

AFOSR Grant Submission and Review Processes

At one time, AFOSR programs were operated much like ONR programs, with the program officers being very much independent decision makers. However, a new division head came in and instituted a standing panel of external reviewers, at least for the Life Sciences area. This panel no longer exists, but program officers are now required to obtain at least three external reviews for each proposal. These reviews are merely advisory to the program officers who are still the primary decision makers. Although few researchers realize it, the advisory status of reviews is the rule across all the government funding agencies, certainly at NSF. At NSF, I have observed that the relative importance of the reviews versus the program officer varies a great deal. Not all NSF programs have panel reviews, although that has been the rule for the behavioral sciences.

For grants submission, AFOSR uses the grants.gov form and system. However, Dr. Larkin informed me that proposals intended for him have sometimes failed to reach him. He strongly recommends sending proposals directly to the relevant AFOSR program officer. Everything I said about the importance of finding and talking with the relevant ONR program officer applies to AFOSR as well. When I referred my neuroscientist friend to AFOSR, I had great difficulty persuading her to make a phone call to a program officer, even though she already had a long and successful scientific career. She was not used to calling program officers at NIH (although that can be useful also). Once she made the call, in her case, funding came soon afterwards.

When I first looked at the AFOSR site researching for this chapter, it had not been updated for a long time and the program officer information was obsolete. Calling the telephone number given for a program may work, or you can call the division head's office to identify the appropriate current program officer. While I was working on this chapter, the AFOSR website was updated but became much more difficult to find. A search for AFOSR or even the direct entry of what was its Web address (afosr.af.mil) now takes you to the website of AFHRL (Air Force Human Resources Laboratory, with headquarters in Dayton, Ohio). Technically, AFOSR is a subordinate organization to AFHRL, so you must be somewhat persistent now to find its site. However, the offices of AFOSR are currently in Arlington, Virginia, in the same building as ONR, only about two blocks away from NSF.

The Army Research Institute

External research grants for basic research in the behavioral sciences have been given out of a small basic research office within the Army Research Institute for the Behavioral and Social Sciences (ARI), a large applied research laboratory currently located in Arlington, Virginia. (Other areas of science are handled by the Army Research Office [ARO], located in the Research Triangle Area. Occasionally, ARO has handled MURI competitions and project management in behavioral science areas, meaning the responsible program officer is likely to be a mathematician or computer scientist.) Traditionally there were three applied labs within ARI, one dealing with training, one with personnel management, and a third dealing with human factors research. The human factors lab has now moved to a different organization and is located on the north side of the Washington area.

ARI's Research Interests

Almost every year, ARI issues a statement of its current interests, the research topics for which proposals are being invited. In 2011, the announcement of interests was not issued until April with a submission deadline of September 30. Even though a researcher, a current ARI grantee, told me it had been issued, I had difficulty finding it. It did not appear on the ARI website. This happened because ARI does not have its own contracting office and uses the services of other agencies to do its contracting. The announcement of interests had been issued on a site called FedBizOpps, a successor to the Commerce Business Daily, on which all kinds of government contracting opportunities are announced. Lucky researchers may have efficient university contracts and grants offices that will alert them to relevant announcements of opportunity. Again, direct contact with program officers is advised. You should be able to get on a mailing list to receive these announcements when they are issued.

This is what the announcement said about current research interests:

> While all proposals will be considered, ARI has identified the following domains as especially germane to its basic research needs. This list is neither comprehensive nor exclusive and ARI is especially open to proposals that combine or cut across these domains. Further, proposals that adopt multi- or interdisciplinary approaches to research questions are encouraged. These domains include:
>
> 1. Training and Learning
>
> 2. Leadership
>
> 3. Human Resources
>
> 4. Organizational Effectiveness
>
> 5. Socio-cultural Capabilities
>
> 6. Affect and Emotions

The current head of the Basic Research Office at ARI, as of this writing, is Dr. Jay Goodwin (jay.goodwin@us.army.mil). Talking with him, I found out that the expectation was that only one new grant would be made in each of these areas, because of budgetary limitations. Although the current basic research portfolio includes a large contract aiming to update the cognitive modeling approach heavily used in the human factors lab with approaches taken from John Anderson's ACT-R, the basic research needs in the human factors area are now being met through a different funding approach and a different organization because the applied human factors lab is no longer part of ARI.

Proposal Submission and Review Processes

ARI is not participating in grants.gov. In fact, the ARI basic research awards are no longer grants but are contracts, even though the recipients are usually university researchers. This change was made because some grantees did not do what they promised to do with their money. Contracts provide somewhat more control over the use of money. The periodic announcements provide submission information. The goal, incidentally, is to make these announcements in March with a submission deadline in July and funding in October, the beginning of the federal fiscal year. However, various bureaucratic problems, especially Congressional delays in passing the federal budget, frequently make that schedule impossible to achieve.

Proposals are reviewed by the many psychologists staffing the applied research labs of ARI. For that reason, the review outcome is likely to be influenced by the relevance of the proposal to the applied research programs of the ARI labs and a promise for future applied research to be conducted in the ARI labs.

Basic Research in the Human Factors Area

When the Soviet Union fell, resulting in significant budget cuts across all of DOD, the basic research budget at ARI was suddenly cut from about $6 million per year to about $2 million. About that time, the entire ARI organization was also seriously threatened with abolition. It proved bureaucratically difficult to restore the previous level of funding after that. Instead, basic research funding began to pass through two sub-laboratories of the Army Research Lab (ARL). These are the Human Research and Engineering Directorate (once part of ARI) and the Computing and Information Sciences Directorate. The basic research money in behavioral science spent through ARL has been done as single large awards, with a company as the prime contractor responsible for management of a large team, including university researchers on the total team. The first time around, the prime contractor was Rockwell International with the University of Illinois managing all the university research there or elsewhere. The second time around, the prime contractor was a small business in the human factors business, Micro Analysis and Design. Currently the prime contractor is an overseas company.

This approach to funding may meet the needs of the Army, but it does not seem to provide easy access to funds for the average university researcher. Such researchers can become team members when the projects are recompeted. Or, there may be some opportunities for new team members to be added during the course of the project. To participate in this funding, quite a lot of social networking effort is probably called for.

An Organizational Note on Army Research

As in the Air Force, it appears that the ARO is an organization subordinated to the Army Research Lab. A lab focused on simulators for training, located in Orlando, Florida, is now under the management of ARL's Human Research and Engineering Directorate. ARI is not listed under ARL, nor is the behavioral science basic research part of ARO. This is looking like a bit of an organizational anomaly. Perhaps more organizational change will come.

The Defense Advanced Research Projects Agency (DARPA)

DARPA (sometimes known just as ARPA) was founded in 1958 after the Soviet Union's launch of Sputnik. DARPA rarely supports anything in the realm of behavioral science research. The most relevant work can be found under DARPA's Defense Science Office, under Training and Human Effectiveness. A current program is called Education Dominance, described in this way:

> Warfighters today must master a diverse set of physical and mental skills, often in a very compressed period. Measures of learning in this military environment often rely on qualitative and subjective assessment, with little opportunity to correct or redirect learning in mid-course.
>
> The Education Dominance program will enable students to learn at their own pace, in their own style, with their own digital tutor. In this way, students will not simply memorize information, but will learn and understand the concepts upon which information is built. They will train to a standard of competence, not rote recall, to demonstrate significant improvements in mastery of complex concepts. Novices trained on Digital Tutor will acquire accelerated problem-solving capabilities that will enable them to compete with experienced operational experts. Education Dominance focuses on several key approaches:
>
> - Replicating expert tutor behavior using knowledge engineering techniques.
> - Modeling intrinsic motivation and memory to optimize learning and consolidation.
> - Building student/tutor models based on abstractions of a wide range of student behaviors with live tutors.
> - Incorporating remediation strategies to enable the Digital Tutor to provide targeted reinforcement.

Many years ago, DARPA jointly funded some early work in artificially intelligent tutoring with ONR. After many years of noninvolvement, it appears that DARPA has returned to this topic. However, I believe that the Education Dominance program consists of one very large award to a Silicon Valley entrepreneur.

In the intervening years, there was one very large educationally oriented program called Computer Aided Education and Training Initiative (CAETI) that lasted about five years, aiming at computer-oriented and network-based educational innovations. It happens that I served as a reviewer in the initial phase. Although a few cognitive scientists interested in educational R&D received awards under this program, a typical proposal came from a youngish computer scientist who imagined that he would have enjoyed learning from the proposed system. Apart from the fact that these people were hardly typical students, they may also have been wrong about themselves as young students. Most of the awards went to the usual DARPA contractors, computer scientists in R&D firms and FFRDCs (Federally Funded Research and Development Corporations, a privileged class of R&D firms), many of whom had been funded under a previous high performance computing initiative. Few of the awardees had any background in instructional psychology or developmental psychology. In five years, this program probably spent more money than all of the other DOD agencies together have spent on educational and training technologies over their entire history, with few products that showed even promise of actual educational use. I was also present at one of the last program review meetings where the emphasis was on such potential applications. As of this writing, nothing about the CAETI program, the awards that were made, or the products can be found on the DARPA website.

Much of the work that is organizationally close to this program is actually reverse engineering—creating artificial systems that can emulate the capabilities of biological systems. For example, the biography of the current director of DARPA, the first woman director of DARPA, notes her earlier work as an outstanding DARPA program director, and one of her programs was called Dog's Nose, aiming at artificial explosive sniffing capability. Her doctoral degree is in Mechanical Engineering.

In the recent past, there was a short-lived program called Biologically Inspired Cognitive Architectures (BICA). This program was a pet project of the then director of DARPA. Initially it did not aim at a close fit to human cognitive architecture and was therefore quite distinguishable from my own Cognitive Science Program at ONR. However, it soon evolved to something that aimed to solve all the major problems of cognitive psychology and cognitive development in a very short period. At this point, the BICA program became a threat to my own program because ONR management was likely to ask why they should bother to spend a few million if DARPA was spending 10 times as much. The BICA program suddenly ended, perhaps because the grantees and contractors could not produce dramatic results in 18 months: existing grant promises were not even fulfilled. (A current search of the DARPA site for BICA-related information yielded nothing—not even documents such as research reports.) Indeed, the last few remaining uncommitted dollars I had as I retired as an ONR program manager were spent on some continuing work on a dropped BICA project that I considered particularly interesting.

DARPA tends to spend very big bucks, so it can be a very tempting source of support for researchers. A number of well-known cognitive scientists have received substantial and long-continuing support from DARPA, such as Ken Forbus, Roger Schank, and Allen Newell. These people have all been on the artificial intelligence side of cognitive science. A behavioral scientist interested in getting support from DARPA would be advised to collaborate with someone like that. Current DARPA funding opportunities are listed on the DARPA website and are also officially announced on FedBizOpps. Submission requirements and also planned review processes will be specified in those announcements. Realistically, awards tend to go to an established community of DARPA contractors, and it is my impression that it is difficult to break into that community. A substantial social networking effort may be required. In addition, DARPA awards pose management challenges that few academic researchers are equipped to meet. These are large awards and the expectation is that people will be hired to do the work very quickly, much more quickly than the usual processes of academic institutions allow, so that significant results can come very quickly. Also, the arrival of promised incremental funds tends to be unreliable in timing and may not happen at all. The institution has to be able to handle these financial gaps. In one instance, funds that Roger Schank expected to get never arrived, leaving Yale University holding the bag for several million dollars. Somewhat similarly, DARPA joined me in supporting George Miller's WordNet project, providing about twice as much money per year as I had been able to supply. But then, there was a year in which the money did not arrive for a very long time, so I had to have Miller submit a revised proposal to me for graceful termination of the project so that I could spend the money I had allocated to WordNet. Finally, some money did arrive from DARPA, but an additional two years of support that were promised at that time never materialized.

Large R&D firms are much better equipped to meet these management challenges because they can reassign existing staff to start new projects quickly or reassign staff to other projects when funding does not materialize as expected. Even though much of the DARPA money is nominally basic research (6.1) money, the projects tend to have a technological demonstration character (similar to what other DOD agencies fund with 6.3 funds as "advanced technology demonstrations") and are expected to produce impressive (and expensive) demonstrations for admirals, generals, and congresspeople. For the agency, this has been a successful strategy in maintaining high levels of funding. Although you will find DARPA characterizing itself as an agency supporting cutting-edge, high-risk research, often other agencies such as ONR have actually supported the high-risk basic research before DARPA became involved.

Final Thoughts

All of us who have been involved in evaluating many proposals naturally develop an interest in articulating, if only to ourselves, what characterizes a good proposal, and our views are remarkably similar. NIH information packets sent to researchers seeking funding have generally contained an article on this subject. At one point in my career, I wrote a short piece about proposal writing that was never published or distributed in that way. Below is my version of this message, now with some specialization to DOD agency funding.

Prior to writing a proposal, researchers must identify an appropriate agency or program to which they will submit their proposal. This chapter has attempted to provide relevant information for that purpose. However, a general strategy not previously mentioned is to look at the footnotes giving credit for the support of the work in papers about research similar to what one wants to do. These may be informative. For example, some researchers interested in developing artificially intelligent tutors for medical instruction came to me because they noticed that ONR was credited with supporting a large fraction of research in artificially intelligent tutoring. This led to my very first grant dealing with natural language interaction in intelligent tutoring. Similarly, checking Elizabeth Loftus's early research on eyewitness testimony reveals some unusual sources of research support.

Turning to advice on the writing of the proposal itself, here are my main points of advice:

Know Your Audience

Applicants should keep in mind both the needs of the probable audience for the proposal and the purpose for which the proposal is written. It is wise to find out or imagine for oneself as much as possible about the characteristics of possible reviewers and the circumstances under which they will be reviewing. Proposals should be written in clear fonts of reasonable size to meet the obvious needs of all readers. They should not be of excessive length. Typically, reviewers are pressed for time. A typical length for research proposals in the United States is 30 pages double spaced. Applicants should avoid appending extensive extra materials such as books, articles, and reports. If the content of such materials is important to the discussion, they should be summarized in the text of the proposal for reviewers. The main body of the proposal should be comprehensible without reference to other materials. If the expected reviewers will be from diverse backgrounds, it is important to avoid jargon specific to one's own specialty and to make the narrative comprehensible across disciplinary boundaries. Avoid inscrutable acronyms and other in-jargon.

As detailed earlier, in the DOD agencies, the audience may be a single person—a program officer—or the most important member of the audience may be a program officer even though other reviewers are involved. Occasionally, review panels may include persons with little professional knowledge of your field, such as military officers representing the ultimate customers for research products. So, it is important to try to get to know the relevant program officers. If other business, such as serving on an NSF review panel, takes you to Washington, you may well be able to arrange a personal meeting with the program officer. As of this writing, the Ballston area of Arlington, Virginia, is research central. ONR and AFOSR are located in the same building, about two blocks from NSF, and DARPA is about three blocks away in the other direction, at the Virginia Square metro station. Currently, ARI is located in the Crystal City area of Arlington, also accessible by metro. If they are not otherwise committed, most program officers will be willing to meet with you. It is part of the job to do so. When standing review committees are used, as was done in AFOSR, you will probably be able to find out who is serving on the panel. If a panel will be put together on an ad hoc basis, you can probably find out if all of the reviewers will have research expertise or if some of them may be essentially lay people—representatives of the customer communities.

Because of heightened security concerns since the 9/11 terrorist attacks, it is now necessary to make appointments with program officers in advance; it is no longer feasible to just walk into the buildings and look for people to talk with. (It once was possible to walk into ONR; there were no security guards at all when I first went to work there.) For the same reason, the research agencies may be forced to move to less convenient, somewhat fortified locations, in the near future.

The Proposal

The purpose of a proposal is twofold. The first is to convince the reviewers that the research question is of sufficient importance and significance to merit research support. The second is to convince the reviewers that the researcher is competent to carry the research to a successful outcome. To accomplish these goals within the suggested page limit, applicants must make a strategic selection of points to be discussed.

Literature Review. To present the significance of the research as a contribution to knowledge, there should be a review of the research literature, which is structured to provide a conceptual framework converging on the specific research question addressed. It should be clear why the question is important and what the significance of the possible research outcomes will be. The literature review should be comprehensive but not exhaustive. If the applicant is taking one approach or one side of a controversial issue in preference to others, the existence of other views and of the reason for the applicant's decision should be discussed briefly. Do not request support for doing a literature review. You are expected to know the relevant literature in advance.

Plan of the Research. The research questions should be concisely and explicitly stated. The research plan should be described in specific and concrete terms. The proposer will find it helpful to remember that the purpose is to convince the reviewers of the proposer's competence to carry out the proposed work. It is better, for example, to describe the statistical techniques that will be used than to assert that the appropriate statistical techniques will be applied. The same point applies to linguistic methods or ethnographic methods or "cognitive task analysis"; the reviewers need to understand what will actually be done. Both the questions and the research plan should show evidence of the participation of persons with pertinent expertise. Although 10 experiments might be proposed, one or two should be described in sufficient detail to demonstrate competence.

Other Concerns. Facilities and equipment and other necessary research arrangements should be discussed. If data involving human subjects are to be collected, there must be evidence of access to appropriate subject populations. Expecting a program officer to provide you with access to a military subject population will be a fatal flaw unless the program announcement specifies that such a population will be available. A duly constituted human subjects committee must have approved the experimental protocols.

Over the years, human subjects requirements have become more onerous and animal subjects requirements even more so. At ONR, it became necessary to have human subjects approval in place before the grant could be made, even though the nature of the research was such that human subjects approval would not be a problem. Although many researchers like to delay the human subjects approval process until a grant is received, that is no longer a good strategy.

An Alternative Path to Research Funding

As I have mentioned in passing, the military services have various in-house laboratories where behavioral science research is done. If you wish to pursue a research career and do not wish to teach, employment in one of these laboratories may be an option for you. Although you will encounter some internal competitions for research support, research support really comes with the job. Generally, the research in the laboratories is somewhat applied but not necessarily classified or combat related. Recently, DOD has initiated a program of fellowship support at both the graduate and undergraduate level. The generous support provided does come with a service requirement to work in the laboratories for a while. The upside of the service requirement in these difficult times, is that it also means a guaranteed job. Although I have not covered the National Aeronautics and Space Administration (NASA) in this chapter, there are similar behavioral science job opportunities in the NASA labs. For those who find the kind of research that DARPA supports interesting, it might be appropriate to seek a job in an FFRDC or other similar R&D corporation.

Although research management jobs are few in number, some behavioral scientists, like myself, may find research management an attractive option. It is a good option for those with broad interests and a taste for the big picture of their science and little need for personal recognition. If you become more interested in granting than in getting grants, consider applying for such a job yourself!

References

Chipman, S. F. (2003). Overview: The U.S. Office of Naval Research Training Technology R&D. *Proceedings of the NATO Human Factors Symposium, Advanced Technologies for Military Training.* Genoa, Italy, October 13–15, 2003. (Obviously, other papers presented in this symposium would also be informative.)

Chipman, S. E. F. (2010). Applications in education and training: A force behind the development of cognitive science. *Topics in Cognitive Science, 2,* 386–397. (This article provides a thirty-year history of cognitive science research related to education and training.)

Driskell, J. E., & Olmstead, B. (1989). Psychology and the military. *American Psychologist, 44,* 43–54.

Melton, A. W. (1957). Military psychology in the United States of America. *American Psychologist, 12,* 97–103.

Nichols, P., Chipman, S., & Brennan, R. (Eds.). (1995). *Cognitively diagnostic assessment.* Mahwah, NJ: Lawrence Erlbaum Associates.

11

Writing Grant Proposals for Military Agencies

Eduardo Salas and Marissa L. Shuffler

The military has historically served as a reliable sponsor of basic and applied research in a broad range of areas. Indeed, the Department of Defense (DOD) supported an almost $80 billion research and development (R&D) program in fiscal year (FY) 2010 (Silver et al., 2012). Furthermore, although a vast majority of this budget was dedicated to weapons systems and related technology development needs, an increasing focus has been paid to the social and behavioral science needs of the military. In FY 2010, approximately $14.7 billion of the overall DOD R&D budget went to behavioral, cognitive, and social science research. Military agencies such as the Army Research Institute (ARI), Army Research Laboratory, Center for Army Leadership, Office of Naval Research, the Air Force Office of Scientific Research, and the Air Force Research Laboratory all serve to fund extramural and intramural research programs that range from basic (6.1), to applied (6.2), and advanced development programs (6.3) in the area of human systems. From a social and behavioral science perspective, researchers can contribute to the military by understanding and developing tools for multiteam systems, leadership training and development, cognitive and neural modeling of decision-making processes, the influence of culture in dynamic and changing environments, and cognition of groups and teams, just to name a few.

Certainly, there are many areas of research that can be funded through military agencies, particularly in the brain and behavioral sciences. However, obtaining this funding is not always easy, as there are often many research teams competing for a single call for proposals or broad agency announcements. The purpose of this chapter is therefore to provide guidance from two different perspectives regarding how to identify, secure, and maintain military funding. As authors of this chapter, we provide the perspective of a well-established researcher with 15 years serving as a Senior Research Psychologist and the Head of the Training Technology Development Branch of the Naval Air Warfare Center Training Systems Division, as well as extensive experience obtaining multimillion dollar grants as a professor and program director at a major research university. We also provide the perspective of a relative newcomer to the field, with six years of experience writing successful grants and proposals for military funding. Together, we hope that these two differing perspectives will provide a rich source of tips and strategies that can be put forward by both newcomers and more experienced grant and proposal writers.

We begin by outlining our philosophy and assumptions toward approaching the grant process, followed by a discussion of this process overall, including how to determine which organizations may fund relevant research, how to find funding opportunities, and the actual submission process. Next, we review several myths and misconceptions that may lead researchers astray and are therefore critical to avoid. We follow this with key tips for success for the entire grant process, from finding grant funding sources to submitting the proposal, and everything in between. Finally, we conclude with a few last words of wisdom to encourage researchers to "buy the ticket" into the world of grant writing for military agencies.

Assumptions and Philosophy Toward Military Research Funding

To provide an understanding of our approach toward securing and maintaining military funding, we first present several key assumptions, as well as our overall philosophy toward military research funding. First, there are no specific prescriptions in terms of how to guarantee military funding. Each agency and circumstance is different, and researchers must be adaptable and fluid in responding to what the agency and proposal is looking for. Thus, we are not necessarily providing the "right" way to seek funding, but instead a set of tips and strategies that are based on experiences leading to successful outcomes.

Second, the tips and strategies provided within this chapter are designed to be applicable to all forms of research (basic or applied), to all agencies, and to consulting (both in terms of services and research). It is important to note that these tips and strategies have primarily been developed in terms of relationships with U.S. government agencies, but most should still be useful for interacting with foreign military agencies. For example, as will later be discussed, understanding the jargon and "lingo" of a granting agency is critical, whether it is the U.S. Army or the Canadian Defense and Development Research organization, which sponsors similar work for studies related to the Canadian forces.

Third, the tips and strategies provided are designed to cover all aspects of the grant process, from the formation of new relationships with sponsoring agencies to long-term, ongoing relationships. That is, we do not specifically focus only on how to submit a grant proposal or how to build a network of researchers to respond effectively to grants, but we also provide information regarding what to do from the beginning of the process in terms of securing a contract or grant to the maintenance of an ongoing relationship with sponsors and fellow researchers. This provides a more holistic perspective on what must be done throughout the entire relationship to develop and maintain funding effectively.

Our final assumption is that the tips and strategies provided herein are our own insights, lessons learned, and experiences that should help shape the process. However, they are by no means a finite set. They are designed to help get researchers thinking and reflecting, so that as each researcher goes through this process, he or she can create and pass along new tips and strategies. The politics of research funding can create a very dynamic environment, so new strategies may be necessary for success as policies change, new research areas emerge, and new needs arise on behalf of the funding agencies. For example, as will be discussed in further detail later, the increasing rise in calls for interdisciplinary and team research has led some federal funding agencies to resort to funding only teams of researchers as opposed to sole principal investigators. This type of change can have a major effect on how researchers should approach applying for funding and exemplifies what researchers should be attuned to in the dynamic environment of military and government funding.

In addition to these assumptions, we also offer an overarching philosophy toward applying for military funding. The purpose of military funding is to provide answers to both basic and applied questions, which can in turn lead to better tools, training, tactics, and procedures for individuals, teams, and organizations as a whole. Thus, researchers seeking military funding should want to make a difference in these organizations, as well as truly be interested in solving their issues. This does not necessarily mean agreeing philosophically with every military policy or action set, but instead it means being dedicated to helping those who must carry out the decisions made through the best training and resources possible, as well as potentially helping to positively influence decisions so that military actions are always as best informed as possible. To work with the military, there must be a passion for actually doing the work and not simply wanting to secure just any type of funding. Therefore, our philosophy towards working with military agencies is this: researchers interested in working with the military should be open to understanding all sides of military issues and problems, and should be driven by the scientist-practitioner model in which research ideas are developed and cultivated from an inherent interest in solving these issues in the military's present and future. Although each researcher may need to establish his or her own personal philosophy toward working with the military, having a clear understanding of why one is interested in pursuing this type of work will help in developing and successfully writing grants, as it will help to define intent and purpose to the reviewers.

The Process of Securing and Maintaining Military Funding

The process of applying for grant or contract funding with a military organization can seem daunting, especially for someone new to the language of the military or proposal writing in general. However, in some ways applying for funding from military agencies is no different from applying for funding to other government agencies such as the National Science Foundation or the National Institutes of Health. These agencies typically have guidelines for what types of research is accepted, requirements for what must go into a proposal, specific deadlines by which proposals must be submitted, and a protocol for how progress will be checked and quality maintained across the course of a funded research project or program. Researchers must therefore be aware of each of these aspects and understand how they might vary for a military funding agency. In the following, we break down the major aspects of the proposal process into three components (understanding the type of research funded; finding funding opportunities; and submitting a proposal) and provide strategies for success at each aspect of the grant writing process.

Understanding the Types of Research Funded by Military Agencies

The first aspect of the funding process for military organizations begins before a call for proposals or broad agency announcement is put forth by the sponsoring agency, in that researchers should first understand the organizations themselves and what types of research they fund. As discussed previously, within the Department of Defense, funding usually is placed into one of three categories: basic (6.1), applied (6.2), and advanced development programs (6.3). Basic research is research designed to expand knowledge or understanding regarding a given topic. From a military perspective, exploring basic research serves to lay a foundation for areas that may be of interest to the military but not enough information is currently known to begin answering more applied questions. In the behavioral and social sciences, research questions could be: What team processes are important for team effectiveness? How does culture impact socialization into a group? What neural processes underlie human decision making? As a further example, one basic research question that has been pursued by the authors of this chapter is the understanding of multiteam systems, or systems composed of multiple teams working together toward an overarching goal or set of goals (DeChurch & Mathieu, 2009). These multiteam systems have recently gained the attention of the military as they have become an integral part of many military operations, yet it is not clear as to how to optimize their functioning as little is known about their basic processes. Thus, this is a driving basic research question that has been explored using funding from multiple military agencies over the past few years.

Answering these basic research questions can help researchers better understand applied research issues as well. Applied research is focused upon answering practical problems or issues, as opposed to expanding current knowledge for knowledge's sake. This type of research is some of the most necessary for the military, as applied research problems appear almost daily, particularly during times of rapid deployments. In the social and behavioral sciences, examples of applied research problems might be the need to better train soldiers on a particular skill necessary when in theatre, methods for improving the relay of information across a chain of command, or new technology that personnel can use to diagnose medical injuries in the field. Applied research projects often lead to the development of training programs, selection systems, new tools, and other technologies specific to the military agency's needs as laid out in the call for proposals. Drawing upon the previous example of basic research in multiteam systems, this work has most recently been expanded to the applied research context by asking the question, how can we best train Army multiteam systems with teams comprised of different functional backgrounds so that they work together as effectively as possible? This is an example of how basic research may be further propelled by building upon prior work to expand into more applied areas.

A third type of funding that can be obtained from military agencies is that of advanced development program research. This area of research provides funding to projects that aim to further develop promising technology and tools developed initially as basic or applied research. In the social and behavioral sciences, advanced development research is not funded as often as basic and applied research as funding is more limited. However, when funded, these projects may include the further development of prototype immersive training programs into the actual training programs and supporting technology, or the further development of prototype support tools into useable tools that can be used in the field. Continuing the multiteam system research example, although no current research exists at this stage for multiteam systems, one possible area for advanced development might be to expand preliminary applied research training that has been developed for multiteam systems into an immersive online training simulation where real military multiteam systems can train together from various locations to optimize performance when in the field.

Within each of these broad categories of research funding, different military organizations have different specific research topic needs. These research topics are driven by the specific military branch that provides funding and resources to the organization, and are often driven by current missions or orders from higher officials. For example, immediately following the repeal of "Don't Ask, Don't Tell," several of the research organizations were requested to investigate how this change would affect factors such as cohesion within different military branches. Additionally, given the ongoing missions in culturally diverse nations, several military officials have requested that attention be paid to training military personnel to be able to operate effectively in such cultural diversity. Overall, each agency has its own agenda in terms of areas of research to be pursued, and a structure within the organization that facilitates addressing these areas. For example, the Army Research Institute is composed of several different research groups targeting different topics. The basic research office explores cutting-edge basic research issues acknowledged by the Army as important to soldier and mission success, while other offices focus on more applied problems, such as soldier selection, leadership development, and training.

Within funding organizations such as ARI, different offices or research groups can put out their own calls for proposals, or they can fund research through broad agency announcements (BAAs) sent out regularly. These BAAs are designed to allow for funding in areas of interest across an organization and can be targeted at basic or applied research interests. BAAs include broad categories of interest with suggestions for specific research needs while still allowing for researchers to come to the potential sponsor with ideas for research that the organization may not have thought of on their own but are relevant to the organization's needs.

In terms of strategies for success in understanding research areas, it is important that researchers do their homework in regards to military agency or agencies of interest, preferably prior to a call for proposals or broad agency announcements being posted. This may mean reading recent technical reports or academic publications put out by the organization in order to discern what topics may be relevant. Doing research on the organizations and their policies is also useful, either through reviewing their website or networking with individuals from the organization at conferences or other professional events. Additionally, staying current on military policies, politics, and missions can aid in being able to predict both basic and applied research needs, particularly the applied needs. Furthermore, when appropriate, researchers can contact sponsors with potential ideas, ideally in the form of a white paper, after doing research to determine a topic that might be of interest. Finally, in addition to networking with the sponsoring organization, researchers should also work to expand their own networks so that as opportunities come along, they will be in contact with others whose skills and expertise may complement their own. Networking is a critical aspect of the proposal process, as will be discussed in more detail later.

Finding Funding Opportunities

Once researchers understand which organizations may be viable options for funding research in their areas, the next step is to find funding opportunities. There are a few different methods for doing this, including submitting an unsolicited white paper, finding specific calls for proposals or broad agency announcements, and responding to small business innovation research (SBIR) or small business technology transfer (STTR) solicitations. First, submitting an unsolicited white paper can be done when researchers believe that they have ideas for research that are worthy of funding, but there may not currently be a call for proposals out that exactly fit the research being proposed. Such white papers consist of a 5- to 10-page summary of the need for the proposed effort, an overview of the proposed project plan, and an estimate of the budget. They may also include references and examples of prior performance to illustrate the abilities of the researcher or research team. If the potential sponsor likes the idea, the agency may then be able to work within the organization's policies to find potential avenues for funding and request a full proposal. Submitting these types of white papers requires a relationship with the potential sponsor as well as a keen understanding of current issues relevant to the military agency. For example, the senior author of this chapter has submitted these types of white papers in the past after hearing a potential sponsor present at conferences or other public events where specific needs are called out. This subsequently has created a dialogue between the research team and potential sponsor, leading to funded work. When there is an identified need and researchers feel that they have the skills and expertise needed to address this need, an unsolicited white paper may be an advantageous route to go, but can be risky in that there is no guarantee the potential sponsor will be interested or able to fund such an effort.

Another more common way to find funding opportunities is to look for calls or requests for white papers and proposals posted by military agencies. Typically, these opportunities can be found on the agencies' websites, or through websites such as Federal Business Opportunities (www.fbo.gov). In these requests, the sponsoring agency will lay out a summary of the requested effort, which typically provides a justification for the need for such research, the anticipated level of effort required (e.g., number of full-time equivalent hours, total project length, anticipated funding amount), and requirements for submission (e.g., page length, deadline, financial information needed, examples of past performance). At times, the sponsoring agency will first request a white paper prior to the submission of full proposals, and then will request full proposals from specific white paper submitters. This can help with narrowing down the total number of proposals received for a particular effort, as these organizations receive a large number of proposals regularly. It is very important to carefully read calls for proposals to ensure that all requirements are met in the final submission, as an incomplete submission will not be reviewed.

As BAAs have previously been discussed in detail, we will not review them again here, but instead reiterate their importance in serving as an avenue for researchers to bring ideas to a military funding agency in a solicited manner. Similar to calls for proposals, BAAs often first request or recommend a white paper. However, for BAAs, these white papers are typically followed with feedback from the sponsor, which can be infinitely valuable in developing the subsequent proposal. Even if a white paper is not required, it is highly recommended that one be submitted to get this feedback, as it can change the entire direction of a proposal and may prevent the researcher from making mistakes that reduce the likelihood of funding, such as addressing a research topic that is no longer of much interest or having a project be too costly.

Finally, SBIR and STTR solicitations are BAAs or calls for proposals specifically geared toward small businesses. These solicitations are designed to provide a specific pool of federal resources to support the growth of small businesses in the United States to stimulate technological innovation and growth while meeting federal research needs. Although the lead organization must be a small business, it is important to note that small businesses are allowed to partner with universities (and even encouraged to do so), opening up this line of solicitations to a broader audience. Military research organizations use SBIRs and STTRs regularly, but each agency has its own individual program within the guidelines set by Congress. The details of how the SBIR/STTR program works can be found online (www .sbir.gov), but the general structure involves three phases of funding. In Phase I, researchers receive a small sum of funding to establish the technical merit and feasibility of a research effort over a short period, typically six months. The purpose of Phase II is to continue work from Phase I for projects found to have promise, typically running for two years beyond Phase I. The only way to win Phase II funding is to have first conducted a Phase I project. Phase III involves the commercialization of products or tools produced during Phase II using additional funding from the agency sponsoring the work. In the brain and behavioral sciences, Phase III work is not typical for most projects but is possible.

To pursue these different lines of funding, there are several strategies that researchers can use. First, researchers must actively look for funding opportunities. This means subscribing to relevant electronic mailing lists, where such opportunities may be posted for the discipline of interest, networking with sponsors at different professional events to learn about potential opportunities or better understand what problems and issues may be future funding opportunities, and regularly checking websites such as www.fbo.gov to review upcoming proposals. Second, researchers should develop and maintain a running list of potential ideas that are current to the needs of agencies of interest. Staying abreast of current literature and attending military and industry conferences can help to provide ideas for answering problems the military may be facing. By having ideas ready at a moment's notice, researchers will be able to respond to requests for proposals and develop white papers quickly and efficiently. Finally, researchers should be open to thinking "outside of the box" when it comes to potential funding opportunities. Although a funding opportunity may not initially seem to fit the skills of a research team, it may only take partnering with a new group or organization to develop a white paper or proposal that will be successful. For example, the lead author of this chapter learned of an opportunity to explore issues of culture through complex computational modeling; however, computational modeling was well outside of the author's expertise. Instead of choosing not to submit, he instead decided to seek out partners with this skill, resulting in a successful proposal that combined both social science and computer science experts. Therefore, thinking creatively about how to respond to a call for proposals can be quite advantageous.

Submitting a Proposal

The final aspect to the grant writing process is the actual preparation and submission of the proposal itself. Once a potential funding opportunity is identified, there are several critical steps to take to be successful. First, it is imperative to read the entire call or request for proposals from start to finish. There are many details regarding the requirements for a proposal to be considered complete, and it is important not to miss any. Additionally, given that military grants and contracts will likely reference specific military terms, it is important to note these and be sure that the research team has a complete understanding of them and how they may impact the overall approach.

Once the proposal call is carefully reviewed, it is important to make an assessment in terms of whether or not a proposal can be successfully put together. In making this assessment, it is important to evaluate the interest in the topic, the ability of the researcher or research team in putting together a credible set of ideas and methodology, and the competitiveness of the researcher or research team. Conducting such an assessment can help the researcher or research team in beginning to formulate a strategy or approach for the proposal, and can also help to identify where there may be expertise weaknesses so that new team members can be added if needed.

Following this assessment, the next step in the process is to assemble a team for the proposal. Depending on the expertise of the researcher and the complexity of the proposal, this may mean bringing together multiple coprincipal investigators. It may also mean including a military expert on the team (e.g., retired or former military, civilian with extensive history working with the military), especially if interactions with military personnel are expected. One aspect to consider at this stage in the process is the need for multidisciplinarity in the research team. There is an increasing emphasis by military agencies for research teams to have breadth in their knowledge, as problems and needs are becoming more and more complex. Furthermore, as technological advances have increased, the military often looks to technologically rich tools as answers to the problems they face. For the brain and behavioral sciences, this may mean partnering with experts in computer science, modeling and simulation, computational modeling, or similar areas. Other critical team members may be identified in the call for proposals, such as researchers with certain areas or levels of expertise (e.g., a senior psychologist with a Ph.D., a data analyst with a master's degree or higher). It is important to make sure all of these requirements are met and are clearly laid out within the proposal.

The next step is to coordinate with those who will be putting together the financial aspect of the proposal. For a university researcher, this may be the office of research within the university. Identifying requirements and deadlines with these individuals early on is crucial, as military agencies very rarely make any exceptions in terms of extending submission deadlines or changing requirements. This administrative support can also be useful in terms of helping the research team ensure that all requirements are met prior to the proposal deadline.

Once the research team has been assembled and the proper administrative support notified, researchers can begin to actually prepare the proposal. Outlining ideas and brainstorming is an excellent way to begin, and for military proposals, doing research regarding the military's perspective on the topic of interest is also important. If possible, it may be helpful to identify questions early on that can be posed to the sponsor. For most military agencies, there is typically either a direct point of contact provided in the call for proposals, or a contact who can collect questions to be posed to the sponsor. At times, these questions must be asked by a certain deadline, so it is important to put these together early on in the proposal process. The end goal of this step in the process should be a detailed outline that contains all of the necessary requirements.

At this point in the process, the proposal writing should begin. Although the specific format of the proposal may vary depending on the requirements, the general way to frame responses for military proposals is (1) to provide an introduction to the ideas to be presented; (2) to lay out a set of technical objectives so it is clear to the sponsor what will be achieved through this work; (3) to clearly define the approach and methodology to be taken in order to accomplish these objectives; (4) to identify the deliverables to be produced so that the sponsor understands what the payoff of this investment will be; and (5) to provide an overview of the timeline and justification of costs. The earlier that this can be completed, the better, as it leaves time for feedback from others. Furthermore, once the writing begins, team members may realize a need to incorporate new aspects or change an approach to meet the proposal requirements. Typically, as the sponsor receives questions regarding the proposal, it is common for the answers to be provided in a public forum so that all potential researchers have the same advantage. Responses to these questions can at times mean significant changes to an approach. Therefore, several drafts may be needed before the proposal is completely finalized. The final step is to submit the actual proposal. Again, this is a step where attention to detail is absolutely vital, as there is usually no room for error with military agencies in this respect. Indeed, the authors of this chapter have had a proposal rejected by a military agency because, due to an overload of the electronic submission system at the final submission time, the proposal was submitted five minutes late.

There are a few key strategies that can make the military proposal submission process go smoothly. First, to be successful at responding to military calls for proposals, researchers must really understand military language. The military is rich with jargon and abbreviations that may be confusing to civilian readers, and an apparent lack of knowledge in the language that comes across in a proposal will likely mean an unsuccessful proposal. To avoid this problem, researchers should immerse themselves in the language of the military branch of interest—even across branches, terminology and language can vary greatly. Reviewing military literature (e.g., field manuals, websites, technical reports, pamphlets) relevant to the topic can be helpful, and can also help expand an understanding of the military's particular philosophy or stance regarding an issue. For example, social science researchers interested in pursuing leadership training and development research for the Army should read the Army Leadership Field Manual (FM 6-22) to get a sense of leadership-relevant terminology and perspectives. In addition to field manuals, researchers may also want to engage with current or former military members to have someone readily available to answer questions or help clarify. Indeed, sometimes having a military subject matter expert included in a proposal as a staff member can help to reassure the potential sponsor that the research team will be equipped to understand the perspective of the military.

Another key strategy that can help with successful proposal submission is to seek feedback from others. Although it is important to be aware of others who may be directly competing with you during a proposal process, gaining feedback from those not involved in the submission can be invaluable in helping to ensure that ideas are clearly laid out and presented succinctly. For researchers relatively new to the process, getting the perspective of a more experienced mentor or advisor can help in catching basic mistakes or refocusing a proposal to be stronger. For more experienced researchers, getting input from researchers familiar with the military context may be helpful to ensure that ideas are relevant to the population of interest.

Finally, it is important that during the submission process, research team members coordinate effectively. On larger efforts, there may be multiple individuals putting a proposal together, and it is important that everyone understands the overall goals and objectives. Holding an initial brainstorming meeting and subsequent meetings to lay out tasks and to check on progress can help to prevent problems close to proposal submission time. Furthermore, these meetings can help teams find weaknesses in their proposal early on, and can ensure that all requirements are met by holding certain individuals accountable for their completion.

Overall, the grant and contract submission process for military agencies can be challenging, but it provides researchers with an opportunity to stretch their ideas into new areas, and to aid in solving real world problems for the military. Perhaps most importantly, researchers who can "think like the sponsor" throughout the process should be best prepared in terms of making sure that their ideas are relevant and their approach is strong. Although the strategies identified here are certainly not the only ones that make the process successful, they should aid in providing insight and clarity at each of the stages of the process.

Myths and Misconceptions About Grants and Contracts

Given this discussion of the submission process, we next move to clarifying some of the common myths and misconceptions in pursuing military grants and contracts. We believe it is important to distinguish these as they can impede the successful grant process. By clearing these up early, researchers should have more realistic expectations regarding how to proceed with a successful proposal. Table 11.1 provides a summary of the myths and misconceptions that follow.

First, submitting a proposal to a military organization will not guarantee funding. Military organizations do have access to funds that can support research in the brain and behavioral sciences, but this funding is often dedicated toward very specific needs to meet current demands in the field. Furthermore, military organizations funding this research must be able to justify the cost of a particular grant or contract to their supporting agencies, as they often must get the funding from budgets outside of their own, especially to explore dynamic topics that arise because of new challenges. At times, even the military research organizations must compete with one another to secure funding for their research needs, making it important that every dollar spent is done so wisely.

Indeed, these research organizations must always be prepared to defend and justify why a certain project was funded. For example, although not a military organization, the National Science Foundation (NSF) was recently criticized in a congressional report for inadequate oversight and the mismanagement of funds (Mandel, 2011). In turn, the NSF had to defend its choices for funding certain lines of research and subsequently changed some of its reporting policies and other practices to meet these criticisms. Military organizations face this exact same potential for criticism and therefore must select only the most worthy proposals for funding.

Thus, researchers must understand that given the amount of scrutiny proposals must receive to ensure that they adequately meet the purpose and needs of a military research organization, not every proposal will be funded. Furthermore, at times military research organizations may choose—or be forced, because of changes in the availability of funds—to decide not to fund any proposals for a given call for proposals. As researchers, both the authors have experienced this situation, with many hours being spent on preparing proposals and white papers for potential funding opportunities that later fell through. However, as will be discussed later, it is important to view these not as missed or wasted opportunities but instead as chances to learn and develop in the writing process.

Table 11.1   Myths and Misconceptions of Military Grant Writing

Myth/Misconception	Reality
1. If I apply, of course I'll get funded.	Grants are not entitlements; they must be won through good ideas and well-written proposals.
2. If I pick a hot topic, it will guarantee funding.	Hot topics can be risky, as needs of the military can change quickly.
3. The more I propose, the better my chances will be of getting funded.	Proposing something that is too complex or out of the scope of the research team's abilities is dangerous.
4. I'm the world's expert, they have to fund me.	It is about what you propose, not who you are—the ideas proposed must use the skills of the expert.
5. I'm not asking for much money, so it will be funded.	Sponsors make judgments about the balance of dollars spent on products; you need to propose something that will be worth the money, even if it means spending more.
6. I know the sponsors, it is a sure bet.	Networking is helpful, but the person you know may not be the one reviewing or funding the proposal.
7. There is no point in competing, it is just a "good old boy" network.	A well-designed, well-written proposal can win even when there are incumbents with past history.

Second, a "hot topic" does not equal a funded proposal. Although some calls for proposals are very specific in terms of what is to be investigated, others, such as broad agency announcements, can be more open to a range of ideas. Researchers often look for what they believe are cutting-edge topics that will catch the attention of reviewers and therefore ensure funding. For the military, such hot topics may be based off of current news reports regarding actions or perceived needs, such as culture-specific training for soldiers based on the region of the world in which the military is currently operating. Or, these hot topics may be derived from buzzwords receiving attention in a particular research discipline, such as a new type of technology or new construct of interest. For example, the topic of team adaptation, or preparing teams to handle novel or unique situations, has been a growing area of interest in the behavioral sciences due to the increasing use of teams in the workplace, and has received attention by the military as well (Burke et al., 2006).

Although research on hot topics may be necessary and at times encouraged by the military, simply selecting a topic because it has been in the news or recent academic or trade journals does not guarantee funding. Just as hot topics may arise because of changes in the environment faced by the military, new changes can occur from the time a proposal is conceived to the time it is funded—and even in the time it may take to submit. For example, although cultural training for Middle Eastern countries has been a hot topic for the past several years, given current military policies and strategies, this type of training may no longer be as in demand. Furthermore, by the time a topic is a buzzword or considered "hot" in the academic world, funding may have already been spent by the military to research this particular issue. For example, the military has funded much of the research behind recent publications on team adaptation, so by the time this has become a topic of interest to the broader academic community, it may no longer be something that will be considered as a stand-alone topic of interest for the military. Additionally, when military organizations are interested in hot and cutting-edge topics, simply writing about the topic is not enough to garner funding. These types of hot topics may be risky ventures from the perspective of a funder, with high stakes made to potentially yield high returns. Therefore, successful proposals on a hot topic must be well researched and supported by effective approaches and methodologies, as well as conducted by a team of researchers who either have experience exploring new topics or have laid out a clear plan of how their areas of expertise will contribute to new gains in knowledge that will be beneficial to the military community. Proposing research on a hot topic is not necessarily a bad idea or wrong approach, but requires a well-developed plan that is clearly tied to outcomes that will be viewed as worth the financial risk to the funding organization.

Third, proposing a more complex research plan does not increase the likelihood of being funded. Oftentimes researchers believe that having a complex set of research goals along with a complex methodology will lead to a funded proposal. However, determining the level of complexity to propose is a balancing act. A very simplistic plan may leave reviewers questioning whether the effort will yield results worth funding. However, an extremely complex research plan may be viewed as unrealistic or overambitious, especially if there is little or no past performance from the research team reflecting skill in managing complex research programs. Being too complex can also confuse reviewers in terms of what the ultimate goals are of the project, and how they will specifically be achieved. Additionally, complexity also increases the riskiness in terms of whether or not all the different parts of a complex project will actually be able to produce results. Furthermore, proposing a very complex project over a short period of time or for a very low overall cost may leave the reviewers questioning the ability of the researcher(s) in terms of being able to realistically judge the financial and temporal demands of a project. However, this is not to say that researchers should never propose highly complex projects; instead, researchers should be aware of what the call for proposals is asking. Some calls for proposals specifically look for high risk, high reward projects and therefore may welcome complexity in proposals that are well designed and staffed appropriately.

Fourth, being a leading expert (or having one on the research team) will not guarantee funding. Expertise is certainly in high demand when it comes to proposing research programs. In the military, where research oftentimes needs to be completed very quickly to meet the demands of current operations, having researchers who are experts can help to ensure that they will not need an extensive period of time to bring themselves up to speed on the details of the topic at hand. However, expertise does not ensure funding; having a well-designed proposal is what matters. When reading proposals, reviewers want to see that ideas are well thought out and realistic in terms of execution. The use of expertise must be incorporated effectively into these ideas. For example, proposing an expert for a few hours' worth of work on a very intricate and complex research plan that clearly demands more of the expert's time for successful implementation will not lead to funding. Alternatively, having an expert spend extensive amounts of time on more trivial tasks may also be viewed as a poor use of resources. Furthermore, having the world's leading expert on a poorly designed and haphazardly thrown together effort will reflect badly upon not only the current proposal, but may also harm that researcher's reputation. Finally, although expertise can be of benefit to proposing successful efforts, sometimes having a relatively new researcher who can propose well-constructed plans offering new insights and new perspectives may be viewed by reviewers more favorably than something from a researcher with expertise in a very well-established area. Thus, researchers must carefully balance their inclusion of both new researchers and experts when developing research teams for military proposals.

Fifth, asking for only a small sum of money does not encourage military organizations to fund research. As mentioned previously, most military research organizations have budgets that must be carefully spent to ensure that organizations are getting the most for their money. Although proposing a small budget may logically seem like a good idea since it means the organization will not have to invest much, it does not mean that funding will be awarded. Sponsors must make judgments about the balance of money spent and the quality and quantity of products received in exchange. Proposing too small of a budget for a large research project may mean sloppy results and a hastily completed set of products. Conversely, proposing a small budget in exchange for a single product may also not seem like a good investment to a sponsoring organization, unless it is a groundbreaking product that meets specific needs or will lead to improved future research efforts. Military research organizations tend to award projects at a minimum level of $100,000, with some extending to well beyond that. For example, the Army Research Organization has awarded multiple awards of $5,000,000 for five-year efforts investigating issues related to culture, collaboration, and negotiation, key topics for the Army as they continue to operate in culturally diverse environments. These efforts result in a large number of products as they involve researchers from multiple universities, and provide a great deal of knowledge and useable training tools in exchange for their cost. As budgets permit, military research organizations are willing to provide the funding necessary to conduct well-designed research efforts, and oftentimes these larger efforts with a single research team may be favored over a series of much smaller projects from multiple research teams that may not provide the same quality of products or allow for the research teams to go as deep as needed in the area. When permitted, contact with a potential sponsor may be the best way to get a sense of what type of budget is acceptable for a project. Although they are not necessarily able to give a precise dollar amount for a budget, they can provide a historical range or average cost of a funded project for certain types of calls, such as broad agency announcements. In other instances, calls for proposals may provide a recommended number of hours to be spent on the project. Thus, using such guidelines is highly recommended when determining the scope of a project.

Sixth, knowing the sponsors is not a sure bet that funding will be awarded. Researchers often establish positive relationships with military research organizations over the course of time as they conduct multiple research projects for the organization. Additionally, it is entirely possible that a potential sponsor may be a former colleague, fellow classmate, or former supervisor with whom the researcher already has an established relationship. Having this relationship, even if it illustrates a history of positive past performance, does not mean that funding for a newly proposed effort is guaranteed. From a military research perspective, it can be beneficial to branch out to new researchers over time to incorporate new ideas that may better address new challenges or issues. Or, based on the needs of the military at a particular time, the proposed research team may not have the right blend of skills or expertise needed to solve a particular issue. Furthermore, similar to the issue of expertise, if the proposal is not well designed or is not of high quality, it may not meet the criteria for funding. The reviewer of a proposal may not necessarily be the person who knows your name or reputation. Therefore, it is critical to always put forward a strong proposal, even if it seems like the funding is guaranteed.

Seventh, new researchers sometimes assume that there is no point in competing in a call for proposals, as the military is primarily a "good old boy" network. Although having an established history of strong past performance with a military organization may be viewed positively by reviewers, this does not mean that reviewers only consider researchers with such a history, or those only within their social or professional networks. As discussed previously, reviewers for military organizations look for well-designed ideas, regardless of who submits. Indeed, one of the authors of this chapter worked on a proposal for a proposed research effort with a military organization where there was an incumbent who had been working with the organization for several years. Initially a discussion was held among the research team members about whether or not it was even worth pursuing the effort, as the incumbent had a long history of work with the organization, and the proposed effort was a continuation of similar work. However, it was decided that the risk was worth taking, and the proposal was submitted and won by the author's research team. In speaking with the sponsor after the award, it was revealed that while the sponsor was generally satisfied with the incumbent's work, the new team's proposed effort was a better fit to the needs of the organization at that point in time. Therefore, it is important to not assume that newcomers will have an unequal chance to secure funding, even in situations where incumbents currently hold funding.

In sum, researchers often make assumptions when entering the proposal process, which may lead to overconfidence in a proposal or even a decision not to submit at all. Perhaps the most common theme to all of these myths and misconceptions is that the proposal itself is what makes the decision in terms of whether or not an effort receives funding. A well-written proposal that is clearly thought out and effectively designed in terms of methodology and budget will stand for itself when presented to reviewers, regardless of the number of world renowned experts, past history with the sponsoring organization, or hot topics proposed. Researchers must not get sidetracked during the proposal process by the aforementioned myths and misconceptions, but instead should focus on developing an effective proposal that meets the needs of the sponsoring organization in a cost-effective manner that best uses the strengths of the research team. Thus, the following section focuses in on key tips to aid in the overall process of finding, applying for, and winning military grants and contracts, which should help researchers avoid some of these common myths and misconceptions.

Tips for Securing Military Grants and Contracts

To close this discussion of military funding, we now turn to eight general tips that can be implemented to further increase chances of securing funding. These tips are designed to provide advice that can be followed before, during, and after the proposal process. They are not all-inclusive, but instead serve as a few concluding thoughts regarding what can help make the process of submitting to military agencies as successful as possible. Table 11.2 provides a summary of all eight tips.

First, researchers must "buy the ticket." To even think about winning the lottery, you must buy a ticket. The same holds true for obtaining funding from military agencies—if researchers do not write and submit proposals, they will never have a chance to receive any funding. This is a very simple tip, but it is certainly an important one. ***Tip #1: Be willing to submit proposals.***

Table 11.2   Tips for Submitting Successful Military Agency Grant Proposals
1. Be willing to submit proposals.
2. Create and maintain a reputation—give yourself a chance!
3. Get to know the business and where the opportunities are.
4. Always have good, relevant, and doable research ideas ready to "buy the ticket."
5. Get to know your administrative supports.
6. Network, network, network!
7. Build and maintain interdisciplinary partnerships that complement your skills.
8. Persevere and don't give up!

Second, to have a chance at winning funding, researchers must be credible in the eyes of the potential sponsor. Sponsors look for well-written proposals from researchers who have evidence that they can follow through with the research and deliver on what they say they will do. Although previous experience with the military or the sponsor is one way to gain credibility, it can also be gained by having an impressive resume or vita. Researchers should therefore actively publish, present to both civilian and military audiences, and participate in professional networking events. For those who currently have military funding, making sure to consistently deliver what has been promised is critical. If sponsors know that they can rely on you to produce high-quality and timely work, it will bode well for future efforts. *Tip #2: Create and maintain a reputation—give yourself a chance.*

Third, you must know where to "buy the ticket." Getting to know the business of military funding is therefore critical to successful proposals. Knowing the business involves having a good understanding of the different branches of the military, getting to know the types of issues they face, and staying on top of national and world dynamics that may affect research needs. Additionally, this means getting to know more about military funding agencies themselves, in terms of their requirements, organizational structure, review process, expenditure requirements, language, and other business aspects. Researchers must understand that funding for the military is a business, and this business cannot be ignored. *Tip #3: Get to know the business and where the opportunities are.*

Fourth, researchers should always have ideas ready to go. Once you begin to understand the needs of various military research organizations, it is important to keep track of ideas that may be relevant to addressing these needs. Remember, at the end of the day, the purpose of military funding is to solve military problems. Therefore, ideas need to be relevant to these needs, but they also may need to be new, innovative, and at times even risky. Ideas can focus on solving a problem long term or short term, but they must have a scientific or practical payoff. Everyone can create good ideas, and therefore it is important to keep track of them in some form, whether it is writing them down in a notebook or keeping an electronic list available at all times. Also, once ideas are started, don't leave them alone—expand them, discuss them with colleagues, refine them, and update them as new research emerges. *Tip #4: Always have good, relevant, and doable research ideas ready to "buy the ticket."*

Next, your administrative support can be lifesavers during the proposal submission process. Researchers in a university or other organizational setting should therefore get to know those who will support their efforts. This can include financial and budget administrators, office managers who can help with the physical submission process, graphics support who can aid in creating helpful illustrations, and students or junior staff who can assist in conducting research to help support idea generation and development. It is important to get to know both the individuals as well as the operating procedures of their offices. Missing a funding opportunity because you were not aware of a university requirement that a proposal must receive a special type of review or must be submitted through a certain type of system can be distressing, especially if all of the work has already gone into preparing the proposal. *Tip #5: Get to know your administrative supports.*

In addition to getting to know administrative supports, it is important to get to know others who can help expand your professional network. Perhaps one of the best ways to succeed in achieving military funding is to build and maintain a large network of researchers, potential sponsors, and other colleagues who can assist you in the proposal process. Attending conferences and professional events is vital to this, not just to present your own ideas but to speak with and hear ideas from potential sponsors and colleagues. Coordinate with individuals currently in your network to meet their colleagues who may be potential future collaborators. Furthermore, maintain the relationships you have already established, especially with potential sponsors. Importantly, do not only approach these individuals when you want funding. *Tip #6: Network, network, network!*

Along these lines, while building your professional network, it is important that this network includes researchers outside of your discipline. As discussed previously, the problems and issues being faced by the military today and for the foreseeable future require a range of skills and expertise. Building connections with those outside of your immediate discipline can therefore serve to create interdisciplinary partnerships that can complement your own abilities as a researcher. To do this, attend conferences outside of, but relevant to, your discipline. For example, an organizational psychologist interested in virtuality may want to attend an engineering conference where researchers are presenting on the creation of virtual technologies. Do some research to find other disciplines that might be conducting research that is similar or complementary to your own. Look within your own network to see who might have connections to others who could complement your own research. Don't be afraid to contact someone who is outside of your network to begin building a relationship for future collaboration. These initial conversations may very well lead to a successful proposal down the road. *Tip #7: Build and maintain interdisciplinary partnerships that complement your skills.*

Finally, none of these tips work unless you are patient. The authors' experience has been that it may take several tries to secure funding, even if you are credible and have strong ideas. It takes several attempts in some careers to get a grant, so researchers must not be disappointed if the first proposal is not funded. Hard work, good ideas, and perseverance will eventually lead to funding. *Tip #8: Persevere and don't give up.*

Final Thoughts

The purpose of this chapter has been to highlight key tips and strategies aimed at helping both new and experienced researchers in securing and maintaining military funding. We have reviewed the basic process for applying for military funding, as well as provided insight regarding common myths and misconceptions, and highlighted a few important tips for success. Although much of the advice offered may also apply to funding agencies outside of the military, it is important to remember that the military does have its own unique operations and policies, and that it cannot be assumed that what works for one funding agency will work for all. We hope that researchers will be able to use the information provided herein to develop strong proposals that result not only in buying the ticket, but also in winning the funding lottery.

References

Burke, C. S., Stagl, K. C., Salas, E., Pierce, L., & Kendall, D. (2006). Understanding team adaptation: A conceptual analysis and model. *Journal of Applied Psychology, 91,* 1189–1207.

DeChurch, L. A., & Mathieu, J. E. (2009). Thinking in terms of multiteam systems. In E. Salas, G. F. Goodwin, & C. S. Burke (Eds.), *Team effectiveness in complex organizations* (pp. 267–292). New York: Psychology Press.

Mandel, J. (2011, May 26). Senator Cogburn sets sight on waste, duplication at science agency. *The New York Times.* Retrieved from www.nytimes.com/gwire/2011/05/26/26greenwire-sen-coburn-sets-sight-on-waste-duplication-at-55538.html.

Silver, H. J., Sharpe, A. L., Kelly, H., Kobor, P., & Sroufe, G. E. (2012). Social and behavioral science research in the FY 2012 budget. In Intersociety Working Group (Ed.), *AAAS report XXXVI: Research and development FY 2012* (pp. 205–213). Washington, DC: American Association for the Advancement of Science.

12

Preparing Institute of Education Sciences Applications

There's (Almost) an App for That

Lynn Okagaki

I've missed more than 9,000 shots in my career. I've lost almost 300 games. Twenty-six times, I've been trusted to take the game winning shot and missed. I've failed over and over and over again in my life. And that is why I succeed.

—Michael Jordan

Although there isn't yet an app for preparing grant applications for the Institute of Education Sciences (IES), there are a number of tips researchers can follow to improve their proposals. Successful grant writing is a combination of having great ideas, meeting the objectives of the funding agency, articulating ideas clearly, following the rules, and exercising persistence. There are researchers who have great ideas that are theoretically and empirically well grounded and who propose projects that are methodologically impeccable. Yet, they strike out because reviewers are unable to understand the proposal. Some researchers submit strong proposals, but they fail to submit a required form or they miss the application deadline. Sometimes the proposal is a wonderful proposal, but it does not address the agency's objectives for its grant program. Some researchers will get rejected once or twice and decide that it is not worth the effort. Writing a successful research proposal for a federal science agency takes time and effort, but there are steps that researchers can take to increase their chance of receiving an award.

This chapter addresses writing proposals for IES, the science office of the U.S. Department of Education. The chapter is divided into four sections. First, I provide some background on IES to help researchers understand the purpose of the IES research programs. The second section is an overview of the IES funding process. Third, I discuss the requirements for IES research programs and provide specific strategies for writing IES research proposals. Finally, I conclude with practical suggestions for preparing the project narrative.

Understanding the Funding Agency

In 1971, the RAND Corporation conducted a comprehensive review of education research in the United States, including case studies, correlational studies, small-scale experiments, and quasi-experiments. At that time, policymakers were looking for answers to basic policy questions—what programs and policies should be implemented to improve education outcomes for U.S. students. The RAND researchers concluded that education researchers had very few answers to the practical questions of education decision makers and practitioners. They wrote:

> [E]ducational research has tended to be small in scale, narrow in scope, diffuse, maldistributed, and lacking in focus. By comparison with other major sectors, the amount of research activity devoted to educational problems is surprisingly small. . . . The body of educational research now available leaves much to be desired, at least by comparison with the level of understanding that has been achieved in numerous other fields. (Averch et al., 1972, p. 157)

Fast-forward to 1999, when the National Research Council published a report on the state of education research in the United States. The panel concluded:

One striking fact is that the complex world of education—unlike defense, health care, or industrial production—does not rest on a strong research base. In no other field are personal experience and ideology so frequently relied on to make policy choices, and in no other field is the research base so inadequate and little used. Comparatively little research is funded, and the task of importing even the strongest research findings into over a million classrooms is daunting. (National Research Council, 1999, p. 1)

Almost 30 years later, the conclusions drawn about education research in the United States were remarkably unchanged. Policymakers were frustrated; education research was not turning our education system into an effective operation for improving student outcomes. If our students had been doing well, the fact that education research was not contributing to the improvement of the education system might have gone unnoticed. However, in 1999, although U.S. eighth graders scored above the international average in mathematics and science on the Third International Mathematics and Science Study-Repeat (TIMSS-R), they scored significantly lower than students in 14 countries on both assessments (Gonzales et al., 2000). In 2002, on the National Assessment of Educational Progress (NAEP), one out of three 4th graders and one out of four 8th graders and 12th graders scored below the basic level in reading (Jerry & Lutkus, 2003). That is, these students were unable to understand a grade-appropriate text. Similarly, about one out of three 4th graders, 8th graders, and 12th graders were below the basic level in mathematics on the NAEP 2000 assessment (Santapau, 2001). Although teachers were hard working and dedicated to their students, we were not achieving the desired education results.

Education is at its core an intervention. Education is intended to provide students with the knowledge and skills to live meaningful lives and to contribute to society. A good education increases the choices that students will have in life and enables them to take better advantage of the opportunities that come their way. Policymakers, community leaders, and the private sector have concluded that our education system is not doing what the country needs it to do. Consequently, at the turn of the 21st century, policymakers were frustrated that the education sciences were seemingly unable to accomplish what the sciences had achieved in other fields, such as medicine, public health, and agriculture. This was the context in which IES was created with the Education Sciences Reform Act of 2002. IES was charged with providing "reliable information about . . . educational practices that support learning and improve academic achievement and access to educational opportunities for all students" (Education Sciences Reform Act of 2002).

What is the practical implication of the agency's historical context for researchers? It is that IES focuses on *applied* research that ultimately is intended to improve academic achievement and access to educational opportunities. IES thinks about research in terms of what will benefit students, teachers, administrators, and policymakers. Policymakers judge the success of the agency by the degree to which it can produce or identify tools, programs, and policies that enable educators and the education system to improve outcomes for students.

Getting the Big Picture

This section is an overview of the IES funding process, and much of it is about the mundane—the documents that provide information on how to complete an application, deadlines, and the review process. I do not go into detail because the specific details may change in the future (e.g., application deadlines, forms, application receipt portal). However, the basic concepts will apply to any grant competition.

Request for Applications

Grant competitions begin with a funding announcement. For IES, the funding announcement is called a request for applications (RFA). IES will publish a notice in the Federal Register (www.gpoaccess.gov/fr/) and will post announcements on its website (http://ies.ed.gov) to let the public know when a new RFA is released. The RFAs are posted on the IES funding page (http://ies.ed.gov/funding). When this chapter was written, IES typically released its RFAs in late February or early March of each year. The RFA provides information about (a) scientific requirements for the proposed research, (b) amount of funding that is available, (c) application formatting requirements, (d) submission process and deadlines, (e) review process, (f) award decisions and start dates, and (g) people to contact for more information about the IES research programs.

Reading the RFA is the first step to developing a proposal. Unfortunately, it is a step that many researchers seem to forget about or not invest much time in. In the RFA, IES explains the purpose of the research grant program. Some researchers will look at the title of the RFA and because they do not see the exact words they are looking for, they assume that their research project is not appropriate for the grant program. I often would hear a researcher say, "IES doesn't fund X," when in fact, IES did fund work in that area, and if the researcher had read the RFA, he or she would have learned that IES did support such work. Conversely, sometimes researchers invest substantial time in preparing and submitting a proposal that does not fit the IES research programs or does not conform to the requirements in the RFA. Reading the RFA is the first step; it is also the most important step.

IES releases several RFAs each year. For the last several years, the two major RFAs are for the Education Research Grants Program and the Special Education Research Grants Program. Each of these grant programs covers a number of topics that represent long-term programs of research (e.g., Reading and Writing, Cognition and Student Learning, Early Intervention and Early Learning in Special Education). Each topic is an area in which IES is investing to accumulate a body of research that will result in effective interventions for improving student outcomes or improving the efficiency and management of school systems. In addition to these two RFAs, IES typically releases RFAs for (a) education or special education research centers that will conduct a program of research that focuses on understanding and developing solutions for specific education problems; (b) predoctoral and postdoctoral research training programs; and (c) other specialized grant programs (e.g., Evaluation of State and Local Education Programs and Policies).

In a later section, I discuss the scientific requirements in IES RFAs, but let's continue with basic information about the submission and review process.

IES Grants.gov Application Submission Guide

Currently, IES receives grant applications through the grants.gov system (www.grants.gov). Applications must conform to the guidelines detailed in the *IES Grants.gov Application Submission Guide* (http://ies.ed.gov/funding) and the *Grants.gov User Guide* (http://grants.gov/assets/ApplicantsUserGuide. pdf). Because several federal agencies use the Grants.gov portal for receipt of grant applications, the *Grants.gov User Guide* provides generic instructions for completing the application package. The *IES Grants.gov Application Submission Guide* was specifically designed to help investigators complete an IES application for submission through Grants.gov.

Researchers should keep two things in mind with regard to the Grants. gov submission process. First, although the instructions in the *IES Grants. gov Application Submission Guide* may seem a bit tedious, it is important to read and follow them. The *Guide* is designed to take the applicant through each step of the application package. If there is an error in the application, it will not go through the Grants.gov submission process. If this happens, the applicant will receive a message about the problem. However, for those applicants who submit close to the application receipt deadline, there may not be sufficient time to correct the problem and resubmit before the deadline. Applications must be received by the posted deadline to be reviewed. Although advice to submit early may seem trivial, in my nine years at IES, the vast majority of applications were submitted within a few hours of the deadline, and there were always applications that were rejected because they missed the deadline.

Second, Grants.gov is not run by IES. Consequently, if applicants need help with the Grants.gov submission, they will need to go through the Grants.gov help desk. IES staff members will not be able to fix problems with the Grants.gov process.

Application Package

The Application Package contains all of the forms that need to be completed for the submission of the proposal. The Application Package is posted on the Grants.gov website. Each RFA has an application package that is associated with it, and the RFA includes instructions for searching Grants.gov for the correct application package. Using the wrong application package results in the application's being submitted to the wrong competition.

Application Deadlines and Award Start Dates

Currently, IES accepts applications twice a year—early in the summer (typically in June) and early in the fall (typically in September). However, some of the research grant programs only accept applications at one of the application deadlines. If a research program accepts applications in summer and fall, there is no particular advantage for submitting at one time over the other. What is important is that the researcher plans sufficient time to prepare a strong proposal. It wastes reviewers' time when they have to read and give feedback on a poorly written proposal.

In the RFA, IES identifies the earliest anticipated start date for a project. This date is the earliest date for which a researcher can expect to receive the funding to start a project. There are times, of course, when the earliest anticipated start date is not the most practical time for beginning a project. For example, for June applications, the earliest anticipated start date is typically March 1 of the following year. The principal investigator may have other projects to wrap up before starting this one or may find it more advantageous to start the project at the beginning of the summer rather than in the middle of a semester. Applicants should also note that IES sets the latest possible start date for projects funded under a specific grant competition.

Typically, this date is September 1 and has to do with the fiscal year ending September 30 for the federal government.

Review Process

When IES was established in 2002, we used the peer review system for the National Institutes of Health (NIH) as the model for our scientific peer review. In particular, those responsible for the scientific review of applications are separate from the program officers who work with researchers on the preparation of proposals and subsequently monitor grants. The IES Deputy Director for Science and staff in the Office of Standards and Review manage the processing of applications, recruit scientists to serve on review panels, assign applications to panels and specific reviewers, and ensure the integrity of the review process. Standards and Review is also responsible for determining whether applications are "compliant and responsive" to the RFA. Compliance refers to following the rules specified in the RFA. Does the application meet the guidelines for format (e.g., font size, margins, page limits)? Was the application submitted on time with all of the required components? Responsiveness has to do with the type of research requested in the RFA. For example, for the special education research grant competitions, IES typically specifies that the research must focus on children with or at risk for developing disabilities and details how risk for developing disabilities should be established. If an application to a special education research competition does not meet these requirements, it may not go to review because it is not responsive to the purpose of the research program.

In the RFA, IES specifies the peer-review process and the review criteria for the grant competition. For most research grant competitions, IES uses a triage process. Applications are assigned to at least two primary reviewers who independently evaluate the strengths and weaknesses of the application against the criteria specified in the RFA. For most RFAs, the review criteria address four areas: (a) significance of the project, (b) research plan, (c) personnel, and (d) resources. Reviewers score each criterion and provide an overall score for the application. The average overall score is calculated for each application, and applications are ranked based on their average overall score. These scores are used to triage applications so that only the most competitive applications go to full panel for discussion and review at the panel meeting.

Typically, each reviewer receives seven to ten proposals to evaluate. After triage occurs and prior to the panel meeting, each reviewer is then expected to read all of the applications that will be discussed at the panel meeting (generally around 25 applications). For most IES competitions, the proposals are 25 single-spaced pages in length, not including appendices and other forms. Practically speaking, what does this mean for the reviewer? Work—a lot of work. Members of IES panels come to Washington, D.C., twice a year for two-day panel reviews. Preparing proposal reviews and attending the panel meetings come on top of their regular job. Practically speaking, what does this mean for the applicant? Obviously, doing everything possible to ensure that the proposal is well written helps. If nothing else, it reduces reviewer irritation, which is always a good thing. One other point is important. In the panel meetings, the primary reviewers summarize the research proposal and present their critiques. Oftentimes, specific questions about a proposal will arise, and panel members look through the proposal for further clarification. Providing headings that organize the proposal and numbering pages will help reviewers find information in the proposal more easily. The easier it is to find information in the proposal, the better the chance that the reviewers will be able to find critical information when they are discussing the proposal in the panel meeting.

Summary

This section has focused on the basic procedures for submitting a research proposal to IES. It may be mundane, but it is important. Federal science agencies establish procedures to make competition for research grants as fair as possible and to maintain the integrity of the scientific review process. Rules about page limits, font sizes, and submission deadlines are intended to ensure that the process is fair. No agency wants to disqualify a scientifically strong application because the rules were not followed, but the agencies must observe their rules to keep the process from being manipulated for political, personal, or any other reason.

IES Education and Special Education Research Grants Programs

Overview

As the title of its authorizing legislation implies, IES was created to "reform" education sciences. In particular, its mission is to transform education sciences into a scientific enterprise that is more rigorous in its methods and more relevant to the goal of improving the education system in America. A direct consequence of this mandate is that IES established explicit and detailed methodological criteria in its RFAs and identified the general problems that proposals need to address (e.g., improving reading outcomes for students or increasing school readiness for young children). For this chapter, I focus on the two major IES research grant programs—Education Research Grants and Special Education Research Grants. For these grant programs, applications are submitted under a specific topic (e.g., Effective Teachers and Effective Teaching; English Learners) and a specific research goal (e.g., Development and Innovation). Understanding the basic issues that pertain to these two grant programs provides a strong foundation for preparing proposals for any IES research grant competition. In this section, I begin with the research topics and then describe the five types of projects that IES funds, or in IES parlance, the five research goals.

IES Research Topics

Under the Education and Special Education Research Grants programs, there are several topics (e.g., Reading and Writing; Mathematics and Science Education). Applications are submitted under topics and among other things, the topic identifies the education outcomes that are the focus of a study. In general, the topics are broad education challenges that need solutions (e.g., improving science achievement or language development), targets for intervention (e.g., teachers, school leaders), or types of interventions (e.g., technology) that could improve student outcomes. Each topic has specific requirements—primarily with respect to the content or problem that is addressed (e.g., reading or writing outcomes), the population that is the target for the intervention (e.g., students from kindergarten through Grade 12; children with autism spectrum disorders), and types of measures that need to be included (e.g., measures of classroom management practices and student academic outcomes). For the most part, the topics are self-explanatory but there are specific details that are important for researchers to recognize. For example, under the Special Education Research Grants program, some topics are limited to research on students with disabilities (e.g., transition outcomes for special education secondary students), whereas other topics will also include students who are at risk for developing disabilities (e.g., technology for special education; early intervention and early learning in special education). Further, the RFA specifies that when research includes students who are at risk for developing disabilities, there must be a process for individually identifying those who qualify as being at risk for developing a disability and that process needs to be described in the proposal as part of the sample selection process. It is not sufficient to say, for example, that children from low-income families are at risk for developing certain disabilities.

One practical implication of IES having many topics and each topic having specific content and sample requirements is that researchers need to carefully read the RFA to determine which topic best fits their research project. IES recognizes that some projects may be appropriate for more than one topic. For example, Education Technology essentially overlaps with all of the other topics. If a researcher is proposing to develop an intelligent computer tutor for high school physics, the proposal could be submitted under the Mathematics and Science Education topic or under Education Technology. If the research team is primarily weighted toward technology researchers, they might choose to submit under Education Technology. Conversely, if the team is primarily content experts, then they might go with the Mathematics and Science Education topic.

In most cases, there is no practical advantage for selecting one topic over the other. For example, an evaluation of a reading intervention for fourth-grade English learners may be appropriate for both the Reading and Writing topic and the English learners topic. In such cases, IES indicates that an applicant may choose to submit under either topic. Most likely, the application will be reviewed by the Reading and Writing panel, which includes researchers who have expertise in literacy instruction for English learners. Researchers are always encouraged to contact IES program officers to discuss the appropriate topic for their proposal. However, conversations with program officers are infinitely more productive when the researcher has carefully read the RFA first.

Education Outcomes

Recall that the Education Sciences Reform Act mandates that IES generate information about educational interventions "that support learning and improve academic achievement and access to educational opportunities." Under the Education Research Grants and Special Education Research Grants programs, every project has to include student or child outcomes. The type of outcome depends on the specific topic. For example, for the Reading and Writing, IES simply specifies that the research must include student outcomes in reading or writing. What researchers sometimes forget is that they need to include student outcomes even if they are examining teachers' behaviors or studying school management practices. For example, if a researcher has a professional development program that is designed to change the way in which middle school math teachers provide algebra instruction, the proposal should include relevant measures of students' mathematics performance as well as measures of teachers' behaviors. Given the agency's mission, it is not enough to demonstrate that one can change what teachers do. Research on teacher professional development also has to examine what happens to students' learning outcomes. The point here is that investigators must make sure that their proposal meets the requirements for the topic under which they submit the proposal.

IES Research Goals

Through its two major research grant programs, IES supports intervention research and divides this research into five types of research projects: (a) Goal One—Exploration, (b) Goal Two—Development and Innovation, (c) Goal Three—Efficacy and Replication, (d) Goal Four—Effectiveness, and (e) Goal Five—Measurement. Together, these five types of projects are known as the IES goal structure. Understanding the differences across these types of projects and the basic requirements for each goal is critical to writing successful IES proposals.

Goal One: Exploration

Exploration projects have to do with understanding the association between education outcomes and malleable factors. There are three key ideas here: (a) education outcomes, (b) malleable factors, and (c) association.

Education Outcomes. As discussed in the section on IES research topics, the specific student outcomes vary by topic, but every project has to include student or child outcomes. The key here is understanding that Exploration projects have hypotheses that include specific student outcomes.

Malleable Factors. By malleable factors, IES refers to those things that can be changed by the education system, such as student behaviors, curricula, instructional practices, professional development programs, or management practices. In Exploration projects, researchers are looking for potential targets for interventions—something that can be changed in ways that are correlated with student outcomes. For example, under Exploration, a researcher could propose to examine the relations between different types of writing instruction and student outcomes by assessing children's writing performance at the beginning and end of a year, observing the instructional practices, and statistically testing the relations between instructional practices and gains in writing performance. In this example, the malleable factor is writing instruction. If the researchers find that certain practices are associated with larger gains in writing performance, then instructional practice is a target for intervention. Suppose a researcher wanted to find out if girls are better in writing than boys—in essence, an examination of the relation between gender and writing outcomes. This would not meet the requirements because there is no malleable factor under the control of the education system; schools cannot manipulate the gender of their students.

Association. Exploration projects are about examining the correlation between malleable factors and education outcomes. Under this goal, investigators are *not* allowed to examine causal relations. IES makes a clear distinction between research designs that support causal conclusions and designs that support associations. Under the Exploration goal, investigators should *not* ask causal questions (e.g., Does the Super Writing Program lead to better writing outcomes for fourth graders than typical writing instruction?) and should *not* propose research designs that are intended to answer causal questions (e.g., regression discontinuity design). Exploration projects are correlational studies. Finally, under Exploration, researchers can also propose to examine mediators or moderators of the relation between malleable factors and student outcomes.

Thinking Ahead to the Next Grant. For each goal, IES describes what is expected from a grantee at the end of a project. These expectations are intended to help researchers think about how their project would contribute to scientific knowledge of education and how it would prepare them for the next research project. For example, if an Exploration project leads to the identification of a malleable factor that is associated with education outcomes, then the researcher has empirical evidence to support a proposal to develop an intervention to change the malleable factor in ways that will produce better student outcomes.

Goal Two: Development and Innovation

The purpose of Development projects is to develop new or modify existing education interventions. There are three components to these projects: (a) developing or refining an intervention to improve education outcomes, (b) testing the feasibility of implementing the intervention, and (c) obtaining pilot data on the promise of the intervention for improving student outcomes.

Iterative Development. The first component and the primary focus of Development projects is the development or modification of an intervention. IES expects researchers to describe an iterative development process for their intervention. Diamond and Powell (2011) explain the iterative process that went into the development of their teacher professional development program. For example, as part of the program, teachers watch video clips of a master teacher demonstrating specific instructional practices. There were a number of questions the research team considered in developing these modules. How long should each video clip be? What text needs to preface the clip so that the teacher will focus on the important actions in the clip? If each session includes multiple clips for the teacher to watch, how should the clips be arranged to ensure that teachers will actually click on them and watch them? Developing a version, testing it to find out if it functions as intended, modifying the new version, testing it, and revising it until it operates as intended is what IES means by an iterative development process.

Feasibility of Implementation. The second component—feasibility of implementation—addresses the question of whether the intervention can be deployed in the type of setting for which it has been developed and implemented by the intended end user in the way that it is intended. Suppose a researcher works on the development of a fourth-grade science program with a small group of master teachers, and they go through an iterative process to make sure that the intervention works in the way that the researcher believes is optimal. But, the program is intended to be used by regular fourth-grade teachers! To test the feasibility of the intervention, the researcher should have regular fourth-grade teachers implement the program to see if they are able to use it in the way that the researcher intends for it to be used. Further, even if the teachers *can* implement the program as intended, the researcher needs to consider whether teachers and school leaders will *want* to use the program.

Promise of the Intervention. Third, the Development project concludes with a pilot test of the promise of the intervention for achieving the intended outcomes. Data from a pilot test are more compelling if a comparison group is involved, but the pilot test does not need to be a causal analysis. When this chapter was written, IES limited the pilot test to no more than 30 percent of the grant budget so that researchers would focus on the development of the intervention. Keeping to this limit, many IES Development projects are conducted with small experimental or rigorous quasi-experimental evaluations to have more compelling pilot data to support a proposal for an Efficacy and Replication grant.

Thinking Ahead to the Next Grant. Two criticisms of many education interventions are that the developers (a) have not clearly specified how and why the intervention should lead to improvements in student outcomes and

(b) have not clearly operationalized what it means for the intervention to be operating as intended. To address these shortfalls, IES indicates that at the end of the Development project, there should be (a) a fully developed intervention; (b) a well-specified theory of change for intervention (i.e., how and why it is supposed to work) with a detailed description of what it would look like if the intervention were operating or functioning as intended; (c) a fidelity measure to assess whether the intervention is delivered as intended; (d) feasibility of implementation data (i.e., a demonstration that the intervention can be implemented in their intended settings by people who are like the people who will ultimately use the intervention); and (e) pilot data demonstrating the promise of the intervention for producing the intended outcomes. Having these products will be important when the investigator goes to the next step, which is the Efficacy proposal.

Goal Three: Efficacy and Replication

The purpose of Efficacy projects is to evaluate the impact of an education intervention when implemented in schools with a small and well-defined sample. What does this mean? First, Efficacy studies address a causal question: Does the intervention produce a positive effect relative to a specified counterfactual or comparison condition? Second, the intervention needs to be implemented in schools or other formal education delivery systems. Third, Efficacy studies evaluate the intervention under limited or more homogenous conditions. They are designed to have high internal validity but limited generalizability. In essence, efficacy trials determine if an intervention *can* work under specific conditions but not whether the intervention *will* work if broadly deployed. Further, in efficacy trials, the intervention is tested under what may be considered to be more ideal conditions. That is, the researcher may provide more support than would typically be available in the schools. For example, the researcher may be observing in the classrooms and giving feedback to the teachers to ensure that the intervention is implemented in the way that the researcher intends for it to be implemented.

IES recognizes that many researchers are eager to test their intervention under diverse conditions in large evaluations. However, IES intentionally limits these initial impact evaluations to be on a relatively smaller scale. Over its first decade, IES found that most education interventions are not potent and robust enough to produce substantively important, positive effects on student outcomes when deployed under diverse conditions and rigorously evaluated. By funding Efficacy studies and limiting their size, IES can support the testing of more interventions in hopes of finding the few that have sufficient potential to improve student outcomes when widely deployed. In addition, IES can encourage researchers to do more research on the implementation of their interventions. The field is learning that understanding the conditions that support or hinder strong implementation of interventions is critical to improving our education system.

Under Goal Three, IES also funds Replication studies. Suppose a math curriculum has been tested in schools in two rural districts that have a high proportion of students from low-income families and was found to produce a positive impact relative to the existing curriculum in those schools. Before one would evaluate this curriculum at scale, it is important to determine if it can be used under other circumstances—for example, with English learners or in urban schools. Conducting Replication studies before moving to an Effectiveness evaluation allows researchers to gain valuable information about the robustness of their intervention for improving student outcomes and the conditions that are associated with the quality of the implementation of their intervention.

Thinking Ahead. Ideally, at the end of an Efficacy study, the researcher will have (a) a study that meets the standards of the What Works Clearinghouse for a causal evaluation, (b) data indicating whether or not the intervention produces a positive impact on student outcomes relative to a comparison condition, (c) support for or revisions to the theory of change for the intervention, (d) data identifying organizational procedures and tools that may be necessary to achieve sufficient fidelity of implementation of the intervention, and (e) data on moderators and potential mediators of the intervention. Thus, at the end of the project, researchers should either have data to support a proposal for a Replication or Effectiveness study (if the intervention produced a substantively important, positive impact on student outcomes) or have gained a better understanding of the way in which the intervention operated and those factors (e.g., fidelity of implementation, mediators, moderators) that may play a role in its operation. In the best of all worlds, if the intervention "fails," the researcher will have sufficient information to decide if this is a theory failure (i.e., the idea underlying the intervention did not work or was not sufficiently different from the theory underlying current practice to make the intervention more potent than current practice) or an implementation failure (i.e., the intervention was not implemented well enough to produce an effect). If the researcher understands why the intervention failed, the researcher may be able to generate ideas for developing a new intervention or modifying the existing one in ways that will make it more likely to improve student outcomes. This situation takes the researcher back to a Development proposal.

Goal Four: Effectiveness

The purpose of Effectiveness evaluations is to determine if an intervention, which has strong evidence of its efficacy, will produce a positive impact on student outcomes when it is implemented under conditions of routine practice and when evaluated by an independent evaluator. Below I deconstruct this statement and discuss how IES expects to generate evidence of the generalizability of intervention effects.

Strong Evidence of Efficacy. The first key idea is that the intervention must have strong evidence that it produces meaningful improvements in student outcomes. Strong evidence could be based on two or more well-designed and implemented efficacy trials that resulted in substantively important improvements. What makes an improvement "substantively important"? Think about the answer from the perspective of a school superintendent or chief state school officer. Suppose the Anaconda Reading Curriculum was evaluated against two other reading curricula and students in the Anaconda program showed three months gain compared with students in the other programs at the end of the year on the state reading assessment. A superintendent is likely to consider that much gain to be educationally meaningful. Conversely, a statistically significant effect that translates into a one- or two-week advantage does not make much difference if students are an entire year behind in reading.

Implemented Under Conditions of Routine Practice. The second important idea for Effectiveness evaluations is that the intervention must be implemented under conditions of routine practice. This means, for example, that the intervention is implemented by the schools as if they had decided to use the intervention totally apart from participation in any evaluation, as if they had purchased it and implemented it on their own.

Independent Evaluation. Third, the evaluation must be conducted by an evaluation team that is independent from the developer or distributor of the intervention. The evaluation team cannot have any financial interest in the intervention. This requirement does not preclude developers or publishers from having some involvement in the evaluation. For example, suppose a publisher would like to have its curriculum evaluated. The publisher may, for example, provide the curriculum to the schools at a reduced cost. The principal investigator, however, needs to be someone who is independent of the publisher. Those who are involved with the random assignment, design, implementation of the evaluation, and analysis of data need to be independent of the publisher. Now, suppose the publisher also wants to provide professional development training to the teachers in the intervention group. If school districts typically received the professional training when they bought the curriculum, then it would be acceptable for the training to be provided as part of the implementation of the intervention. If, however, the training was something out of the ordinary—that is, not part of routine practice—then it would not be allowed for an Effectiveness evaluation.

Generalizability. Finally, another factor to keep in mind for Effectiveness evaluations is that IES does not expect any single Effectiveness evaluation to cover a diverse sample of students and school conditions. Similar to what IES expects to happen through Efficacy studies, IES intends to accumulate knowledge about the generalizability of results to a wide range of students and conditions through multiple Effectiveness evaluations. When adequately powered, education evaluations tend to be costly. Rather than funding a few large and expensive Effectiveness evaluations that include sufficient diversity to assess the impact of an intervention when widely deployed, IES is funding more but smaller Effectiveness evaluations to increase the likelihood that IES will identify some interventions that are effective under conditions of routine practice. So far, very few interventions have been found to be effective for producing educationally meaningful impacts under conditions of routine practice and when evaluated by an independent evaluation team.

What Works, for Whom, Under What Conditions, and Why. At the end of an Effectiveness project, the investigator should have (a) evidence of whether or not the intervention produces a net positive impact relative to a comparison condition when the intervention is implemented under conditions of routine practice and is rigorously evaluated by an independent researcher, (b) support for or revisions to the intervention's theory of change and contributions to scientific understanding of education, (c) have garnered a better understanding of the organizational supports needed to implement the intervention with fidelity, and (d) have determined the influence of one or two key, theoretically selected moderators on the relation between the intervention and student outcomes. Not only does IES care about answering the "does it work" question, but the agency believes it is critical to know for whom, under what conditions, and why an intervention works or does not work. Effectiveness evaluations should be designed to gather data on the organizational conditions or supports that may affect implementation of the intervention. The "for whom does an intervention work" and "under what conditions does an intervention work" questions may be addressed through moderator analyses. Reviewers will expect research questions or hypotheses that address fidelity of implementation and other moderators. Investigators should be thoughtful in framing these questions, careful that design allows them to answer these questions, and adequately power the study to answer the questions. At the end of the project, if the intervention fails to produce a positive effect, the investigator should have sufficient implementation data (see, e.g., Fixsen, Naoom, Blasé, Friedman, & Wallace, 2005) so that one can determine if failure reflects a theory failure or an implementation failure.

Goal Five: Measurement

Measurement projects are intended to support the development and validation of new measures or the validation of existing measures. IES encourages development of instruments that will be used by practitioners for screening, formative assessment, progress monitoring, or outcome assessment, but also funds development of measures to be used for research purposes. Below I outline some practical issues that investigators need to be mindful of with Measurement proposals.

Student Outcomes. Validation of new instruments needs to be against student outcomes. For example, if an instrument is developed to measure teachers' instructional practices in mathematics, the instrument might be validated against video recordings of instruction or principal observations or other measures of teacher practices. In addition, however, the investigator must validate the measure against student outcomes. That is, does the instrument capture aspects of instruction that are correlated with students' performance?

Measurement Versus Intervention. A common mistake that researchers make is combining measurement development with an Efficacy study of the use of the measurement to improve student outcomes. For example, suppose a researcher wants to develop and validate a progress-monitoring instrument for development of knowledge in physics AND wants to know if *using the instrument* will provide teachers with feedback that will guide their instruction and improve student outcomes. Under the Measurement goal, the investigator can develop the instrument and validate it against other measures of knowledge and skills in physics. However, the second question—does using the progress-monitoring instrument improve instruction and increase students' knowledge of physics—is a causal question about the efficacy of an intervention (i.e., the progress-monitoring measure) for improving student outcomes. This question cannot be addressed under the Measurement goal. When we consider the researcher's second question, it becomes clear that the researcher essentially wants to develop an intervention—a progress-monitoring tool. Although the investigator could develop and validate the instrument under the Measurement goal, to do the research that is needed to develop an intervention and have the necessary data to support an Efficacy proposal, the researcher should develop a proposal that conforms to the guidelines for the Development goal. The program officers can help investigators sort out these types of issues before the investigators have committed significant amounts to developing their proposal.

Summary of Research Goals

From the perspective of the researcher, it would be wonderful if funding agencies would provide funds for long-term programs of research—say, 10 years' worth of funding at a time. Researchers would not have to spend so much time writing proposals and could focus more easily on getting the important work done. Funding agencies, however, recognize that not all ideas pan out. IES has intentionally taken a research process that goes from identification of potential targets for intervention through the development and evaluations of interventions and broken it into individual projects. Exploration projects should lead to development or modification of an intervention. Development projects should lead to Efficacy evaluations. If Efficacy evaluations result in positive impacts that are educationally meaningful, they should lead to Effectiveness evaluations. IES has found that few Effectiveness evaluations find interventions to be robust and potent enough to produce positive impacts when implemented under conditions of routine practice. By breaking down the research process into smaller pieces, IES increases the likelihood that strong interventions will ultimately be identified.

Practical Tips for Preparing the Project Narrative

The project narrative is the main component of an application. The narrative is what most of us think about when we write a grant proposal, and reviewers pay the most attention to the project narrative. It is composed of four sections: (a) Significance (i.e., what will be done and why it is important); (b) Research Plan (i.e., how the work will be done); (c) Personnel (i.e., the expertise and commitment of those who will do the work); and (d) Resources (i.e., assuring the availability of basic resources and partnerships [e.g., collaborations with schools] for doing the work are available). In the RFA, IES details what information should be provided in each section. Below I provide practical tips for preparing the narrative.

Significance

Under Significance, the investigator describes the purpose of the project (e.g., hypotheses, research questions), the theoretical and empirical foundation for the hypotheses and research questions, and the practical rationale for the project. The specific issues that need to be covered in this section differ across goals and are described in the RFA. Although there are differences across goals, there are common problems that emerge across goals.

First Paragraph of the Proposal

After the reviewer has read the first paragraph of the project narrative, the reviewer should know the purpose of the proposed research project. In the first sentence, researchers should state the topic and goal to which the proposal is being submitted (e.g., This proposal is submitted to the Mathematics and Science Education topic under Goal Three—Efficacy). Although the investigator identifies the topic and goal for the proposal on the cover sheet, sometimes what is on the cover sheet does not match what is in the proposal itself. Reviewers generally will ignore the cover sheet and go by what is in the project narrative. Because the criteria differ by topic and goal, it is an easy safeguard to state the topic and goal at the beginning of the narrative. In the second sentence of the narrative, tell the reviewer what the purpose of the project is (e.g., to conduct an efficacy evaluation of an instructional approach for teaching fractions). I cannot overemphasize how important it is for the investigator to make the purpose of the proposal clear at the beginning of the narrative. Invariably there are proposals that leave reviewers so confused that they do not know what the investigator wants to do. If the reviewer cannot figure this out, the proposal will go nowhere. In addition, if reviewers have to wade through several pages of introduction before they find out what the purpose of the project is, they are likely to become frustrated (and successful grant writers avoid frustrating their reviewers!).

Confusion About the Malleable Factor or Intervention

A problem that occurs across topic areas is that the malleable factor (Exploration proposals) or the intervention (Development, Efficacy, and Effectiveness proposals) is not explained clearly enough for the reviewers to understand the focus of the proposal. For the malleable factor, researchers need to remember that it is something that can be changed. The idea of the malleable factor is that if the Exploration study finds that variation in the malleable factor is associated with student outcomes, then the malleable factor is a target for an intervention. To convince reviewers that the project is worth funding, there should be a theoretical rationale that links the malleable factor to the student outcome. In addition, it should be clear that the malleable factor is something that the education system can control or manipulate if it is to be a target for a future education intervention.

For Development, Efficacy, and Effectiveness proposals, the reviewers need to have a clear understanding of the intervention. The researcher needs to succinctly describe the intervention so that the reviewer has a good picture of what is supposed to happen. Based on this description, the reviewer should know the components of the intervention, who engages in each activity, when activities happen, what happens during them, how long the components last, and how they will be implemented.

However, just knowing what the components are is not enough. Sometimes investigators describe the activities that will occur and neglect to delineate the content that will be delivered. For example, the researcher might describe a teacher professional development program by saying that coaches will observe teachers and provide feedback to them every other week. This type of description leads reviewers to wonder what the coaches will be looking for during their observations and what type of feedback they will provide.

Reviewers also want to know why the intervention should work. To address this question, the investigator needs to present the theory of change for the intervention. The theory of change delineates how the components of the intervention relate to one another and explains the mechanism by which the intervention should lead to improved student outcomes. A well-articulated theory of change shapes the evaluation and provides a framework for the proposal. One of the key presentations in the IES summer research-training institute on cluster-randomized trials is the session on specifying the conceptual and operational models. For more information on describing the theory of change, readers can watch the first lecture by Dr. Mark Lipsey (www.ipr.northwestern.edu/qcenter/NCER2008/).

Inconsistent Research Questions or Hypotheses

The research questions or hypotheses frame the entire proposal. In the Significance section, the researcher provides a theoretical and empirical rationale to support each question. In the Research Plan, the research design has to be appropriate to answer the posed questions. The investigator has to make sure that the dependent and independent variables identified in the research questions are captured in the proposed measures. Finally, the proposed analyses need to match the research questions and hypotheses. Unfortunately, the consistency that should flow throughout the proposal does not always occur. Sometimes this happens when proposals have multiple authors, with each one taking responsibility for a different section. Sometimes it happens because the proposed project has morphed over time, and sections were written during different phases of the evolution of the project. Researchers have to make sure that they read the proposal from beginning to end before it is finalized and check that the questions and hypotheses posed in the beginning are consistent throughout the proposal.

Research Plan

In the Research Plan, the investigator explains how the work will be done. It needs to correspond to the research aims that are presented in the Significance section. The research design has to be appropriate for the questions that are posed and described in sufficient detail so that the reviewers understand what the investigator intends to do. The elements of the Research Plan vary across the IES research goals, and the RFA provides detailed information about what should be included for each goal.

Sample

For any study (including secondary data analyses), there needs to be a clear description of the sample, including selection criteria, and a rationale justifying why this is the appropriate sample. For Development projects, investigators need to remember that to test the feasibility of implementation of the intervention, they need to work with a sample that is similar to the intended end users of the intervention. For longitudinal studies, reviewers will want an estimate of the attrition rate and procedures to reduce attrition from the study.

Measures

For any study, the investigator will need a clear description of the measures, their psychometric properties, and the rationale for selecting the measures. Researchers need to describe not only the outcome measures, but, as appropriate to the type of project, also measures to assess the fidelity of implementation of the intervention and whether the intervention is operating as intended. Reviewers will want to know the procedures for collecting and coding data. If observations are conducted, what are the procedures for maintaining inter-observer reliability? A common mistake is when the measures that are described do not match the research questions and hypotheses. The researcher needs to make sure that the outcome measures will provide the data to answer the research questions. For evaluations, the researcher should make sure that the proposed measures cover the key points for the intervention's theory of action.

For evaluations, including the Development pilot study, as well as Efficacy and Effectiveness studies, a critical measurement issue is balancing the sensitivity of a measure for capturing change relative to the focus of the intervention and the degree to which the measure will be of interest to principals or superintendents. If a measure is closely aligned with the intervention, then it is more likely to show change but also less likely to be of interest to anyone but the researcher. In general, including both a sensitive measure to ascertain if the intervention is doing anything at all relative to the comparison group, as well as a broader measure that education leaders will care about is a good idea.

Research Design and Analysis Plan

All studies require a detailed explanation of the research design and data analysis plan. This description needs to be clear, and it needs to correspond with the research questions and hypotheses. Although the design and analysis requirements vary across goals, there are some general issues for investigators to consider.

Make the Methodologist a True Collaborator. First, the methodologist should be part of the team from the very beginning. When the methodologist writes the section on the design or data analysis plan in isolation from the rest of the team, one risk is that the design and analysis will not match the research questions because the proposal has evolved over time. Another problem that occurs is that the methodologist does not fully understand what the data will look like (e.g., what kind of data will result from each measure), and the analysis plan will not work with the intended data.

Address the Issues in the RFA. In the RFA, IES identifies issues that pertain to the design and analysis plan for each goal. Generally, issues are explicitly mentioned in the RFA because they have emerged as common problems in proposals. Consequently, researchers should pay attention to these issues. For example, under the Exploration goal, researchers who plan secondary data analyses should document their access to the data sets, and if data sets will be linked, reviewers will want sufficient information to be assured that the linking can be done.

Under the Efficacy and Effectiveness goals, a critical issue is the research design. Although random-assignment experiments are preferred, IES also funds strong quasi-experimental studies. IES requires research designs that meet the standards of the What Works Clearinghouse for establishing causality (http://whatworks.ed.gov). The What Works Clearinghouse has standards for randomized trials and regression discontinuity studies. For the Special Education Research Grants program, single-case experimental designs are allowed for low-incidence disability populations, and the What Works Clearinghouse has standards for establishing efficacy through single-case designs.

A common problem across goals, but particularly for the Efficacy and Effectiveness goals, is calculating the power analysis correctly. During the panel meeting, reviewers have been known to recalculate the power analysis that is in a proposal. Along the same lines, if the investigator does not have an empirical basis for assumptions regarding attrition rates, estimated effect sizes, intraclass correlations, and other parameters, reviewers will question these assumptions and the ramifications the assumptions have for determining the power of design. Investigators must be sure to clearly specify the data-analysis plan and ensure that the plan is appropriate for the structure of the data. Generally, evaluations that are conducted in schools will involve clustered or nested data (e.g., students are grouped in classrooms or schools, which are nested in districts). Investigators who are interested in learning more about the design of and analysis of data from clustered randomized trials may find the videos from the IES summer research institute on clustered randomized trials to be useful (www.ipr.northwestern.edu/qcenter/NCER2008/).

Personnel

The Personnel section does not need to be long. Essentially, the investigators need to demonstrate that they have the expertise to do the project and that they will devote sufficient time to carry out the project. It is helpful if there is a clear link between each of the key personnel and each major task in the project. The application will also include biographical sketches, which provide additional information on the expertise of the personnel. Reviewers will question whether key personnel have allocated sufficient time to do the project. For example, if a senior researcher is on for 2 percent of his or her time, reviewers will wonder if that individual has made a serious commitment to the project.

For projects that are conducted in field settings, it is extremely important that someone on the team has experience working with personnel in schools and districts. The primary reason for a project failing to be conducted as planned is that the research team loses their sample. For example, a district has agreed to participate in an evaluation, but then the superintendent changes, and the new administration does not want to do the evaluation. Implementing studies appropriately in schools is difficult. Efficacy and Effectiveness grants are multimillion dollar awards. It is extremely important that the team has expertise and experience in working with schools and managing a project of that size.

Reviewers will look at investigators' publication records to assess their expertise but also to look at prior grants received. When a researcher has had prior grants, reviewers will look to see what the researcher accomplished from those grants and what was published from that work. For example, if the researcher had a Development grant, did the researcher produce an intervention that showed promise? Is the current proposal a project to evaluate that intervention? If not, is that intervention currently being evaluated by some other team?

Finally, an issue that has arisen more frequently in recent years has to do with conflicts of interest. In the RFA, readers will see this issue addressed in the Personnel section. Essentially, reviewers are becoming more sensitive to how a research team will preserve the objectivity of the evaluation when the team includes individuals who developed or distribute the intervention. IES suggests that investigators ensure that random assignment, data collection, data coding, and data analysis are handled by individuals who are independent of the developer.

Resources

The Resources section does not need to be long. The researchers need to show that the lead institution and the collaborating organizations have the capacity to support the work. Often researchers will use their institution's boilerplate language about space, information technology support, and library resources. This language does not hurt, but researchers need to focus more explicitly on what is needed to conduct the proposed project. The most important aspect is to show that each organization, including schools and districts, understands what is involved in the project and what their responsibilities will be. Because the involvement of schools and school personnel is critical to most IES projects, being able to show that there are other possibilities for district and school partners in case the proposed partners drop out is helpful. For example, some investigators indicate that if Districts A and B decide not to participate in the study as currently planned, another district has indicated interest in the project already. Similarly, if a project requires access to data that are not under the researcher's control (e.g., a state's longitudinal student data system), the researchers should show that they have access to that data.

Top Nine Tips for Successful IES Grantsmanship

First, the most important tip is to read the RFA. Researchers who are familiar with grant competitions at the National Science Foundation or NIH may be used to more open, field-initiated competitions. The IES competitions are field-initiated *within* topic and goal. Hence, there is much more structure provided in the RFA because IES is funding specific types of research. Investigators should take seriously the directives in the RFA (i.e., any recommendation prefaced with "must" or "should"), because the reviewers take them seriously. In addition, the RFAs do change over time. Hence, researchers should not assume that the requirements will be exactly the same from one year to the next. This last caution is especially important for proposals that are being revised and resubmitted. The resubmission will be evaluated against the RFA under which it is submitted.

Second, after reading the RFA, researchers should talk to the program officer about their idea. The program officer can help researchers better understand the nuances of the research programs and provide insight into the issues that reviewers focus on.

Third, although the authors of the proposal may read and reread the proposal for clarity and consistency, it helps to have an outsider—a colleague who is not involved with the project—read the proposal. What is clear to the authors is not necessarily clear to the individual who is coming to the proposal with fresh eyes. Reviewers are more like the latter than the former.

Fourth, because proposals evolve for time and writing on computers involves cutting and pasting, it is all too easy to deviate across sections on a variety of issues, such as the purpose of the project, the hypotheses and research questions, the sample (e.g., size, characteristics), measures, and the goal under which the proposal is submitted. Before a proposal is submitted, the investigators should reread the proposal from beginning to end to make sure that the details are consistent throughout.

Fifth, it is helpful to reviewers if the project narrative follows the outline and uses the headers that are in the RFA. Although following the outline under each goal is not required, it is a simple way for the investigator to make sure that he or she has addressed each of the issues detailed in the RFA. Further, it makes it easy for reviewers to find information on specific issues.

Sixth, be persistent. Very few proposals are funded on the first submission. If a proposal is not funded, the researchers should read the reviews, and then talk to the program officers. The program officers can help the researchers interpret and understand the comments.

Seventh, for proposals that are resubmissions, IES allows researchers to respond to reviewers' comments in an appendix. No matter how the researcher feels about the reviews, the researcher should address the comments as completely as possible. Moreover, it is not wise to write things in the response (or anywhere else in the proposal) that imply that the prior reviewers did not do a good job in their critiques. Irritating the reviewers does not help one's proposal. Vent to colleagues, not to reviewers.

Eighth, submit the proposal well before the deadline. Why spend weeks preparing the proposal only to have it disqualified because it is late? If the proposal is late by a few seconds or a few hours, it is still late.

Ninth, take advantage of the resources that IES provides. The program officers are happy to discuss ideas and give feedback to researchers. IES conducts webinars on preparing applications. There is a "Resources for Researchers" webpage (http://ies.ed.gov/resourcesforresearchers.asp) that includes resources such as methodology resources, tips on applying, information on longitudinal data sets, and instructional videos primarily on research methods.

Final Thoughts

Preparing research proposals is time-consuming and hard work. Is it worth the effort? Writing a proposal helps us clarify our ideas. It forces us to delve into the literature, develop our ideas, and construct a logical and compelling argument. Comments from reviewers can spur our thinking even further and improve our research. Beyond these benefits, successful proposals bring resources that enable researchers to do the work that they want to do. Grants can help faculty attract the best doctoral students and provide resources to enable the faculty and their students to travel to conferences and interact with other leading researchers. For researchers who are willing to do the hard work to prepare the proposal, following the suggestions in this chapter can help increase the odds that the proposal will be a successful one.

References

Averch, H. A., Carroll, S. J., Donaldson, T. S., Kiesling, H. J., & Pincus, J. (1972). *How effective is schooling? A critical review and synthesis of research findings.* Santa Monica, CA: The RAND Corporation. Retrieved from www.rand.org/pubs/reports/2006/R956.pdf.

Diamond, K. E., & Powell, D. R. (2011). An iterative approach to the development of a professional development intervention for Head Start teachers. *Journal of Early Intervention, 33,* 75–93.

Education Sciences Reform Act of 2002. Retrieved from http://ies.ed.gov/pdf/PL 107–279.pdf.

Fixsen, D. L., Naoom, S. F., Blasé, K. A., Friedman, R. M., & Wallace, F. (2005). *Implementation research: A synthesis of the literature.* Tampa: University of South Florida.

Gonzales, P., Calsyn, C., Joselyn, L., Mak, K., Kastberg, D., Arafeh, S., Williams, T., & Tsen, W. (2000). *Highlights from TIMSS-R.* Washington, DC: National Center for Education Statistics. Retrieved from http://nces.ed.gov/pubsearch/pubsinfo.asp?pubid=2001027.

Green, L. W., & Glasgow, R. E. (2006). Evaluating the relevance, generalization, and applicability of research: Issues in external validation and translation methodology. *Evaluation & the Health Professions, 29*(1), 126–153.

Hallfors, D., & Cho, H. (2007). Moving behavioral science from efficacy to effectiveness. *International Journal of Behavioral and Consultation Therapy, 3*(2), 236–250.

Jerry, L., & Lutkus, A. (2003). *The Nation's Report Card: Reading highlights 2002.* Washington, DC: National Center for Education Statistics, Institute of Education Sciences, U.S. Department of Education. Retrieved from http://nces.ed.gov/pubsearch/pubsinfo.asp?pubid=2003524.

Jordan, M. (n.d.). [Quotation]. Retrieved from http://www.brainyquote.com/quotes/authors/m/michael_jordan.html#ixzz1kmqMEM00.

National Research Council. (1999). *Improving student learning: A strategic plan for education research and its utilization.* Washington, DC: National Academies Press.

Santapau, S. L. (2001). *The Nation's Report Card: Mathematics highlights 2000.* Washington, DC: National Center for Education Statistics, Institute of Education Sciences, U.S. Department of Education. Retrieved from http://nces.ed.gov/pubsearch/pubsinfo.asp?pubid=2001518.

13

Securing Support for High-Quality Scientific Research and Development in Educational Sciences

Eva L. Baker

Securing funds for research and development (R&D) projects depends on knowledge, luck, and experience, in varying doses. In this chapter, I'll attempt to compile and distill proposal writing experiences and present them as rough rules of thumb. The focus here is education with two caveats. First, many practices I describe may well apply to other fields. Second, federal and state departments outside of the agency designated for research in education, the Institute of Education Sciences (IES), have vibrant and well-funded programs supporting research in the schools, including other arms of the Department of Education.

In the pursuit of financial support, we have had great successes, and obviously, some failures. To begin, let's assume that the readers are interested in obtaining funds from a source external to their primary organization. In many commercial situations for instance, one needs to propose new ideas to one's own management, so the commentary may be relevant to those working in the nonpublic side of education.

What Proposals Are About: Research, Development, Evaluation, Dissemination

Let's start by considering the core functions of research and development to be played out in funded projects. Many proposals fail because the authors have an unclear or inaccurate model of the fundamental attributes and processes that are desired by the funding agency.

Research

What is research? At its center it is the production of new knowledge. New or new interpretations of knowledge are found. Knowledge can be discovered by reviewing prior work, by constructing new strategies and testing them, or by investigating an application that is new for a subgroup of students or to a particular topic. The study might be very fundamental, investigating previously unacknowledged relationships with no immediate application to practice. In education, however, much research is very practical. Studies might address whether short teacher development systems work, the best way to teach prealgebra to young underachievers, or investigate alternative reading practices leading to success of English learners. R&D has frequently been linearly depicted with fundamental research at the outset, followed by exploratory development, and then moving to applied research, practical development, evaluation of interventions, and broad dissemination or "going to scale." This model is represented in some of the IES proposal guidelines (IES, 2012). In real research, findings from practice may significantly inform theory, leading to later revisions of practices. It has been clear to me, however, that many studies cannot and should not be neatly pigeonholed into mutually exclusive R&D categories, such as exploratory development or evaluation. It is desirable that agencies provide enough flexibility for research that blurs the boundaries of their guidelines. For one point, agency foci and guidelines change with some frequency, and as a constituent, you can have influence on the changes.

Development

The goals of development are to make something and to create a credible claim for its efficacy. The evidence base for development is the extent to which the intervention or product meets its goals, often in tested comparison to common alternatives. In scientific development, a research base is also at the heart of the intervention design. Such development differs from artistic- or craft-based creation because of its dual emphases on a scientific knowledge for design and its commitment to evidence needed to claim its effectiveness. Examples of development may be large, like an entire reading system, smaller, like a tool, such as automated scoring of open-ended examinations (Shermis & Burstein, 2003); very targeted, such as a game teaching math or resilience (Baker, Griffin, & Chung, 2011); or a model to analyze and validate new kinds of achievement tests (Mislevy, Steinberg, & Almond, 2002).

In education, these developmental approaches are thought to yield "improvement." Most, if not all, of scientific development is intended to solve a problem, that is, improve on a situation, rather than exclusively contribute to the knowledge corpus (Cronbach & Suppes, 1969). Yet, development and research interact, and studies about instructional pedagogy are conducted in coordination with the development of mathematics videogames (Delacruz, 2011). Why should the grant writer care about these abstract relationships? Because writing a proposal is not a one-time thing, but a piece of a larger intellectual process. If the writer sees relationships between research and development, then he or she can traverse the boundaries between them and conduct studies that have meaning to both.

Evaluation

Evaluation studies address topics such as needs assessment, implementation of innovations, and effects of new developments in narrow or broader settings. For the most part, such studies answer the questions "Did it work?" "How well?" and "How do you know?" generalizing only to the group tested. These studies may employ qualitative techniques—for instance, observations, interviews, or detailed ethnographic procedures. Conversely, many evaluations rely on quantitative information, such as surveys, tests given before, during, or on a follow-up basis after the intervention to determine effectiveness. Evaluations may use a wide variety of designs, found in experimental studies, with randomized assignment of subjects to treatment and control conditions. Less stringent designs may permit the identification of reasonable comparison groups. An important, underdeveloped part of evaluation and research as well is the relevance and quality of the dependent measures used to derive evidence to support claims. For example, because educational policy focuses on standardized achievement tests, IES most generally requires their use in efficacy studies. Yet, it is well known that, for targeted interventions on a focused content or skill domain, targeted outcome measures are needed, and off-the-shelf standardized tests are likely to underestimate relevant domain performance. In addition to apt measures, good evaluations not only look at relevant intended effects, but also they investigate the intervention's staying power (using delayed measures) and generalizability of effects (examining learning in a different situation or with different constraints). The relationship of processes to outcomes used in the intervention are of interest to explain findings; for example, number of trials, incentives, help, or feedback and outcome performance may help explain poor findings. Comprehensive evaluations attend to side effects, those unanticipated positive or negative outcomes that accompany interventions. Consider findings from the Programme for International Student Assessment conducted over a period of years by the Organisation for Economic Co-operation and Development (OECD, 2010, 2011). These studies compare achievement at different age ranges of students in a large number of countries, most recently 67 countries. One finding is that many students who achieve at the highest level of mathematics or science report having little or no interest or intention to pursue the field as a career. This finding is generating alternative ways to teach high-level mathematics and to develop engagement and continuing motivation.

Dissemination

Funded research also addresses dissemination, either separately or as part of a research, development, or evaluation study. Dissemination, for education agencies, used to mean a count of how many people had been exposed to set findings, such as how many people in audiences when presentations were made, how many on mailing lists, or how many products had been purchased. We have learned now to take dissemination seriously, and almost all of our funded projects create tools for teachers and other practitioners to use to change their practice as a deeper mechanism of dissemination. Our view is it is better that they apply the idea in their own setting than hope that they can extrapolate from a journal article (if read at all) and apply findings to their own environments.

The remaining sections of this chapter will explore how to go about securing funds, from the notion of idea generation and sources of potential support to a moderately detailed guide on the actual creation of and issues to be considered in a serious proposal.

The R&D Market in Educational Sciences

There is an idea, often in the minds of the very new or the very experienced scholar, that their own personal intellectual ideas are of unassailable, intrinsic merit. They believe their ideas need only be well explicated in a conference presentation or research article and the world, and funders, will beat the veritable path to their door. Occasionally, this self-validation fantasy may be true. More likely perhaps, is the recognition at some point that the research world, like much else, operates in a competitive environment. Gaining support for research and development demands a competitive perspective. If there are more potential R&D performers than there are resources to fund desired scholarly pursuits, choices among individuals or scholarly teams will be made by funding officers. It is fair to assume that these choices are unlikely to be arbitrary; rather, they will be guided by the match of the proposed work to the desires of the funding source, whether the proposal follows a prescribed general framework or requirements for a specific functional tool. Intellectual acumen is often recognized, but history has shown that choices are made by comparing strategy, quality, and clarity of documents that propose a plan and justification for conducting the needed R&D. There is also a matter of who is proposing and what history individuals reviewing or making decisions have with the topic, the proposal team, and the institution. Such vagaries can rarely be managed.

Although "marketing" may have a derisive, commercial connotation for some in the scholarly community, especially since the idea of "market" has overrun almost all serious institutions in capitalist societies, the reality is that any proposal must compete. The proposal must not only detail the plans and procedures underlying an individual project or program of work, but also it must be written in an appropriately persuasive style. That style must argue for the work, explain why other potential competitive strategies are not desirable (like the Pepsi challenge), and do so in an academic rather than a baldly self-aggrandizing manner. To understand the market means to understand both the range and depth of funding sources for the scholar's desired activities as well as the interests of likely competitors. For example, one characteristic of the emerging R&D market is its clear tendency to support interdisciplinary work. Such work has been funded by agencies looking to combine psychology, computer science, and medicine, for example, or astrophysics, biochemistry, and ceramics. Sometimes, the combination of disciplines is left up to the proposal writer, and often the desire for research integration from different disciplines or fields of study is tacit rather than explicit. Often multidisciplinary efforts are arrayed in larger centers for a significant time period compared with single investigators funded for relatively short-term research projects. Whether the market will focus itself on fewer, larger entities, or seek to distribute research funds in smaller amounts and over shorter periods will always depend both upon economics of scientific research and the personal preferences of supporting agencies and their research program managers. Note that within research agencies themselves, there is internal competition for funds for specific programs, so the managers of research have already survived one level of competition, before your competition becomes public.

Purposes and Strategy of Proposals

Clearly, researchers use a variety of sources to determine what purposes they will pursue. Some are natural outgrowths of their prior academic training and experience. Some are developed after identifying emerging issues that the scholar finds interesting and believes can be addressed by new insights, methods, and outcomes. Some academics flock to where the money is, subtly or dramatically adapting their own priorities to those of available resources. With greater pressures on academic institutions, the incentive systems of their organization may invoke conflicting goals: high-quality, mission-specific, programmatic research, and high levels of funding.

The reasons for external resources are many, beyond contributing knowledge and practice. They may include the desire and responsibility to provide financial support for undergraduate students, graduate students, and new researchers. Scholars may hunt, even with some desperation, for research support to meet expectations if advancement or promotion depends significantly on the value of the revenue brought in to the home institution. Incentive for research activity also depends upon the personal image held about scholarly role, and these images are widely varied. Is the goal to become a preeminent scholar leading the theory development in a field? Is the drive less for deep contributions and more to attain visibility to practitioners or policymakers, to shape the direction of policy and practices in a near-term, applied setting? Perhaps the scholar wishes to develop studies whose reports can be written in lay language to reach a wider audience. Might the scholar have in mind early on a plan to transform research and development findings, if successful, into a commercial venture? And, then, there are those investigators who develop a passion that drives their work, whether to improve literacy for young children, help homeless kids achieve, or raise the U.S. mathematics performance. These passions may develop because common practical problems have not been solved. All of these options are found in almost every institution and in many disciplines, and it is common for scholars to combine more than one purpose in their efforts. They are mentioned here because the novice scholar may only think of choices that support the next promotion hurdle, without anticipating alternatives relevant for the future. Any choice of purpose should match the current (as well as changing) role and institutional pressures attending the scholar and research collaborators.

General Strategic Principles

Independent of personal purpose, there are some general strategic principles that should be considered to guide the writer of proposals for R&D support for IES and other education funders. These principles speak to the issues of audience, plausibility, feasibility, and competitiveness. Let us consider each in turn, although it will be obvious that they are overlapping in their application.

Audience

Although it is an undeniable fact, some proposal writers prepare the proposal to please themselves, rather than imagining the audience that will review it. Analogous to the research by Scardamalia and Bereiter (2006) on student composition skills, a writer can choose to tell about a project to an ill-defined scholarly audience or to tailor the proposal to elicit a responsive reading from individuals who will be making the decision about funding. As noted earlier, in many agencies and in more private foundations, the decision maker(s) may have had a seminal role in developing the program, usually by a process requiring them to obtain resources from their management in competition with other research program managers. Their task requires them to design the general framework of the work, sometimes to spell it out in greater (and sometimes inappropriate) detail to communicate its intent to potential contributors in a formal solicitation. They may also select a group of reviewers to be responsible for advising the program manager on the quality of the solicitations and to evaluate whether competitors had sufficiently understood and developed proposals that met the intent of the proposal development. In some cases, where proposal writers misinterpret intent, the solicitation for research may be withdrawn or, perhaps, delayed and given further clarification. In other cases, for instance in some foundations and agencies, the program manager makes the key decisions, ratified by a higher level of management. Moreover, educational agencies and foundations have been noted to reflect stronger points of view and willingness to support research conforming to that viewpoint.

Sensitivity to audience is essential, whether one has been invited to prepare a proposal or whether one is in competition with other scholars. Some funding agencies look for high-risk ideas. Others, through the peer-review process, may be intrinsically more conservative in their focus. There are a number of ways to understand the audience for research apart from what is explicitly indicated in the procurement document. One is to do background research on a range of agencies that support educational research. Within the Department of Education, there are a number of sources of funding. The principal research agency, IES, is designated as the major focus for research. It has a very specific set of rules for what kind of studies will be supported and identifies a relatively defined set of rules that guide the types of "research" it supports. Aside from methodological studies, its major focus appears to be on the development of interventions to support schooling. Strong emphasis in its guidance and review panels is devoted to quality of design, theoretical framework, and "efficacy" studies. Its focus, for instance, on randomized controlled designs, has developed as a reaction to some poorly conceived education research examples. One frequent requirement for methods at IES is a focus on standardized tests, noted earlier. IES is divided into four centers: the National Center for Education Research, the National Center for Education Statistics (NCES), the National Center for Education Evaluation and Regional Assistance, and the National Center for Special Education Research. Each of these has its own requirements and expectations. NCES is the home of National Assessment of Educational Progress, statistical compilations, such as the Condition of Education, and smaller studies available for competition addressing design, analysis, and validity issues. For educational research, one might well find support from other units of the Department of Education. Additional well-known agencies supporting education sciences are the National Science Foundation and the Office of Naval Research in the Department of Defense. Within these organizations, there will be programs that vary in their goals, expectations, and funding cycles. These expectations range from very basic research on learning, for example, to applied studies focused on developing or contrasting innovation to meet particular needs. Copies of previously funded research projects from education research sources, including foundations, are usually available on a website and can help guide the nature of planned and proposed work. If all previous awardees of research grants or contracts have included a strong applied element, it is likely that application should be a part of your proposal. Step one on the path to audience understanding is to read statements by the agency and, if possible, to get to know, either through the literature or personal meeting, relevant program officers. Ideally, the "getting-to-know-you" effort should occur in advance of a particular solicitation of interest. One must also understand that agencies' preferences and objectives change as a function of politics. It is important, for instance, to read the priorities released by the Secretary of Education or the National Board for Education Sciences of IES to discern if emphases have changed.

Comparing old priorities, offered under a different administration with current statements may be enlightening about subtle differences in expectations. If given the chance, you should be willing to serve as a member of a peer review panel for a particular agency. In that role, you can internalize the expectations and preferences of the research management.

Plausibility

In general, reviewers will look at who is proposing the research, and usually a significant proportion of the score given to a proposal is based on the quality of staff and institutional capacity of the proposer. If a new researcher decides to propose a very large endeavor, one that may have multiyear funding, it is unlikely that R&D funds will be awarded unless the quality of the ideas is far and away superior to any competitor. In general, new researchers should build their résumé and credibility by obtaining smaller research awards and using them to develop their publication record. In addition, it may always be an excellent idea to involve leading scholars in the field of interest as partners. They may be subcontractors, consultants, or have advisory positions for elements of the study. The agreement of such luminaries to participate in the proposal bolsters the reputation of a newer researcher and may well teach them valuable lessons. Even with such academic support, the proposer needs to be aware of the management requirements, including staffing and quality control, in addition to financial management. These topics will be explored later in this chapter.

Feasibility

What is the likelihood that the proposed work will actually occur as planned? When studies are conducted within one's own institution, feasibility first depends upon securing the approval of the institutional review board (IRB), which determines that the general methods meet standards and do not violate any precepts involving the use of human subjects and informed consent. New researchers may wish to consult members of the IRB for advice at the time a proposal is under development. Even in those cases where IRB gives approval, there is still the issue of recruiting participants in sufficient numbers to engage in the study. A good dose of realism should be reflected in the proposal, for instance, describing back-up strategies if the primary recruitment method yields an insufficient number of participants. Feasibility comes into play when the topic of the research may edge on personal information, affective states, and cultural values. Although deception is now rare in research, researchers need to understand participants' concerns. These include not only privacy and individual identification (usually handled by the IRB process), but also the perception by the subject that the study crosses some personal line. A third issue is the recruitment of institutions, such as schools. In these cases, letters of agreement are usually expected to be included in the proposal. Sadly, these letters may have little real value, for the time from proposal submission to award may be six to nine months. In that time, about one third of the superintendents of any district might change, policies governing student or adult personnel may be modified, and emphases by governance bodies may make a topic appear to be less relevant to the goals of the institutions.

Nonetheless, a key to success has been establishing good relationships with local and sometimes nationally situated schools. How can one establish such relationships? First, when local schools ask for me or another colleague to speak, at a board meeting, a large conference, or an afterschool professional development session at one school, our answer is always yes. We know we have to show we understand schools before we ask them to participate in research studies. Second, we often offer free training or seminars to draw school people to the University of California, Los Angeles, again with the motive of learning more about their interests and sharing our perspectives. Third, in every education study we conduct, we have teacher or principal partners as experts, helping us design interventions, write test items, and review our materials. Setting up a true sense of collaboration promotes a willingness to agree to participate in longer studies. Most recently, it has been essential to show that the research study itself will have potential payoff for students who are not performing well on goals that are part of the state testing program.

The practical matter of recruiting schools or teachers almost always runs into difficulty. For instance, in some cases, school districts will ask for volunteers for the study, a practice that limits generalizability of findings. Parental permission is usually required as well, and the yield may skew the intended sample of students. Studies may need students just as summertime begins.

Then, there is the issue of how much time will be used, for instance, to change patterns of behavior or to obtain significant learning. If the time is short, the likelihood of achieving results is weak. If the time is extended, then oversampling is required, because children are absent or change schools. Resulting attrition may affect the representativeness of the intended sample.

Competitiveness

If research support were based on a strict meritocracy, then competitiveness would depend upon the quality of ideas, methods, and importance of goals proposed by credible scholars. Such ideals are not always the case. In some situations, it is important to sweeten the competitive status of the proposal in a number of ways. These include adding supplementary outcomes, desirable but not required in the solicitation, and institutional resources, if permitted by the funder, proposed to supplement the study. Availability of additional local resources depends upon decision makers at the home institution and may include actual dollars, in-kind contributions such as equipment, compensated research time of faculty research assistance, and clerical help, as examples. In some cases, cost is a criterion for selection, and lower cost proposals are more likely to succeed. In other procurements, cost is defined, and proposals may be designed to fit the resource constraints. In some cases, cost is explicitly not an issue to be considered in the review and is handled as an administrative matter. Nonetheless, it is wise to make sure that costs are consistent with what the funder has previously awarded. The most difficult part of competitiveness is judgmental: deciding which aspects of the solicitation should be emphasized and the desirability of the team of performers, given the likely competitors. Help in this area can come from talking to more experienced researchers familiar with the funder and those who have prior success with the topic. A surprise is how forthcoming our colleagues usually are.

Figuring Out Sources of Support

How do you know where to propose? There are numerous options to help you. First is the history of institutional support in your department or section, that is, to determine who has funded similar work before. Second, one can scan websites like the Federal Register (www.gpoaccess.gov) and the Commerce Business Daily (www.cbdweb.com) to see what federal agencies support work of interest. Often there are unexpected sources that show up there, such as psychological research in the Department of Energy. Third, through one's development or foundation office, one can understand what is possible and likely in the foundation or private giving area and explore the Foundation Center website for information (www.foundationcenter.org). For example, foundations such as Bill and Melinda Gates, the Spencer Foundation, and the Hewlett Foundation have long supported education. Certain foundations are best if the focus is technology. Others are better if one is looking at higher education or social justice issues. Reading the foundation reports to see what and whom they have funded and the estimated cost of projects are essential elements of homework. Fourth, good knowledge of the field and learning where other scholars have received resources can be helpful. Talking to potential program managers in foundations and agencies can be very enlightening, for they are often very generous in suggesting peoples' names or institutional options for work they do not normally support. If they have some interest, they may ask you to send in a short concept paper, describing your research goal, method, and cost, and then give you feedback, or they may alert you to upcoming cycles of solicitations. Remember, however, that a quick "no" is a great gift. On the websites of most funders, there will also be useful information about cycles of proposals, time from submission to award, resource levels, and review procedures. In addition, these sites will usually have the desired format, if there is one, for the submission of the proposal.

Proposal Prospects

Assuming you have monitored websites and had useful conversations with funders and colleagues, you will reach the point when you are looking for a solicitation (sometimes called requests for proposals generally or broad agency announcements) in the federal world. Let's assume that the amount of money offered is about right and the topic and methods, if any are suggested, fit your goals. You may have the option, as noted earlier, to join others as a subcontractor, where the main recipient (the prime contractor or grantee) is in charge of the overall project and monitors the financial and technical quality of your work. If you choose to be in a subcontracting relationship, it is very important to clarify terms and expectations before writing a word. It is far too common that an organization will invite you to participate as a subcontractor to eliminate you as a competitor. Subsequently, when budgets are reduced (as they often are), it is probable that you would be dropped from the team by the prime contractor. If you are removed as a subcontractor, you have no recourse. So working out the conditions in advance is critical. What will happen if the budget is cut? Will subcontractors get their fair share of the reduction? Will they be protected by the prime ("held harmless")? Where is the work to be done? At your home institution? At an off-campus site? How will continuations and other options be handled? Who on your team and theirs will be points of contact? What will be the turnaround for collaborative review during the awarded research? What kinds of financial oversight will be expected, other than that normally provided by your organization? If you are prime contractor, or the leader of a partnership of one or more subcontractors, you will need to have thought through answers to these questions. Often a "teaming agreement" is signed for the duration of a particular procurement to spell out essential conditions. The matter of resource allocation is central. Before you write word one of the proposal, you need to discuss resources to get at least a firm estimate or proportion of the total. What kind of split in resources do *you* want? You could, under certain conditions where your work is especially expensive— for instance, large-scale data collection—receive the largest share of the planned project budget, even if you were not the prime contractor. It is often common to negotiate an approximate split such as 40–60, so that you can size your project to the available resources. It is likely that the mechanics of the contracting process are overseen by respective offices of contracts and grants at your university or institution. You may need to contact them early to get advice, give them notice, and may need to deal with the financial team serving your local department, school, or organization.

If you have a significant role in the proposal, you may be central to assembling the team of institutions and individuals. As suggested earlier, finding key individuals is essential.

One way to do this is to read the solicitation carefully and determine the names or references used. Calling such individuals and asking them to join in your proposal will have two benefits: first, you may strengthen your plan with their ideas and gain credibility from their participation; second, you may find out who is competing against you and make the judgment about your own group's competitiveness. Don't hesitate to call even the most well-known individuals to join your effort. Our experience has been that the better they are known, the more gracious they are, and they may very well wish to assist emerging scholars or to join a team whose membership they admire. Make the calls yourself, even if you don't have prior contact. Many may be happy that you called; they may be too busy, but may suggest you contact them again at a future time, either to participate in the proposal, should you win the award, or to join in another proposal opportunity. They may also give you advice, the kind of tacit knowledge they have assembled about the area, the funder, and even the program officer. I have found such calls to be immensely useful, even if they did not lead to an expanded team.

Assemble the Team

Next, assemble the team, physically or virtually, after securing a statement of interest and willingness to help. Clarify who are the principal investigators and project directors for the overall project and for subcontracts. The principal investigator(s) are responsible not only for the overall execution and quality of the work, but also for the financial management of the project (or projects, if a larger center is being sought). The project director is usually the person who manages day-to-day operations. In smaller awards, these functions may be handled by the same person. Bring in the clerical staff and editors, if any, who will be responsible for putting together the final document. Discuss general format requirements and strategy for the document. For example, innovative formats may not be desired unless explicitly specified. Sections of the proposal should mirror the sections called for in the procurement.

Agree on protocols for using virtual, shared space, who may update, specified section and version numbers (not left to the automated update when a document is opened), and the way the transactions will occur and be reviewed. If it is a complex project, agree on an overarching theme to link disparate parts of the project and write it early, even if only communicated roughly in bullet format.

Decide who is the lead writer for various sections of the proposal, who will be reviewers on the team, and if you have time, who will review the entire document externally before it goes to its final draft. Estimate the number of drafts needed and figure out due dates for each wave. Obviously, the introductory, thematic section may be needed before certain other sections can be written.

Proposal Requirements

Read the solicitation again, very, very carefully. The solicitation, asking for the proposal, may be clear or disorganized. It may demand too many products for the resources available. The agency oversight may be at typical review points or be more demanding. For example, on a number of current projects, we have weekly teleconferences with the program managers, and sometimes levels of reporting are far more detailed than expected. The solicitation may indicate such management, requiring a certain number of oversight trips, presentations to the funder's higher up staff, workshops, and reports for various audiences. Some of this demand meetings that are not explicitly called out, so to be safe, it is good to have a cushion for them. Be sure to include trips and other dissemination requirements in the budget because they functionally subtract from the resources available for the research study itself. Commonly, the project will ask for collaboration with other awardees. Collaboration may mean simply sharing information at prearranged times, developing collaborative approaches to solving problems, or working through and executing joint dissemination efforts options. Depending on expectations, collaboration may be a big-budget item. In addition, the funder may reserve the right to ask for revisions, and a common error is to plan too little time and money to assure revisions take place. As noted earlier, subcontractors are supposed to be collaborators with the prime and other members of the team. It is important that one's contribution be appropriate to the budget and recognized within the project. From my own experience, small subcontracts or consulting sometimes have resulted in my unattributed ideas, often exact words, being used by the prime as their own work.

A critical path through reading the solicitation document involves first determining what kind of procurement instrument is being used. Is it a contract, with a specified set of deliverables? If so, changes in scope during the project will need to be approved by the funder. Is it a grant, which often gives the investigator more leeway in proposing timeline, methods, and R&D outputs and may be more flexible? Is it a cooperative agreement? Cooperative agreements are legally grants, but require ongoing consultation with the funder throughout the project on major (and sometimes) minor issues. IES uses cooperative agreements and their flexibility in larger projects and center awards varies with the program officer. Understanding the difference between procurement options, such as grants and contracts in contrast to other research resources, such as gifts, can be extremely helpful. For example, contracts may be fixed-priced, which means that no more money will be forthcoming if the deliverables or products fail to meet the funders' standards. This may be a high-risk proposition, for if the agency rejects the project's output after all money has been expended, the project team must complete it on its own resources. Conversely, if you think that the project desired is not very difficult, or if you have experience, a tool or other "trick" to make the project successful for far less money than is available, then a fixed-price contract will give you the full amount promised upon the successful submission of the products, and the unspent money can remain under your control at your institution. But, it is a gambler's instrument. Most grant awards are called "Best Effort" awards, and just like dissertation studies, even if you do not find what you intended, you will be compensated for your effort. You must certify that you have done your best, and back that up with careful financial reporting. The trend, it seems, is to move toward contracts, formerly the major vehicle for commercial providers, and use them more frequently in academia. Many grants have taken on attributes of contracts, with deliverables, milestones, and predicted funding patterns required.

To understand more about expectations, find out when and where the public question-and-answer period will take place to allow proposers to clarify ambiguities in the procurement. This may take place online or in person, and typically questions and responses are published, although there may be a delay in posting them, which can be a disadvantage if the due date is close. One should know that usually one does not interact with the program officer or those in oversight positions when the proposal competition is open, unless the topic excludes the proposal. There are variations on what is fair to discuss, but generally in the federal government, such conversations are not permitted and can lead to protests by losing competitors.

Writing

To begin writing you must determine the functional format requirements. Are there restrictions or targets for total pages, word count per page, spacing, font and its size, the use of color, binding, and other such issues?

Following the understanding of the general procurement instrument and how that affects your work, I would negotiate the path through the solicitation by starting at the end. I suggest first reading very carefully the criteria to be used to judge the quality of the proposal and the differential points that will be allocated to elements, such as quality of personnel, institutional capability, methods, goals, feasibility, and innovation. Focus as well on the particular word length required, and what fits in the main proposal. Does the budget section count? Can you provide additional references, lengthier resumes, or supplementary graphics in appendices? It has been my practice to divide the required and supplementary sections in accordance with the proportions awarded for each section. For instance, if theoretical context is worth 10 points, in a 100-page document, I would have 10 pages devoted to the topic. These components help you structure the document.

Read whether the funders intend to share the proposal. In the federal government, the Freedom of Information Act allows individuals to request funded proposals in most cases. The funder may have intentions to share your proposal, although they may ask for identification of proprietary sections. It has been our practice to put copyright notices on the entire proposal and requests not to cite without permission. It has also been our experience that sometimes our work is shared. Determine what the ownership plan is for the outcomes of the project. Will ownership of intellectual properties reside with the proposing group, or will the funder expect that the work will be made publically available (open source)? It has been our experience, for instance, that some funders happily share pieces of drafts or early projects with those we would consider competitors without seeking our approval. Can you foreclose that option in the proposal? Can you commercialize the output if desired? On the opposite side, some solicitations are for work that you cannot publish, because of secrecy or classified status, or because a commercial company wants rights of review for any document emerging from the study. You may well have to possess a specific security clearance to win some awards. Your university may have rules proscribing such projects that cannot be published. Similarly, there may be provisions in the solicitation saying that the funder has the right to review in advance potential publications emanating from the study. My own university will not permit such prior review of research published. Because I wanted to do the work, I undertook a study of a large project as a consultant. The evaluation, I thought, was generally positive, but apparently the funding agency did not agree. They did not publish the work or its summary, and the contract forbade me from doing so. I'll not do that again.

Crafting the Proposal

Like any good combination of analysis, explanation, and persuasion, the document has to make the case, explicitly, for why this project is going to yield important results, why its methods are appropriate, and how the funder will be able to meet its own goals through the work you perform. It is also important to feedback to the proposing agency, ideas that they regard as central and allocate sufficient space to those elements that they regard as important.

The sections of the document are specified in the solicitation but will include elements such as objectives, importance, literature or theoretical or practical support, methods, and so on. The proposal typically begins with a statement of overall goals or objectives that may be specified in more detail in a later section. In the background, or argument in the narrative, some compromises must be struck. Just on a writing level, the proposer must seek a balance between keeping the main elements of the proposal in front of the reviewer, such as linking cognition and emotion in games, and providing sufficient detail so that everyone can understand what actually would be done. For instance, unless otherwise specified, it is a good idea to limit the review of research to the pages specified. It may be shortened by making assertions about findings, and then listing in parentheses the key studies that support the claim. This is opposed to a common practice of analyzing each relevant study in-depth, a desirable effort, were there sufficient space, and if it can be done without overshadowing the major strands of work to be proposed. Ideally, the section should have subheads related to each important element in the procurement, justifying the approach taken. This justification does not mean sweeping under the rug contrary or potentially ambiguous findings. These should be included and treated appropriately, but probably not at length. If one goal of this section is to communicate deep understanding of the areas in question, another is to frame the detailed objectives or hypotheses of the work.

Objectives of the project should be clear, operational, and directly linked to the measures and outcomes that are intended. This relationship may be well presaged in the objectives section, although details of outcomes, their audience, quality criteria, and formats will occur in a later section.

Methods

Most agencies want a lot of detail here: who, what, when, and how long to judge the comprehensiveness, clarity, and feasibility of the design and procedures. Some procurements will emphasize (or for instance, IES requires) great clarity about certain strategies. Is a randomized control design being used? How are subjects selected as well as assigned? What are the power requirements for students that use mixed models, for instance, some districts, some schools, some teachers, some grade levels, some students with different background characteristics? What is the major unit of analysis (unit of randomization) and how adequate is the sample to examine interactions and nonrandom effects? Sometimes the actual models to be used to compute power should be included, if they are not widely disseminated. If an intervention is to be designed and tested, what is the planned effect size? This estimate of variance accounted for is obviously linked to power in hypothesis testing.

Measures, Metrics, Criteria, Tests

Some agencies specify the outcome measures to be used, such as a standardized test in a particular area or administered by the states in which the study is conducted. Obviously, such specification creates problems for innovative content to which such measures may not be sensitive and also requires the development and validation of measures that supplement the prescribed tests to show effects. Unless already developed (where technical quality information can be provided), the proposer needs to include design and validation plans for any new measures. This stricture also pertains to the use of questionnaires, where in education and other areas, the use of one item "scales" are common. It is important to gather validity information in these areas, but it is often difficult, especially if growth on the measures is expected to occur over a considerable time. One strategy to use is a kind of discriminant validity, where people who are known (or at least thought) to possess the skill or attribute are contrasted with those who do not (expert-novice studies in learning) and evidence is obtained to determine the degree to which the measure detects differences between groups. This approach does not require long periods of time waiting until a group has been taught the intervention. A second, complementary approach is to use close interviews of performers as they respond to the measures, perhaps involving their thinking aloud about responses as they make them. Data collection and analysis of this type of investigation can be time-consuming even for small samples, but well-chosen representatives of key subgroups can provide convincing information.

Capability Statements for Organizations and Individuals

Capability statements should be carefully crafted and adapted to each procurement rather than your rolling in a standard boiler plate. Prior work that is relevant to the required focus needs to be referenced and awards, honors, and significant findings need to be highlighted.

It should be clear that the staffing selected for the project should have a representative expert in each of the major areas to be explored, and this expertise should be reflected in their résumés. For individuals, résumés (often required in paragraph form) also need careful attention to assure that high-value efforts and those particularly relevant to the proposed work are emphasized. Even in the appendix, if space allows for fuller résumés, it may be wise to use "Selected Publications" to focus the reviewers' attention on history of performance in the proposed area. Some agencies expect lists of recent publications, recent financial awards, including amount, duration, oversight officer, and the like.

Costs

An old saw is that one should calculate proposal costs from the bottom-up, that is, which people, spending what time, plus what other special resources (recruitment incentives, consultants, travel, equipment) will be required. Once done, in the ideal, you would double the resulting total and add a zero. Would that were possible! It is true that researchers may often underestimate the cost of projects and may need help both substantively in deciding on what to invest in and practically in how to craft a budget.

The first shock may be that the project is responsible for the benefits costs of project employees, for example, health, retirement, and social security. These benefit percentages may vary with type of personnel—faculty, professional research staff, administrative staff, graduate students, for example. In most cases, graduate student fees and tuition are required costs, so that hiring a graduate student may be financially less desirable than a postdoctoral researcher. However, because university research exists in part to support students, costs here are not especially pertinent. However, they must be budgeted.

A big surprise to many is the matter of indirect costs. For universities, university-wide percentages for indirect costs have been negotiated with the federal government. This means that a proportion, let's say 60 percent of the value of project direct costs, will be added to the cost of the study. This does not mean the university gets $6 out of every $10, but it does mean that a significant amount of money is not available for project expenses. In particular, for each $10 you spend, the university takes another $6. This money belongs to the university; sometimes a proportion goes to the state in state-funded universities and is often returned in part to the dean of the unit for discretionary use or to departments or individual researchers. Proposers can attempt to negotiate a return from the dean on the value of their proposal drawn from indirect funds. But, the rate for research is fixed by agreement with a federal oversight agency. No particular agency can abrogate these limits. If the research is conducted off campus and does not use campus facilities, buildings, janitorial services, and so on, then indirect costs levels will have been established for that situation, although the proposing team may need to pay for rental space, furniture, and so on, off campus.

Other ways in which indirect costs can be reduced depend on project type, for instance, if the project is a training project rather than a research project. In addition, some private foundations have upper limits, such as 20 percent of project costs that they will provide for indirect costs. Often universities accept this level, even if it is below what is actually needed to meet costs of the research, because of the prestige of the granting agency and the importance and visibility of the grant.

For commercial companies, indirect costs are usually divided into categories involving general and administrative costs, which pertain to the organization, for example, accounting costs. A second area, overhead, is general technical costs that are useful to the project but are not billable as direct costs, for example, the maintenance of a reference database or journal subscriptions. A third area, if allowable, is the fee or profit the company specifies. With the federal government, all of these levels are subject to audit, and sometimes companies may not be permitted to bid without proof of a successful audit by the oversight agency.

In addition, there are direct costs that may be billed to the project, such as equipment (either new or recharged based on use), paper, copying, report preparation, and conference expense. Some of these are estimated using archival information, whereas others can be directly calculated. Some agencies do not permit the charging of food, even for an all-day business meeting on the project. Some universities do not pay for food from any source for its local employees. Few institutions pay for alcohol at dinner, unless there are unrestricted funds available for such expenditures. The lesson is that, sometimes, the principal investigator pays for such expenses privately, if they are deemed by her to be required for project success (excluding alcohol). Projects may not pay expenses of, or give free food to, government personnel.

Audit Liabilities

Legally, costs assigned to a project must be legitimate. So, it is not possible for an investigator to supplement one study with funding from another with a different purpose, even if the projects share staff. The proposer should be aware of the regulations audits impose, for as principal investigator, he may be personally responsible for financial errors made under his supervision.

After the Writing

Even though the writer has had many choices during the crafting of the proposal, there are the requirements in the solicitation that must be met. The proposal must arrive on or prior to the date and time specified. Remember time-zone differences. There are no exceptions, even if FedEx or another carrier was delayed by a snowstorm. One carrier once lost our proposal en route to the agency, despite our using tracking software for a minute-by-minute tracking. It arrived late. Even though it was insured, they were willing to reimburse us for the cost of the delivery only, not for the cost of proposal preparation. These stringent standards are not simply the convenience to the funder. If different proposers have more or less time to complete their submission, the process loses its fairness. More practically, complaints, suits, or other legal measures may be taken by unsuccessful authors. Similarly, now that proposals are uploaded on servers for agencies, make sure that personnel are trained and start early enough to anticipate the last-minute rush.

Final Thoughts

This chapter has ranged from the abstractions of R&D to the details of tracking a delivery service. Putting together a proposal is difficult, both intellectually and on the procedural level. It requires considerable knowledge usually acquired only through experience and strong intuitions. It requires more savvy and effort than proposals in former years, where the goal might be for a professor to support a graduate student and take one trip a year to his or her primary professional association. In many universities, interdisciplinary centers are replacing disciplinary research, and the complexities of their management are many, including but not limited to knowing how to manage the quality of work.

Nonetheless, the conduct of personally developed research by a team is one of the most rewarding parts of a university or R&D life. It is the lifeblood of what scholars do, is essential to developing our students, and contributes strongly to our ability to understand phenomena that may lead ultimately to impact in the field. Despite the cautions and the conundrums, I highly recommend it.

References

Baker, E. L., Griffin, N. C., & Chung, G. K. W. K. (2011, April). *GAMECHANGER: Using technology to improve young children's STEM learning* (Proposal to the Defense Advanced Research Projects Agency). Los Angeles: University of California, National Center for Research on Evaluation, Standards, and Student Testing (CRESST).

Cronbach, L. J., & Suppes, P. (Eds.). (1969). *Research for tomorrow's schools: Disciplined inquiry for education.* New York: Macmillan.

Delacruz, G. C. (2011). *Games as formative assessment environments: Examining the impact of explanations of scoring and incentives on math learning, game performance, and help seeking* (CRESST Report 796). Los Angeles: University of California, National Center for Research on Evaluation, Standards, and Student Testing (CRESST).

Institute of Education Sciences. (2012). *Overview of IES research and research training grant programs.* Washington, DC: Author. Retrieved from http://ies.ed.gov/funding/overview.asp.

Mislevy, R. J., Steinberg, L. S., & Almond, R. G. (2002). On the roles of task model variables in assessment design. In S. H. Irvine & P. C. Kyllonen (Eds.), *Item generation for test development* (pp. 97–128). Mahwah, NJ: Erlbaum.

Organisation for Economic Co-operation and Development. (2010). *PISA 2009 results: Executive summary.* Paris: OECD Publishing. Retrieved from www.oecd.org/dataoecd/34/60/46619703.pdf.

Organisation for Economic Co-operation and Development. (2011). *Lessons from PISA for the United States, strong performers and successful reformers in education.* Paris: OECD Publishing. Retrieved from http://dx.doi.org/10.1787/9789264096660-en.

Scardamalia, M., & Bereiter, C. (2006). Knowledge building: Theory, pedagogy, and technology. In K. Sawyer (Ed.), *Cambridge handbook of the learning sciences* (pp. 97–118). New York: Cambridge University Press.

Shermis, M. D., & Burstein, J. (Eds.). (2003). *Automated essay scoring: A cross-disciplinary perspective.* Mahwah, NJ: Erlbaum.

14

Diversifying Your Funding Portfolio

The Role of Private Funders

Susan M. Fitzpatrick and M. Brent Dolezalek

Securing external funding in support of their research program has become part of the job description for academic faculty. In this chapter, we hope to provide researchers in the psychological sciences with some insights into the grant-making mechanisms and priorities of a subset of private funders likely to come onto the radar of researchers looking to identify potential sources of support. The types of funders we concentrate on in this chapter are (1) independent and family foundations, for example, the James S. McDonnell Foundation and (2) disease-specific public charities, also called voluntary health organizations, such as Cure Autism Now. For simplicity's sake, we will refer to these organizations within this chapter collectively as "foundations." However, it is important to remember that these two categories of foundations have very different structures and that within these two categories each individual funder is more different than similar.

In general, independent and family foundations disperse in the form of grants an Internal Revenue Service–mandated percentage of the income generated from an endowment, much like the way colleges and universities use income generated from endowments to fund projects and programs. Public charities support research with funds raised from a large number of donors through a variety of mechanisms including events, donor solicitations, and corporate sponsorship. This chapter does not address the research support provided directly to institutions or to individuals by high-net-worth individuals (known as Major Donors in development-office speak), by venture funds, or from corporate foundations. Using the James S. McDonnell Foundation as a model, we also concentrate on private funders that use advertised requests for applications/requests for proposals with specific application guidelines rather than private funders who tend not to engage in strategic programmatic giving but rather make grants to institutions with which they have special relationships. In general, foundations in the latter category communicate directly with senior university officials and rarely consider unsolicited applications.

The chapter presents general principles for approaching foundations and offers guidance about how to discover the individual characteristics of a foundation that will be important to consider prior to application or proposal preparation. The information presented in this chapter comes with an important caveat: We are providing you with our perspective of how private funders operate based mostly on our own experiences as program officers at the James S. McDonnell Foundation. Needless to say, private funders are highly individualized and idiosyncratic. The most important take-home message of this chapter is the following: Success at receiving support from private funders means taking the time to investigate a foundation's history, philosophy, and personality and taking what you learn seriously when making a decision to move forward with an application.

The fact that private funders are like snowflakes in that no two are alike in the way they identify and select projects to support can naturally lead to frustration on the part of applicants, who may feel that they are already spending too much time searching for funding. On the positive side, however, the diversity of interests and decision making creates the opportunity that ideas early in their inception or projects that depart from the reigning dogma or from the status quo could get a sympathetic reception. But, this tension does mean you have to be smart about the way you approach foundations.

To help you better understand the role private funders can play in the overall support of your research, it is important that we place foundation funding in the more general context of overall support for research in the United States. Suffice it to say, and this underscores the importance of the advice we provide later in this chapter, foundations account for a tiny sliver of the overall funding pie. For investigators searching for funds, foundation dollars can be an important sliver, but their scarcity requires that for your search to bear fruit, it must be targeted and specific.

In 2009, the most recent year for which complete figures are available, the United States invested $400.5 billion in research and development. Federal government and industry funds accounted for 82 percent of the total expended while universities and colleges represent 14 percent (Figure 14.1). The remaining 4 percent ($17.5 billion) is the research and development expended by nonprofit institutions. Although the absolute value of these numbers can change from year to year, the percentages have remained fairly constant for the past two decades. It is important to point out that the $17.5 billion sliver also represents nonprofit support for *all* science. Psychology (or for social/behavioral research) has traditionally represented a small percentage of foundation support for science. Unfortunately, in this way, foundations are

Figure 14.1 $400 Billion U.S. Investment in Research and Development for 2009 (National Science Board, 2012)

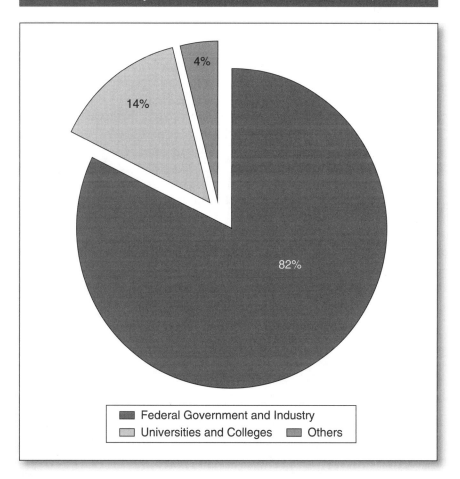

mirroring a reality also true of the federal funders (Figure 14.2; Britt, 2010). Taken at face value, these numbers might be very discouraging for researchers looking to foundations to make up the shortfall in their budgets. The numbers could suggest that foundations are of minor importance in the past and future development of U.S. science and technology and of only minor interest to academic researchers tasked with raising external sources of support for their research programs. The numbers, however, do not tell the entire story.

Before we become too discouraging, we think it worthwhile to introduce a historic digression so we can put private funding for scientific research into a context that tells a more interesting story and one not captured solely by

Figure 14.2 $55 Billion of R&D Funds for Science and Engineering at Universities and Colleges, 2009 (Britt, 2010)

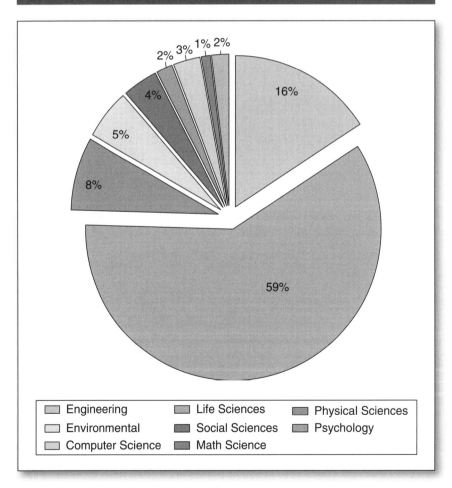

the numbers. In the first few decades of the 20th century, prior to the establishment of large government-sponsored funding agencies, private philanthropy was a major contributor to scientific research. Since World War II, however, the dollar amounts contributed by private foundations to scientific research, as indicated earlier, account for a small fraction of the total national investment. Yet, an examination of what American philanthropy has done, currently does, and might do in the future to sustain academic research suggests that looking only at relative dollar amounts *does* not tell the whole story. Foundations, by strategically and creatively looking for opportunities, have been and can be essential to the development of American science (Kevles, 1992; Kohler, 1991; National Research Council, 2006). Foundations have been and are the source of valuable "venture funds" used to launch new careers, new ideas, and even new academic disciplines.

Identifying a Niche

One of the ways foundations make an impact with limited funds is by carefully targeting funds in such a way that even modest investments could yield significant returns. A side benefit of establishing a well-defined niche is that doing so can create a natural limit to the number of applications submitted. Foundations typically award a small number of grants. As anyone whose research deals with signal-to-noise problems knows, it is very difficult to make principled decisions when selecting a few grantees from a large number of applications. It is important for potential grant seekers to understand that foundations that craft initiatives and specify their funding niche are very likely getting more fundable proposals than the available dollars can support. It is highly unlikely for a foundation to fund a proposal that falls outside the publicly stated areas of interest or outside of the published guidelines. Each foundation used different criteria to help carve its niche, but a few of the common strategies employed by foundations include the following:

- Narrowing topically—identifying areas within a broad topic that tend to be underfunded and underresearched. A foundation interested in memory disorders, a rather large space, might target their giving to research focusing what is known about memory functions and what keeps elderly seniors able to live independently.
- Selecting a rung on the career ladder—many foundations define their funding space by limiting support to applicants at particular career stages. Foundations tend toward supporting early career scientists (trainees or junior faculty), considering an investment at the start of a research career as likely to yield returns throughout a researcher's professional life span.

- Bridging the gaps—foundations have a history of success formalizing "informal colleges" by providing support for new research questions emerging from the edges of traditional academic disciplines and by supporting research questions requiring concepts and methods from multiple disciplines.

It is easy to see how foundations develop funding schemes using such strategies. A grant seeker doing investigative homework should not be surprised to read of a foundation program targeting junior investigators working on a defined set of questions requiring research integrating concepts and tools from multiple academic disciplines. In your search for potential funders, it may very well be true that no foundation occupies the niche you have carved for yourself. Our advice: Do not to try to force a match when there isn't one.

The Psychology Funding Landscape

There was a time in the not so distant past when psychology faculty could typically support their research programs with a base of institutional support supplemented with one or two grants from a federal funding agency, typically the National Institutes of Health (NIH) and/or the National Science Foundation (NSF). Although there may be a few isolated Ivory Towers left, in today's tight funding climate and era of diminishing institutional support, it is increasingly likely that psychology researchers will need to become more entrepreneurial and *extramural* when it comes to garnering research support. As is already true for the biomedical sciences, building and maintaining a robust and successful research program is likely to require assembling a diverse array of funds composed of grants from federal, institutional, and private sources together with some investment or sponsorship from the corporate or for-profit world.

A decade ago, while analyzing private support for scientific research, the James S. McDonnell Foundation examined the acknowledged sources of support for articles published in 34 issues of the weekly journal *Science* selected from all issues published between August 1998 and June 1999. Typically, foundations are interested in funding research early in its inception, and we were curious to see if there would be much overlap in the papers acknowledging private support versus public. We were somewhat surprised to find that 42 percent of the more than 530 research articles identifying their sources of research support reported several funding sources with some funding from private donors in their acknowledgments. Limiting the analysis to articles characterized as biomedical and life sciences pushed the percentage of papers acknowledging some private support to greater than 50 percent. The message we took away from this data is that, at least in some fields, diverse sources of funding were increasingly becoming the norm. More recently, we decided to take another look at this rather simple metric in the limited context of neuroscience. We performed the same analysis on a smaller set composed of the 124 research articles published in *Nature Neuroscience* between 2003 and 2008. From the acknowledgments section of each article, we counted the number of papers acknowledging financial support from public funders only, a mix of public and private funding sources, private funders only, and no sources. We also noted how many papers acknowledged support from funders representing more than one country. The findings are summarized in the pie graph in Figure 14.3.

Figure 14.3   Funding Source Acknowledgments for *Nature Neuroscience*, 2003–2008

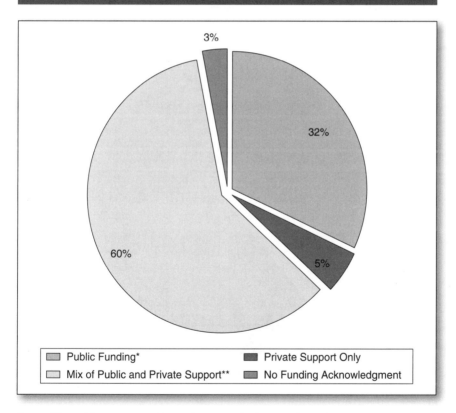

Source: Nature Neuroscience (11 journals, 124 articles from 2003–2008).

*Six included a mix of international public sources;

**Thirty-one acknowledged a mix of international funding sources.

Considering it might be interesting for the purposes of this chapter to see how the pies would look in the context of psychology, we performed the analysis with a one-year snapshot from two journals, a classic psychology journal, *Psychological Science,* and the *Journal of Cognitive Neuroscience,* representing a fast-growing research discipline closely allied with departments of psychology (Figures 14.4 and 14.5). Granted, the analysis selects a minuscule sample of all the psychology research papers published annually, and we would probably be wise not to make too much of it. Still, the results are intriguing. A quick glance demonstrates that psychology research might be lagging biomedical and neuroscience research in diversifying its funding base. Perhaps the most surprising finding comes with comparing the data from *Psychological Science* with the other journals we coded. We would not

Figure 14.4 Funding Source Acknowledgments for *Psychological Science,* 2011

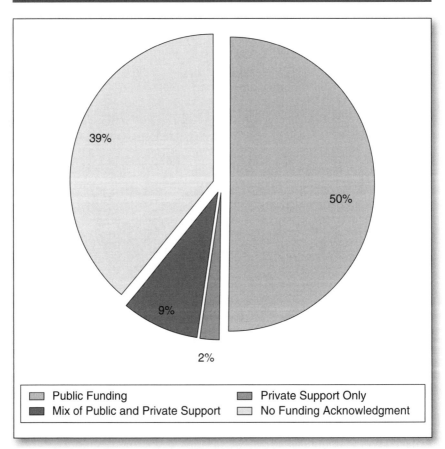

Source: Psychological Science (12 journals, 231 articles from 2011).

have guessed that almost 40 percent of the *Psychological Science* papers would not acknowledge a source of funding. It is not clear what to make of this, but we suspect that the picture will change in the coming decade. We foresee a time when the acknowledgment section of psychology papers may increasingly read like this exemplar from the October 2011 volume of *Psychological Science* by Kendler et al. Their paper titled "The Impact of Environmental Experiences on Symptoms of Anxiety and Depression Across the Lifespan" acknowledges U.S. public funding from NIH, international public funding from the Netherlands Organization for Scientific Research, the Swedish Research Council, and Swedish Council for Working Life and Social Research, and private support from the Carman Trust and the W. M. Keck, John Templeton, and Robert Wood Johnson Foundations.

Figure 14.5   Funding Source Acknowledgments for the *Journal of Cognitive Neuroscience*, 2011

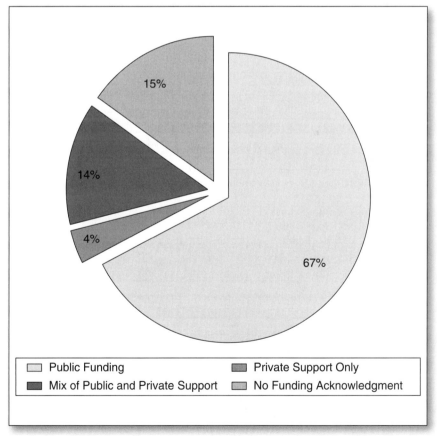

Legend:
- ▢ Public Funding
- ▨ Mix of Public and Private Support
- ▨ Private Support Only
- ▢ No Funding Acknowledgment

Source: Journal of Cognitive Neuroscience (12 journals, 322 articles from 2011).

Foundations Supporting Psychology

A list of foundations with programs relevant to psychological science is provided in Table 14.1. It is difficult to get an accurate picture of total foundation support for psychology primarily because there is no comprehensive database gathering such information. Aggregated information such as that tallied by the Foundation Center (www.foundationcenter.org) is often provided at too coarse of a grain to make meaningful determinations or to guide a researcher seeking support. We recommend that researchers work closely with the professionals in institutional advancement offices (also known as "development") to identify potential funders. Development officers have the skills and tools needed to carry out more sophisticated searches for relevant opportunities to apply for funding. The University of Minnesota–Morris serves as a good example of a development office identifying funding sources relevant to psychology (University of Minnesota–Morris, Grants Development Office, n.d.).

Table 14.1   Programs With Connection to Psychology

Foundation	Website	City, State/Country
Alfred P. Sloan Foundation	www.sloan.org	New York, NY
American Psychological Foundation	www.apa.org/apf	Washington, DC
Andrew W. Mellon Foundation	www.mellon.org	New York, NY
Annie E. Casey Foundation	www.aecf.org	Baltimore, MD
Carnegie Corporation of New York	www.carnegie.org	New York, NY
Charles A. Dana Foundation	www.dana.org	New York, NY
David and Lucile Packard Foundation	www.packard.org	Los Altos, CA
Fetzer Institute	www.fetzer.org	Kalamazoo, MI
Ford Foundation	www.fordfound.org	New York, NY
Foundation for Psychocultural Research	www.thefpr.org	Pacific Palisades, CA

Geraldine R. Dodge Foundation	www.grdodge.org	Morristown, NJ
Glaser Progress Foundation	www.glaserprogress.org	Seattle, WA
Harry Frank Guggenheim Foundation	www.hfg.org	New York, NY
The Haynes Foundation	www.haynesfoundation.org	Los Angeles, CA
Jacobs Foundation	award.jacobsfoundation.org	Zurich, Switzerland
James S. McDonnell Foundation	www.jsmf.org	St. Louis, MO
John D. and Catherine T. MacArthur Foundation	www.macfound.org	Chicago, IL
John and Mary R. Markle Foundation	www.markle.org	New York, NY
John Frederick Steinman Foundation	http://goo.gl/N1BRT	Lancaster, PA
John Simon Guggenheim Memorial Foundation	www.gf.org	New York, NY
John Templeton Foundation	www.templeton.org	West Conshohocken, PA
Pew Charitable Trusts	www.pewtrusts.org	Washington, DC
Robert Wood Johnson Foundation	www.rwjf.org	Princeton, NJ
Rockefeller Brothers Fund	www.rbf.org	New York, NY
Russell Sage Foundation	www.russellsage.org	New York, NY
Spencer Foundation	www.spencer.org	Chicago, IL
Staunton Farm Foundation	www.stauntonfarm.org	Pittsburgh, PA
Wellcome Trust	www.wellcome.ac.uk	London, United Kingdom
William T. Grant Foundation	www.wtgrantfdn.org	New York, NY
W. K. Kellogg Foundation	www.wkkf.org	Battle Creek, MI

Source: University of Minnesota, n.d.

In addition to support from private foundations with an interest in behavioral research, psychology can garner funding from disease-specific charities and voluntary health organizations supporting research related to the cognitive and psychosocial aspects of diseases affecting brain function and impacting behavior negatively. Foundations with interests in depression, Alzheimer's disease, Parkinson's disease, schizophrenia, autism, stroke and brain injury, and many other insults and injuries affecting the nervous system could offer funding programs relevant to research in psychology. It is now well accepted that individuals with brain disorders have life-changing alterations in mood, cognition, and behaviors. A better understanding of the social and psychological impacts of neurological disorders could inform the design diagnostics and outcome measures. Importantly, psychology working with more traditional biomedical disciplines could contribute to the development of appropriate treatment options directed at multiple levels of analysis. It might be worthwhile for psychologists, perhaps working through their professional societies, to partner with neurological disease advocates in advancing a more comprehensive approach to research informing diagnosis and treatment.

In this context, an important point worth highlighting is the disparity in funding sources for research related to the consequences of abnormal development or neurological disease (or described as such) and research focused on an understanding of normal cognitive and psychological processes. NIH funding for neurological disease and mental disorders is more than 34 times that of NSF's support for psychology (approximately $3 billion compared to $100 million) (NIH Almanac, 2012; National Science Bound, 2012). We think the future of psychology and the health of the nation might benefit from some rebalancing of this ratio.

Best Practices for Applying to Foundations

1. Read Everything

Most foundations, particularly if they support academic research, have very comprehensive and informative websites providing details concerning:

- Goals and missions
- Program guidelines
- Eligibility
- Application guidelines
- Selection criteria
- Frequently asked questions
- Lists of prior grantees
- Names of reviewers

Our advice is to read everything provided. Pay special attention to the list of prior grantees as they provide a peer comparison group you should carefully weigh your credentials against. Also, pay special attention to the reviewers. At the James S. McDonnell Foundation (JSMF), we select reviewers to strategically advance the foundation's programmatic goals.

2. Follow Not Just the Letter but the Spirit of the Guidelines

In our experience, potential grantees jump directly to the application guidelines, missing important information about the limits (for both the letter and the spirit) of eligibility. For example, a foundation might state that applicants must have obtained a Ph.D. within the past 12 years. An applicant exactly 12 years post-Ph.D. is technically eligible. However, a careful reading of the posted information indicates that the goal of the program is to help faculty transition from pre-tenure to posttenure positions with the expectation that for most candidates this will occur somewhere between 6 and 10 years post-Ph.D. The generous 12-year guideline is to provide some space for individuals with atypical career paths or who have had to take time to meet personal or family obligations. An application from a senior associate professor 12 years post-Ph.D. will more than likely be eliminated from consideration early in the review process. To decrease the number of ineligible proposals, it is becoming more common for foundations to ask potential applicants to complete an "eligibility quiz" prior to receiving application guidelines.

3. Use Good Judgment

Foundations typically have small staffs. For example, JSMF has four full-time staff. We consider the JSMF website our hardest working *fifth* staff member since it is available for communicating with potential grantees about the foundation's programs and funding opportunities 24/7.

Although we often hear or read that federal funding agency program officers encourage potential applicants to contact them with any questions, this kind of contact is usually not encouraged by foundations. Most foundation program officers wear multiple hats with responsibility for several or in some cases all the funding programs. We also spend a large percentage of our time out of the office. A system relying on one-to-one, person-to-person communication through the telephone or even e-mail is not an effective way to transfer information. In general, at JSMF we advise grant seekers to carefully read and review the material posted on the website prior to contacting the foundation. If you do need to contact the foundation for clarification, it is best to use whatever preferred method the foundation advises. JSMF requests e-mails to an address specifically designed for this purpose. In our experience, approximately 90 percent of the e-mailed inquiries we received could be answered with even a cursory review of the JSMF Web pages. Calling JSMF is the most unlikely route to a quick response. It is not that we do not want to be accessible. We want a leveled playing field where all applicants have access to the same information. We know that part of the motivation for calling is not to get an answer to an obvious question like font size or page numbers but to form a personal relationship and to get feedback on the general scope of the proposed project. At JSMF, we prefer that you are the best judge of whether or not your research program fits the guidelines. It is important to keep the purposes of guidelines in perspective. Guidelines are called guidelines for a reason—they keep proposals consistent, important for making principled comparisons, but they also allow for judgment calls to be made on the part of applicants. Submitting the application is only the first hurdle in a very competitive process. It will not surprise you that there is an inverse correlation between the number of times an applicant contacts the foundation for assistance and the funding success of the submitted application.

4. Conscientiousness Pays Off

Although it should go without saying that following the posted instructions for submitting a proposal is essential, you'd be surprised at how often this step is overlooked. Applications that are missing required information, have pages out of order, are difficult to read because of small font size or a poor-quality scanned file, or that are submitted after the deadline are not competitive. There may be some foundations kind enough to contact an applicant and give him or her an opportunity to correct errors, but we would not suggest you count on second chances. Remember, most funders are receiving many more applications than can be funded.

Prior to submitting an application, double-check that it includes all required components. We know this tidbit of advice may appear to be too fundamental to mention, but our experience indicates otherwise. Applications should be scrutinized to make certain they conform to the guidelines concerning format, style, page or word limits, and attachments. Applications should be complete, containing all requested information, assembled as listed in the application guidelines. We craft JSMF's guidelines so that they can also serve as an application checklist.

We cannot emphasize enough how important it is to submit an application on time. At JSMF, we try to have as tight a turnaround time as is possible and the review process begins within hours of the application deadline.

We do not believe it is fair to allow some researchers to submit late or incomplete applications. At JSMF, as is true for many other funders, application deadlines are firm. Now that most foundations use electronic submission processes, we also recommend that you do not wait until the closing minutes of eligibility to upload your application. Any technical snafu could jeopardize all the hard work that went into the preparation of the application.

5. The Budget: Driven by the Science

One component of an application that we at JSMF pay special attention to, and we know this is true of other private funders as well, is the budget and budget justification. Budgets are reviewed both in-house and by our external advisory panels. Each foundation, and even different programs within a foundation, can have very different allowable items. In general, foundations do not allow for the recovery of indirect costs that have been negotiated between universities and federal funding agencies. It is important to make sure your institution will accept the budget restrictions of a foundation prior to submitting your application. A foundation should not be the first reader of your proposal.

Have Other Eyes on Your Proposal

Junior investigators should avoid the temptation of rushing the preparation of a proposal so that it has to be submitted before it has had a thorough in-house review by an experienced senior investigator. Asking a senior colleague to review the completed proposal, with a copy of the application guidelines attached, will not only help catch the errors and omissions that could cause an otherwise promising proposal to miss the first cut, but also it will most likely save the application from failing because of some other common traps. Every program officer will tell you that nothing is worse than getting that sinking feeling in the pit of your stomach when you read what appears to be a promising proposal on an interesting topic that just never manages to make its case. There are times that we read a proposal, hoping the next few paragraphs will finally tell us what it is the researcher *actually* plans to do! Another common pitfall for young investigators is overstuffing a proposal. We sometimes get the feeling, while reading a proposal, that the applicant convinced himself somewhere along the line that if some is good, more is better. We have read proposals requesting three or four years of support that would take decades to complete. Most foundation application requirements are not onerous; project narratives rarely are longer that two or three thousand words. An experienced colleague can quickly detect weaknesses that are likely to contribute to a proposal being triaged out of consideration early in the review process.

Final Thoughts

In summary, our experience suggests that a successful proposal meets the following criteria:

- Arrives on time, submitted as required
- Is complete and prepared according to guidelines
- Conforms to eligibility
- Is well matched to program goals
- Is budget appropriate
- Narrative prepared to meeting guidelines and is readable, articulate, informative, and engaging; problem is defined and proposed work makes sense in context of the problem

Our final words of advice are to keep in mind that researchers and foundations are partners. Researchers want to pursue interesting and important scholarly work and foundations want to fund interesting and important research that is well matched with their program goals. Before committing time and energy applying to a foundation, take the time to determine if you are a good fit to the foundation's mission and program goals by carefully reading the program description. If the program description sounds promising and is consistent with your research area, you shouldn't stop there. Browse through the list of grants funded in that program area, and read the grant descriptions, if available. Some foundations post grant titles only, but others, like JSMF, provide a public essay of each grant as written by the principal investigator. Keep in mind that programs evolve over time and aspects are often tweaked from year to year, so it's important to note that there may be a difference between more recent grants and grants awarded several years ago. Foundations are boutique, not retail funders. Unlike NIH or NSF, foundations are not charged with fueling the entire academic research enterprise. Their limited resources must be deployed more strategically. To successfully meet this goal, foundations need researchers with interesting ideas.

References

Britt, R. (2010). Universities report $55 billion in science and engineering R&D spending for FY 2009; redesigned survey to launch in 2010. *National Science Foundation InfoBrief*, NSF 10–329. Retrieved from www.nsf.gov/statistics/infbrief/nsf10329/.

The Foundation Center. (2012). *Foundation directory online*. Retrieved from http://fdonline.foundationcenter.org.

Kendler, K. S., Eaves, L. J., Loken E. K., Pedersen, N.L., Middeldorp, C. M., Reynolds, C., Boomsma, D., . . . Gardner, C. O. (2011). The impact of environmental experiences on symptoms of anxiety and depression across the life span. *Psychological Science, 22*, 1343–1352.

Kevles, D. J. (1992). Foundations, universities, and trends in support for the physical and biological sciences, 1900–1992. *Daedalus, 121*(4), 195–235.

Kohler, R. E. (1991). *Partners in science*. Chicago, IL: The University of Chicago Press.

National Institutes of Health (NIH). (2012). *Almanac–Appropriations: Section 1*. Retrieved from www.nih.gov/about/almanac/appropriations/index.htm.

National Research Council. (2006). *Evaluation of the Markey Scholars program*. Washington, DC: The National Academies Press.

National Science Board. (2012). *Science and engineering indicators 2012* (NSB 12–01). Arlington, VA: National Science Foundation.

University of Minnesota–Morris, Grants Development Office. (n.d.). *Opportunities by discipline—Psychology*. Retrieved from www.morris.umn.edu/grants/FUNDING-disciplinePSYCHOLOGYpage1.htm.

15

Seeking Funding From Private Foundations

Morton Ann Gernsbacher

In this chapter, I will talk about seeking research funding awarded by private foundations. I will be using the term "private foundations" as the term is often used in discussions of research funding, namely, as a contrast to funding agencies, such as the National Science Foundation (NSF) or the National Institutes of Health (NIH), which award grants from federal revenues.

Furthermore, I will be using the term private foundations to refer to both charitable foundations, like the Red Cross, which solicit funds from the public, and private foundations, like the Bill and Melinda Gates Foundation, which are endowed by an individual or family. Complicating the issue even more is the fact that most private foundations operate in the public sector, so the term "private foundation" might be a bit misleading. But, as I stated at the outset, I will use the term "private foundation" as it is used in discussions of research funding, namely, as a source of research funding that doesn't derive from federal (or state or municipal) revenues.

The Variety of Private Foundations

The private foundations that fund behavioral and brain science research vary along several dimensions, including the size of their operating budget and—not unrelated—the size of their grant-program portfolio. Many behavioral and brain scientists have heard of the relatively large John D. and Catherine T. MacArthur Foundation (www.macfound.org/about/), which "supports creative people and effective institutions committed to building a more just, verdant, and peaceful world." The MacArthur Foundation reported total assets of $5.7 billion at the end of 2011; it received nearly 7,000 grant proposals during the preceding 12 months, and through its foundation staff of nearly 200 employees, it awarded $230 million of grant funding during 2011.

Many cognitive scientists have heard of the relatively large Alfred P. Sloan Foundation (www.sloan.org/about-the-foundation/). The Sloan Foundation "makes grants to support original research and broad-based education related to science, technology, and economic performance." The Sloan Foundation was established in 1934 by Alfred Pritchard Sloan Jr., then-president and chief executive officer of General Motors. The Sloan Foundation reported total assets of $1.7 billion at the end of 2010. In addition to awarding grants for basic research in the behavioral and brain sciences, the Sloan Foundation awards grants to "outstanding filmmakers and screenwriters who bring innovative, compelling stories about science and technology to the screen" (www.sloan.org/major-program-areas/public-understanding-of-science-and-technology/film/film-schools/recent-winners-of-film-school-prizes/?L=0).

Medium-sized foundations include The Spencer Foundation (www.spencer.org/content.cfm/mission), which is "dedicated to the belief that research is necessary to the improvement in education." Since its founding in 1971, The Spencer Foundation has awarded grants totaling $250 million. Another example of a medium-sized foundation is the James S. McDonnell Foundation. The McDonnell Foundation was founded in 1950, and since then has awarded grants totaling $347 million (www.jsmf.org/about/). The McDonnell Foundation's grant program is guided by its 21st Century Science Initiative, one focus of which is the study of human cognition. However, as the foundation cautions, grant applications "proposing to use functional imaging to identify the 'neural correlates' of cognitive or behavioral tasks (for example, mapping the parts of the brain that 'light up' when different groups of subjects play chess, solve physics problems, or choose apples over oranges) are not funded." Nor does the McDonnell Foundation fund "[f]unctional imaging studies using poorly characterized tasks as proxies for complex behavioral issues involving empathy, moral judgments, or social decision-making."

As the names of these foundations suggest, many were established in honor of or at the bequest of an individual. One of the most common household names is the benefactor of the W. K. Kellogg Foundation (www .wkkf.org/who-we-are/our-history.aspx). Indeed, Will Keith Kellogg is described on the foundation's website as "the cereal industry giant and inventor of Corn Flakes." Another example is the William and Flora Hewlett Foundation (www.hewlett.org/about), which "has been making grants since 1967 to solve social and environmental problems at home and around the world," and the David and Lucile Packard Foundation (www.packard.org/), which "for more than 45 years . . . has worked . . . to improve the lives of children, families, and communities."

Perhaps less well known as a household name, but recently in the news for purchasing the Hawaiian island of Lanai, is Lawrence J. Ellison, who established the Ellison Medical Foundation (www.ellisonfoundation.org/). The foundation "particularly wishes to stimulate new, creative, research that might not be funded by traditional sources or that is often under-funded in the U.S." Ellison was also the founder of Oracle database software, was reported by Forbes (in 2010) to be the third richest person in the United States, and dropped out of both the University of Illinois and the University of Chicago during his twenties.

Other foundations are the offspring of financially profitable corporations, such as the Ford Foundation (www.fordfoundation.org/grants), whose "grant making focuses on reducing poverty and injustice; promoting demo-cratic values; and advancing human knowledge, creativity and achievement" and the Carnegie Corporation of New York (carnegie.org/about-us/mission-and-vision/), which aims to "promote the advancement and diffusion of knowledge and understanding."

And, still other foundations are well-known public charities, for example, the long-running March of Dimes. On the March of Dimes website, you can read an extensive history of its founding, and for several years, you could join a unique type of advocacy: helping the March of Dimes keep Franklin D. Roosevelt on the dime. Another example is the American Cancer Society, which for "more than 60 years ... has been finding [and funding] answers that save lives—from changes in lifestyle to new approaches in therapies" (www.cancer.org/Research/ResearchProgramsFunding/index).

Learning About Private Foundations

Where can you, as a researcher, find out about these private foundations? And, more importantly, how can you find out which of these private founda-tions might fund your research project? Sometimes there are staff members working at your college or university whose job it is to help investigators find funding opportunities. For example, the University of Wisconsin–Madison maintains an Office of Research and Sponsored Programs, and this office subscribes to several online databases of grant information.

However, I've had my best success locating private foundations to fund various aspects of my own research program the same way I find everything from long out-of-print *Fraggle Rock* episodes to discount airline fares. I suggest you turn to Google or a similar search engine. For example, using a Google search with the unquoted terms *foundation research child development*, I found within the first 20 hits many of the familiar foundations that support research on child development, such as the W. T. Grant Foundation, the Foundation for Child Development, and the March of Dimes.

Whether you identify these foundations through your own Internet search or through a search assisted by your university research office, the next step is to begin perusing the foundation's website. Typically, the first thing you'll read is the foundation's mission statement.

For some foundations, their mission will be obvious from their foundation's name. For instance, the International Dyslexia Association's mission is to "support and encourage interdisciplinary research [to] facilitate the exploration of the causes and early identification of dyslexia" (www.interdys.org/whoweare.htm). The Foundation for Alcohol Research's mission is "[t]o achieve a better understanding of the effects of alcohol on the health and behavior of individuals; [t]o provide the scientific basis for prevention and treatment of alcohol misuse and alcoholism; [t]o fund innovative, high quality research; [t]o support promising new investigators, [and] [t]o communicate information effectively with the research community and other interested parties" (www.abmrf.org/Mission.asp). Thus, for what we can consider cause-based foundations, their purviews are relatively obvious from their foundation's names.

The purview of other foundations is not always apparent in their names and also often is obscured in their mission statements. For instance, the mission of the William T. Grant Foundation is to support "research to improve the lives of young people" (www.wtgrantfoundation.org/about_us/mission_statement). What's not to love about that mission? But, will your proposed study on prosocial development in preschoolers be of interest to this foundation? It's hard to say from only the mission statement.

As another example, the Kellogg Foundation's mission is to support "children, families, and communities as they strengthen and create conditions that propel vulnerable children to achieve success as individuals and as contributors to the larger community and society" (www.wkkf.org/who-we-are/our-history.aspx). But, does the Kellogg Foundation support scientists whose research relates to how those goals can be achieved? To find out—to get a clear vision of any foundation's funding priorities—I recommend looking at a list of its previously awarded grants and grantees.

For example, when you look at a list of grants recently funded by the Foundation for Child Development, you will find that they recently funded a study investigating the "Cognitive and Socio-emotional Outcomes of Children of Immigrants," a study identifying the "Cognitive Consequence of Exposure to Multiple Languages," and a study exploring the "Immigrants, Parenting, and Infant/Toddler Well-being" (http://fcd-us.org/our-work/new-american-children/ysp-profiles). When you download a list of recent grants awarded by the Human Frontier Science Program, you will find that they recently funded a project titled "Imaging Neuronal Activity and Connectivity Across Neocortical Areas" and another titled "The Striatal Cholinergic System and Attention for Learning: From Neurotransmission to Personality" (www.hfsp.org/awardees/newly-awarded).

When you click to read the completed projects funded by the Russell Sage Foundation, you learn that grants titled "Race, Ethnicity, and Identity, 2010," "Intergroup Experience in the Stereotype Content Model," and "Identity Threat and the Racial Achievement Gap" were recently funded (www.russellsage.org/research). When you look at the Fetzer Institute's website, you learn that "[s]ince 2001, the Fetzer Institute has supported more than thirty scientific studies on compassionate love and altruistic love. Nine new studies explore compassionate love within a broad range of relationships, including marital, parent-child, families, inter-group, and relations between religious and cultural groups" (www.fetzer.org/resources/compassionate-love-research).

Another way that I've found to identify potential private foundations is the academic version of *People* magazine reading: I view research articles that are related to my own research interests, and I look to the acknowledgments section. There I might find that one of my memory-research colleagues was awarded a grant from the Dana Foundation, that a reading researcher was awarded a grant from the Haynes Foundation, and that a cognitive neuroscience colleague was awarded a grant from the Brain and Behavior Research Foundation (which was formerly called NARSAD). Similarly, I recommend perusing your colleagues' vitas or websites to see what funding organizations have supported their work, or provided them with junior or senior level fellowships or awards.

To summarize: Good sources for finding out about appropriate private foundations for your own research are the foundations' own mission statements, but do be advised that these statements can be, intentionally or inadvertently, vague or overly circumscribed compared with the research that the foundation actually funds. Therefore, it's often even more beneficial to look at the lists that most foundations provide of their previous grants and previous grantees. One can also check the lists of advisory board members to get a sense about the foundation's priorities. And, I really like reading the acknowledgment sections of published articles to identify relevant foundations, as well as snooping around in my colleagues' vitas and on their websites to see which foundations have provided my colleagues with grants and awards.

Applying to Private Foundations

So, let's say that you have identified what looks like a potential foundation—how do you start the application process? As simple as it sounds, the most important piece of advice is to follow the directions. And, follow them scrupulously. In this way, applying for funding from private foundations is very similar to applying for funding from federal sources. There are rules and regulations, and they need to be followed.

Indeed, as the Kellogg Foundation states in the introduction to its online application: "As you might expect, we receive more requests each year than we are able to fund with our limited resources. We are not able to fund requests that do not fit our funding guidelines." These guidelines can constrain who can apply, when you can apply, and how you can apply.

Some foundations, like the William T. Grant Foundation, have been known to walk you through a series of questions that help you determine if you are an eligible grantee. The interactive feature of its website asks you questions such as, "Are you an early career researcher at a university or a not-for-profit institute interested in a highly competitive program for junior scholars?" If you answer "yes" to this question, you are taken to the next branching question, such as "Do you have a terminal degree, awarded within the past seven years?"

I truly can't stress how important it is to read all of the instructions and to follow them to a T. If the foundation says that the budgetary limit is $60,000 per year, then don't propose a penny more. If the foundation says that the maximum duration of the grant is 24 months, then don't propose a second more. If the foundation says that a principal investigator salary will not be supported, then … well, you get my point.

There are some general principles you will want to keep in mind when applying to private foundations.

First, make clear why you are applying to that foundation in particular. Private foundations are usually quite targeted in what they fund and often prefer not to fund proposals that just as easily could be funded by a large federal agency such as NSF or NIH. So, you will want to emphasize the fit of the proposed research to the particular mission of the foundation.

Second, clarify what the benefit of the research is in terms of the particular mission of the foundation. With an organization such as NSF, the main concern is scientific benefit, with societal benefit perhaps a strong second. Private foundations have all kinds of missions, and they are particularly interested in benefits in terms of their particular mission, rather than just generally in terms of scientific progress or social benefit. So, target the benefits section to the foundation.

Third, remember that your first shot is probably your last. Whereas federal agencies often entertain revisions, foundations typically do not. So, your first shot has to be your best!

Pros and Cons of Seeking Foundation Support

This brings me to the pros and cons of applying for private foundation support. Let's start with the cons. In most cases, funds provided by private foundation grants are limited, and often quite limited, meaning more the size of an NIH small exploratory grant than an NIH program project. However, I've found that $60,000 a year provides a great springboard for starting a new research project or collecting necessary pilot data.

Another drawback is that grants from private foundations are typically not renewable; they are fixed terms, sometimes extending only one or two years. Moreover, you can typically only go to the well once, meaning that many private foundations don't fund multiple applications by the same investigator, even if the topic varies.

Furthermore, you—and more specifically, your institution—shouldn't expect high indirect cost recovery rates. Often, the indirect cost recovery rate is 15 percent or even lower. Furthermore, often the principal investigator salary is not an allowable budgetary item, and purchasing major equipment may not be within the foundation's budgetary guidelines. Also, in contrast to many federally funded opportunities, private foundations often offer a more limited number of application deadlines, sometimes only once a year. However, the turnaround is typically faster. Don't expect to get the depth of feedback on your unsuccessful (or successful) application that you would get if you applied for a federal grant. Most often, you'll just receive a two-sentence letter saying that the foundation is unable to support your application (or a phone call saying that they are). If you are fortunate enough to be awarded a grant from a private foundation, be prepared to write frequent, but short, progress reports.

Offsetting these cons, what are the pros? Often, you are allowed or required to test the waters prior to submitting a full application by submitting a short Letter of Intent. Even the full application in many cases is relatively short, definitely shorter than the traditional 25 pages we used to submit to federal agencies. Funding decisions for private foundation grants are often based more on the quality of the ideas than on a demonstrated track record. Therefore, junior faculty, senior faculty who are retooling their research toward a new area, or faculty who don't run large RA-loaded factories have just as good of a shot as anyone, if the ideas they propose are of interest.

Lastly, my experience has been that working with private foundations often involves developing a personal relationship with the foundation staff, and sometimes with the founders. The first grant I received from a private foundation was announced to me by a personal phone call from the president of the foundation.

Final Thoughts

If you are seeking a relatively small amount of funding and are all right with the idea of funding that may not be renewable, private foundation funding is worthy of your consideration. Keep in mind, though, that private foundations pay little or no overhead and so you will want to make sure that the college or university in which you work will support your application. Sometimes, they may be reluctant to do so for fear of losing money on the grant. Thus, in addition to having to plead your case to the foundation, you may also have to plead your case to your institution as to why they should accept funding at a potential loss to the institution. Whatever you decide, good luck in finding funding for your research!

16

Funding Opportunities at the National Aeronautics and Space Administration

Cynthia H. Null and Bettina L. Beard

his chapter summarizes the funding mechanisms of the National Aeronautics and Space Administration (NASA). Further, it provides a guide to the funding sources at NASA and to assembling the components of compelling proposals.

Become Acquainted With the NASA Enterprise

One of NASA's primary objectives is not only to provide a worldwide understanding of the systems and processes on our planet, in our atmosphere, and in the cosmos, but also to stimulate economic development in the United States. This objective is addressed through education as well as fair and open competition to outside sources for the work required by NASA's four mission directorates—Aeronautics Research, Space Operations, Exploration Systems, and Science (www.nasa.gov/about/directorates/index.html). Each directorate is further divided into focused programs. The majority of the funding opportunities in the brain and behavioral sciences are at the Aeronautics Research and Exploration Systems Mission Directorates. Programs in these directorates include the work of the International Space Station, the Space Shuttle Program, the Launch Services Program, and the Space Communications and Navigation Program.

Although NASA has world-class facilities and almost 19,000 civil servants,[1] most of the research and development is done out-of-house. NASA typically allocates 85 percent of its $18.7 billion budget to *directed* grants and contracts[2] to the private sector (i.e., industry, education and other nonprofit organizations). Research sponsored by NASA must be relevant to its programs in addition to being of high intrinsic scientific and technical merit, affordable and realistic in cost. The first steps toward a successful proposal are to read NASA's Strategic Plan, visit each program's webpage, and attend program technical interchange meetings.

The URL www.hq.nasa.gov/office/procurement/forecast/ will take you to the acquisition forecast for each of the NASA research centers listed here:

Ames Research Center: www.nasa.gov/centers/ames/home/index.html

Dryden Flight Research Center: www.nasa.gov/centers/dryden/home/index.html

Glenn Research Center: www.nasa.gov/centers/glenn/home/index.html

Goddard Space Flight Center: www.nasa.gov/centers/goddard/home/index.html

Jet Propulsion Laboratory: www.nasa.gov/centers/jpl/home/index.html

Johnson Space Center: www.nasa.gov/centers/johnson/home/index.html

Kennedy Space Center: www.nasa.gov/centers/kennedy/home/index.html

Langley Research Center: www.nasa.gov/centers/langley/home/index.html

Marshall Space Flight Center: www.nasa.gov/centers/marshall/home/index.html

Stennis Space Center: www.nasa.gov/centers/stennis/home/index.html

NASA Solicitation Mechanisms

NASA generally uses two types of broad agency announcements to solicit proposals for basic and applied research: The NASA Research Announcement (NRA) and the Announcement of Opportunity (AO). AOs announce research opportunities, typically through contract, having well-defined deliverables and relatively heavy oversight to prevent cost and schedule overruns. Contracts awarded through an AO can be for hundreds of millions of dollars and may have periods of performance lasting 10 years or more for space flight missions. Investigators in the brain and behavioral sciences will most often be interested in NRAs. Proposals that respond to a specific NRA are called "solicited proposals." NASA receives and processes several thousand solicited proposals each year. NRAs range from one to five years, but most awards are for three years. NRAs are typically aligned with the sponsoring program or project mission and goals, although often not specifically in order to stimulate creative responses. The response time to NRA announcements typically is 90 days. NASA sometimes initiates an omnibus solicitation in which the needs of several projects and programs are combined in an overarching solicitation.

NASA uses peer review based on factors in the NRA to select proposals for funding. Unlike the AO's request for proposals, which contain a statement of work or specification to which proposers respond, NRAs provide for the submission of competitive project ideas, conceived by the proposers, in one or more program areas of interest that it specifies an end product or service.

To stimulate technological innovation and to encourage the commercial application of research results, small businesses may present an innovation that meets the technology needs of NASA's mission directorates and that has significant potential for successful commercialization. Details can be found at www.zyn.com/sbir/bnews.htm.

NASA also solicits new and innovative education products, tools, and services from qualified external organizations. Rather than alignment with NASA mission directorates, education solicitations align with changes in science, technology, engineering, and mathematics education trends, identified gaps in the education investment portfolio, or new priorities identified by Congress or the administration.

NASA Award or Funding Instruments

Awards depend on the type of proposing organization, which is self-identified on the proposal cover page and typically aligns to the proposing organization's financial reporting identity as required by federal law. Table 16.1 lists the various award instruments.

Regardless of the award instrument, NASA agrees to provide a specific level of support for a specified period of time. Funding is usually provided annually because of the fiscal year federal budget process, although there can

Table 16.1 The Award Instruments That NASA Uses

Award Instrument	Objective	NASA Involvement
Grant[3]	General enhancement of the field of scientific and technical programs of interest to NASA	No substantial technical involvement is expected between NASA and the recipient, nor does the government direct the research
Cooperative Agreement		Substantial technical interaction and cooperation between NASA and the selected recipient(s) to achieve NASA's desired objectives (e.g., to develop and operate a research institute, an extensive educational/ public outreach activity, or a specified technology capability)
Contract	Acquisition by purchase, lease, or barter of property or services from the contractor for the direct benefit to or use by the government	Contracts are negotiated and have deliverable products (i.e., a study in a specified area of basic research)
Interagency Transfer	One U.S. government agency obtains needed supplies or services from another U.S. government agency	

be exceptions to this rule. NASA occasionally sponsors programs that fund selected tasks for up to five years, although in such cases the selected tasks are subject to full peer evaluation after the first three years in order to qualify for continued funding.

Notification of Release of NASA Research Solicitations

Requests for Information

Requests for information (RFI) are sometimes issued prior to the NRA. An RFI includes rates, experience, estimated cost, and relevant reasons for a potential application that NASA can use to get a sense of how well the proposer communicates with the client. Failure to adequately meet the expectations or omission of necessary information disqualifies one from the short list.

Submitting a Solicited Proposal to NASA

The following section will take you through the solicitation, proposal submission, and review process, identifying best practices and lessons learned from our viewpoint as writers of NASA solicitations and as reviewers of the responses to these solicitations.

Figure 16.1 presents a representative timeline of the acquisition process. Starting at the left, NRAs that anticipate the award of both contracts, and grants or cooperative agreements must be synopsized in the Federal Business Opportunities[4] (FBO) website at least 15 calendar days prior to release. NRAs that expressly exclude the award of contracts are not necessarily posted on the FBO but can be found on the Grants.gov website[5] no later than three days after release.

The primary method of dissemination for NASA-specific NRAs and AOs is the NASA Acquisition Internet Service (NAIS).[6] The NAIS is a searchable collection of online servers operated at each NASA field installation, and all are interconnected. The NAIS posts all synopses, solicitations, award notices, acquisition forecasts, regulations, forms, and small business assistance. It is possible to personalize e-mail notifications to fit one's interests. NASA postings on the Internet can also be searched through the NASA search engine.[7]

Links to open and recently closed NRAs and NASA Cooperative Agreement Notices are posted on the NASA Solicitation and Proposal Integrated Review and Evaluation System (NSPIRES)[8,9] on the day of release. When possible, NSPIRES also provides advance notices of future NRAs with a best estimate of the release date. Several weeks after the NRA release, specific journals may report news about the opportunity.

It is important to revisit the site where you first learned of the NRA. When program changes, program funding, or any other reasons require cancellation of an NRA, the office issuing the NRA will notify potential

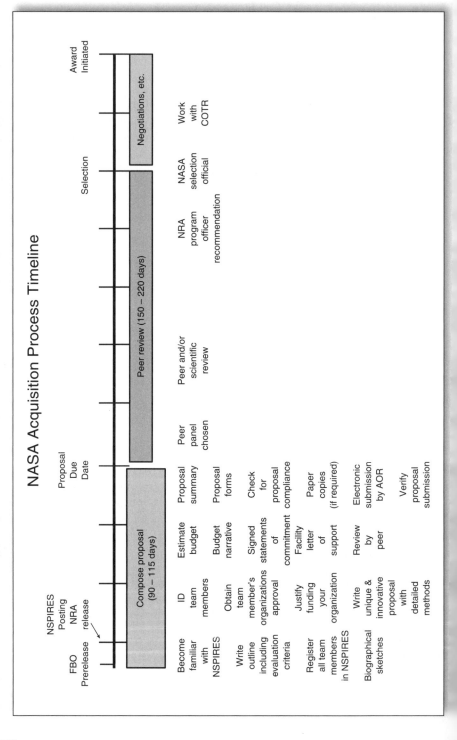

Figure 16.1 Timeline of the NASA Acquisition Process

proposers by using the mailing list for the NRA. Keeping an eye on the FBO and on NSPIRES solicitations will help you know if NASA is seeking research and development activities in your line of interest.

Assuming a solicitation speaks to your area of expertise, begin the proposal writing by becoming familiar with the NSPIRES structure and downloading the appropriate application packages and tools.

Organizing your thoughts in a straightforward and detailed outline will make the proposal submission process manageable. To be competitive for selection, proposals must fully satisfy the evaluation criteria. These criteria may include relevance to NASA missions, relevance to NASA programs, realism and reasonableness of proposed costs, staying within the page limitations, and scientific and/or technical merit. The reviewers will be qualified peers who are knowledgeable, though not necessarily specialists, in the objective(s) solicited by the NRA. According to the *NRA and CAN Proposer's Guidebook*,[10] "Experience has consistently shown that the characteristics of successful proposals are that they are technically meritorious, logical, complete, convincing, easily read, affordable, and responsive to the advertised NASA program."

During this early phase of the proposal-construction process, it is a good idea to practice submitting your proposal on NSPIRES. To allow this, all individuals and organizations named in the proposal must be registered in NSPIRES. If multiple proposals with the same title and principal investigator are submitted through Grants.gov, NASA will attempt to review and accept the version with the latest time and date stamp. However, it is the responsibility of the proposer to withdraw old versions of proposals.

What Goes Into a Good Grant Proposal

Every proposal should identify a principal investigator who is responsible for the quality and direction of the proposed research and for the proper use of awarded funds regardless of whether or not he or she receives support through the award. The proposing organization has the authority to designate the principal investigator and to designate his or her replacement, if that becomes necessary. NASA approval is required for replacement of a principal investigator after proposal selection.

Although NASA program personnel may be contacted to discuss general program objectives with prospective proposers, they cannot provide specific advice on budgetary or technical issues beyond those published in the NRA that would give an unfair competitive advantage unless this same information were openly available to all interested proposers.

Proposals should be brief and concentrate on substantive material essential for a complete understanding of the project. Experience shows that few proposals exceed 15–20 pages. Write in a way that an engineer or someone not in the behavioral sciences field can understand easily. Any necessary detailed information, such as charts, should be included as an attachment rather than in the main body of the proposal.

Budgets should be adequate and realistic, and provided with the details necessary to justify and facilitate understanding of the proposed costs. A relatively low cost does not necessarily provide a competitive advantage to a proposal unless all other factors are equal; likewise, a proposal judged to be of especially high scientific/technical merit is not necessarily rejected because it requests a budget beyond the norm advertised for the program.

The Budget Narrative must describe the basis of estimate and rationale for each proposed component of cost, including direct labor, subcontracts/subawards, consultants, other direct costs (including travel), and facilities and equipment. Provide the source of cost estimates (e.g., based on quote, on previous purchases for same or similar item[s], cost data obtained from Internet research), including the company name and/or URL and date.

On occasion, a proposal may include aspects that are considered undesirable or unnecessary (e.g., the development of hardware, the pursuit of a certain research objective, plans for excessive travel, or the support of certain personnel). In such a case, and at the option of the cognizant NASA Program Officer, a proposal may be evaluated more than once: first as originally proposed, and then again as "de-scoped" of one or more of its original provisions. In such a case, the rating of the de-scoped proposal may justify its consideration for funding consistent with the policy for Partial Selections and a revised proposal may be requested.

Partnering With NASA

Proposals that include a partnership with a facility at a U.S. government organization (including NASA Centers and the Jet Propulsion Laboratory), must include all funding requested from NASA for the proposed investigation in the budget and be reflected in the budget totals that appear in the budget forms. Any required budget for that government coinvestigator and/or facility should be included in the proposal's Budget Narrative and should be listed as "Other Applicable Costs" in the required Budget Details. If the proposal is selected, NASA will execute an inter- or intra-agency transfer of funds, as appropriate, to cover the applicable costs at that government organization.

If a principal investigator from a U.S. government organization (including NASA Centers and the Jet Propulsion Laboratory) proposes to team with a coinvestigator from a nongovernment organization, then the proposing government organization must cover those coinvestigator costs through an appropriate award for which that government principal investigator organization is responsible. Such nongovernment coinvestigator costs should be entered as a "Subcontract/Subaward" on the Budget Summary.

Partnering With an Existing Lab

A proposal is more likely to be funded if the cost of production of a lab is not included. NASA facilities are available for proposers to include in their proposal as summarized in Table 16.2.

If the proposed use of a facility goes beyond the publicly stated availability, a statement, signed by the appropriate government official at the facility verifying that it will be available for the required effort, is sufficient.

The Investigators

If you are a junior principal investigator, consider a coprincipal investigator with more success, especially with a track record of receiving greater amounts of money. However, one should not include a famous name as coprincipal investigator or as a consultant but not define a useful job for them. Inclusion of unjustified personnel can lead to a downgrading of a proposal's rating.

Table 16.2   NASA Facilities

Ames Research Center	www.nasa.gov/centers/ames/business/index.html
Dryden Flight Research Center	www.nasa.gov/centers/dryden/daof/overview.html
Glenn Research Center	http://facilities.grc.nasa.gov/explore/explore_all.html
International Space Station	www.nasa.gov/mission_pages/station/research/facilities_category.html
Langley Research Center	www.nasa.gov/centers/langley/news/factsheets/Facilities.html

Review and Evaluation Process

NASA begins its evaluation process as soon as possible after the deadline for proposal submission. NASA uses several evaluation techniques. In all cases, however, discipline specialists in the area of the proposal provide reviews. Some proposals are reviewed entirely in-house, others are evaluated by a combination of in-house personnel and selected external reviewers, while still others are subject to a full external peer review either by mail or through assembled panels. Due regard for conflict of interest and protection of proposal information is always part of the process. Review panels are instructed not to compare proposals to each other; and NASA program personnel conduct all comparative evaluations. Evaluation criteria include relevance to NASA's objectives, intrinsic merit, and cost. Regardless of the evaluation technique, the decision to fund or not fund an unsolicited proposal is made by NASA technical personnel.

The following URL can be used to track the process of a grant and/or cooperative agreement prepared by the NASA Shared Services Center on behalf of one of the NASA Centers/HQ: www.nssc.nasa.gov/grantstatus.

Final Thoughts

This chapter summarized NASA's solicitation mechanisms, provided a timeline of the acquisition process, detailed the components of a successful grant proposal, described how to partner with NASA researchers and presented the review process used at NASA. Paired with an exceptional research idea and sound research method, these tips should pave the way to a successful research proposal.

Notes

1. http://wicn.nssc.nasa.gov
2. The 2012 president's budget request can be downloaded at www.nasa .gov/news/budget/index.html.
3. Search the NASA *Grant and Cooperative Agreement Handbook* to download a pdf version of the document.
4. www.fedbizopps.gov
5. www.grants.gov/
6. http://procurement.nasa.gov
7. http://prod.nais.nasa.gov/cgi-bin/nais/index.cgi
8. Grant Information Circular (GIC) 06-03 and Procurement Information Circular (PIC) 06-12.
9. http://nspires.nasaprs.com/
10. www.hq.nasa.gov/office/procurement/nraguidebook/proposer2011.pdf

PART III

Collaborative Grant Proposals

17

Building a Strong Institutional Research Training Program

Jon Atherton, Nathan Hansen, and
Jeannette R. Ickovics

One of the greatest challenges in research is the need for uncompromising focus on that which defines and sustains the successful scientist: her or his own science. In a time of unprecedented competition for research funding and unrelenting constraints on time and resources, it is critical to retain this focus. But, such dedication also provides one of academia's greatest anomalies; namely, that outstanding training and reciprocal research mentorship are essential prerequisites to becoming a successful research scientist.

It is for this reason more than ever that investing time as a training director or mentor through a training grant can be enormously beneficial professionally and personally. Constructed on the right foundations, such grants offer active collaboration across an array of research projects, encouraging interests, honing skills, and strengthening commitment to research for mentor and mentee alike. The purpose of this chapter is to highlight the rudiments of a strong training grant application to any one of a number of funding agencies that support institutional training programs. Examples include the National Science Foundation's Integrative Graduate Education and Research training program, which offers training to undergraduate students as well as to graduate and postdoctoral scholars; the National Center for Educational Research training programs in the Education Sciences, which provides predoctoral students with the opportunity to train in education interventions (e.g., curricula, professional development); and the "hybrid" training programs offered by the National Institute of General Medical Sciences, such as their Behavioral-Biomedical Sciences Interface program, which provides learning experience that integrate coursework, laboratory rotations, and programmatic activities that reinforce training at this interface.

Here we provide a set of considerations and topics that are easily applied to these and most other funding scenarios by focusing on the most sizable and scalable training mechanism: the National Institutes of Health (NIH) "T" grant. We look beyond the administrative formula and extrinsic structure of the application to bring to light the intrinsic elements that have shaped and sustained our "T32" training program since 1999. In doing so, it is important to recognize that our perspective comes from a research-intensive university, where our goal is to equip scholars with the strongest foundation of knowledge, skills, and experience to achieve and sustain careers as independent scientific investigators. We begin with some fundamental principles about training grants and their benefits, and then provide guidance on the primary sections of the application itself.

What Is a Training Grant?

Institutional training grants, which allow an institution to award and administer Ruth L. Kirschstein National Research Service Awards (NRSA), exist to ensure a diverse pool of highly trained scientists is available in appropriate scientific disciplines to address the nation's biomedical, behavioral, and clinical research needs (note that NRSA awards can be given to individual scientists by NIH through "F" grants as well). This grant mechanism has been the principal means of external support to predoctoral and postdoctoral training since the enactment of the NRSA legislation in 1974 (National Research Council, 1994). By comparison, NIH's similar "R25" mechanism typically provides research *education* that emphasizes didactic training through short courses, workshops, mentor networks, and activities that otherwise complement the primary appointment of the full-time postdoctoral trainee.

Research training programs are designed to allow the training director/principal investigator to select trainees and develop a program of study and research experiences necessary to provide high-quality training for a next generation of scientists. The program must be of sufficient depth to enable selected trainees, upon completion of the program, to have a thorough exposure to the principles underlying the conduct of research. Full-time training "slots" are limited to individuals who are committed to a career in research and who plan to remain on the training grant or in a non-NRSA research experience for a minimum of two years. A training grant should also provide skills necessary for scholars to apply for subsequent support through an individual fellowship, mentored career development award (K) program, or independent research project (R) grant. Training grants offset the cost of stipends, tuition and fees, and training-related expenses, including health insurance for appointed trainees, but offer no direct financial support to would-be directors or participating mentors.

At the Center for Interdisciplinary Research on AIDS (CIRA) at Yale University, our *HIV Prevention Training Program* (T32 MH020031) supports both predoctoral and full-time postdoctoral fellows, who work closely with a research preceptor from among the ranks of our affiliated faculty researchers. The overall goal is to provide the strongest foundation of knowledge, skills, and experience to young investigators at the pre- and postdoctoral levels, who can establish and sustain careers as scientific investigators, contributing to advances in HIV prevention, specifically, and public health, in general. Our training program also provides a unique focus on professional development, setting clear expectations for scholarly research productivity, the establishment of a program of research, and the creation of professional identity in preparation for an academic career.

Why Write a Training Grant?

Nationally, the total number of postdoctoral trainees in the United States was estimated to be more than 48,000 in 2005, with more than 70 percent of these "slots" funded by the federal government. NIH is the single largest source of support for postdoctoral scholars in biomedical research, and the NRSA training grant remains the most direct method of funding for individual postdocs (National Postdoctoral Association, 2009). In 2011, more than 40 percent of predoctoral fellows at the Yale School of Public Health were funded through NIH institutional training grants. Yale School of Medicine's Ph.D. programs also benefit significantly by bringing in many predoctoral scholars (60 percent in 2011) for whom funding would otherwise be unavailable. Institutional training grants account for one quarter of all postdoctoral fellows at Yale University, and despite remarkable improvements in health since the mid-20th century, a number of new health problems and the threat of emerging diseases throughout the world belie an unequivocal need to provide extensive training in biomedical research (National Research Council, 2005).

Although the value of training programs at the institutional and national level is clear, the motivation to apply for a training grant might seem less obvious for the would-be training director or mentor. Though the benefits may at first appear intangible, a training grant can offer great reciprocal value to both mentor and mentee. Working with pre- or postdoctoral fellows is stimulating in every sense, and particularly the one that counts. To continue to do research at a research-intensive institution, scientists must succeed in the unremitting cycle of turning grant applications into funding, and to do this they must continue to publish. It is in this simple metric that a training grant benefits mentor and mentee alike. The mentee grows exponentially working alongside and learning from the established scientist, refining her or his own scientific direction and publishing as many first authored papers as possible over the training period. A successful postdoctoral training period means publication, and within our Fellowship, we encourage postdoctoral fellows to aim for at least three first-authored journal publications per year, along with additional coauthored papers where the mentor is first author, or in collaboration with other fellows and faculty. Coauthorship is thus a visible product of a scientific collaboration, with both mentor and fellow expanding their scientific credentials. In fact, a successful writing team with faculty, postdoctoral fellows, and graduate students can allow multiple papers to be produced simultaneously, allowing mentors and mentees to each develop first-authored papers, and with authorship credit going to all team members who contribute to a manuscript, and thus exponentially increasing the productivity of all team members.

Additional benefits of institutional training grants are their tremendous capacity for developing new collaborations and their potential to expand one's portfolio of scientific projects. The matching of fellows with mentors is a critical first step. It provides the opportunity to facilitate such collaboration. In our program, we continue to expand our pool of mentors by identifying applicant fellows from a broad range of different disciplines and inviting mentors to work with these fellows. Mentors are expected to attend many of our training seminars and "Research in Progress" meetings and interact with the training program—in effect, new mentors are signing up for at least two years of intensive research connectivity with their trainee as well as with other mentors and scholars across the program. As a result, our training program has facilitated numerous productive collaborations within CIRA and across Yale. Further, after 13 years, we have a wide network of faculty members at top universities within the United States and abroad with whom we continue to collaborate in the development of grant applications and manuscripts. Thus, a training grant allows research collaboration to increase both within the host institution and potentially across multiple external institutions as successful fellows move on to pursue their independent research careers.

Fellows also enable mentors to significantly expand their research portfolios by taking on project management and clinical responsibilities, and freeing mentors to focus more time on developing grant applications and manuscripts. As grant writing is an essential skill for fellows to develop, fellows can assist in the development of mentors' grant applications and also develop applications of their own. In our program, we encourage fellows to focus on manuscript development during the first year of training to strengthen their curriculum vitae in preparation for the job search, which typically begins in the fall of the second year. They are then encouraged to actually write their own grant application during the second year of training.

Note that unlike employing a postdoctoral associate on a regular research project, a fellow supported by an institutional training grant is fully funded by the training program and, in some sense, is a "free" resource to the mentor. In exchange, the mentor is required to provide intensive research training experience, including ample face-to-face mentoring, engagement in ongoing research projects, and access to data to develop first-authored papers. It is important to remember that the fellow is not employed by the mentor: the fellow's time should be largely her own. Thus, our program reinforces that, while fieldwork, project management, and clinical work are important for the fellow's training, ample time should be protected for writing. Teaching, which is time-intensive, is discouraged for postdoctoral fellows unless it can be shown to benefit the fellow's training program.

How Do I Write a Training Grant?

Before we explore the substantive sections of a training grant in detail, in Table 17.1 we list what we consider to be the essential elements to keep in mind as you set out to write your training grant. These "Essential Elements" are derived from our experience writing numerous competitive and noncompetitive training grants, but also impart the benefit of hindsight following our active participation *within* a training fellowship.

Our training grant is built upon the need to provide research training in a specific scientific field, and delivered by willing mentors who conduct

Table 17.1   Ten Essential Elements for a Successful Training Grant

1. **Locate Socket: Insert Data.** Is funding available for a training grant in your area of scientific inquiry? If so, is there a justifiable need for training, and does a pool of qualified scholars exist to fill that need?

2. **Why You?** Define what is unique and innovative about your training program—what sets you apart from others? Why will scholars choose you? Why will NIH choose you?

3. **Don't Go Fishing—Phone a Friend.** Your closest scientific collaborators are on your page and are therefore best placed to form the core group of training directors who will undertake much of the mentorship and program input in the first years (and beyond).

4. **Do Cast Your Net.** With directors in place, begin early dialogue with other potential mentors and a wider group of resource faculty.

5. **No Commitment Necessary (Yet).** Beyond your core group, your wider pool of mentors won't be called upon until a mentee match is made, and it may not be for some time.

6. **Build Infrastructure.** A multidisciplinary and multidepartmental approach is the hallmark of a great institutional training grant. Show the wealth of existing resources around you.

7. **Define Program Structure.** A strong program plan will complement the central mentorship component of your grant by setting out a balanced syllabus of scientific meetings and presentations that supports the end goals of your scholars.

8. **Small, Medium, or Large?** The number of trainee slots requested is justified by the availability and research expertise of the available mentor pool. Don't aim too high. An imbalanced mentor/mentee ratio is a potential risk to your application and is likely to hamper subsequent scholarly productivity.

9. **Tables. Tables. Tables.** An institutional training grant is an epic piece of work that takes time to assemble. It's never too early to contact your mentor pool for their other support and mentoring history. Ask for samples from other training grants at your institution.

10. **Don't Skimp the Help.** Good administrative support is an essential component to your training grant application (see #9) and to subsequent program delivery.

relevant research in an environment that supports mentor/mentee productivity. The *Background, Program Plan,* and *Recruitment and Retention Plan* are the sections of the training grant application where these defining elements are unpacked and articulated in significant detail. Here we describe the specific structure of these sections—which must fit within the combined 25-page limit currently set by NIH—and suggest content based on our three successful competitive grant cycles. We also discuss the recent addition by NIH of a separate (but related) section covering training in the Responsible Conduct of Research.

In Table 17.2, we list the components required for a new grant application requesting mixed pre- and postdoctoral scholars (U.S. Department of Health and Human Services, 2012). Unless otherwise instructed in the specific funding opportunity announcement (the current NIH program announcement for T32 training grants can be found at http://grants.nih. gov/grants/guide/pa-files/PA-11-184.html), it is critical that applicants become familiar with and follow the instructions in the NIH Application Guidelines (http://grants.nih.gov/grants/funding/424/SF424_RR_Guide_ General_Adobe_VerB.pdf; supplemental instructions for preparing institutional National Research Service Awards are contained in Section 8). Downloadable form files are available at http://grants.nih.gov/grants/ funding/phs398/phs398.html. In addition to becoming familiar with these guidelines, a first step for any new applicant should be to consult the appropriate staff contact in the NIH institute or center most closely aligned to the field of research (a table of specific Information, requirements, and staff contacts is available here: http://grants.nih.gov/grants/ guide/contacts/parent_T32.html). Instructions on how to create a short- and long-term budget, including specifics on stipends, tuition/fees, health insurance, and other "training related expenses," are provided here: http://grants.nih.gov/grants/guide/notice-files/NOT-OD-12-033.html.

New page limits for plans for instruction in the Responsible Conduct of Research (RCR) were issued by NIH in March 2011 (http://grants.nih. gov/grants/guide/notice-files/NOT-OD-11-039.html), and gave investigators a separate, three-page section to describe arrangements for relevant instruction. Plans must explicitly state how an institution will address responsible conduct of research retraining with close adherence to further guidelines (http://grants.nih.gov/grants/guide/notice-files/not- od-10-019.html), which provide that instruction must be undertaken at least once during each career stage, at a frequency of no less than once every four years.

Table 17.2   Principal Components of a T32 Training Grant

1. Face Page

2. Table of Contents

3. Budget Period

4. Budget for Entire Proposed Period

5. Biographical Sketch of Program Director(s)

6. Resources

7. Background

8. Program Plan
   - Program Administration
   - Program Faculty
   - Proposed Training
   - Program Evaluation
   - Trainee Candidates

9. Recruitment and Retention Plan to Enhance Diversity

10. Plan for Instruction in the Responsible Conduct of Research

11. Human Subjects

12. Vertebrate Animals

13. Select Agent Research

14. Literature Cited

15. Multiple PD Leadership Plan (if applicable)

16. Consortium/Contractual Arrangements

17. Participating Faculty Biosketches (not to exceed four pages each)

18. Data Tables

19. Letters of Support

20. Appendices

Training grant "data tables" require you to describe training faculty and the prospective candidate pool in infinite detail. Do not underestimate how long this will take and the many hands you will need to complete the task. Helpfully, blank data tables, detailed instructions, and sample tables are provided by NIH for each table (http://grants1.nih.gov/grants/funding/424/index.htm#data). Although some of this information should be held at the department or institutional level (for example, NIH-required Tables 1 through 4), others, particularly Tables 5 and 6, require in-depth information about individual scholars that is more likely to be held by individual training programs or possibly individual mentors. A complete list of NIH training grant tables required for a new, mixed pre- and postdoctoral application is provided in Table 17.3. We urge you to start immediately by contacting administrators and faculty members for biosketches, for other support pages, and for details about their mentoring history.

Table 17.3   Training Grant Data Tables for a New, Mixed Pre- and Postdoctoral Training Program

1. Membership of Participating Departments and Programs
2. Participating Faculty Members
3. Institutional Training Grant Support Available to Participating Faculty Members, Department(s), or Program(s)
4. Grant and Contract Support of the Participating Faculty Members
5. A&B. Separate tables for Pre- and Postdoctoral Trainees of Participating Faculty Members
6. A&B. Separate tables for Publications of Research Completed by Pre- and Postdoctoral Trainees
7. A&B. Separate tables showing Admissions and Completion Records for the Participating Departments and Programs During the Past Five Years for Pre- and Postdoctoral Applicants
8. A&B. Separate tables showing Qualifications of Recent Pre- and Postdoctoral Applicants to Each Participating Department/Program
9. A&B. Separate tables showing the Qualifications of the Current Pre- and Postdoctoral Trainees Clearly Associated With the Training Program
10. (Optional). Admissions and Completion Records for Underrepresented Minority Trainees, Trainees With Disabilities, and Trainees From Disadvantaged Backgrounds Clearly Associated With the Training Program

Background: Rationale, History, Need

NIH research training activities can be in basic biomedical or clinical sciences, behavioral or social sciences, health services research, or any other discipline relevant to the NIH mission. Therefore, the first, important step is to define the need for the training that you and your colleagues intend to satisfy. In our training grant, a review of the epidemiology of HIV/AIDS revealed a critical need for training a new generation of scientists with the skills and commitment to conduct HIV prevention research in the United States and abroad. Indeed, in addition to the alarming statistics at the center of the AIDS epidemic—with upward trends in incident HIV/sexually transmitted disease infections attesting to the need for sustained targeted prevention efforts—other research priorities called out for new talent. For example, reducing comorbid mental health conditions; reducing disparities based on income, gender, and ethnicity; developing interventions in clinical settings; and an almost boundless list of important research questions concerning individuals, families, and communities in the United States and across countless international borders (Joint United Nations Programme on HIV/AIDS and World Health Organization, 2007).

The high standard of interdisciplinary, collaborative prevention science set by HIV-related behavioral researchers in turn provided—in fact required—a rich training environment to stimulate a wide array of studies, publications, and career trajectories. The potential for a training grant to exist can therefore be fairly judged by observing the momentum in your research environment, the number of faculty members engaged within an area of research, and the environment to support it.

Program Plan, Part A: Administrative Strengths, Leadership, and Scientific Expertise

The strength of any training grant rests squarely on the foundation of expertise, experience, and commitment of the training director(s), and the wider pool of relevant research mentors. All things being equal, these people are a fellowship's greatest resource by virtue of their expertise and capacity for guidance, and in most cases by their unconditional offer of collaboration in active research studies. The training director is required to be a senior scientist and proven leader in the field. The director must have existing experience as both a scientist and a mentor and have strong management skills. It follows that would-be training directors are often groomed through several years' active participation as a mentor in an existing training grant or departmental training program. Indeed, these qualities could (and we think should) be shared across a team of codirectors, who form the core group willing to take on an equal stake in managing workload, participating as individual mentors, and providing general mentorship oversight across all program participants. The time commitment to collaborative research or scholarly work with one or more fellows is open-ended and considerable. Where predoctoral fellows are being requested, this should not only be possible but expected since normal teaching obligations coincide with advising fellows and supervising their dissertations.

Beyond individual virtues, this core group should ideally self-select based on existing research collaboration. They will be known quantities in both personal and professional terms. In our experience, it has been invaluable to rely on a core team drawn not just from existing research collaborators but also former postdoctoral trainees who have become faculty mentors themselves. This cycle is borne out by the active participation of current faculty members who came through the training program and have now developed exciting and accomplished research programs of their own. Including such training faculty provides significant value both through their relevant research and in relation to their experience of the particular training program. The central strength and longevity of our program is due in large measure to this reinvestment, which continues to set strong career mentorship and the success of our fellows as the first principle of the program.

Complementing the core team of directors, two levels of faculty should be clearly defined in the program plan. As the pool of core research preceptors for the training program, the substantial record of research and research training of *primary training faculty* must be described in significant detail. They should be outstanding investigators, recognized for their research and contributions to the particular field of your application, and have strong training records at both the predoctoral and postdoctoral levels. For many T32s, there is an expectation that primary mentors will be funded investigators in the sponsoring institute; applicants should check such requirements with individual funders. Mentors should also span a broad array of disciplines to show the potential breadth and scope of your training program to accommodate a similarly wide mix of scholars. For example, CIRA's training program brings together faculty representing psychology, anthropology, sociology, epidemiology, public health, biostatistics, adult and pediatric infectious diseases, operations research, medical ethics, law, and health policy.

Resource Faculty should be available to provide additional scientific, ethical, and biostatistical consultation to fellows as needed. Their role is primarily to serve on thesis committees, to provide expertise in specific content or methodological areas, and occasionally to serve as mentors for training. All of these faculty members will contribute to the educational mission of the proposed training program through their ongoing teaching as well as research efforts.

The program plan should also set out how activities of the training program will be monitored by a training steering committee, which typically consists of the codirectors and other senior figures from across the institution and for whom participation would be commensurate with their priorities as active investigators and leadership responsibilities. This committee provides overall management and evaluation of recruitment, selection, and training of fellows; coordination of programwide activities such as seminars and conferences; and review of fellow progress, performance, and responsibility for resolution of any training-related problems if they arise (e.g., grievances, ethical conduct). The existing CIRA External Advisory Committee also provides oversight of the training program. At its annual meetings, the Committee reviews the status of the program and provides advice on any issue brought to its attention by the training directors.

All training faculty should exhibit a strong history of collaboration and cross-interactions, which is evidenced by shared grant support and in a number of joint publications. One characteristic that distinguishes our training grant at CIRA is its emphasis on interdisciplinary research. Today, interdisciplinary collaborations at CIRA, involving a combination of investigators and methods from different disciplines, represent 58 percent of active, externally funded affiliated projects. These many examples of ongoing interdisciplinary research continue to offer unprecedented training opportunities, which we continue to highlight in subsequent competing training grant applications. We have found it valuable to structure such a significant number of mentor (and mentor–mentee) research collaborations under convenient subheadings, for example, disaggregating by specific population groups in local, national, or international contexts, or thematically in accordance with particular research collaborations. Within a dedicated NIH-funded research center such as CIRA, we have been able to demonstrate our strength in research collaborations and a combination of perspectives under headings such as "basic social and behavioral research," "interdisciplinary research methods," "community-based research," "law, policy and ethics," or "international research." A strong program plan will return to these same headings consistently throughout the grant application.

Evidencing research facilities and an environment of active collaboration among NIH-funded researchers is a clear indication of the opportunities awaiting fellows. A primary goal of CIRA scientists is to contribute to HIV prevention science through externally funded research, the publication of findings in scientific journals, and the dissemination of findings in ways that can have a direct impact on programs and policy. Accordingly, our training grant applications have always emulated this goal, benefitting from the center's considerable growth over the past 10 years. Today, we draw on the resources of more than 70 scientists representing 22 disciplines and 7 schools at Yale, as well as across partner organizations and other universities. In part, CIRA's growth and expansion reflects the success of our NIMH-funded training program.

Program Plan, Part B: Proposed Training and Environment

Having established a broad base of resources, the Program Plan should establish the distinctive philosophy of the proposed training program and set out the unique activities and resources available for both pre- and postdoctoral trainees. Before doing so, it is always worth restating the basic components and unique features of the program. This is also a good juncture to set down and rationalize the specific number of pre- and/or postdoctoral slots requested (this will have been set out in plain numeric form in the budget and budget justification), with the practical description of training activities serving to demonstrate how fellows will fit into the wider program. Our approach to training continues to emphasize flexibility and individual tailoring of fellows' coursework and research mentorship, while recognizing the importance of core training in methodology, ethics, and the responsible conduct of research (themselves not exclusive to our unifying theme of professional development). Expectations upon fellows themselves should also be codified, for example, where they will present research findings or prepare an extramural grant application by the end of the training period.

For predoctoral fellows, this should include key milestones and the time commitment expected for a typical training period; for example, describing formal course requirements, examinations, degree petitions, prospectus' submissions, the process of developing and completing dissertation research, and the roles of dissertation advisory committees, readers, and academic advisors in considerable depth (syllabi and other detail materials should be kept for appendices).

Complementing the formal coursework and classes of predoctoral scholars, our training grant provides significant coverage of the unique activities in which all fellows are expected to participate. Again, this will provide detailed evidence to substantiate the formidable institutional resources that will be leveraged. For example, our predoctoral scholars take advantage of formal seminar series offered by each division within the Yale School of Public Health. Here, the grant should describe speakers from within or outside your institution and the benefit of opportunities for fellows to meet with speakers or join faculty in informal settings. Outside courses and meetings should also be described where specialized training can be justified as the best way to acquire state of the art science, knowledge, or skills.

For both pre- and postdoctoral scholars, we also pay particular attention to the support available to each fellow in establishing individualized training plans. At the onset of the first training year, each of our fellows meet with the training director and her or his primary mentor to discuss specific research interests and objectives, and to establish a tailored plan to attain these objectives. Fellows provide a brief semiannual assessment of their work to assess achievement of these objectives. In addition, postdoctoral fellows have their research reviewed biannually (each semester) by the steering committee. These meetings are to ensure that the training program and research preceptor are meeting the fellow's needs, to provide feedback, and to evaluate the training program itself. Significant focus is given within the fellowship to "hands-on" conduct of research, analysis, paper and grant writing in collaboration with a faculty mentor and other faculty. The program plan should describe the guidance, mentorship, and faculty expertise that will be provided to fellows throughout the fellowship to help them successfully conduct their research, produce research products, and present them in a professional manner. For example, our fellows are expected to write high-quality scientific articles for publication and prepare conference presentations, based on their participation in CIRA projects and on the undertaking of their own projects begun during the first year of fellowship.

Significant coverage should also be provided to describe the process by which primary research mentors are selected. As a rule, fellows participate in the current research of their mentors and develop their own supervised research projects with that faculty member. They may also select a secondary mentor, who is typically a faculty member from another discipline who shares similar interests and can contribute another perspective to the fellows' research endeavors. Describing primary and secondary mentors will provide further evidence of the interdisciplinary experience and broad scope of knowledge available to fellows. Our intent is to allow the fellow to gain direct knowledge, familiarity, and experience in the theoretical bases, intervention approaches, assessment measures, and research design strategies used in HIV prevention research and to show the adaptability of the training program in the event that a fellow requires additional skills to complete his or her work (e.g., additional biostatistical training in categorical data analysis techniques, group intervention facilitation skills, or the wider collaboration with another member of the training faculty or with outside experts). Typically, the fellow will be involved in many aspects of the research endeavor, ranging from study design, data collection, intervention implementation, to data management, analyses, and paper writing. Participation in weekly research team meetings that address such issues as recruitment, logistical concerns, and project progress, should all be evidenced to show how postdoctoral fellows will be encouraged to design and implement their own independent research.

Our training grant has established a wealth of institutional resources and codified the benefits to individual scholars of formal course work and structured classes (in the case of predoctoral fellows) and through the formation of individual relationships with primary and secondary mentors. Complementing these core elements, a strong training program should also establish exclusive activities that engage program directors, mentors, and fellows in a group or "fellowship" setting. Our Interdisciplinary HIV Prevention Fellowship seminar series was established in 1999 and has continued to be a strong and valued asset throughout successive competitive renewal applications. This weekly seminar series was designed to address specific critical issues in HIV prevention research, including the Responsible Conduct of Research, HIV Prevention Science, Conduct of Community Research with a focus on both domestic and international settings, and Professional Development. Three special seminars are defined in our training grant and rotate on a biweekly basis.

Our Research in Progress meetings develop fellows' ability to conduct research that meets the highest scientific standards. We consider review of research proposals and other scientific products (manuscripts, talks, posters, etc.) emanating from fellows' research one of the central components of postdoctoral training. The purpose of Research in Progress is to enhance the quality of manuscripts and grant proposals produced by NIH postdoctoral fellows by sharing these materials with a multidisciplinary group of colleagues with a range of expertise. The program is designed to be constructive rather than evaluative, and we especially encourage fellows to present even preliminary research proposals and data for peer review so that discussions of scientific merit and feasibility occur at a time when they can have maximum impact. The simple practice of giving regular research presentations also serves to keep fellows on track in developing research products, and provides a friendly environment in which to hone speaking and presentation skills, as well as valuable experience as reviewer within the peer review process.

A Professional Development series provides fellows with the opportunity to discuss issues related to their academic careers, including development of a research program and professional identity; professional networking and establishing a mentorship network with an eye to future employment; navigating the tenure process; and identifying career opportunities and strategies for success in research and academic settings. Fellows also use these sessions to present their research findings in anticipation of "job talks" that take place when interviewing for academic positions.

A Grant Writing Seminar supports fellows to develop and write their own NIH-formatted grant application by the end of the training period. Initial ideas are presented and reviewed during the Research in Progress seminars. In this way, we hope to equip scholars with an oven-ready grant to take to their next academic position.

Our Interdisciplinary HIV Prevention Training Grant has also drawn significant benefits through its relationship with Yale's CIRA. Fellows become participating members of specific research cores, keeping current on the latest scientific inquiry while also consulting with core members on their own products. All fellows have an excellent opportunity to initiate independent research through CIRA's Pilot Program, which was established to fund pilot research for new investigators, including our postdoctoral fellows. CIRA's Development Core runs quarterly Career Development Consultations, designed to help junior faculty members and postdoctoral fellows with quality guidance from experienced colleagues in building long and productive careers in HIV/AIDS. Seminars and workshops offered by CIRA's Interdisciplinary Research Methods Core are highlighted as further resource for fellows to engage in topics, including quantitative methods and biostatistics (e.g., social network analysis, meta-analysis, community intervention trials, cluster analysis, recursive partitioning, experience sampling methods, and graphical methods for data exploration), qualitative methods and ethnography (e.g., ethnographic methods in international settings, community-based participatory research), and mathematical modeling and cost effectiveness (e.g., cost effectiveness of HIV screening, mathematical models for translating behavioral measures to epidemic impact). CIRA's Community Research Core offers fellows a wealth of connections to HIV/AIDS service organizations and community-based organizations. The Yale AIDS Colloquium Series, cosponsored by CIRA and Yale's Institution for Social and Policy Studies, brings researchers, policymakers, advocates, representatives from nonprofit organizations, and others to CIRA to discuss topics in AIDS research and policy. In addition to our fellows, the audience includes Yale faculty, staff, graduate and undergraduate students, health care providers, and members of the local community, providing an important communitywide forum for the discussion of HIV/AIDS prevention, research, treatment, and care. These opportunities were designed to foster strong interactions and intensive information exchange with respected figures in the field of AIDS policy and research.

Annually, CIRA sponsors AIDS Science Day, an interdisciplinary conference on AIDS research. All CIRA and CIRA-affiliated faculty, and other faculty, fellows, and students undertaking AIDS-related research at Yale have the opportunity to present their findings to an invited scientific audience of peers and community members. Nearly all of our postdoctoral fellows have presented their own research at AIDS Science Day, either as an oral or poster presentation. Postdoctoral fellows are also encouraged to attend national meetings (and international meetings when suitable) to present their data, meet other scientists, and to learn about new ideas and techniques. Postdoctoral fellows may also attend outside courses when specific training is desired. Note that workshops and seminars are to be preferred as they are more focused and less time intensive than completing a course. In addition, while attendance at conferences and training workshops/seminars are encouraged and supported, these activities can become a distraction and interfere with the productivity of fellows in writing their own original research for peer-reviewed publication. We advise our fellows to cap conference and workshop attendance at two per year.

Our predoctoral fellows are trained within the Yale School of Public Health, where they undertake formal coursework, qualifying examinations, and complete the doctoral dissertation. Leveraging the resources of both Yale and an independent NIH-funded research center continues to be of critical value in sustaining our training program. A unique sequencing of courses, community-based programmatic activities, and field or laboratory research provides students with an array of opportunities to define their specialty and to tailor their course of study. The program of coursework is designed by the student and faculty adviser and monitored by the doctoral committee. Provisions are made for individual and small group instruction to meet the needs of each doctoral candidate. There are joint degree programs with the Yale Schools of Medicine, Nursing, Management, Forestry, and the Center for International and Area Studies in the Graduate School. In addition, students may make individual arrangements for joint degree programs with the Divinity and Law Schools. Schools of Public Health have a tradition of interdisciplinary doctoral-level training and a commitment to improve the health of the public. Through innovative research, policy analysis, and education that draw upon interdisciplinary scholarship from across the graduate and professional programs at Yale, we train our graduates to serve communities at the local, national, and international level. Students benefit from an emphasis on problem solving and strong training in a variety of disciplines, combined with an interdisciplinary approach fostered by close relationships with other professional schools at Yale. Our training program has gained strength from this approach: a predoctoral program within one of the nation's leading schools of public health and a postdoctoral program in a center that draws from many disciplines but is administratively housed within this school. This provides consistent administrative leadership, an intellectual community, and training in the skills required to nurture academic careers.

Program Plan, Part C: Program Evaluation

The next component of the program plan should set out a rigorous evaluation plan to facilitate consistent review of the quality and effectiveness of the training; obtain feedback from current and former trainees; and monitor trainees' subsequent career development. This section should briefly set out the structure and mechanisms that will satisfy each of these components. We have used four principal mechanisms. First, the training director organizes semiannual meetings of fellows to discuss their experiences, gather feedback, and agree on needs related to the training program. Second, primary mentors report on their fellow's progress semiannually at steering committee meetings. The training director is also responsible for soliciting additional feedback and comments from other program faculty regarding progress and training needs. Any major concerns are brought to the attention of the steering committee. Third, fellows have the opportunity to evaluate their training experiences themselves using confidential evaluation forms. These forms evaluate knowledge obtained, mentorship of faculty members, and overall experience in the program. The training directors summarize these for review by the steering committee. Fourth, a review by CIRA's external advisory committee takes place annually. These four mechanisms are essential to the continuing development of the training program and provide almost constant feedback to ensure optimal mentor–mentee relationships and a tailored training experience that reflects the ever-changing fellowship dynamic. A consistent and recognizable evaluation plan is also critical as the primary means by which existing and former fellows provide career development feedback, which, of course, returns us to the central purpose of the training provided. Annual updates should be collected from all trainees to ensure a current record of research positions and research products are held by the training program and thus reported to the training grant funder. Beyond quantifiable metrics, we encourage you to describe mechanisms for sustained connectivity—such as through websites and social media—with the growing network of fellows who will come through your program. Continuing to foster relationships with past trainees can and does provide obvious benefits in the development of future collaborations within and beyond the immediate training environment.

Program Plan, Part D: Trainee Candidates

This section should describe the pool of candidates available to your fellowship and the process and criteria to be used for recruitment, review, and selection. Candidacy for support on NIH T32 Training Grants is restricted to U.S. citizens or those with permanent resident status. Within our program, prospective predoctoral fellows must meet all of the general requirements of the Yale Graduate School. Recruitment of graduate students thus occurs through the Graduate School and School of Public Health websites, brochures, and advertisements. Applicant screening is a two-stage process. First, applications are screened through the School of Public Health doctoral committee, which includes faculty from every division. Qualifications initially are evaluated by members of the doctoral committee based on GRE scores, undergraduate record, letters of recommendation, and statement of career goals. We look for candidates who have some training in health sciences and are strong quantitatively, with at least one year of college-level mathematics. Many of those admitted to our doctoral program come with a master's degree. Second, any applicants who pass through the initial assessment and who express an interest in HIV research are sent to the training directors, who convene a specific training program selection committee, with training grant faculty representing each division within which we expect to place doctoral students. Selected candidates are brought to Yale for an interview, with faculty chosen based upon the student's expressed research interests. This process involves as many of the training faculty as possible to assure the selection of the best candidates.

Recruitment procedures governing postdoctoral fellows should also follow the hiring protocols of the parent institution. We advertise through our program website, increasingly through social media, extensive distribution by mail of program announcements, advertisements of the availability of positions in professional journals, and announcements at meetings of professional societies. Again, our recruitment efforts are strengthened by the extensive network and media coverage available through CIRA. Traditional media remain highly valuable, and announcements are placed in newsletters and journals of relevant scientific associations and at doctorate-granting institutions (schools of public health, social work, and nursing; departments of epidemiology, and psychology, sociology, anthropology; and postgraduate medical training programs in psychiatry, infectious diseases, and family and community medicine). Faculty members also have longstanding relationships with scientists at other doctorate-granting institutions, and they can be instrumental in identifying candidates interested in your particular area of research. Contact with researchers at other institutions has been an invaluable source of potential candidates and serves to foster wider links between institutions.

Each step in the hiring process should be described. As a guide, we require candidates to submit the following materials as part of an online application process: (a) curriculum vitae; (b) professional statement that includes research background, interests, and short- and long-term career goals; (c) letters of recommendation from two faculty members or researchers familiar with the candidate's qualifications; (d) reprints or copies of articles, scientific presentations, or writing samples of scholarly work; and (e) undergraduate and graduate transcripts. Candidates are also asked to specify the projects and/or investigators with whom they prefer to work. In describing the candidate selection process, we consider a rigid weighting or scoring system inappropriate for selecting fellows from varied backgrounds and with different experience levels. Rather, the CIRA training grant continues to prioritize candidates who demonstrate commitment and motivation to pursue careers as research scientists. However, provided these criteria are satisfied, a candidate's particular strengths, weaknesses, needs, and interests should ultimately be considered in the context of the best possible mentor fit. If no such fit can be made, the most promising candidate is unlikely to prosper within your program.

Recruitment and Retention Plan to Enhance Diversity

Both new and renewal training proposals are required to submit a plan for recruitment and retention to enhance diversity. Those who are starting out to design a new training grant might find it useful to think about what diversity means within their field of study. As an HIV center within a school of public health, we consider the diversification of the biomedical workforce and the attraction of the most talented researchers from all groups an inseparable requirement and obligation. Therefore, training directors should recognize that passive recruitment efforts are not sufficient and that active outreach is necessary to meet goals to include underrepresented race, ethnic, disadvantaged, and disabled scholars (categories that are established and defined in detail by NIH). Again, all members of the training faculty who attend scientific meetings or give lectures and seminars or collaborate with colleagues in other universities should be formally urged not only to meet with individuals suggested by their host but to specifically request meetings with members of underrepresented minorities (undergraduate and graduate students) to discuss with them the next stage in their education and provide them with information about training programs.

This section should also describe aggressive recruiting efforts for pre- and postdoctoral scholars, including at centralized offices for diversity and inclusion, graduate schools, and throughout and across a host of professional, social, and pipeline networks. Once applications have been gathered, they should be given fair and thoughtful consideration, with applicants from underrepresented backgrounds undergoing the same review process as all other applicants. However, it is incumbent upon training directors to actively seek a mix of backgrounds as a coequal criterion alongside mentor fit and scholar qualification and motivation.

Equally important, new training grants must demonstrate a track record of involvement in the training of underrepresented scholars at various levels: postdoctoral, graduate (including medical school), and undergraduate. Faculty receiving supplemental awards from NIH to train underrepresented minority fellows should also be highlighted. Similarly, T32 renewal applicants are required to evidence specific examples where faculty mentors have worked with training scholars from underrepresented backgrounds.

Training in the Responsible Conduct of Research

All NIH pre- and postdoctoral fellows are required to be trained in the Responsible Conduct of Research (RCR), and the new T grant applicant should look upon this as an opportunity to provide formal, integrated training that directly supports the fellows' career development. The format of this section can thus be seen as a natural extension of Part B of the Program Plan (Proposed Training and Environment), though note that the RCR section is separate from the Program Plan and has a three-page limit of its own. The structure of this section is determined by the topics and subject matter required by NIH, each of which will be met in different ways either explicitly as part of discrete fellowship activities or through existing formal structures and training opportunities across the wider institution. We have developed a new tailored training on the RCR, requiring fellows to attend a series of five lecture–workshops throughout the academic year as part of our weekly seminar program (see later). In developing this type of curriculum, T32 applicants should once again draw on the experience in research ethics and conduct within their institutional setting, as we have engaged with the Yale Bio-Ethics Center and existing compliance areas of Yale's grants and contracts administration with oversight for conflict of interest avoidance, biosafety, animal care, and other matters.

Substantial face-to-face discussions regarding bioethics and the RCR is integrated into training for all of our fellows. Per NIH guidance, we use a combination of didactic and small-group discussions (e.g., case studies) as part of our weekly fellowship seminar and/or use centralized resources across Yale University, as follows:

a. *Conflict of interest, personal, professional, and financial:* As part of the Yale University Conflict of Interest Office, all fellows are trained and complete an External Interest Disclosure form. Many universities make similar commitments to ensuring that the research, consultation, and other activities of faculty and nonfaculty employees are conducted in accordance with the principles of openness, trust, and free inquiry that are fundamental to the autonomy and well-being of a university.

b. *Policies regarding human subjects, live vertebrate animal subjects in research, and safe laboratory practices:* We address policies regarding human subjects in several ways, including but not limited to all fellows completing Yale University HIC and Health Insurance Portability and Accountability Act training and certification. In addition, we address these issues as part of our grant writing seminar (though most of our fellows are limited to human subjects, and are not involved in animal or laboratory practices). This has also become part of a weekly RCR seminar series for fellows.

c. *Mentor/mentee responsibilities and relationships:* This is part of our written guidelines to all fellows and their mentors. These issues and relationships are central to our training program, and we address them during recruitment of fellows as well as throughout our four-part evaluation process.

d. *Collaborative research, including collaborations with industry:* This is integrated into our grant writing, research, and professional development seminars. To date, we have not had fellows actively collaborating with industry partners.

e. *Peer review:* Peer review is an ongoing process and set of skills. We conduct Research in Progress (with peer review) at least two times per month. Fellows also use the formal Peer Review system that is part of CIRA and meets monthly with even wider faculty input.

f. *Data acquisition and laboratory tools; management, sharing, and ownership:* This is integrated into our grant writing, research, and professional development seminars. It is also addressed specifically as part of our RCR seminar series.

g. *Research misconduct and policies for handling misconduct:* This is integrated into our research and professional development seminars. We have also added a separate session on this as part of our RCR training curriculum.

h. *Responsible authorship and publication:* This is integrated into our ongoing research in progress seminars (at least two times per month), and is addressed as part of our professional development seminars. We have also added the topic as a separate session within our RCR seminar series.

i. *The scientist as a responsible member of society, contemporary ethical issues in biomedical research, and the environmental and societal impacts of scientific research:* This is integrated into our ongoing seminars and is addressed as part of our professional development seminars. We have also included a separate RCR seminar broaching historical and "contemporary issues" in the ethical conduct of research.

Final Thoughts

Writing a training grant is a significant and challenging undertaking. However, applying for and maintaining such a program provides substantial benefits to individual program directors, to mentees, and to the wider productivity of the scholars within and across institutions. We hope that this chapter provides some guidance should you decide to pursue a training grant at your institution. We advocate that the satisfaction of mentoring pre- and postdoctoral fellows, engaging in rich collaboration, and seeing scholars succeed as independent investigators is more than worth the effort and an ideal—and necessary—complement to the development of one's own career in research.

References

Joint United Nations Programme on HIV/AIDS (UNAIDS) and World Health Organization (WHO). (2007). *AIDS epidemic update.* Switzerland: UNAIDS.

National Postdoctoral Association. (2009). *Fact sheet on U.S. postdoctoral stipends.* Washington, DC: Author.

National Research Council, Committee for Monitoring the Nation's Changing Needs for Biomedical, Behavioral, and Clinical Personnel. (2005). *Advancing the nation's health needs: NIH research training programs.* Washington, DC: National Academies Press.

National Research Council, Committee on National Needs for Biomedical and Behavioral Research Personnel. (1994). *Meeting the nation's needs for biomedical and behavioral scientists.* Washington, DC: National Academies Press.

U.S. Department of Health and Human Services, Public Health Service. (2012). *SF424 (R&R) application guide for NIH and other PHS agencies.* Washington, DC: Author.

18

Interdisciplinary and Interinstitutional Collaboration on Research Grants

Hard but Fun!

Denise C. Park

It is increasingly common for successful research grants to involve collaboration across multiple disciplines. As the breadth of reach and diversity of problems approached through the psychological sciences increases, scientists find themselves reaching out more often to colleagues from other disciplines to work collaboratively on a problem that exceeds their own individual expertise. In my own research life, almost every successful research grant I have written in the past 15 years has involved some type of interdisciplinary collaboration, typically with researchers in medical schools or in the field of bioengineering.

Note: The author thanks Jackie Gauer for her assistance in preparing and editing this manuscript. The author thanks the National Institute on Aging for its generous support of so many collaborations, and finally, she thanks the many collaborators from whom she has learned so much.

Collaboration across disciplines has so many positives: It is exciting to see a problem through the lens of another discipline—it has expanded my horizons and has even led to paradigmatic shifts in my own research. There truly is a special thrill in learning how a bioengineer, a psychiatrist, or a neurologist thinks about a problem relative to my own perspective, and there is an excitement and energy in these interdisciplinary relationships that I believe greatly enhances scientific creativity.

The intellectual positives of interdisciplinary collaborations are innumerable, but there are many issues to consider before embarking on an interdisciplinary collaboration. You genuinely need to ask yourself how flexible you are in thinking about a problem; how effective you are at building and leading a team of diverse individuals and keeping everyone on board; and also the ability of you and your department to address complex budget issues and negotiations between different departments and even universities. Interdisciplinary collaboration takes time—a lot of time. You will be learning new vocabularies, new techniques, and new world views. You will be stunned at times to find that you fundamentally disagree with the way your colleague from another discipline approaches a problem, and find yourself groping for common ground so that you can move the project forward. It is frankly a pain in the neck to meet your collaborators in their departments at locations distant from your own lab and department, particularly on large campuses where parking is an insoluble issue. It is a never-ending challenge to adapt to other academic cultures, particularly the interface between a college of arts and sciences (home of most psychology departments) and a medical school (where most of my collaborations have occurred). These are different cultures that operate under quite different constraints.

Just to provide some perspective for the reader as I discuss these issues, I have been funded on many different research proposals on some facet of cognitive aging over the past three decades. Most of my grants have been awarded by the National Institute on Aging, part of the National Institutes of Health (NIH), but some have also come from private foundations. Every grant I have ever had has involved collaborations of some sort. In my initial grants, I collaborated with senior psychologists at other institutions who had interests very similar to my own in cognitive aging. Later, as I studied medical adherence and medical decisions in older adults, I worked with practicing physicians in the community and even had a funded proposal with some colleagues in the law school. In my neuroimaging work, I began to work extensively with bioengineers, radiologists, and physicists. I have most recently become increasingly interested in neuroplasticity, genetics, and neuropathology in seemingly healthy adults and collaborate extensively with neurologists, psychiatrists, and exercise physiologists. Finally, I have also held two large NIH grants that involved cross-cultural research in China and in Singapore that were among the most exciting but challenging projects I have ever conducted. I believe it is these interdisciplinary collaborations that have kept my research vital and my love of and excitement about my research so high for so many years.

The focus of this chapter is on describing how to integrate your collaborators into a good, fundable grant, and I will consider a range of issues that address interpersonal, financial, and institutional issues. First, I will address general issues associated with interdisciplinary collaborations. Then, I will consider the easiest interdisciplinary collaborations in which to engage—cross-disciplinary collaborations within your own institution. Following that, I will address some issues to consider when collaborating across universities and will close with a discussion of international collaborations as well as collaborations where one is the secondary rather than primary investigator.

Why Collaborate and With Whom?

The only good reason for collaborations of any sort is that such a relationship will strengthen the science of the project you are proposing. I almost always do work that goes beyond my own discipline and training. Once I focus on a problem that excites me and I think is important, I then concentrate on building what I call the "A Team." The A Team consists of a group of scientists who are excellent and highly credentialed in their area of expertise; they are available to do the work; and I usually know the individuals well enough to know that I can work with them and that they work well with others. If I do not have the expertise I need at my own institution, I go outside and get it. It helps if you have a collaborative history with the individuals and some shared publications or preliminary data. However, this is not always essential. Twice in my career as a young investigator, I contacted national experts whom I didn't even know, but whose work I greatly admired (for the curious, this would be Anderson Smith at the Georgia Institute of Technology and Howard Leventhal at Rutgers University). Both agreed, and both grants got funded, resulting in lifelong friendships and decades of collaborations that worked beautifully. Having said this, I was lucky that these were both exceptional individuals, and I do not recommend this approach. Moreover, this was many years ago, when conference travel was special, and, believe it or not, faxes, e-mail, and cell phones had not yet been invented. Skype was something we watched on the *Jetsons*. It seems to me that, given our present hyperconnected scientific community, one should have had quite a bit of opportunity for contact with any proposed collaborator and likely will have had considerable communications and discussions before developing a research proposal together.

When choosing collaborators, it is essential that you consider whether they will strengthen or weaken your position in the eyes of a reviewer. Say, for example, you are a social psychologist with expertise in dating behaviors and are proposing to collect blood for genetic samples and have no history in genetics. It would thus be critical that your genetics collaborator have an impeccable reputation and unquestionable resources to get the job done, since you will be relying heavily on this person for the genetics facet of your work. A great colleague who has knowledge of this area but few publications and limited "on paper" expertise will weaken your hand. Keep the notion of the "A Team" in mind.

This sounds a bit silly, but I believe it is essential that you really like and enjoy your collaborators and that the collaboration is based on both intellectual and personal affinity. You are more or less committed to your collaborator for a five-year period. A bad collaborator is not much different than a bad marriage—the only good thing about a collaboration is that you can gracefully exit when your five years are up without the trouble of divorce—but five years is quite a long time, and "divorcing" your colleague during these five years will be almost impossible without damaging the project. So be careful.

In a similar vein, recognize that it is almost certainly a big mistake to develop an interdisciplinary project simply because there is a request for proposals (RFP) and you think you have a good chance to get some funding, even though you are not superinterested in the topic. The good news is that you probably won't get funded because the excitement and energy needed for success will be lacking from your proposal. The bad news is that, if you somehow do get funded, you will actually have to do the work. A close colleague and I call doing things we must do but don't want to do (like writing a "methods" section) "digging ditches." Sometimes you have to do things that bore you—it is part of being successful—but don't invite unnecessary ditch-digging into your life. Never, ever propose to do work that you are not interested in—you will be so sorry about a year after you get funded.

The Time Costs of Collaboration

I think the most precious professional resource each of us has is time. It is irreplaceable. When one chooses to commit to spending time on something, it means one is choosing not to spend time on something else. It is painful to get a wonderful invitation and realize you must turn it down because you have already made a commitment to do something that you really don't want to do. It is critical to recognize that interdisciplinary collaborations take time, often lots of time. Meetings are harder to schedule and more time-consuming to schedule the more people are involved. You frequently have to hold them at inconvenient times to accommodate others, and the cost of determining a course of action that is agreeable to all can require an exceptional amount of meeting time. There are going to be conflicts in collaborations—at the minimum, there will be intellectual conflicts—that take time to resolve. Although it is exactly resolving these conflicts that makes interdisciplinary work exciting and moves the bar higher on the quality of work you do, they do have a price and require resilience and considerable people management skills that have little to do with scientific ability.

Additionally, the financial and institutional review board (IRB) complexities involved in interdisciplinary collaborations often require a great deal of time and patience. Executing a subcontract, negotiating budget cuts with your collaborators, agreeing on expenses—all of these things take time. It is also important to have solid departmental and/or institutional infrastructure as collaborations become more complex and involved. Frequently, grants professionals in your academic unit can address some negotiations between the two departments or institutions involved in your project. If you have excellent administrative support, do not unnecessarily insert yourself into complex budget issues that are better handled between administrative professionals. As a simple rule of thumb, I would argue that the more distal one's collaborators are either conceptually or geographically, the more time collaboration will take.

I would like to discuss particularly the collaboration between a traditional academic department and a medical school. These relationships take extra time, and it is because the cultures are so different. I have found that collaborations are much easier between a psychology department and other traditional departments like engineering or physics than they are between psychology and a medical school department like psychiatry, even if the investigator in psychiatry was a psychologist. The additional draw on time mainly has to do with money and budgets. I discuss this in the following section.

Budgets, Subcontracts, and the Financial Costs of Collaboration

One of the knottiest issues in collaboration is compensating each collaborator fairly for their costs. It is fair to say that interdisciplinary collaborations, particularly those that involve two institutions or more, are expensive. It turns out that different departments, colleges, schools, and universities all have unique ways of compensating their faculty. Some investigators are required to produce their entire salary from external funding. This is particularly true of investigators at medical schools, but it can also be the case for individuals affiliated with research centers at major universities. At the least, nearly every researcher requires three months of salary for summer. Increasingly, as budgets get tighter, researchers get less and less compensation for salary from their grants, while at the same time institutions are demanding more and more. This results in painful decisions and incredibly tight budgets. It is extraordinarily important that you understand what a collaborator needs from a project to be participatory in it. You should expect that if your project pays only a small fraction of the salary of someone who is required to pay all of their salary to survive, you will get only a small fraction of their time. They have little choice. So recognize that you could be working with someone who has their time distributed across as many as a dozen grants and that if you need a full and sustained partnership for your project, you will need to pay for it. Also, in these situations, it is important to recognize that once a number is put in a budget for an investigator, it can be quite difficult to renegotiate it later on, as it becomes quite literally that individual's livelihood.

You should also be prepared to consider the implications of large raises, promotions, or institutional changes in your collaborators' situations, as these all have budget implications for you. It is reasonable to insist that the project has "x" dollars set aside for any individual and that the amount cannot be increased, except in the unlikely situation where a sponsor is willing to increase a budget to accommodate these changes. Grant budgets are indeed a zero-sum game. At the same time, if your circumstances change where you find you really need more money for a project and are tempted to cut a subcontract, I would think twice. I believe it is of utmost importance to keep your commitments to others, even if circumstances or budgets change. This has costs, but it also has gains, in terms of being viewed as a trusted and valued colleague. Sacrificing your own needs a bit in favor of a colleague's needs makes for long-term, enduring relationships. Capricious budget changes or decisions will very quickly make you an undesirable collaborator.

You may come up with the idea of including a well-known and thus expensive senior collaborator in your grant for an institutional contribution of their time or for a week or two of paid time. As a general rule, I am not a big fan of this approach on a research grant, as I think it often looks gratuitous to reviewers, although it is a highly acceptable practice for training grants and mentoring grants where the wisdom and advice of a senior scholar can go a long way. I also think it can work well if you are a young scientist and include a senior investigator for little salary, as again the mentoring role will be acknowledged by reviewers, particularly if you have a history of publishing with the individual and he or she is housed at your own institution.

Writing an Interdisciplinary Grant

It is not uncommon for collaborators to write a grant together, with one scientist writing one section and another writing others. Generally, I do not think this is likely to lead to success. When reviewing grants, it is sometimes easy to see two writing styles and redundancy or omissions that occur when two people write independently. I strongly believe that the principal investigator (PI) should write nearly the entire grant, perhaps leaving brief sections with very specific paragraphs or technical components to be completed by the collaborator who is more knowledgeable than the PI on a given topic. Even when relatively small technical insertions of this sort are needed in my grants, I closely query my collaborator about any component I don't quite understand and then translate the text into language that I do understand. I figure that if I don't understand it, it is quite likely that the reviewers will not understand it either. Don't think that impenetrable mumbo jumbo on something esoteric will be effective—I suppose it works occasionally, but it is a high-risk strategy. Although I believe the PI should always write the grant, I always ask my collaborators to work closely on edits with me and usually accept all of their edits. If you have trouble abandoning your own wording or are going to contest every change your colleague suggests, you are probably going to be most successful and effective as a solo investigator or in collaborations that do not span disciplines. This isn't necessarily a bad thing, but it is something you should know about yourself so that you don't waste that precious resource of time.

Interinstitutional Collaborations

It is important to recognize that interinstitutional collaborations are considerably more difficult logistically and are also more expensive than any other type of collaboration. They are more difficult because you are dealing with two different institutional cultures and because these relationships require that a formal subcontract detailing the work, costs, and time frame for the collaborating group to be issued. This is a written agreement between the two institutions that must be executed jointly by institutional grant officers. Then, once the contract is issued, your collaborator has to bill the project and then the bill must be paid from your grant. These plans and invoices can often go awry, particularly when the sums of money involved are small. Small sums are frequently involved in subcontracts when you are covering only a month or two of your colleague's time, and the research activity is all paid from the primary grant. The larger the subcontract, the more likely it is, in some ways, that things will go smoothly, as the institutions will be keenly aware when payment isn't issued. My experience is that the most troublesome subcontracts are small ones. The effort involved in executing and paying them is pretty much the same as for a large one, and these small subs rather easily fall between the cracks. On more than one occasion, bills have been delayed for prolonged periods and it has become difficult to settle payment. As a PI, it is important to be sure the subs are issued, billed, and paid. A second related issue is that once two or more institutions are involved, one must submit and coordinate protections for human subjects through two or more IRBs, which again can be quite challenging. None of these issues are intellectually demanding, but seeing them through requires tact, patience, good organization, and a highly competent staff. As the PI, you have little control over the execution and completion of some of these matters, yet these can be significant stumbling blocks to initiation and completion of the work. Adding to the situation is the fact that costs will be higher for your project. Costs are higher on many projects because of the complexity of the arrangements for indirect cost charges on subcontracts. This is a very complex topic, and the view is that indirect costs are the purview of your institution and not you as an investigator. It is unwise to get overly involved in how indirect costs are paid—you cannot likely influence your institution in any way on what they will accept for your federal project (private foundations may be more negotiable with your institution). Nevertheless, it is critical that you get competent advice very early in project budget development from your institution about indirect costs for subcontracts, or you may find an unpleasant surprise of higher costs than you expected for this as you get close to submitting the proposal.

International Collaborations

Collaborative relationships that span countries and even continents are becoming increasingly common. Cultural psychology, the study of how cultural values shape behavior, has become an increasingly important area of research in the psychological sciences. This has led to interesting and important international collaborations, as have studies of trauma, health, poverty, and many other important topics. Moreover, in our "flat world," researchers with common interests pay little attention to international borders and frequently collaborate on projects of shared expertise even though they are widely separated by geography and cultures. Not surprisingly, it turns out that there are some unique issues to consider when developing grants that cross international borders, even if your proposed colleague is only a few miles across the U.S. border in Canada or Mexico. NIH requires that any international collaboration be particularly well justified. This is easy to do if the focus of your project is cultural or national differences in a given phenomenon. For example, we investigated the hypothesis that differences in perceptual processes between East Asians and Westerners that were ascribed to cultural values would decrease with age and also examined cross-cultural differences in age-related cognitive decline. An initial project was funded with my U.S. institution (the University of Michigan) and the Chinese Academy of Sciences as the subcontractor. A second funded project involved neuroimaging research across cultures with the University of Illinois (my institution) as the primary grantee but with a subcontract to Duke University/ National University of Singapore Medical School. The challenges in developing a cross-cultural project are numerous, but the work is incredibly rewarding. Issues to consider include the need for large travel budgets, differences in salary requirements across the two countries, and differences in languages and work styles. It took me some time to realize that there was an expectation of very rapid turnaround for publications from the research in China and Singapore compared with the United States, and that productivity of scientists was monitored on a quarterly basis compared with an annual basis in the United States. I was considerably more relaxed about the time frame from data collection to publication, and this reflected different evaluation systems in the different countries. I also found that we would have lengthy meetings for several days, and if I did not take detailed notes when I was out of the country, jet lag would take its toll and we would end up not sure to what we had agreed. Detailed written summaries after meetings are particularly critical for international collaborations.

International grants are not for the faint of heart, particularly when there is less development of academic infrastructure. In order to submit the grant, the project at both sites is required to have, at a minimum, pending IRB approval. This means that your collaborative country must have or must form an IRB that meets specified U.S. standards and the project must be submitted for review to this group. This is something to be prepared for well in advance of submission. It is also the case that a full subcontract between the sites will be required. All of the issues described earlier about subcontracts become more acute if the foreign site has never participated in a U.S. federal subcontract. I would advise PIs contemplating an international grant to be very certain of the capabilities of their administrative infrastructure at their own institution to see an award through and to be prepared to learn quite a bit oneself about what processes need to occur. I also suggest that the PI consider making a case to include direct costs for some direct administrative support for the project in the form of a half-time or even full-time administrator (depending on the project's size) to address the extremely high administrative burden that occurs with international collaborations.

Serving as a Collaborator on Another PI's Project

If you collaborate with many different colleagues on your own research grants, the situation will undoubtedly emerge where you will be asked to be a collaborator by another PI. The same considerations apply as discussed earlier. Make sure you are interested in the work and enjoy the collaboration. Be certain that you have sufficient effort and support to cover the work you are expected to do. Also, consider the risks for your own focal efforts in getting too involved in a project where your effort requirements are substantial, but the research does not significantly expand your intellectual horizons. Be especially careful of getting involved in many projects for small amounts of effort where your primary contribution is data collection or statistical analysis and you lose intellectual focus. I have found that I have very much enjoyed the secondary collaborative role when I was working on projects that were most distal to my own interests and where my expertise overlapped little with the PI. For example, I really enjoyed applying my expertise in cognition to an interesting disorder in rheumatology that appeared to have consequences similar to cognitive aging. I also greatly profit from a collaboration I have now with a terrific bioengineer who is keenly interested in using neurovascular health to correct functional magnetic resonance imaging signals in the brain as people age. In these projects, I have been able to play an important role in shaping a question that I had never thought much about that ultimately changed the way I think about my own work. I have had the privilege of working with some of the best scientists in fields remote from my own and have learned so much in the process, as did my graduate students and postdocs.

Final Thoughts

Interdisciplinary collaborations are increasingly the focus of "big science" as well as more and more critical to almost every domain within the psychological sciences. The closer we get to solving real-world problems, the more frequently we will work with other kinds of scientists such as epidemiologists, physicians, engineers, geneticists, chemists....the possibilities are both exciting and endless. My very first grant had a collaborator from another institution, and I have found that collaboration with scientists across many disciplines and universities has been one of the most rewarding aspects of my career. Moreover, it has been a nearly painless way to maintain intellectual excitement, make wonderful friends, and enhance career opportunities for my students and postdocs. In short, it has been hard, but it has been fun. If I have an idea about which I am very excited, I never let geography or institutional affiliations create insurmountable barriers to research. Collaborative relationships will only grow in importance in the future—the biggest barrier to interdisciplinary collaborations are, in my estimation, complex IRB requirements that can require many months of iterations to secure final approval from all institutions and severe limits on grant budgets that make such relationships unfeasible financially. If you are passionate about a research project that is important and can feasibly be investigated, you should go for it. All of the difficulties collaborations entail will be readily surmounted with scientific excellence.

PART IV

Conclusion

19

"Aha! Plus Data"

Reviewers, Program Officers, and the Public Are People Too

Susan T. Fiske

W riting successful grant proposals is a science, and the experts writing in this volume tell us how to convince our target audience. The process is knowable and feasible but competitive in a volatile political and fiscal environment. One author (Rissman, this volume) estimates her team spends 50 percent of its time writing proposals, and everyone reports 90 percent rejections, consistent with the agency funding lines, so the first lesson is that we all get rejected, and the other guys are not getting grants so easily either (Barr, Salas, each this volume). People typically blame some liability of their own identity—ivy/state/liberal arts college, youth/age, social/bio topic, radical/conservative methods—but the simpler explanation is the 90 percent rejection rate. We suffer the same rates at top-notch journals, so we must take our lessons from persisting at that all-too-familiar experience (Dovidio, this volume).

What's more, writing a grant organizes one's research program, even if not funded (Okagaki, Sternberg, Young, each this volume). So, when that bright-eyed senior or first-year graduate student enters your office saying, "I want to work with you," you have a study in your pocket and a rationale for the student to read. I met my own advisor that way, and now grants have kept my eye on the big-picture aims of our research, guiding the logical next steps, despite the semester's mayhem.

"Aha, Plus Data"

Of course, it's better to be funded than rejected. That's why you and I turned to this volume. The secret, these authors tell us, is the mix of ideas and evidence—the same as a journal article. No one ever wrote a successful grant proposal without an "Aha!" experience. Good ideas come from a variety of sources, but that's another chapter or two (Fiske, 2003, 2004a, 2004b).

Contrary to our parental instincts, ideas are cheap; they come with the zeitgeist. People often invent similar ideas in parallel because they are minding the same gaps. We do not own our ideas, just the work developing and operationalizing them. The other necessary ingredient, then, these authors tell us, is pilot data. An outstanding grant requires a demonstration: the proposal is feasible, probably right, and here's an existence proof.

Reviewers, Program Officers, and the Public Are People Too

If an idea and its data sit on your hard drive, nobody heeds them. Your grant audience is not disembodied agencies, abstract organizations, or a distant populace, but individual people: specific program officers, predictable peer reviewers, and interested taxpayers. Keep these people in mind, the authors tell us (e.g., Eichenbaum, Levenson, Riley, Rissman, Sternberg, Young, each this volume); ignore their perspectives and convenience at your peril. Somebody has to want you to get funded, and without an advocate, your ideas and pilot data will not survive the Darwinian competition (Baker, Fox, each this volume). And, if any one of these audiences wants you *not* to be funded, you probably are cooked. Think like the sponsor (Salas, this volume). Besides an idea and pilot data, grant readers want what other people want: they seek good fit, shared norms, good stories, and determined persistence.

Find the Fit

No one likes to be mistaken for someone else. Such an insult implies the communicator did not bother to discover or remember who you are and what you like. Program officers and reviewers are no exception, and offending them is undiplomatic, at least. Plus, it wastes everyone's time to send your grant to the wrong group of minds.

Finding the fit, these authors tell us, is simple yet time-consuming. But, supplicants cannot be cavalier about benefactors' time. Each agency and foundation has a webpage; explore its mission, mechanisms, precedents, programs, and personnel. Not surprisingly, the funders here are especially keen on would-be grantees doing this homework before contacting them (e.g., Chipman, Fitzpatrick, Null & Beard, Okagaki, Riley et al., Young, each this volume). To be sure, talking to the program officers further hones the fit and guards against changing priorities that outpace webpage-update lags. Federal agency program officers universally recommend talking to them—it's part of their job—but private foundation officers are too short-staffed and recommend against it, as their webpages are likely to be simple, direct, accessible, and up-to-date.

How does a novice find the right sources in the first place? These authors represent a variety of standard and not-so-standard funders: the National Institutes of Health's numerous institutes and centers, the National Science Foundation's many programs, the Institute for Educational Sciences, the military agencies' basic and applied venues, and the private sector (for a list of foundations related to psychology, see Fitzpatrick, this volume). Unexpected sources lurk as close as a Google-keyword Web-wide search (Gernsbacher, this volume).

Read the Rules

Students who read the syllabus and do the required work pass the course; students who don't, don't. None of us, as teachers, would claim this is more than the minimum, but we are appalled when students do not even bother to respect the rules. Of course, the A students do much, much more, but we know they've at least read the syllabus because they follow it. Grantors expect the analogue of proposers: As all the authors agree, do them the courtesy—and yourself the favor—of reading their guidelines and following their rules. Of course, more is required to pass beyond perfunctory rejection of a mistimed, misformatted, or misdirected proposal, but too many proposers fail even this elementary step more often than rock-bottom self-interest would predict. From program missions to mechanisms to margins, no detail is too small to matter. Funders will not give you a pass on a stated rule, any more than professors ignore a requirement clearly stated on the syllabus. Follow not only the letter, but also the spirit of the rules (Fitzpatrick, Gernsbacher, this volume); smart people thought them up for a purpose.

Address the Audience

Presentation Matters. Cognitive science tells us that fluency creates liking; people like input that goes down easy. Social psychology tells us that similarity creates liking; people like authors who share their history and values. Both fields tell us that people like stories; people like narratives with progress, novelty, and excitement. Program officers, reviewers, and the public are people like us. Before any of them wants to advocate for funding our work, they have to understand it, and they have to like it. Enthusiasm comes from narratives that motivate in specific ways.

Narrate. Even the most rigorous scientists value a good story of discovery (e.g., Barr, Dovidio, Eichenbaum, Levenson, Sternberg, each this volume). Scientists' version of the heroic journey begins with a hook to a problem. Problems must excite and challenge the reader, but not be overly cute, toy problems (Chipman, this volume). An epic journey begins with respect for the forbears who tackled the problem before, and then learns from their efforts to carry on. Insulting the forbears is a bad idea because one of them or their followers might review your proposal. The proposed solution must be novel, but the protagonist proves it doable. After delivery, the future will be better for all science, agency, and society.

Aim Well. The protagonist has a specific quest; the principal investigator must articulate specific goals. The section of grant proposals most dissected in this volume is the abstract or specific aims. First impressions count. The first sentence counts, so consider writing it last, when you know precisely what you propose. The authors all agree wholeheartedly that having and communicating a clear purpose matters more than any other element (e.g., Levenson, this volume).

Guide. Journeys need guides and maps, and a dense grant proposal can feel like a journey, but it should be a guided tour of human wonders, not an unmarked trail through the jungle. Headings are our guideposts, and figures are our maps. Although they take up precious space, a heading is worth a hundred words (Chipman, Okagaki, each this volume), a table is worth a thousand (Atherton et al., this volume), and a figure is worth a million (you hope!) (Dovidio, Rissman, each this volume).

Explain Everything. Assume nothing on faith (Dovidio, Levenson, Park, Young, each this volume). The principal investigator should be the world's expert, so by exclusion, everyone else is not. Even nearly-as-expert peers appreciate seeing a good explanation of a shared domain; it shows a logical mind, clear communication, and good grasp of the issues. Reviewers often must stretch to cover unfamiliar areas, so they need to become expert on your behalf, if they decide to serve as advocates for your cause. In judging confusion and clarity, the reader is always right (Dovidio, this volume).

Keep Flowing. As principal investigators write, they develop their ideas. The good news is that this represents insight and growth; the bad news is that it creates inconsistency. People do and should write Specific Aims (or the equivalent first), but then link the aims to the later methods and analyses (Fox, this volume); be consistent. The abstract or Specific Aims provide the big picture. One trick is to print out that single page and post it next to your computer, as a reminder to relate everything else back to the main points.

Convince and Compel. A grant proposal is a persuasive communication arguing for a perspective. A cogent message is clear, compelling, and concise, but complete (Riley et al., this volume). Our ideas do not speak for themselves, so we must present and defend them (Baker, this volume).

Show Them the Data. The most convincing argument is evidence, and the most exciting argument is new evidence. Pilot data keep everyone from wasting time and money. Proposers should not pursue a problem without encouraging results; reviewers should not have to evaluate untested wish lists; and the public should not have to support unpromising speculations. Pilot data are crucial, all the authors agree (e.g., Eichenbaum, Fox, Rissman, each this volume).

Anticipate Criticism. Nothing is more impressive to a reviewer than thinking of a problem, only to see it addressed in the next paragraph. Having a vocal (but not paralyzing) inner critic is a honed skill. Being able to see your work the way critics do is difficult—and essential (Eichenbaum, Fox, each this volume). In the same spirit, anticipate setbacks, note alternative explanations, and offer alternative methods (Okagaki, this volume).

Recruit Eyeballs. A colleague pre-reviewing your grant can save you six to eight months of review, rejection, and revision (Fitzgerald, Okagaki, Young, each this volume). You can't review each other's grants anyway, because of conflict of interest, so trading advice makes good use of resources in a department that will benefit if you get funded. Moving outside your department and comfort zone requires collaboration, another recommended strategy.

Go, Team. Collaborate to get outside eyes but also to fill expertise gaps. Multidisciplinary approaches are the name of the current game (e.g., Fox, this volume). Collaborations also energize, across career levels, as in work with training-grant trainees (Atherton et al., this volume), across disciplines (Park, Rissman, each this volume), and across cultures (Park, this volume). But, make sure the collaborations are real; don't simply add an important consultant for name-dropping rights (Fitzgerald, Park, this volume). Our science is increasingly a team effort (Baker, Null & Beard, Salas, each this volume).

Perseverance Furthers

Admittedly, a 90 percent rejection rate is discouraging, but the rate is 100 percent if you don't try (Barr, Rissman, Sternberg, each this volume). If you don't ask, you don't get. So go for it!

References

Fiske, S. T. (2003). The discomfort index: How to spot a really good idea whose time has come. *Psychological Inquiry, 14,* 201–206.

Fiske, S. T. (2004a). Developing a program of research. In C. Sansone, C. Morf, & A. Panter (Eds.), *Handbook of methods in social psychology* (pp. 71–90). Thousand Oaks, CA: Sage.

Fiske, S. T. (2004b). Mind the gap: In praise of informal sources of formal theory. *Personality and Social Psychology Review, 8,* 132–137.

Author Index

Subject Index

Page references followed by (table) indicates a table; followed by (figure) indicates an illustrated figure.

SAGE research**methods**

The essential online tool for researchers from the world's leading methods publisher

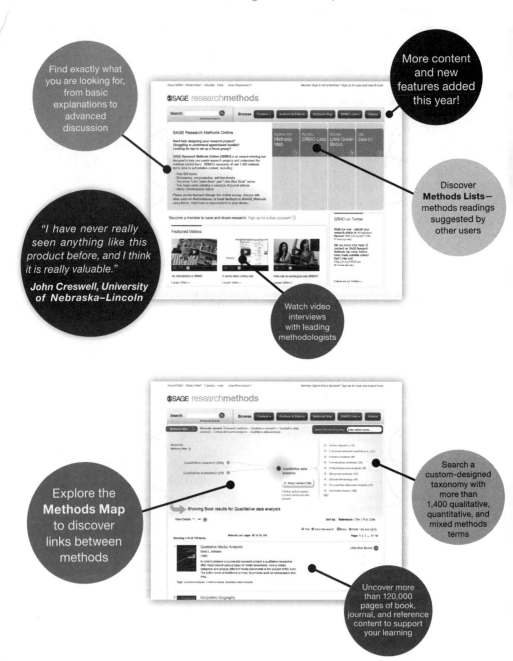

Find exactly what you are looking for, from basic explanations to advanced discussion

More content and new features added this year!

"*I have never really seen anything like this product before, and I think it is really valuable.*"
John Creswell, University of Nebraska–Lincoln

Discover **Methods Lists**— methods readings suggested by other users

Watch video interviews with leading methodologists

Explore the **Methods Map** to discover links between methods

Search a custom-designed taxonomy with more than 1,400 qualitative, quantitative, and mixed methods terms

Uncover more than 120,000 pages of book, journal, and reference content to support your learning

Find out more at
www.sageresearchmethods.com